# HAND-HELD VISIONS

# HAND-HELD
# VISIONS

## The Impossible Possibilities
## of Community Media

### DeeDee Halleck
### With a foreword by John Downing

Fordham University Press
New York • 2002

Communications and Media Studies, No. 5
ISSN 1522–385X

**Library of Congress Cataloging-in-Publication Data**

Halleck, DeeDee.
    Hand-held visions : the uses of community media / DeeDee Halleck.—1st ed.
        p.   cm. — (Communications and media studies series ; no. 5)
    Includes bibliographical references and index.
    ISBN 0-8232-2100-8 (hardcover) — ISBN 0-8232-2101-6 (pbk.)
    1. Halleck, DeeDee.   2. Television producers and directors—United States—Biography.   3. Video recordings—Production and direction.   I. Title.   II. Communications and media studies ; no. 5
    PN1992.4.H36 A3   2001
    791.45′0232′092—dc21
    [B]                                                        2001040637

Printed in the United States of America
            05   06     5   4   3   2
First Edition

Dedicated to my grandchildren,
Sol Maria, Natalie, Tolan, Peter Vladimir,
Owen, Rowan, and Liam,
and my adopted grandchildren,
Jake, Ana, Niger, Senque, and Anaya.

# CONTENTS

# FOREWORD

HISTORIES OF MAINSTREAM media, and of varying media technologies, are easy to find. They have their importance, when they are not designed as puff-pieces for the wonders of corporate control. Histories of alternative media are, by contrast, few and far between, though a real history of the labor movement, of the movements for black and Latino and women's empowerment, and of similar struggles, ends up somewhat unreal if the communications and media dimensions of these movements are left out of the account.

In this book, DeeDee Halleck brings us into the front lines of the fights she and other video activists, American and international, have waged—in her case for two generations—to make video and other media accessible to the poor, to the technically uninformed, to those given no voice by the power structure's media. As we read these pages, countless highly politicized situations burst into life before our eyes, whether in Managua or New York or Delhi or Rio, and there in the midst or on the immediate sidelines is DeeDee, tirelessly campaigning, insisting, explaining, urging, reminding, connecting.

And doing: with Paper Tiger Television, Deep Dish TV, and children's video production; concerning prisonization, the quincentennial of the conquistadors, the AIDS crisis, and the 1990–1991 Gulf War; and slamming *The New York Times*.

Above all, these pages bring us headfirst into the *process* of making radical alternative video. Dr. Robert Huesca of Trinity University, San Antonio, Texas, in his study of the Bolivian miners' radio station, has argued that it is indeed the process that is pivotal, not just the product/programs, nor even the role of such media in moments of political crisis. This book's collection of essays, polemics, and histories offers something very unusual in this regard, a spirited tour through the mo-

ments of hope and struggle and determined persistence in the
face of huge countervailing odds. In these pages, it is possible
to taste and to smell and almost to touch the process of radical
media-making.

So while sociologists might be more systematic, the fur
would not fly, or even stand on end. This collection is an in-
domitable call to arms, to throw our energies into radical alternative media, and an extraordinary memoir of what that
meant within the United States—and some other places too—
over the last four decades of the twentieth century. It is a call
to courage and a reminder of how much courage and vision
we need.

JOHN DOWNING

# ACKNOWLEDGMENTS

ACKNOWLEDGMENTS FOR BOOKS can last longer than credit rolls in films, and I will take full advantage of that to appreciate those without whom this book and my work would have been impossible. I know that in my haste I will leave some out, but I hope they realize that this is of course a reckless approximation, not a definitive list.

Thanks first and foremost to Joel and to my children and stepchildren, Molly, Tovey, Peter, Ezra, Andrea, Erin, and Jon, my immediate family, who have had to wait patiently and for the most part with good humor though my endless conference calls, editing crises, and board meetings.

Thanks to Robin Andersen, without whom there would be no book. Her visionary leadership in regards to communication publishing at Fordham University Press is bearing fruit. I am very appreciative of David Anderson's careful copyediting.

Several of my mentors have passed away but their spirits are still very much alive in the struggle for social justice and media democracy: Herb Schiller, Shirley Clarke, Conrad Lynn, Flo Kennedy, Lyn Blumenthal, Archie Singham, and Jaime Barrios.

Thanks to Ed Herman and George Stoney, colleagues whose work informs and inspires so many media activists. I am grateful for my comrades Eddie Becker, Joan Braderman, Chris Burnett, Maggie Cammer, Daniel Del Solar, Jesse Drew, Brian Drolet, Karen Einstein, Virginia Escalante, Joyce Evans, Simin Farkhondeh, Bruria and David Finkel, Elsa First, Sara Flores, Catherine Gund, Adrienne Jenik, Michael Kassner, Cambiz Khosravi, Tetsuo Kogawa, Kole Ade-Odutola, Tuli Kupferberg, Ernie Larsen, Lee Lew Lee, Peggy Leo, Geert Lovink, Nathalie Magnan, CheChé Martinez, Monica Melamid, Jesus Papoleto Melendez, Sherry Milner, Neil Morrison, Hye Jung Park, Sheila Pinkel, Luana Plunkett, Rick

Prelinger, Fanny Prizant, Lourdes Prophet, Norma Quintero, Karen Ranucci, Michael Ratner, Martha Rosler, Ed and Miriam Sanders, Elka and Peter Schumann, Tamar Schumann, John Schwartz, Cathy Scott, Joan Snyder, Melinda Stone, Johanna Vanderbeek, Bea Velasco, May Ying Welsh, Judith Williamson, Joan Yoshiwara, and Patty Zimmerman.

My association with many groups and collectives has informed my work and taught me the wisdom (and the pain) of consensus decision making: Highlander Folk School, Community Government at Antioch College, Live Arts (Middletown, New York), the Gate Hill Co-op (The Land), Wintersoldier, Videofreex, TeePee Video Space Troupe, Women Make Movies, Artists Meeting for Social Change, Communications Update, Image Union, the Low Power Television Center, Paper Tiger, X-Change TV, Germinal (the Ché Cafe), Institute for Media Analysis, Red Lion Collective (UCSD), Deep Dish Network, Vidéazimut, Instructional Telecommunications Foundation, Green Network, Independent Media Centers, and Democratic Media Legal Project.

Much appreciation to those educators and media teachers from whom I learned much: Eric Barnouw, Greg Bordowitz, Loni Ding, Ariel Doughtery, Julio Garcia Espinosa, Ted Glass, Jose Antonio Jimenez, Herb Kohl, Roger Larsen, Iraida Malberti, Chris Marker, Branda Miller, Clare Oglesby, Sheila Page, Pedro Rivera, Bruce Speigel, Ellen Spiro, Amos Vogel, Arturo Zamora, Susan Zeig. Thanks to all the video pioneers of Image Union, especially Tom Weinberg, Parry Teasdale, Skip Blumberg, and the Videofreex. Thanks to Liza Bear, Vickie Gholson, and Michael McClard of *Communications Update*.

Thanks to all the original Tigers: Diana Agosta, Pennee Bender, Alan Steinheimer, Caryn Rogoff, Daniel Brooks, David Shulman, Shu Lea Cheang, Karen Einstein, Mary Feaster, Melissa Leo, Marty Lucas, William Bodde, Fusun Atesar, Roger Politzer, Martha Wallner, Roy Wilson, Yvette Nieves, Hilary Kipnis, Linda Cranor, Esti Marpet, Jesse Drew, Carla Leshne, John Walden, Jane Cottis, Bob Kenney, and Margaret Difani. Kudos to the game Paper Tiger subjects: especially Brian Winston, Ynestra King, Harry Magdoff, Bill Tabb, Michael Channan, Jean Franco, Donna Haraway, Peter Wollin, Sheila Smith Hobson, Page Dubois, Lynn Speigel and Myrna Bain. Thanks to the Deep Dishers: Steve Pierce, Cynthia Lopez, Beverly Singer, Fiona Boneham, Kai Lumumba Barrow, Iannis Mookis, Loudi Prophette, Tom Poole, Lauren Glynn Davitian, Safiya Bukhari, Elliot Margolies, Bob Hercules, Jerome Scott, Louis Massiah, Alexis Lowenstein, Molly Fink, Orlando Richards, Jesse Epstein, Mike Torres.

Thanks to my all my students, especially Zulma Aguiar. Dominique Chausse, Mark Chavez, Vesna Kulasinovec, Todd Lehr, Federico Lopez, Derrick Maddox, Oly Norris, Julie Puzon, Bonni Rooney, Hermilla Torres. I am indebted to my colleagues at the University of California, San Diego: especially Susan Davis, Dan Hallin, Dan Schiller, Yueshi Zhao, Michael Schudson, Peter Smith, Vickie Mayer, Zeinabu Davis, Babette Mangolte, Jean Pierre Gorin, Terri O'Brien, Jim Smith, Bill Campania, and the late Helene Keyssar. Some of my research has been supported by the UCSD Faculty Senate, for which I am grateful.

Thanks to the visionary communications policy warriors: Nicholas Johnson, Nolan Bowie, Peter Franck, George Gerbner, Henry Kroll, Larry Hall, Michael Couzens, Greg Rugierro, Jeff Cohen, Andrea Buffa, Helen DiMichelle, Steve Dunnifer, Ralph Engelman, Bob McChesney, Barbara Abrash, Anita Schiller, Danny Schecter, and Emma Bowen (gone but not forgotten).

Thanks to the courageous curators who have exhibited community media and Paper Tiger: Karen DiGia, John Hanhardt, David Madsen, Bill Horrigan, Craig Baldwin, Vickie Dempsey, Robin Reidy Oppenheimer, Micki McGee, Kathy High, Chris Hill, David Jensen, Richard Herskovitz, Jean Weiffenbach, Kathy Geritz. Thanks to those who have had the courage to support community media: Janet Sternberg, Steve Lavine, the late Bill Kirby, Marge Nicholson, Alice Myatt, Tom Reese, Harriet Barlow, Victor Wallis, David Haas, Michelle Syverson, and especially Robin Lloyd.

Thanks to those artists who keep the standards high: Richard Serra, Joan Jonas, Yvonne Rainer, Antonio Muntadas, C'Love, Max Schumann, Mary Frank. And the culture jammers Guillermo Gomez Peña, Coco Fusco, Brian Springer,

Igor Vamos, Carrie McLaren. Thanks to the founders of the IMC movement: Sheri Herndon, Dan Merkle, Jeff Perlstein, Manse Jacobi, Jon Stout, Erik Galatas, and the tech crews and the hundreds of IMC card-carrying members. Thanks to my *compañeros* of Barcelona: Gloria, Joan, Nuria, Xavier, Toni, Iñaki, Laura, Rosa.

I am in awe at the enthusiasm, courage, dedication, and talent that has continued to burn in the Paper Tiger collective through the work of Michael Eisenmenger, Jessica Glass, Linda Iannacone, Tara Mateik, Jamie McClelland, Amy Melnick, Ana Noguera, Carlos Pareja, Denise Graberman, Carlos Salsedo, Rachel Daniel, Jennifer Whitburn, Mark Read, Matt Height, Lyell Davies, Satya, Heather Hendershot, Andrew Bellware, Josh Lefkowitz, Satya, YuYu Din, Samuel Delgado, Aldumen Gomez, Sara Zia Ebrahimi, Laura Wiltshire, Javier Justiniano, Joshua Kalin.

The train rolls on.

# INTRODUCTION

FOR FORTY YEARS I have been intrigued with the possibilities of creative expression with simple consumer-level technology. My work on a variety of projects that involve media making by "nonprofessionals" began in 1961. It was in that year that I worked with children on the Lower East Side of New York City to produce films by scratching the emulsion off 16 mm film stock. What started as a simple exercise that was documented in a short 16 mm film called *Children Make Movies* happened to appear around the time that Marshall McLuhan was touting the utopian possibilities of a mediated world. The children's film project, made for $88 with a couple of rolls of leftover film stock (short ends, they were called), was met with enthusiasm by a group of newly coined "media educators," who used it as an example of the democratizing potential of "hands-on" media education. It was shown at several early conferences on youth and media, among them one organized by John Culkin and Marshall McLuhan at Fordham University and a UNESCO convocation in Oslo in 1962.

Since that time I have been a "media educator" in a variety of situations: at a reform school in upstate New York, with elementary school children and teachers as an NEA artist-in-residence in Kentucky, Texas, and Nebraska school systems, at senior centers, mental hospitals, farm worker centers, art galleries, film schools, and several universities in an effort to foster creative use of equipment and technology and to encourage critical viewing of mainstream productions and networks. I have taught at the Department of Communication, University of California, San Diego; Cinema Studies at NYU; the School of Visual Arts; C.W. Post, Long Island University; and several other institutions. The titles of the courses which I have taught are a record of my interests: Towards a Technology of Liberation; Making Our Own: Women and Media;

Media as a Social Force: Community Production for Social Change; Continent in Transition: Film and Video in Latin America; Media in the Classroom for Arts Educators; Communications General: Technologies and Community; History of Alternative Media in the United States.

My goal has been to develop in myself and others a critical sense of the potential and limitations of mediated communication through practical exercises that generate a sense of both individual and nonhierarchical group power over the various apparati of media and electronic technology. These interests coalesced in 1981 with the formation of Paper Tiger Television, a production collective which has now produced over three hundred programs providing critical views of print and electronic media.

This book is a collection of essays, presentations, and lectures written over the past forty years. Some have been published in journals, and some were presentations I made at conferences and seminars as a spokesperson for community media. Although they come from a variety of situations, the reader will find certain common themes: communication democracy is perhaps the overarching subject.

In the past thirty years I have been especially interested in the use of consumer-grade video for community use. This work has a base within the public access movement in the United States, and I have been an active participant in the Alliance for Community Media, a national organization which supports and sustains the public access movement. I have also been active and served on the board of Vidéazimut, an international organization to encourage democratic use of communication technology. Through my research I have been in contact with video groups in many countries of Latin America (Guatemala, the Dominican Republic, Brazil, Colombia, Nicaragua, El Salvador, Cuba, Haiti, Mexico) and in Europe (Spain, the Netherlands, the U.K, France, Germany, Denmark) and Asia (Taiwan, Japan, South Korea, the Philippines). For many of these groups I have been a conduit for information about public access in the United States, and I have helped to expand exchange of programs between groups in these countries through programming films and videos from this international community in festivals, art centers, film theaters, and universities around the United States. Many of the programs have also been collected for transmission on satellite via the Deep Dish Network, which I cofounded in 1986, a network of several hundred community channels in over forty states.

I hope that these discussions of community-based media in the United States, Latin America, and Asia will be useful in creating alternatives to corporate commercial media. Many educational, cultural, and social organizations both in the United States and around the world are realizing that they need to rethink the current models for media and technology. Non-Governmental Organizations everywhere are beginning to take media seriously. A vibrant community of media educators provides the technical means and creative encouragement that foster work that is not dictated by commercial pressures or academic constraints. There are many successful projects that have been generated by videomakers, community radio producers, teachers, librarians, and artists, but very little dissemination of this work so that others can utilize and grow from these many experiments.

Most media research focuses on mainstream television and filmmaking, with scant attention to efforts to create popular forms of participatory media. I hope that this book will serve as a resource for those who are committed to seeking new ways of organizing communication. I start with a discussion of my own development as a teacher, producer, and active participant in the struggle for media democracy. Many of these essays were written in the heat of battle, so to speak. I hope this can give the readers a historical perspective on the community-based media movement and a sense of the determination and resolve that have enabled often fragile and much embattled local community video organizations and independent media makers to survive in a climate that is dominated by global media corporations.

# 1

# From the Atomic City
# to the Chelsea Hotel

DeeDee as a beatnik, painting on the beach, 1958. *(Charles Rotmil)*

# Introduction

I GREW UP in the city of the atomic bomb, Oak Ridge, Tennessee. Although my childhood was infused with the town's celebratory ecstasy of technological triumph that surrounded the "splitting of the atom," this municipal pride of my hometown was tempered by my parents' humanism and growing concern about the specter of nuclear war. "Plunk Your Magic Twanger" and "Perpetual Shadows" go back to that history. "Perpetual Shadows" is a tribute to the work of Erik Barnouw, whose film *Hiroshima/Nagasaki* made clear to me the true horror of atomic weaponry.

How does one get from a gung ho atomic town in East Tennessee to the fringes of beatnik culture on the Lower East Side? By dropping out. In 1958 I left Antioch College after two years of study and went to New York City, adrift in the Beat Generation. I was introduced to Marshall McLuhan in 1961 when he was in residence at Fordham University and at center stage of popular culture. I was flattered by his interest in some experiments I was doing at the time with children and film at the Lillian Wald Settlement. He and Father John Culkin, a Jesuit priest who taught at Fordham and wooed McLuhan to New York City, saw *Children Make Movies*, a document of my workshops on Avenue D, and invited me to speak at several conferences on youth and media. I memorized many of McLuhan's aphorisms and called myself a "McLuhanite," though I lacked the critical background to really understand his oeuvre. Looking at his work in the cool dawn after the fall of the Berlin Wall, I was startled to scrutinize some of his essays. "History Will Dissolve Us" consists of ruminations on my own ambiguous relationship to McLuhan and the phenomenon of his visit to the United States. My paper was presented on the occasion of the twenty-fifth anniversary of the publication of McLuhan's *Understanding Media* and the tenth

anniversary of Media Alliance, a New York State alternative
media organization.

As a dropout, my employment was limited to part-time
teaching gigs. In 1963 I founded the Henry Street Settlement
Film Club with a donated 8 mm camera and a few rolls of out-
of-date stock. We made short films and showed them on a
sheet stretched between the streetlights in the middle of the
block. By 1965 I had three children and a husband in graduate
music school, and we moved out of New York City to Sullivan
County in the Catskills. Although seventy-five miles from
Times Square, I ended up working with very similar groups of
kids: young boys (12 to 16) from the metropolitan region who
had been remanded by the juvenile justice system to correctional institutions upstate. I organized a filmmaking project at
Otisville School for Boys, where dozens of youths made 16
mm, Super 8, and video productions as part of their rehabilitation.

Leading film workshops couldn't support our family, and I
supplemented my income working as a kind of media consultant and facilitator for painters, dancers, and sculptors. I
worked as a collaborator with various artists, including Richard Serra, Nancy Holt, Mabou Mines, Shirley Clarke, and
Joan Jonas. This work was an education into the ways of the
art world and contemporary art history. Those were exciting
years in the newly discovered Soho district, and there was a
sense of community and collaboration, more affirmative and
feminist than in the Beatnik era. Dressed in only a few gauze
stoles, Carolee Schneeman was hanging upside down at Saint
Mark's Church, and there were six-floor walk-up concerts by
Phil Glass and his ensemble and riveting performances by a
heady group of dancer-performance artists called the Grand
Union. I was deeply moved by Yvonne Rainer's performances
in this group. The collaborative unity of both Grand Union
and the Mabou Mines Theater Collective was a major inspiration for what was later to become Paper Tiger Television.

Part of the excitement of the early seventies was the romance with new tools. Raindance, Global Village, and Videofreex had grabbed portapak video and were forging new ways
of making media. The Videofreex and I set up several video

"happenings," at a local park in Middletown, New York, and at the Orange County Fair. We were playing with the phenomenon of video feedback: cameras and monitors with which a curious public could interact. I became a member of Shirley Clarke's Video Space Troupe and spent two years making wild and wacky video installations and performances. "Remembering Shirley" looks at these two years of apprenticeship to that great filmmaker and video artist.

Another influence was photographer Robert Frank. When I had moved to New York in the 1960s, Frank's book of his photographic journey around the United States, *The Americans*, had helped me put my Southern upbringing in perspective. I felt lucky to be able to work with him in Nova Scotia on a film entitled *Keep Busy*. "Keeping Busy on Cape Breton Island" is a diary I kept during the production.

# Plunk Your Magic Twanger: Community Control of Technology

## *January 1991*

OAK RIDGE, TENNESSEE, was a technical town. There was OUR technology and THEIR technology. Television was OUR technology. It was in Oak Ridge that I saw my first TV set in 1947. I was seven. The homemade set was in a neighbor's garage next to boxes of Christmas tree lights and broken bird feeders, surrounded by coils and wires, clutters of tubes and drips of solder. It wasn't a piece of furniture: it didn't have a wood-grained console. It was just a tube wired up to a box of junk. The image was pretty ghostly. It's hard to say whether the reception was poor because the connections were faulty or because the Tennessee hills were too high for the jerry-rigged antenna. About a dozen of us crowded into the space, peering at a circle of dancing snow. It was some guys boxing, but the image was so unclear you couldn't see who was who, even though one of the boxers was black and one was white. You couldn't tell the skin color through the snow.

It was the first time any of us had seen television. It was magic, but magic of the backyard variety—like the wire circles that are supposed to pop apart but only make it on the third try, the bottomless top hat whose plentiful lining is portentously bulging. The seams showed. It wasn't really magic: our neighbor soldered the wires together and tuned in. He had done it himself using an envelope full of clipped schematics from *Popular Science* magazine.

It was OUR technology. Theirs was another matter. We knew where THEIR technology started: mysterious chain link fences circled hundreds of pine-wooded acres hiding laboratories and warehouses. My father had to wear a photo-ID badge to work and present it about five miles from where the actual lab was. Oak Ridge was where they processed the uranium for the first atomic bombs. THEIR technology was secret, grand, and important. Television? That's something in the garage for sharing with friends and neighbors.

In those early days the reception of television was active and communal: something homemade which was shared in a garage on the block. The mass marketing of industrial consoles and the industrialization of network programming soon changed that. Television became something made by THEM for our consumption. I think my early introduction to a funky homemade TV set made me want to bring TV production back to the garage. The first studio cameras were monsters with cables six inches in diameter. Today tiny handheld camcorders have finally brought TV production out of those airless studios to the neighborhoods: the playgrounds and garages, the town councils and the local dumps. Public access to equipment and cable channels has made it possible to share the technology of transmission, just as reception was shared in those early days. Although besieged by the cable corporations, fraught with bureaucratic requirements from the municipalities and burdened with the necessity of having to serve everyone from local narcissists to Nazis, public access has proven that communications can be democratic in the best sense of that overused, often misappropriated word. A thousand flowers have bloomed already—40,000 hours of original programming are transmitted monthly. Not all are peach blossoms. But the product was never the goal. It's the process, of course, but more than the process, it's the potential power that a popular diffuse medium could possibly unlock. Access is dangerous to the system because of that potentia. If one counts the access studios, the media centers across the country, the number of camcorders, and the number of organized solidarity groups and environmental organizations, the potential is quite astonishing.[1] The potential is for democratic communication. That potential is present in the United States: the potential to cut through the hypocrisy of our current information system.

There is a cynical hypocrisy in the hymns to capitalism that dominate the current information networks. We can see how our system is dependent on debt, a tottering stack of credit cards; how, despite the financial boom, our cities are full of misery and joblessness; how our waters and soil are contaminated, our factories rusty, our infrastructure rotting. The savings and loan scandal showed the corruption of our financial system. The machinations of the Gulf and Serbian warmongers cannot hide for long the pathetic state of our own economy and our own repressive state apparatus. There is a hunger for authentic media. How can we work together to help each other to create a television to change our world: a television that is human, responsive to important events, and utilizing the vast reserves of creativity that exist in this country? How can we create a television that is inclusive: that expresses the needs, hopes, and creativity of those now underrepresented on existing channels?

There seems to be consensus around issues of children's programming. Action for Children's Television and other media reformers have raised consciousness about "programming/commercials" for children: the "My Little Pony" and "Ninja Turtles" shows that marketed toys as programming between ads for sugary cereals. These advertising/programs are not new. One of the programs I saw in those days in front of my neighbor's Oak Ridge TV (I can't call it a set—it was more like a pile of wires) was Buster Brown. "That's my dog Tigh, he lives in a shoe. . . . I'm Buster Brown, look for me in there too!" That show was the evolutionary ancestor of the current kids' stuff. The stars were the shoemaker's logo. With the constant repeating of the name Buster Brown, the program sold shoes for almost the entire half hour. But the favorite charac-

---

[1] The media activists working together with grassroots activists against the World Trade Organization in Seattle in November 1999 proved just how strong that potential is. Five half-hour programs called "Showdown in Seattle: The Five Days That Shook the WTO," were produced by over 100 camcorder activists for Deep Dish Television. See Part 9.

ter wasn't the overly cute Buster Brown. There was this naughty frog . . . who could plunk his magic twanger and turn the world upside down. And the TV show would do just that: when the twanger sound effect started, the camera would turn upside down!

Can we rethink the very basis of our television system? Can we start to think of television as an authentic public interest? We need a commercial- and corporate-free television, not a medium designed to make a profit from constructing needs in an already needy world.

When my father would leave for work at the lab in Oak Ridge, Lab Security would check him with a Geiger counter. He was never shown the readings. It was THEIR machine, and the check wasn't for his health. It was for THEIR research.[2]

A few years ago we had a Geigerfest in Woodstock, New York, my new hometown. Ed Sanders, poet, ex-Fug, and recent planning board member, organized it. It was a benefit concert and poetry reading to buy a Geiger counter for the town dump, so we can make sure that the trucks full of waste that use the dump aren't contaminating our groundwater. We raised almost a thousand dollars. It's OUR Geiger counter. We need to have our own measure of the contaminants in our workplace and homes.

*America's Funniest Home Videos* has been one of the most popular shows on television. The tapes that are chosen for national airing are steeped in the same sadism, misogyny, and contempt for the American working class that permeate the rest of television. The actual time given to the homemade tapes is, at most, seven minutes of each program. Most of the shows are endless "wrap-arounds": pathetic and patronizing as the "host" plods through pathetic "intros" and "outtros" of the material. People watch, waiting not for the dopey host or the wide-angle close-ups of the guffawing crowd, but for those moments of fresh humor. They await a flash of recognition of humanity on a box that daily denies it. The public hun-

---

[2] Recent revelations from DOE documents have shown just how egregious and callous much of that research was. Oak Ridge is now admittedly one of the most heavily contaminated spots on earth.

gers for something more authentic, more in touch with the everyday lives of people. Independent producers in the United States have, by and large, expressed this authenticity. Can the independents unite with the access activists, with the community organizers, with the environmentalists, with the Peacenets, with the visual artists, with the performers, with the gays and the lesbians, with the homeless draft-age youth, with the jobless, with the media critics? Can we get together in TV land? Plunk your magic twanger and turn the world upside down!

# Perpetual Shadows:
# Representing the Atomic Age

## *June 1998*

MY OLD HOMETOWN, Oak Ridge, Tennessee, was essentially a government reservation bent on atomic weapon construction. When my family first moved there in 1946, it was still a top secret town, though everyone knew the atomic bomb was developed in its barbed-wire-enclosed factories. In fact, Oak Ridge itself was encircled in yet more barbed wire. Until 1949 there were gates at each of end of the highway that passed through town where guards would study ID cards before they let you in or out.[3] The atmosphere of secrecy and intrigue made it hard to gossip about the place when we went to visit our relatives back in St. Louis. I recall my parents being uncharacteristically vague about just where we lived in Tennessee. There was certainly no discussion of what it was my father did. He was a lowly research engineer working on metals, but as far as I knew he might have been Oppenheimer's assistant. We didn't want to know.

I got the feeling that neither of my parents liked the fact that Oak Ridge was about atomic weaponry—especially since the government had actually used the bomb on Japanese civilians. Oak Ridge knew too much. In that part of Tennessee there wasn't the celebratory end of the war hurrah that seemed to be prevalent at least in *Life* magazine's version of postwar America. However, as the months went by, Oak Ridgers began to be proud of their role in "ending the war." You could buy a pennant at the drug store with the name "Oak Ridge" sur-

---

[3] "Open Sesame! Welcome to the Atomic City!" Headline on *The Oak Ridger*, March 18, 1949.

rounded by little mushroom clouds and circling atoms. One of our school softball teams called themselves the Neutrinos. And slowly Oak Ridge opened up to the outside world. A new red, white, and blue sign went up as the guarded gates went down: Welcome to Oak Ridge: Birthplace of the Atomic Age.

Being an "Army town," Oak Ridge didn't have much in the way of official cultural activities, but many of the scientists were refugees from war-torn Europe, or MIT and Princeton post-docs who were used to the amenities of Western elite culture. My parents were part of a group that started a symphony orchestra. It wasn't hard to fill the second violin section. There were probably more oboe players in Oak Ridge than in the entire rest of East Tennessee at that time. There wasn't much in the way of museums or galleries, until one day it was announced that there would be a new museum of atomic energy. Its slogan was "Atoms for Peace!" The atomic energy industry was getting underway, and there was much excitement about the possibility of having atomic power. People even talked about having little reactors in automobiles. My dad was part of a team to design a plane that would run with a reactor on board. (When the workers on this ill-fated project finally got together for their twenty-five-year reunion, their commemorative T shirt had a white elephant flying Dumbo-like, winking one eye.)

Everyone was excited about the new museum. Finally Oak Ridge would be on the culture map with the culture most suited to its history and place in the world: atomic science! A museum of atomic energy would show school children and tourists the glorious possibilities of the atomic age and of course give a look back to Oak Ridge's seminal role in that history.

For my father the scientist, the idea of a science museum was a dream come true. We were regular visitors every time a friend or relative came from out of town. The museum was a lively place, sort of a precursor to San Francisco's Exploratorium. It had what in those days were quite innovative interactive exhibits, with buttons to push and levers to raise. The type of hands-on experiments displayed in Oak Ridge have found a commercial home in those science stores in U.S. malls which sell science kits as consumer commodities for anxious parents. I especially recall a Van de Graaff generator: you could put your hand on a silver globe and make your hair stand up like a cartoon cat getting electrocuted. There was a simulation of a chain reaction, built like a giant pinball machine. You'd cock a plunger on a spring and then let it let loose, and Wham! a single ping-pong ball would activate hundreds of other ping-pong balls into bopping all around their Plexiglas box in a crazy frenzy. But my favorite exhibit was a machine to irradiate dimes. You could take a dime out of your pocket and put it in a little slot and listen to the buzz and clink as it rolled through a bombardment of electrons. It would come out encased in plastic encircled with a text that said: "Neutron Irradiated at the American Museum of Atomic Energy." To make sure it was irradiated you could hold it underneath the scanner of a Geiger counter and watch as the needle gyrated back and forth to the accompaniment of a loud buzzy ticking sound. Happily convinced that you had a genuine irradiated dime, you could then put it back in your pocket and take it home to your treasure box. I had a collection of several dozen which somehow got lost over the years. My mother, ever the custodian of family history, had the foresight to preserve four dimes for my three sisters and me. After she died we went to her safe deposit box, and there was a box with four irradiated times, one for each of us. I shudder to think of the damage this sort of "fun house" souvenir may have done to ovaries and testicles in close proximity to young pockets. And what about the bank clerk whose desk was backed against those safe deposit boxes?

Aside from the fun and games, there was a history section of the museum that worried me. It consisted of dramatic photographs of mushroom clouds and the airplanes that delivered the bombs. There was a biology section with rows of giant photo blowups of ears of corn and close-ups of rice grains. The first picture of corn was a normal ear. The ones next to it were all weird, misshapen, with some of the kernels the size of lemons and others on the same ear tiny and shriveled like peppercorns. The caption said that this was corn after exposure to the atomic blast and in subsequent generations of progeny from that seed. Similar results were evident in the rice photographs, the grains alternately bloated and shriveled. There were also pictures of water buffalo with weird-shaped horns and a photo of a calf fetus with two heads floating in a bottle.

Missing were any photos of human babies exposed to or born after the blast. Although there were photographs of the destroyed cities of Hiroshima and Nagasaki, there were no human beings in any of the photos. There were no captions detailing the casualties. We had a bomb shelter at our school, and we all practiced "duck and cover" when the siren blew. Perhaps, I thought, everyone went into the air raid shelters or under their desks. But why didn't they show the children? There was only one photograph that had even a memory of a human being: the title was curious. It said "Permanent shadow on such and such bridge." I puzzled over that. A shadow is by its very nature impermanent—it depends on light to create it. It was when I looked at the charred outline of a head and body on stone, that I realized in horror that there had been human beings at Hiroshima and Nagasaki.

The missing "human effects" (as the army euphemistically labeled them) were kept for years in top secret files in the National Archives. Erik Barnouw, Barbara Van Dyke, Paul Ronder, and Geoff Bartz later reconstructed that footage, which had been seized by the U.S. military from Japanese filmmakers. Before the U.S. occupying force had arrived at the scene, producer Akira Iwasaki, with the support of the Japanese Ministry of Education, had arranged to document the devastation of the two atomic bombs. The film crew recorded patient doctors lifting charred skin off children, grandparents sifting through wreckage for signs of their families, weeping mothers holding limp hands sticking out of bandaged forms in hospitals of horror. One of the cameramen, Toshio Sekuguchi, was arrested by U.S. occupation officials while filming the ruins in Nagasaki. All of the footage was declared "classified" and stashed away with the missing photographs from the Oak Ridge Museum to save us from knowing the reality of the atomic age. Barnouw retrieved that footage and was able to make the film *Hiroshima/Nagasaki*, which some have called the most important film of the twentieth century. It brought to both Japanese and U.S. eyes the terrible consequences of nuclear war.

Barnouw knows the necessity of confronting that history, just as his history of broadcasting often shows us the ugly truths of our media system. To build both a lasting peace and an authentic democratic communication system, an unflinching knowledge of our past is a prerequisite, which only historians of Barnouw's integrity can provide.

Irradiated dime from the Oak Ridge Museum of Atomic Energy, 1949. *(Author)*

# History Will Dissolve Us, Or, Time Base Correction in a Post–Cold War World

## *June 1989*

IT IS TWENTY-FIVE YEARS since Marshall McLuhan wrote *Understanding Media: The Extensions of Man*. And it is approximately three weeks since the Berlin Wall was dismantled. It is useful to recall the McLuhan's enthusiasm:

> The electronic age of servomechanisms suddenly releases men from the mechanical and specialist servitude of the preceding machine age. As the machine and the motorcar released the horse and projected it onto the plane of entertainment, so does automation with men. We are threatened with a liberation that taxes our inner resources of self-employment and imaginative participation in society.[4]

> The instantaneous world of electronic media involves all of us all at once. Ours is a brand new world of all at onceness. Time has ceased and space has vanished. Like primitives we now live in a global village of our own making: a simultaneously happening. . . . The global village is as big as the planet and as small as the village post office.[5]

And the optimism of the era:

> It will cost less and less. . . . Access is the key. We're now at the Liverpool stage. Right now it's 90% funk and 10% content. . . .

---

[4] Marshall McLuhan, *Understanding Media: The Extensions of Man* (New York: McGraw-Hill, 1964), p. 358.

[5] *This is Marshall McLuhan: The Medium Is the Message.* This 16mm film, made by Ernest Pintoff in 1968, consists of montages of ads and found footage alternating with interviews with McLuhan, shot with ever-changing colored gel lighting and a psychedelic background.

It'll develop naturally. Where the information is needed it'll flow. The people who have access to video tape equipment initially will be the ones who will be the access points. It's not like print: it's hardware. But we don't have to pound down the doors of NBC. We're trying to evolve our own network that is completely separate from that beast TV trip. . . . As we'll have more and more programming, in five years we'll have Freex buying satellites. That's where we're headed to: time on the satellite. Right now Raindance is trying to buy computer time. It's a natural extension. . . . We have to maintain a generation of information. We have to get into these systems and develop our own databanks, our own networks.[6]

In the eight years between the first and last of those statements, the Vietnam War had escalated from a Green Beret intervention to a full-scale land war in Asia with several hundred GI's and several thousand Vietnamese being killed each week. A massive resistance to the war had grown to the extent that colleges and universities had closed down for varying periods of time. In the African American communities massive resistance and frustration at the death of Martin Luther King, Jr., had fueled insurrections which burned huge swaths of major urban centers.

THE TALE OF THE JOHNSONS

In 1964, the same year that McLuhan published *Understanding Media*, a young fast-talking country lawyer with a keen sense of humor named Nicholas Johnson was appointed to the FCC by Lyndon Johnson (no relation, but knowing Lyndon, narcissism may have been an element). Lyndon was a slow-talking country lawyer whose presidential orders sent those thousands off to Southeast Asia and loaded the planes and the supply depots with barrels of napalm and shrapnel bombs.

Both of these Johnsons had the opportunity to play around

---

[6] Frank Gillette and Michael Shamberg at the Alternate Media Conference, Goddard College, 1972. Videotape footage of the conference is archived at Video Data Bank at the Art Institute of Chicago, 37 S. Wabash, Chicago, Ill. 60603.

with a new toy. Lyndon was given a portapak by the Sony corporation. He used it to practice his speeches. Nick Johnson also played around with a portapak in the early days of that technology: at the Raindance loft, where Ira Schneider, Frank Gillette, and Paul Ryan taught him to do what so many of us videofreaks have done—play with feedback. Pointing the camera into the monitor results in all kinds of trippy psychedelic effects. Think of how history might have changed had Lyndon even by accident pointed the camera at the monitor. Maybe no one ever showed Lyndon. Maybe his narcissism never allowed the camera off his jowly face for one minute. At any rate, Lyndon went on to order more bombs, and Nick wrote a book called *How to Talk Back to Your Television Set*[7] and wedged some public access rules into the FCC ledger—in between voting blocks of the networks and the newly formed cable industry.[8]

Where was McLuhan at this time? He was writing *Culture Is Our Business*, whose subtitle was *War Equals Education: Violence Is the Quest for Identity*. The book jacket promises to examine "the century's one great art form, advertising." It alternates reproductions of ads (Warner's Bra, Northwest Airlines, Western Electric, etc.) with pithy boldface epigrams like "The TV generation is postliterate and retribalized. It seeks by violence to 'scrub' the old private image and to merge in a new tribal identity like any corporation executive."

In looking back at McLuhan it is amazing to me that so many artists and intellectuals downed his theory capsules. He was the L Tryptophan of epigram makers. It is only now that we can see some of the more noxious side effects. We Americans aren't particularly noted for our critical minds, but he certainly contributed to an unquestioning acceptance of mass media for an entire generation—a generation during which the media corporations were able to grow unfettered until we now have what Jack O'Dell, past president of the Pacifica

---

[7] Nicholas Johnson, *How to Talk Back to Your TV Set* (New York: Bantam, 1968).

[8] Both scenes of Johnsons and portapaks are choicely featured in David Shulman's tape on the history of the public access movement, *Everyone's Channel*, available from Video Data Bank.

Foundation, calls the Military Industrial Media complex. Of course, it isn't all McLuhan's fault. If he didn't exist, Madison Avenue, *Vogue*, McGraw–Hill, and *Fortune* magazine (some of his biggest proponents) would have had to, if not invent him, at least find someone else. Surely Bell Labs, IBM, and General Motors could have found other consultants to receive the enormous fees they lavished on the Canadian scholar.

I do not subscribe to the auteur theory of history, and I don't believe that McLuhan's *popularity* was foisted on us. Lots of things are foisted on us that don't get to be so popular. The reason he touched a responsive chord (in Tony Schwartz, another media guru, among other people) is that he was essentially an optimist. Americans like optimists. From Shirley Temple to Jimmy Swaggart, optimists do OK. This is why Jean Baudrillard (a hustler more chic these days and whose technological determinism in many ways mirrors McLuhan) is not exactly a household word, except in the recesses of the Semiotics Program at Brown University and the Whitney Downtown. He's never had his face on *Time* magazine's cover. He's such a downer.[9]

McLuhan's most popular thesis, I think largely misunderstood, was the concept of a global village. If one reads carefully, one sees immediately that in McLuhan's global village the media activity for villagers (and that includes most of us) was seen as passive. When McLuhan talked about media being the extensions of Man (he definitely did not say Persons), for all his cybernetic language, he was talking of media in a Scholastic sense: media as in Gutenberg—media as a way of distributing the Word. Those villagers were under a tree watching a tube. They weren't holding cameras. Of course, many of his readers and fans never for a moment accepted that passivity. With his encapsulated epigrammatic way of both speaking and publishing, he enabled us to pick and choose among ringing phrases.

John Fekete in his book *The Critical Twilight* called McLu-

---

[9] I am indebted to an article by Andreas Huysmans comparing Baudrillard and McLuhan, presented at a conference in Bellagio, Italy, February 1989.

han's technique carpet bombing (an appropriate metaphor for the historical moment): "Some of the harshest critics applaud McLuhan's 'insights' in isolation. Of course these insights cannot be the real basis for a defense of his work, just as there is no defense of saturation bombing that occasionally hits even a military target. . . . Isolated insights like technical military successes are situated in the overall patterns to which they contribute and by which their function is shaped and distorted." Fekete goes on to conclude that in McLuhan "a perception of the massive technocratic manipulation and administration of needs is perverted into a biological extension theory that reinforces technological reification."[10] As Andrew Ross has noted in *No Respect: Intellectuals and Popular Culture*,[11] McLuhan in all his probes and explorations ignored the ugly, exploitative side of technological development. Read McLuhan if you doubt this assessment of the overall pattern of his work. History has enabled us to see his work more clearly, and a lot of what he says doesn't sound so clever any more, which is probably why there are few college courses that even bother to assign his books. For many communication students his name is vaguely familiar and somehow associated with the words "global village"—the way my father associated Fibber McGee with overstuffed closets. So much for the intellectual and cultural giants of our time.

The theme of the global village has resurfaced with the proliferation of satellite-delivered U.S. programs, the marketing of consumer-priced camcorders, and the dissolution of the Soviet empire.

> It has happened as the late Marshall McLuhan, the Canadian expert of communications theory predicted: the next war will be fought with images ["Revolution in a Box: Ted Koppel Reports].

The Ted Koppels and the Dan Rathers are proclaiming the arrival of the true global village. The dull gray masses long

---

[10] John Fekete, *The Critical Twilight* (New York: Routledge and Kegan Paul, 1977), p. 186.

[11] Andrew Ross, *No Respect: Intellectuals and Popular Culture* (New York: Routledge, 1989).

suffering under communist repression can now see *Miami Vice* and the Gap commercials that accompany it to brighten their lives and spur them on to throw off the weight of oppression.

> This year CNN's satellite footprint becomes world wide. . . . The most successful TV programs in the world are ours. . . . The Huxtables and their home are known and beloved around the world ["Revolution in a Box"].

Another aspect of this Second Coming of the utopian global village vision is the explosion of camcorder activity.

> The world is in the early stages of a revolution that it has barely begun to understand. We think we know something about the impact of television because it's been with us for fifty years, but recently TV has begun falling into the hands of the people. . . . This year alone some seven and a half million camcorders will be sold worldwide. . . . With millions of cameras out there today, even though very few are in the hands of journalists, the chances of an important or interesting event being videotaped are much greater than they have ever been before ["Revolution in a Box"].

Of course, for Koppel and Rather the ultimate apotheosis of this activity is not a global town meeting or in fact any semblance of democratic media. No, their vision is more akin to Andy Warhol's famous fifteen. Our very own moment of fame: we can be a part of CBS News.

> One of the newest, fastest growing resources television has is *you*—you and your home video camera. It used to be that people worried about Big Brother watching. Now it seems we've got everybody's brother and his sister behind a camera. In three or four years we'll see twenty million cameras out there. It'll be that much more likely that some type of news will take place in front of someone who can record it. There's a growing demand for this electronic folk journalism and real opportunities for the neighborhood camcorder. If you get any home video of real news, call CBS. And that's tonight's CBS news. Good Night [Dan Rather, CBS News, April 1989].

In other words, if we should luck upon a disaster (with fresh batteries and a blank tape), we might get our train accident or our very own tornado on the CBS News. Taking Kansas to Oz, as it were. If this is the only option, the passivity of McLuhan makes perfect sense.

In homage to McLuhan's gift for metaphor, here's a video metaphor: one of the inventions on which we videomakers have come to rely is the TBC—the time base corrector. For those who have never had a shaky signal or wiggly color, it is the instrument in the video edit room that enables one to take the pulsed track that organizes the video information on one's original material and replace it with a new base, preserving as much of the original material as possible and adding a stability and a strength of signal that enables the material to be copied, broadcast, or processed—changed graphically into almost endless varieties of forms: shapes, colors, edges, dissolves. From the beginning of video, it was recognized by everyone from the Videofreex to Nick Johnson that those wanting to work in video would need such instruments. It was the intention of the pioneering work of people like Kepys and Vanderbeek (who worked at WGBH TV in Boston—the first TV Lab prototype) that the public television system could be a laboratory for those doing experimental and innovative television work. I think it was also a dream of corporations like Bell Labs that appropriation of this kind of experimentation would be good for business.

However, for many of the artists who worked in those systems, both at WGBH and at WNET and within the EAT experiments at Bell Labs and even at institutions such as the Alternative Media Center at NYU, it became increasingly clear that laboratories set up by corporations and/or large institutions have their own priorities. Artists and media activists working within these institutions were often frustrated, their visions belittled, their ideas co-opted. Correcting the artist's base to the institutional base had a certain kind of dropout (to stretch the video metaphor). Time base correction in an institutional context can be a form of appropriation of original material.

In a world of increasing instrumental relations, Media Alliance has been instrumental—in the best sense. To take the

Stand-By program[12] as an example: here is a way to utilize the machinery of corporate media, but administered or *based* outside those institutions. Stand-By allows production houses to write off at full price time on their machines which they give to independent producers through Media Alliance. This time is usually what is called "down time" in the trade. Stand-By is just that: media artists "standing by" to have access on high-end equipment when it is available.

It is interesting that, like the TV Lab, Media Alliance is housed at WNET, but unlike TV Lab, it is independent of any formal administrative and programmatic control by public television. WNET is the landlord, but Media Alliance is *our* base. It is one of an increasing number of organizations and alternative institutions that have grown and flourished in the independent media community. These institutions are the heritage of the pioneering video collectives, the alternative media conferences, the archives, the installations, the research and writing, the taping and editing, and yes, even the utopian epigrams of McLuhan, however unintentional that parentage may be. The dedication and hard work of artists, arts administrators, curators, and technicians maintaining a vision of a liberatory media have created alternative institutions in an authentic *media alliance.* It is in this community effort that our creative abilities, visions, and opinions will be able to develop uncensored and thrive to their fullest potential. It is TBC, but we are at the controls.

But what about *time?* Contrary to the claims of McLuhan, time has *not* disappeared. We are living in an important moment in history. I hope that we can correct our base to this momentous time.

The organizing principle of our country has crumbled with the Berlin Wall; the subsuming anticommunism that has fueled the insanity of U.S. military expansion is a futile anachronism. It is the East that is in flux at this point in time. Our system is rigid and stagnant. Our jails are full, our streets are

---

[12] The Stand-By program uses the unreserved times at commercial post-production houses to provide artists cut-rate use of high-end editing equipment. This was initiated in New York by Kathy High, Robin White, and others and has been replicated elsewhere.

lined with homeless and hungry people. The time demands that we, like the aroused masses in Eastern Europe, examine our bases: this is an opportunity for a questioning of the priorities of *our* society, a time to redirect our vast resources. In a world without the great Red enemy, our own stuffed generals and petrified cold warriors loose all legitimacy.[13]

McLuhan talked of the media as the extensions of man [*sic*], but his models were corporate. Will media be extensions of the military industrial media complex or extensions of creative human endeavor? The technology we have within our grasp need not accept a corporate agenda, but be tools for human empowerment. Our independent media can illuminate paths for a future of hope. Our tools will be extensions of human will, not of alienation and control. Our art can be:

- The eyes of visionaries to see the way to balance in nature and justice in society
- The ears of sympathy for the homeless and jobless
- The hands of friendship and cooperation
- The arms to defend the exploited and oppressed
- The cerebral connections to match global problems with local solutions
- The genitals to glory in our multifaceted sexuality
- The wings to carry the information we need to share, and
- The hearts to beat in time with the celebrations of empowerment.

---

[13] This was written before the Pentagon found convenient new enemies in Iraq and Serbia.

# Remembering Shirley:
# Live From the Chelsea Hotel

## *April 1998*

SHIRLEY CLARKE was my mentor. I learned more from her than anyone else I ever knew—mostly about how to be a mentor—how to energize people, how to push them to do good work, how not to give up when the technology was failing, the people lethargic, or the situation impossible. Shirley pushed things and people to the edge. She never gave up. Alzheimer's claimed her in her late sixties, but she held on.[14] She died in a sweet sleep surrounded by Felix the Cat and Betty Boop, the toys of her youth held tight for all those years.

Shirley was somewhere between Betty Boop and Felix the Cat herself, with a bit of Charlie Chaplin's tramp thrown in. She often wore a bowler hat and tight, smart little suits, like something out of a 1930s chorus line. All she needed were spats to complete the costume. She had style. A small woman with the body of a dancer, she had piercing black eyes, like a beady little mouse. She was witty and bright, and endlessly energetic.

Shirley started as a dancer. Her first films were dance films, such as *Dance in the Sun* (1953) and *In Paris Parks* (1954), a lyrical look at gesture and movement in a public landscape. I saw this early work and *Bridges Go Round*, a piece she did for the Brussels World Fair at the Hunter Art Museum in Chattanooga, Tennessee. It changed my life. Seeing her name on the

---

[14] In her final years Shirley was tenderly nursed by two of her beloved disciples, Piper and David Cort, who bathed her and tucked her in and smoothed her forehead. Her daughter Wendy and many of her colleagues were with her during her last days in a Boston hospital.

credits and the joy and energy of the images made me realize that women could and should make their own films.

Her work in the early 1960s, *The Connection* and *The Cool World*, are landmarks of the American New Wave movement. *The Cool World* is a New York version of Italian neo-realism, every bit as powerful and poignant. It remains (with Robert Frank's *Pull My Daisy*) the best expression of marginal life in that era. Her film *Portrait of Jason* (1967) was one of the first with a gay protagonist in an open and sympathetic (and completely unromantic) manner. Shirley and Viva Superstar shared the screen as talent in Agnes Varda's *Lion's Love*, which was always my favorite Varda film. Somehow Shirley (and Viva) added a New York edge to Varda, who can wax sentimental and cloying.

In the early seventies I found my way up to her workshop space in the penthouse of the Chelsea Hotel. Shirley lived and worked there making live and taped video performance, installation, and documentation with a collaborating group of artists. I was lucky to have been a part of that work. We formed a troupe, those of us who worked with Shirley. She called us the TeePee Video Space Troupe, and the idea was to experiment with performance that integrated video and other technologies. It was the days before video cassettes, and each tape had to be hand-threaded into the portapak decks. Not that it was really about recording per se. Most of what we did was never on tape: the tape was only one of the elements of the constructions, the happenings, the events. It was electronic performance in an interactive mode. The troupe included me, Andy Gurian, Shirley's daughter Wendy, Bruce Ferguson, Vicki Polon, David Cort, Bob Harris, Parry Teasdale, Shalom Gorewitz, Susan Milano, Shridar Bapat, and others. There were regular drop-ins like Agnes Varda, Shigeko Kaboda, Beryl Korot, Nam June Paik, Skip Blumberg, Barbara Haspiel, Steina and Woody Vasulka, Jori Schwartzman, our neighbors at the Chelsea, Carl Lee, Viva (toting one of her kids), photographer Peter Simon, Doris Chase, Andre Vosnevshenski, George Kleinsinger, Virgil Thomson, Harry Smith, Arthur C. Clarke (no relation). At any given time there always seemed to be one or two Japanese dancers around. Sometimes even Andy Warhol climbed that flight of stairs after the last elevator stop, looking for Viva. Louis Malle came by, as did Susan Sontag, Joris Ivens, Peter Brooks, Jean Rouche, and Shelly Winters. The Chelsea had a certain cachet for visitors from Europe, Hollywood, and Japan, and Shirley was queen of the Chelsea.

Around Shirley swirled miles of video cables, cameras, monitors, and telephones. She was wired. Shirley had a new project every night. We were needed to help make it happen. It was sometimes frustrating, often exhausting, but it was hard not to trot over there, because you never knew what you might miss if you stayed away.

One time Arthur Clarke somehow got hold of a laser beam. He unwrapped a long rectangular box with a fat cable, borrowed from some Columbia lab by a fan of *2001: A Space Odyssey*. This was many years before those red needles of light sparkled on every cashier's counter. The laser was exotic and thrilling, and Shirley and Arthur giggled like kids phoning in bogus pizza orders as they plugged it in and carried it out to the edge of the Chelsea roof, aiming it down at the sidewalk. From that distance it was hard to keep steady, but Shrider quickly screwed it onto a tripod tilted over the edge. Passersby on 23rd street stooped to pick up the resulting tiny red jewel. Both Clarkes roared with laughter as they made it jump five feet out of reach. When we tried using the laser in our performances, it etched intricate patterns on several of our camera tubes.

One night we all agreed to do dawn. We broke into five groups and went out to video the dawn. We reconnoitered on the roof with stacks of monitors and cued up the five tapes from the five groups. Shirley rang up for bagels and champagne, and when they were delivered we toasted the pink sky and switched on the decks for a multichannel piece of morning in New York. Shots of steam rising from the street vents, tracking shots of bottle collectors pushing their carts, shots of pigeons in flight mixed and matched across the screens. The natural sounds of the live streets below us mixed with the taped steam hisses and pigeon coos to make a city symphony of sounds as well as sights. Behind the pyramid of monitors flickering the black and white visual poems were the pastel skyscrapers, their windows reflecting the rising red sun ball. One special moment was when pigeons flew right to left across one of the monitors and appeared in the bottom left of the neighboring monitor, as if in one continuous flight. It was one of those synchronicities that we were all sure Shirley planned. We didn't giggle during that event. Exhausted and emotional we sat in the rosy light with tears streaming down our cheeks, the kind of tears that can punctuate a late Beethoven quartet played well. When the tapes spun empty at the end we came together and hugged—like some Omega circle, just more spontaneous and real.

I remember one night, we set up an elaborate elevator installation: a camera on each Chelsea floor aimed at the elevator door and a Pisa-like leaning stack of monitors on the roof re-creating the Chelsea's ten floors. Wires ran up the center staircase picking up the feed on each floor. Then someone would do a performance on the elevator, and we would watch the roof TV stack. We could see the performance only when the doors opened on floor after floor. It was a great idea. It never quite worked. None of Shirley's projects ever "worked" in the conventional sense, but we knew that the ideas totally worked. It was exhilarating. It was being high every night. We were urban guerrillas of the Chelsea penthouse, plotting an electronic coup that would liberate the imaginations of the world.

The image of Felix the Cat was one of the very first images to glow from a cathode ray tube in television experiments in the 1930s. At this moment, high above us on a flickering celestial screen, an implike Shirley in a spiffy bowler hat morphs in and out with Felix in a perpetual softshoe routine. Goodnight, Shirley. May some of us, your students, transmit electric visions as sassy and brilliant as you and Felix, with an edge as sharp and a passion as deep.

Shirley Clarke and Nam June Paik "French kiss" through video. This was an installation built by video pioneer David Cort at the Kitchen on Prince Street, New York City, 1974. *(Author)*

# Keeping Busy on Cape Breton Island: Journal of a Production Assistant to Robert Frank

## August 1975/October 1997

*In the summer of 1975 I kept a sporadic diary during production of a film by Robert Frank and Rudy Wurlitzer called* Keep Busy. *Besides Robert and Rudy, the cast and crew included Joanne Akalaitis, Charles Dean, Alec Gillis, Joan Jonas, June Leaf, Roberta Neiman, Toby Rafelson, Bill Raymond, Richard Serra, Jack Tibbolt, Helen Tworkov, and David Warrilow.*

*In the late 1950s Frank had made* Pull My Daisy *with Al Leslie. The cast had included many of the artists and writers of the Beatnik decade: Allen Ginsberg, Gregory Corso, David Amram, Larry Rivers, Alice Neel, and Dick Bellamy. That film encapsulated an era, with its improvised stream-of-consciousness hipster script and merry prankster antics. In many ways* Keep Busy *was a similar reflection on the cultural scene of the 1970s. The art scene was cooler and, like Frank, craggier in the seventies. There was more self-conscious "performance" and a deeper cynicism. Frank's feelings about the United States, so apparent in his classic photo essay* The Americans, *had finally fueled his departure from the country.* Pull My Daisy *was shot on the Bowery and in lofts on Tenth Street, but* Keep Busy *takes place on the wind-swept cliffs of Cape Breton, Nova Scotia, in northeastern Canada, where Frank has been a landed immigrant for over twenty-five years.*

*In the 1970s the stark landscape of Cape Breton had become a refuge for many New York artists: Phil Glass, Lee Breuer, Pat Steir, Jake Barlow, Hermine Tworkov, Robert Moskowitz, Eliza-*

*beth Murray, and the above cast and crew all were summer regulars. The local townspeople were Scotch-descended former coal miners, now trying to eke out a living as farmers on barren land or as fishermen in waters heavily regulated by what were seen as oppressive fish and game wardens from the distant Canadian government on the mainland. The Scotch culture was and is strongly present in Cape Breton in every word uttered in the rich brogue and in the lively ceilehs (fiddle contests) held weekly during the summers. In Frank's film, John Dan MacPherson, an old fiddler, scratches out a lonesome tune which surpasses in poignancy anything in* Pull My Daisy. *This tune and the "performance" of this "authentic local" old man on screen provide a telling counterpoint to the somewhat arch performances imported to the island direct from the New York art world. Frank treats his Canadian neighbors with a tenderness and affection that he could never rally for* The Americans, *even those self-defined as artists.*

WE ARE PUSHING a creaking cart loaded with hay up a narrow road, six people struggling. The grade is steep, and the ruts in the road don't make it easier. The cart has tires from an automobile on its twisted axles. The right rear tire is completely flat. One of the kids runs to the barn for a bedraggled bike pump, which is passed around as each of us tries various methods of pumping a bit of air into the formless rubber. We toss the pump in the cart and continue pushing up the hill. Doug, one of the Scotch farmers, squints at the three-quarter moon, rising in the late afternoon sky. "To think of it: a man walked on the moon and here we are pushing this cart up the hill."

We are finally at Doug's barn. He has an ancient device for towing the hay in. It consists of two pulleys, a screw mechanism, and a beat-up pickup truck to pull the wench. The screw looks like a big giant wine opener hanging from the barn loft door. The hay is first twisted on the screw, then raised up through the loft opening. A large fluffy bunch is raising up to the loft. CRACK! It falls back to the cart. The rope holding the block and tackle has broken. We splice it together. Once more it tenuously rises, then sinks back to the cart. The fence to which the second pulley is tied has caved in. They get a board and brace it. All set. The pickup sputters, coughs, lurches an inch forward, but then stops and its sputtering motor is silent—the truck is out of gas. Robert looks up at me grinning. "These guys and their farm are too much." We unload the cart with pitchforks and armfuls up the rickety barn ladder. So much for mechanized farming.

Now that the hay is in the barn, the farm children have taken over the loft and are jumping from an overhanging beam into the fluffy hay stack. I take a few turns and find myself in a whooping pile of legs and arms and hay twigs. We laugh and tumble in the pile. One of the kids, a girl of about nine, looks at me with curiosity. My overalls, tousled hair, and willingness to jump in on the fun confuse her. "What are you, a girl or a boy or a mother?" she asks. She seems disappointed when I say I'm a mother.

We walk up the dirt road to Robert's house. He and June Leaf, a painter from Chicago, live above the farm, on a cliff overlooking the sea at the end of a rutted dirt road that used to lead to a coal mine. The "town" is called Mabou Mines.[15] Robert is quite intimidating. I ask Roberta, a crew member from L.A., how she is able to remain so casual and easy with him. "He's an old Jew," she laughs. "He's just like my uncle. When I realized that, I was completely at ease."

I am completely intimidated by Robert, whom many consider the greatest living photographer. Rudy wants me to tell him about my connection in New York for getting cheap color negative so they could shoot in color. I rattle off film stock numbers, processing letters. My speech is a garble of technical jargon. Perhaps it will impress this bristly old pro. "Stop! Stop!" Robert protests. "I don't know what any of those numbers you are giving me mean. I never learned that stuff. This film-making business is complicated enough. I can't bother to learn such things. That's why I don't want to use that film. I use black and white. I'm used to it."

---

[15] This name was taken by Joanne Akalaitis, Lee Breuer, Ruth Maleczek, and others who formed the Mabou Mines theater troupe after a summer in Nova Scotia developing projects.

Robert shows us how to load and unload the Eclair magazines. "You must be careful of these pins. Look how little they are. Little bits of wire. The goddamn French. This shit French camera is so delicate you can't breath deep on it." He watches while I open it and load. I am usually very good with equipment. I handle machines easily and well. But now, all of a sudden, my hands are made of granite. I can hardly hold the magazine, much less open it. The spool on my lap falls to the floor. I bend to pick it up. The magazine slides to the edge of my lap, but I catch it just in time. Robert shakes his head and turns away to face the stove. I know he can't bear to look at a clod like me holding his precious equipment.

Dinner at Robert's house. June is savagely swinging a hammer on the anvil in her studio shed. "I wonder what's wrong with her," Robert asks. After dinner while we are washing the dishes, June remembers how angry she was at Toby for taking pictures in their house. Toby Rafelson had come in, camera swaggering, and visited every room—click . . . click, flash . . . flash. I think what made June especially mad was that Toby even tried to rearrange things to the most picturesque position—like leaning the ax propped up behind the woodstove a *little* bit more to one side so the handle was in frame. "*Stop!*" June had screamed. "Get out of my house!"

Robert says, "I thought so. I thought so. I knew there was something riling you up." June denies any connection between her furious hammering and her anger at Toby. But Robert counters, "Oh, yes. You see, I know you pretty well. And it's true you often hammer furiously. But this time, there was just a little half a degree more than usual."

They talk about Toby. Robert said, "When I saw her walk up the path, I thought to myself, 'Nothing good can ever come out of Hollywood.' " June asks what Toby's husband directed. "*Five Easy Pieces*," Robert answers. "Well, that was a good movie," June says. Robert says nothing.

I ask Robert if the Rolling Stones' film that he made (*Cock Sucker Blues*) will be shown in New York. "There's only one print and it's on the West Coast." The Stones are reluctant to release it—too much drugs. Robert didn't make a promotional film for them, but a searing look at life on the road, warts and all. I wonder why the Stones would commission Robert Frank if what they wanted was a commercial.

After dinner he talks about the neighbors, especially one old guy, MacDougal, who lives alone on the top of the mines hill in a tiny shack. His shack has only a bed and a table and one chair. He cuts wood every day for his stove in the winter, fishes a bit for his meals, and once a week walks eight miles to town to pick up his social security check. He cashes his check and buys as much booze as he can carry back. "Then for two or three days he's a completely changed man," Robert says. "He comes over here and sits right in that chair and sings and carries on. He is a very smart man, and in that condition, he is wonderfully funny. You know Doug who had the hay cart and barn where we were today? Well, Doug came up the path once when MacDougal was here in the kitchen, and he looks out the window and says, 'Well, here comes the minister of agriculture.' " That line seems particularly good after the haying fiasco we have witnessed. Robert laughs until tears come to his eyes, remembering both the line and the scene in the hayfield and at the barn. He sobers up and says, "But you know, when it's been weeks of snow and quiet, it sure is good to see that guy. We need him, and I think he's glad we're here. Doug and his brothers too. They come over and drink coffee, and we feel real close. It wasn't that way at first, but now we're close, very close." Since 1973 Robert and June have spent most of their life at the end of this road, in a desolate corner of Nova Scotia. Unlike many of the New York artists who have found their way to the warm summer beaches of this starkly beautiful island, they do not pack up and head for the States in August. Robert and June have spent many long winters watching the bay slowly freeze over.

*Keep Busy* is the first film Robert has made in Nova Scotia. Some scenes will be shot in Mabou, but most will be shot on deserted Sea Wolf Island, where a lighthouse keeps guard over the bay. This island also serves as a rookery for the local sea birds. The cliffs on the northern shore are white with bird dung.

Before we leave for the island, there is a scene with Joan Jonas, the performance artist and videomaker, in a wreck of a shack near Robert's house. Joan paces around the shack like a restless wolf. It is completely ransacked. Only about a quarter of the roof is still there. But the hole in the roof provides an eerie beam of light that pierces the center of the shack. The floor is full of smashed lobster traps, rotten nets, and buoys. The beams hang low. Joan practices swinging on them. "OK," she says. Robert starts rolling. Joan lunges wildly, swinging from the rafters. She climbs into a large lobster trap and rocks back and forth with her hands on the edge. Sort of like a mad baby in a playpen. "Take one," syncs Robert. The second take is done with a low shot of Joan, who is crouched on the floor. She is huddled on a pile of ropes. She howls wolf-dog-like. The sun has reappeared and is streaming through the roofless ceiling. When she tilts her head back, her eyes catch the beam of light and glow like a cat caught in a headlight. She has become an animal. The last take is even more intense, and when Robert stops shooting, we all look at Joan in silence, deeply moved.

"Where's the chicken?" Robert asks. "He didn't want to come," Alec replies. Joan's shack scene was supposed to have a chicken in it, and Robert misses it. Before we leave for the island, Robert insists that we need some chickens. On Tuesday, as we are getting ready to leave for the island, Robert asks me to pick up Alec and be sure to get his chicken. "OK," I say. "I can persuade it." I used to raise chickens, and I am not intimidated by their shyness. Alec is a Gillis of the Cape Breton Gillises. But to his Scotch heritage he has added a bit of new age style: he is a follower of the Maharishi and sometimes comes to Richard's shed to meditate. Robert prefers Alec's Scotch characteristics. Rudy likes his spacey New Age eyes. At Alec's shack, his old uncle is there. He is an electrician, if that's what you can call a Scotch farmer with some wire cutters and electrical tape. He has done a lot of wiring for Richard Serra's house, where I was staying, and I had thought of him as a sour old man, as crusty and grumpy as they come. Today he is grinning like a Cheshire cat. Alec and

I head off to the woods to try and catch the chicken. "What's with your uncle?" I ask in wonder at his new cheeriness. "Oh, he's just stoned out of his mind," Alec says. "A lot of the old guys around here turn on. There's hemp growing all over this town. It tides them over between social security checks."

We can't catch the chicken. The plucky rooster is scrambling around in the prickly underbrush of the balsam forest. For him there is plenty of clearance. At our level it's a thick barricade of jagged boughs. "Is there any place we can buy one?" I ask. Robert Frank has asked me to get something, and I don't want to come back empty-handed. Alec suddenly brightens. We head for the canteen up the road. Out in back is a ramshackle shed full of moth-eaten, louse-infested, hen-pecked hens. I grab two by their legs from their perch, and we stuff them into a burlap bag, leaving a $10 bill with the canteen owner. Pretty sorry specimens, but, hey, they match the shacks: half-roofed.

Tuesday night is calm. The sky, however, is full of rolling gray clouds. We are supposed to leave for the island. Alec, the only Cape Breton native in our crew, refuses to go. "No, I know what it's like. We can't go." There are A-frame cabins in a wide circle around the field and dormitory rooms in the main house. Plenty of space for cast and crew to wait out the weather, so we head for bed. The actors sit up drinking coffee and murmuring lines back and forth.

The next morning begins with a tremendous thunderstorm. The dogs are freaked and jump in and under various beds. The kids wake up, frightened by the thunder claps. David Warrilow, a seasoned Beckett actor and the star of the film, calms the children with a long story about leprechauns and dragons and whales. David is wearing a maroon silk dressing gown in the rustic camp bunk house.

The thunder shower subsides to a determined drizzle. Rudy wakes Alec up for a native opinion of the weather. "Alec, it's raining. What do you think?" Alec rises from his sleeping bag. He is camping on the bathhouse floor. The windows are shuttered. There is not even a glimpse of the sea or the sky. Through the sounds of gentle rain drops, Alec listens to the distant waves lapping on the cliff below the bathhouse. "It's OK. We'll go." Rudy scratches his head. "OK, Alec. Whatever you say."

The gear is being stowed in the boat. The two sorry chickens, half their feathers missing, are nested in the front at the prow. An emergency flare rolls out of a knapsack and off the seat into the water on the wet boat floor. Joan coughs—her asthma is getting worse. Robert says, "This looks like the beginning of a bad TV serial."

After a choppy ride across the wide bay, we are on the island. We spend the day exploring the empty keeper's house and climbing on the dung-dabbed cliffs. Later, sitting around the campfire, I realize that I have left my sleeping bag in the bunkhouse on the mainland. I search through the knapsacks for extra blankets. Gathering a few together, I attempt to wrap myself up snuggly. Robert has watched my preparations, but his familiarity with the cool Cape Breton nights make him skeptical about my makeshift arrangements. "Look here," he says. "Why don't you use this." He has an extra sleeping bag. "It's light and old and not much use, but it's Swiss, so it can't be too bad." I grab it gratefully and start to zip it up, but the zipper won't work. He frowns. "The bag is Swiss, but the zipper was made in Japan."

The island's most imposing structure is not the lighthouse, which is a small cement silo with a tiny but powerful quartz light whose precision reflectors send out a laser-like beam, but rather the light keeper's house, which was built on top of the hill next to the light—built, as they say, "like a ton of bricks." The government knows what the wind and weather can do in northern Cape Breton, and they meant that house to last. Its rugged, well-painted and shingled structure is a stark contrast to the state of affairs within. The light is now automatic and needs no live-in keeper. The floors are littered with scraps of paper and glass, bird shit, pieces of iron, and the discarded remnants of plumbing fixtures ripped out by other island visitors long ago. On one wall in the kitchen are stacked storm windows—maybe ten or twelve of them. Rudy is preparing for the kitchen scene. He takes a chair and puts it in the corner, then stands back and ponders the effect. He goes to the pile of windows and takes the top one and places it behind the chair, then goes back to survey his scene. Robert has watched him do it. "Rudy, Rudy. Tsk, tsk." He moves the window back to its pile. "It took thirty years to make this place look like this. You think you can improve on it after reading *Better Homes and Gardens*. This interior is sheer genius. Don't presume to change it for the better." Rudy grins sheepishly.

David always wears a white cravat around his neck. Rudy has tried to outfit him in more scruffy clothes. No matter what David wears he always seems to come out looking like one of the mannequins in an Abercrombie and Fitch window. The white scarf is one of the problems. There's something about it that is conspicuously out of place in an abandoned house on a desolate island.

It's the second eating scene. Alec has prepared a plate of potatoes and fish. Robert's idea is to start it with David's head on the plate of food. He is then to lift his face and wipe it off. Robert wants him to wipe it with the cravat. David insists on using his sleeve. Robert acquiesces, but is vindicated by the fact that on the third take, the cravat finally succumbs and is sotted with food. I watch Robert shoot and realize that the face in the plate hasn't been in one take. The camera has stayed with Bill's arrival across the room, only panning to David after his head is already up. The food sleeping sequence must be just for David's character building, or perhaps to get that white cravat into shape.

David is sitting at a table with Robert's dog, Sport, on one side. No one is to get up in the scene. Robert, at Rudy's urging, agrees to shoot it on the tripod. This has been a point of disagreement between them. Initially all the scenes in the house were to be shot with a tripod. Robert balks. Rudy is fearful of Robert's continuous movements. He would like to see more tripod shots. When we were back on the mainland, Robert says he couldn't get a good fluid head tripod, but admits that even if he had it, he wouldn't want to use it. Rudy now insists on using one, and Charley the sound man has brought a state-of-the-art fluid head from Halifax. We set it up in front of David's table. Robert starts shooting. He wants to do a pan back and forth, but the camera has not been secured tightly enough on the head. It swivels on the legs, and when his pan returns, the camera is tilted. Never taking his eye from the eyepiece, he motions to me to loosen the camera in the middle of the shot, indicating that he wants me to take the camera off, and finishes the shot hand-holding the camera. That is the last time we attempt a tripod shot.

Charley the sound man has a gentle, sweet way of reminding Robert of things, as if he were reminding himself. "Like, so we'll sync it at the tail, eh?" Nova Scotians have a delightful way of saying "eh!" It's really a breath—a gasp of breath drawing inward—usually with a sly smile.

Robert always wants to sync it at the end. He wants to let David get into his part, and then he'll start rolling once David's going. That way the syncing won't make him uptight. Even though our syncing is a hand clap and not the usual clunky slate, Robert feels it inhibits the actors to use it at the opening of the scene. "I know it's better this way, and I'll be sure to leave enough film to sync it up at the end," Robert promises. Charley raises his eyebrows. The scene rolls. David is on the floor sleeping in the debris of the light keeper's kitchen. Sport, that good old dog, comes through just in time. He leans over and licks David's face—at exactly the right moment. Sport is savoring the remains of the fish and potatoes caught in David's bushy eyebrows. Robert finishes the shot with a zoom to David's face. A telltale flap, flap is heard, which means the camera is out of film, without doing the slate and clapboard for the shot—a problem in the future for some assistant editor to sync up. Robert winks at Charley. "Well, sometimes I sync it up and sometimes I don't. That shit doesn't matter so much."

By nightfall the sky is completely clear. Rudy is worried about matching scenes tomorrow if the sun is out. The exteriors so far have all been shot under overcast skies. Tonight the stars are crisp in the cool night air. From soggy paper cups we eat mackerel and potatoes which were boiled together Cape Breton style in a big pot over the fire. Joanne waves two large flashlights in hopes that the children are watching from the bunk house on the shore. June and I trade fiddle tunes while the others dance around the driftwood blaze. Robert scratches Sport's tummy. Gulls squabble for sleeping positions on the cliff edge. The lighthouse beam sweeps a wide circumference of sky over our heads.

Robert Frank and Sport on Sea Wolf Island, Cape Breton, Nova Scotia, while shooting the film *Keep Busy*. *(Author)*

# 2

# A Salutary Dose of Poison:
## Teaching Media as a
## Homeopathic Cure

# Introduction

MY INTEREST in making media has always been combined with an interest in helping others make media. Our lives are so dominated by the mediated imagery of mass culture that being able to use the tools of film and television for expression would seem an essential step in any democratizing process. This can happen at a very early age. In 1961 I taught films to elementary school children at a settlement house on the Lower East Side in Manhattan; "Children Make Movies" is both the title of an essay in this section and the name of a film about that project. This simple 16 mm film (cost: $88) was taken up by a nascent media education movement as a model of child-made media and shown in conferences around the country and abroad.

In 1963 I founded the Henry Street Settlement Film Club with a donated 8 mm camera and a few rolls of out-of-date stock. We made short films and showed them on a sheet stretched between the street lights in the middle of the block. We were part of a small community of media workshops: Roger Larsen at University Settlement and the Yellow Ball Workshop in the Boston suburbs, led by Yvonne Anderson. Henry Street kids were mostly African American and Puerto Rican, and most lived in the nearby projects. They ranged in age from seven to fifteen, and they made short animation experiments and live action melodramas.

In the late sixties, I moved out of New York City to Sullivan County in the Catskills. Although seventy-five miles from Henry Street, I ended up working with very similar kids: young boys (12–16) from the metropolitan region who had been remanded by the juvenile justice system to correctional institutions upstate. I organized a filmmaking project at Otisville School for Boys, in which dozens of youth made 16 mm, Super 8, and video productions as part of their rehabilitation, the resulting work exhibited at local libraries, churches, and conferences on juvenile justice. I was commissioned to lead workshops for teachers in other Division for Youth facilities, in collaboration with Young Filmmakers Foundation.[1] It was the days of the "Great Society" when such experimental, creative projects were given value by the federal government, and there were funds for equipment, supplies, and even my salary.

The films made by these incarcerated young men prompted interest in this type of work from local agencies that had programs for "problem teens" in Orange County. I organized a group called "Live Arts," which sponsored a series of art and filmmaking programs at the Martin Luther King Center of the AME Church, at housing projects in Middletown, New York, and at migrant camps in Florida, New York, and rural areas of Orange County.

In the days before VHS rentals, most public libraries had large collections of 16 mm prints. Ever since my classes on Avenue D, I was a library film collection junkie. The idea of selecting films to view was exciting and challenging. I would check out two or three films at the nearest library for the classes I taught. I became very familiar with this unique body of work, and the filmmakers therein, including Burt Haanstra, Jiri Trinka, Norman McLaren, et al. This international community of alternative filmmakers was sustained by the work of the National Film Boards of Canada and Eastern Europe and the dogged persistence of a few independent distributors such as Leo Dratfield, who founded Contemporary Films. The key publication for this world of devotees was the *Film Library Quarterly*, lovingly edited by Emma Cohen. "Films in the Joint" was a report I did at that time for *Film Library Quarterly* about the library films which worked with my classes at the reform school.

"Mini-Moviemakers" was also written for *FLQ* with the intent of inspiring librarians to program films made by children. In the essay I propose organizing screenings around themes,

[1] The Young Filmmakers Foundation was founded by Roger Larsen, Lynn Hofer, and Jaime Barrios. Larsen's book *Young Filmmakers* (New York: Dutton, 1969) was an important document of this early work.

or taking a cue from social science in looking at them for the insight into the lives of children. I was inspired by the work of visual anthropologist John Collier, and the work of John Adair and Sol Worth, who did a pioneering filmmaking project with several Navajo people.[2] I was especially impressed by the insight into the culture and lives of the Navajo that was expressed in their films. It seemed to me that films by young people also reflect aspects of their lives and their culture that are often overlooked or misunderstood by adults. In 1976 I initiated a conference to assess the field of filmmaking by young people. "There's Gold in Them Thar Hills: Prospecting for Child-Made Films" chronicles the organizing of that international meeting, from initial discussions with social scientists to a search for programming. "A Homeopath Aboard" is the story of how youth films are viewed in Europe, where "media literacy" was seen as an important subject as early as the mid-1970s.

---

[2] *Through Navajo Eyes,* by Adair and Worth (Bloomington: Indiana University Press, 1972), is the classic account of this project.

# Children Make Movies[3]

## *October 1961*

THE LILLIAN WALD Recreation Rooms, an affiliate of the Federation of Jewish Philanthropies, is located in a low-income housing project next to the East River on the Lower East Side of New York. The settlement serves a wide variety of ages, interests, and ethnic groups with activities in crafts, cooking, dramatics, sewing, and music. This year a group of the children, ages ranging from five to twelve, made a movie. They were not a selected group of film-interested children but a group solely because their parents came to a Friday evening social held by the settlement. Previous to the film work, the children had been put through a number of programs attempting to interest them and mainly keep them quiet while their parents enjoyed an hour or so of dancing and socializing.

Familiar with many of the films available from the New York Public Library collection, I began to check some out and show them to the children on Fridays. Their interest was often in the technical aspects of film, rather than the content. I was amazed and unprepared for the battery of questions on production and projection. I began to select films from what I found to be the group's interests. They saw a wide variety of films: films with interesting camera techniques, different types of animated films, and some films which were painted directly on the celluloid. I had made a short film of my own, working directly on black leader, by scratching away the emulsion and painting with colored inks.

After seeing my brief scratch film and examining it care-

---

[3] This was first published in *Film Culture* (no. 25) in 1962 and that same year was also reprinted in *Screen Education*, the precursor to *Screen* magazine in the United Kingdom.

fully, the children all clamored to do one of their own. We began what was our first "production" workshop not with work on leader, but with a discussion of animated movements and experiments with "flip movies." The group readily grasped the basic principles of this kind of motion; some were real experts, having explored the medium on the margins of their social studies textbooks, or on bubble gum cards. I gave each child (there were usually thirteen to eighteen in the group) a stack of blank three-by-five oak-tag cards, and demonstrated on one stack the simple motion of a dot growing bigger, increasing slightly with each card, stapling them together. At the end of an hour the room was buzzing with movie producers excitedly showing each other their work. The subjects ranged from a flower budding and slowly unfolding to a "cosmic sun shooting off first small rays, then a whole sky full of piercing rays," to a stock cartoon character blowing up a balloon, bigger and bigger, until it explodes and his face reappears, charred. The next week we began on the "scratch film." Unrolling the leader onto a series of long tables arranged in a U shape, I gave each child a foot of leader and a small straight pin. Their first efforts were bent on getting the feel of the tiny instrument, and making sure that the scratch was on the right side and "showed" when held to the light, then they colored it with felt tip pens. We projected what they had done immediately, and they were incredulous at the speed with which their total twenty feet went through the projector. They wanted it viewed backwards and forwards many times before they were finally convinced. I showed them some of the "painted on film" movies from the library, and the kids were proud to think that theirs were as good as the "professionals'." They were more interested than before and could explain many of the visual problems explored in these films.

Another film I reserved about this time was *Neighbors* by Norman McLaren, the great Canadian animator who had pioneered painting on film. This pixilated allegory on love, war, and greed involved the children to the point of screaming with laughter at the surreal comic beginning sequences, groaning with horror at the brutal fighting, and silenced with thought by the impressive final titles commanding "Love Thy Neighbor." They asked to see it again. When they did, they wanted to know if they could make a film like it. They discussed the techniques possible and decided that "scratching" wouldn't do. I said I'd try to see about getting a photographer. The next week they hit on another idea. The room we were using was also used as a nursery room during the day. It had all the standard nursery equipment, including a large set of Froebel blocks. Often during breaks for reel changing some of the boys would take to the block corner and start constructing. On this evening a fight developed concerning the type of building to be erected, and in the fracas the structure which was up came tumbling down. Forgetting about the fight, the children practically applauded the crash and began to plan how they could use this great dramatic effect. Then the plot came: why not change the *Neighbors* plot (fighting over a flower) to fighting over a block building, with the fighting eventually ruining the point of contention and the people involved. I got Kirk Smallman to film it the next week with two three-minute reels. We didn't rehearse or have exact movements plotted out. The children talked it over briefly, then started acting it out.

When the reels were back from the lab, and Kirk had spliced them together, we screened it, and they went to work making a sound track, titles, and some new footage to connect the block film with their earlier scratch film: shots of the kids at work scratching on film. For the sound track, the kids armed themselves with blocks, waste baskets, and tin pans, and we projected the building sequence. As they watched the action, they acted out, or rather "spoke out," the sounds of what they saw.

As I was surprised to find, films can and should be seen, worked on, and understood by children. It is a medium very close to them: not only are they confronted at the Saturday matinees and "Cartoon Carnivals," but by television in their homes and by "audiovisual aids" in their school rooms. To many of the children of this particular settlement such creative activities as painting, sculpture, and music are lost, for they can't be related to their normal home life. Few of the homes have any painting or sculpture, and few appreciate or recognize serious music. In an afternoon class with primary children, many asked me to keep their paintings, because if they take them home their mothers will throw them away. Rarely will a child want to take anything home.

The reverse was true of the film activity. Here was something which completely awed the parents. The parents can't see the films enough times, or refrain from poking each other that their boy or girl did this or that. The children delight in displaying their knowledge and keep their parents informed as to the different techniques used in the filming of TV programs.

In this age of mass communication, people fear they are becoming machines, forced to obey this or that ad or admonition from the vast networks of power. One way to fight this duped acceptance of the mass media is to interest and instruct people in their production. And certainly, no starting place is better than the children, whose natural curiosity and vigorous imaginations can still function.

# Films in the Joint: What Worked with City Kids in a New York State Reformatory

## Spring 1972

IN 1970 I began teaching at Otisville School for Boys, an up-state New York reformatory with many black and Puerto Rican city kids, ranging in age from fourteen to seventeen. I had applied for a Title One grant for experimental education projects with underprivileged youth. The subject was to be filmmaking. I borrowed films from the local public library. We watched six to ten films a week, not all of which ran their way off the reel in their entirety. I quickly learned that if a film wasn't "making it," it had to be stopped and rewound then and there. These young people have to put up with enough in their lives. Bad films they didn't have to sit through—not in my classes.

The films they liked to see were, first of all, the good ones, and this could include standard dramas or experimental films. All kids (especially these tough sophisticates) can immediately smell a phony, didactic, boring film within seconds of the opening titles. They did prefer, of course, films that had some meaning to their lives. Being stuck "in the sticks" and naturally homesick, they loved films about the city, such as *NY, NY* (Francis Thompson), or *Bridges Go Round* (Shirley Clarke). Some of the film classics that worked were *The Battleship Potemkin* (the food at the training school was a major sore spot—they identified as soon as the wormy meat appeared), *Un Chien Andalou, The General, The Gold Rush*, some Laurel and Hardy (mostly the silent stuff), and W. C. Fields. Some films like *Nanook of the North* needed a little preparation. *The*

*Innocent Eye*,[4] a biography of Flaherty, had some interesting anecdotes which I read to the group and which turned them on to the adventure of filmmaking in the Arctic.

One of their favorite films was *Two Men and a Wardrobe*, Polanski's short student work. The open-ended, many-leveled meanings intrigued them, and they asked to see it three and four times (backwards too). Norman McLaren's *Neighbors* was a hit, likewise *The Hand*, Jiri Trnka's allegory. They liked *Tell-Tale Heart* better than *Hangman*. Both *Time Is* and *Time Piece* were popular, but *This Is Marshall McLuhan*, Ernie Pintoff's attempt to popularize McLuhan's theories, was one of the failures, despite the psychedelic pulsating backgrounds and tinted lights. We never made it through the first reel on that one. *Anderson Platoon* was a devastating commentary on the Vietnam War and sparked a long discussion about the military.

Tom Henderson, an English teacher at Otisville, whose class 7E had a reading level somewhere around second grade, used film a lot and told me his classes liked *The Last Rhino*, *Legend of Jimmy Blue Eyes*, *Black and White*, *Up Tight*, and *Incident at Owl Creek Bridge*. I asked him if he had ever found a good drug film, and he laughed. He's tried them all, but they are just good for a few giggles. The only ones they watched with respect and involvement were the ones made by the Otisville Film Club (i.e., themselves)—*LSD* (a psychedelic bad trip) and *The Beginning of My End* (the story of a heroin overdose)—and the group of films on drugs from the Youth Films Distribution Center. Youth Films also has two good ones on alcoholism: *What's It Going to Get You Peppy?* and *An Unpleasant Evening*. These films were made by teenagers, and they hit home.

Films—on television or in the auditorium—usually make up a large part of any incarcerated person's "rest and recreation." Occasionally the TV in their dorm (euphemistically called cottages) would have one of their favorites: *Cool Hand Luke* was the all-time winner in this regard. Its tough prison scenes resonated with their surroundings. Many of the stu-

---

[4] Arthur Calder-Marshall, *The Innocent Eye* (London: Allen, 1963).

Two students at Otisville School for Boys pose in front of an old-format Panasonic video camer, 1971. *(Author)* (Below): Rafael Valle (left) and Raymond Alvarado with a Bolex (right), setting up a drug-dealing scene with two other Otisville School students as part of the Otisville Art Film Club, 1972. *(Author)*

dents knew all the words and would act out certain scenes while it was playing.[5] At Otisville films are shown occasionally in the school classes, but the main use of feature film is on Sunday nights when 35 mm movies are shown to the entire school population. These films are selected by the recreation teachers from recommended film lists, which means that Doris Day and Walt Disney "sitcoms" are shown regularly. When I (a green "new Jim") first saw the list of milk-and-apple-pie films scheduled, I marched to the head "rec" man and demanded to have a voice in the film choices. He grinned and gave me the film catalogs. After much discussion and research, my classes and I came up with a list and left it with him. It included the film *Popi,* about a Puerto Rican in New York, and had been seen and liked by one of my students. The next few months I searched the "rec" lists in vain for any of the films which we had recommended. I marched to the desk for the second time and asked about my list. None were deemed acceptable. "What about *Popi?*" in particular. Well, that was not approved because it included a woman whose marital status is questionable. So *With Six You Get Egg Roll* won out.

The skirmish was lost, but the kids eventually fought the battle and won. Now the administration shows hipper films. They have to. It all happened because of a riot—a Sunday night riot in the auditorium. And the film choice was the cause: not that it was advocating the violence that ensued. What months of Doris Day didn't do, twenty minutes of Julie Andrews did. After the third *Sound of Music* number the hissing grew, spit balls started flying, and soon even the chairs were aloft: complete pandemonium. They just couldn't take it any longer.

The next day a memo went out (with copies to all the cottages, all recreation staff, all supervisors, all educational staff): from now on "the boys would form a committee for film selection for the Sunday night features." So now they can see G-rated movies of their own choice.

---

[5] This reciting of lines and acting out of favorite scenes was similar to the affection shown by audiences to *The Rocky Horror Picture Show.* The only time the training school kids responded in this way was to *Cool Hand Luke.*

# Mini-Moviemakers:
# Child-Made Films

## Spring 1976

WE MEDIA TEACHERS are used to de-emphasizing the product. It was hard enough to convince greedy school administrators that our classes were not factories to turn out slick industrial-type documentaries about the wonderful new school swimming pool. Even with the kids themselves, we had to constantly point out the essential value of the experience—especially when the film of that one-take scene came back overexposed. Anyone who has ever gone on a shoot with a possessed twelve-year-old director and her (or his) crew and watched the action take shape knows the excitement and connection that develop when things are all coming together. The film that came back from the lab never quite captured the brilliance and group energy of those moments. Or even in the editing: it was watching those kids with film draped around their necks, hanging from their knees to grab that close-up shot off the clothespinned improvised trim barrel, and shouting with glee when it fit in perfectly. Those were the moments we worked for—the actual film was only a by-product. Process, sure. But what about the product? I've got closets full of it. And so do all the other film teachers I know. What do we do with it? Is there an audience?

Of course, the prime audience for kids' films are the kids who made them, and their families and their peers. Most workshop films are shown at some point to an invited audience from the neighborhood. Libraries might show prints of

local youth films and make screening rooms available. Workshops might program work by kids from other locations.[6]

Kids' films work best with youth and adults from cultures
similar to those of the filmmakers. In 1975 I did some workshops in Haverstraw, New York, which has a large Puerto
Rican population. I showed them some Super 8 movies from
the Henry Street Movie Club. The films by city Puerto Rican
children were very well received, while films from my classes
with suburban white youth were less appreciated, even
though they lived less than ten miles away—but across a class
and culture divide. Films made in my classes at Otisville State
School for Boys, a New York State Correctional Facility, are
immediately understood and liked by youth from other reform
schools, no matter what the ethnic composition is. Some of
the subtleties of the Otisville films are lost on kids who have
never been locked up. There is one scene in a film called *Get
on the Good Foot,* by José Rodriguez, which shows a new boy
at the school getting his state-issued clothes. The clothing matron piles up stacks of flannel shirts and boxer shorts. Whenever this film is shown at a reform school, the audience cracks
up at the sight of the boxer shorts with their gingham prints.
They know too well what "state-o" clothes are.[7] There are
countless little details like that are immediately recognized by
correctional inmates.

That doesn't mean that there aren't many films that can
bridge the cultural divide. Lots of them do. But there is a particular kind of complete understanding that occurs with an
audience from the same culture, a moment of recognition.
There have been only the occasional exchanges made by the
individual film teachers themselves to other classes. There is
no national list of children's film classes and no cataloging of

---

[6] Educational Video Center and Downtown Community Television in New
York City both distribute a wide-ranging collection of youth-made video.
Manhattan Neighborhood Network has launched a Youth Channel which
they hope to distribute to other community television channels.

[7] In the seventies boxer shorts were an embarrassment. By the 1990s,
however, they were the height of style. Many of the garments that were
popular in the late eighties and early nineties seem almost to be modeled
after institutional garb: baggy pants, flannel shirts, and those once ridiculed
boxer shorts.

the work that has been done. But there is a tremendous body of work out there, and a lot of it deserves to be seen.[8] The better and more important of the films should be seen by the larger public—by parents, teachers, and anyone who works with children, as they are expressions of the ideas and concerns of a large portion of our population and demand consideration.

In the field of writing, Richard Lewis and Kenneth Koch have organized and collected the writing of young children. In their respective publications, *Journeys* and *Wishes, Lies, and Dreams*,[9] they made writings available to a broad audience. This same sort of anthologizing needs to be done in the field of children's films. The task is not just to put them together, but to place them in a coherent and explicated context that enables people to appreciate them. The problem is that of programming to present the work in a way that allows people to be open to what they have to offer. People bring so many preconceptions and expectations to any experience that they have to be nudged into an alternate way of looking to be able to see something new. What are the ways that films by children can be presented?

One possibility is to look at the films from an almost anthropological point of view. A model for this kind of approach is *Through Navajo Eyes* by John Adair and Sol Worth. Although it is not about children's films, this book describes the first filmmaking efforts of several indigenous people from the Southwest. The book contains an in-depth discussion of five films—a shot-by-shot analysis. When viewed carefully and with the explication offered by the filmmakers and interpreted by Adair and Worth, the films, seemingly simple and uneventful, become complex expressions of a way of life and seeing.

What are the elements of youth films that are dictated by their mass media culture and exposure to certain genres, and what is specific to their ethnic groupings? Youth from different ethnic groups often choose common genres. All film teach-

---

[8] Now with videos there are many more media workshops.

[9] *Journeys* (New York: Simon and Schuster, 1969); *Wishes, Lies, and Dreams* (New York: Vintage, 1971).

ers have had students who have made Frankenstein movies, Cinderella movies, and Six Million Dollar Man movies. I have always wondered what it would be like to put together a bunch of films on one theme: Dracula, for instance. What would happen if we strung together Dracula movies, one each from the following groups: children of migrant farm workers, Lower East Side blacks, Haverstraw Puerto Ricans, suburban whites, and native kids from Wisconsin? How would each of these groups approach that theme? What would the differences be? What elements would Puerto Rican kids emphasize that native kids would leave out? And how about looking at adult Dracula movies and seeing what they have in common and how they differ from the elements the kids' movies contain? I'm not suggesting a month-long festival of Dracula films, but that type of thematic programming might be an interesting way to nudge people into taking a closer look at the details and subtleties of kids' films.

Another area for study of children's films is psychology. Brian Sutton-Smith at Columbia Teachers College directed a research project to study the filmmaking processes as well as the products to learn about developmental stages of childhood. The complex fantasy in films by children suggests that the films are often intimate products of their minds: dreams made visible.

The social sciences have a rich source of material in youth media films, and structured viewing may be one way to develop audiences for the material. Up until now the only children's films that have been seen by wide audiences are the Yellow Ball Workshop films developed by Yvonne Anderson in Massachusetts, and occasionally a Kodak Student Film Winner, predictably slick and "professional." But I'm talking about the films that are harder to watch. They are rough and grubby, but they are also sensitive and moving. They deserve to be seen. If they can be watched with understanding and insight, they are often powerful visions of the world of children. Recognizing the kinds of fantasies, fears, and humor that children have can make us more sensitive to their needs and hopefully allow us to see more clearly the problems and processes in the world we share with them.

# There's Gold in Them Thar Hills: Prospecting for Child-Made Films

## October 1976

GARY COOPER and John Dewey both had a hand in my education. Learning was by doing. Heroism was forging ahead with pluck and determination in total isolation. I've spent a lot of the last seventeen years teaching film to children. Part of the satisfaction of doing it was my sense of heroic loneliness. Who needed models or colleagues? I was learning by doing. Sure, there were others out there. But we were a hardy few. It was a rugged frontier we were exploring.

Hoarded in closets were precious nuggets—the films by my students that I never got tired of watching. Only I knew how good they were. My collection kept growing. I would see the cans on the shelves and think about the other film teachers that I knew. There must be others with similar collections. I had taught film in the sixties. I wondered what were the concerns of youth in the seventies.

Participation in one of the Robert Flaherty International Film Seminars had made me think about the process by which films get made and the need for a democratization of that process—the need for people to tell their own stories. Most of the films we see are made by a very limited socioeconomic cultural group. It occurred to me that a seminar similar to the Flaherty Seminar might be a way of sharing films made by youth. Film teachers could get together and exchange ideas about teaching and discuss the wider implications of what we were doing. We could also take a look at the past—discover our roots. Children had been making films for over twenty years, and no one had really tried to assess the movement historically.

I decided to spend a little time in critical examination and assessment of my work as a film teacher and the film education movement in general. I read a lot of books, saw hours of kids' movies, visited many workshops, and had conversations with film teachers, film programmers, and social scientists.

I showed some films from my workshop at Otisville State Training School to a graduate seminar in Visual Anthropology with John Collier and John Adair, anthropologists at San Francisco State. Their insights into the films made me realize that, if nothing else, films by children were documents full of cultural information. John Adair and Sol Worth's book, *Through Navajo Eyes*, had been a revelation to me in its detailed analysis of five Navajo films. No one had ever looked at kids' films in that detailed way. John Collier, however, warned me against seeing them as just social science data. What had impressed him was their expressiveness—their depth of feeling—and their implicit awareness of social realities. "To evade the emotional intention of the films is to sap their vitality. Any discussion must deal with their emotional and social content. You shouldn't feel that you have to authenticate them by having them scientifically analyzed," he warned. The Otisville films may show details of ghetto culture, but he was more interested in them as expression of youth. "We adults don't listen to children enough. What are the films trying to say?"

Most adults have a lot of resistance to films by children. Especially the ones that deal with their feelings.

> We remember youth as something pitiable, stupid, weak and often contemptible. . . . We underestimate childhood and make most of our jokes at its expense: its will is obstinacy, its indignation is bad temper, its artistry is idling, its poetry is silliness, its enthusiasm is noise, even its passion is only puppy love. We have an evil name for all its natural characteristics; we praise it only when it apes our own. Youth, of course, is quite able to give a good account of itself if it had an unprejudiced hearing, but we do not offer it much of a chance. . . . It is a question of the conflict of standards, you see; and I am proposing that in

the matter of art expression, youth should be permitted to have its own. But first we should open our minds to discover what those standards really are. In my judgment we shall not find him [sic] lacking in the instinct for beauty and for truth; indeed, his power in these age-old fundamentals is often superior to our own.[10]

Mearns was talking about teaching poetry to children, but certainly we can easily update his words to include filmmaking (and female pronouns!).

I talked in San Francisco to Rhoda Kellogg, a pioneer in collecting and discussing the drawings and paintings of young children. For fifty years she devoted her life to children's art. In her book *Analyzing Children's Art*[11] she wrote, "The prejudice against child art is part of the larger prejudice against the mind of the child. Each adult can recall his [sic] own school, when he was made very aware of his inadequate (though potentially adequate) physical and mental capacities. In later years it is difficult for him to respect the activities or art products of the child." She, like Collier, warned against leaning on the social sciences for validation. Her voice was weary, and sighing deeply, she said, "I think that one of my greatest mistakes was to spend so much time trying to get the academics to accept children's art. I developed all these codifying systems, and all they do is look at the work and find which cubbyhole to put it into. I love the work and I wanted others to love it, and I thought that by analyzing it for them they would understand it. Now, of course, they buy my books, but only to find which place on the grid to put the drawings from their classes. Now, that isn't what I had in mind at all." I told her that I was planning a seminar which would, hopefully, get people to appreciate children's films. "Oh, my dear, you have such an uphill battle. Don't you know that this society can *never* accept the fact that children can make art. Why, it goes against everything. Those professionals are never going to admit that children can do it too!"

---

[10] Hughs Mearns, *Creative Power: The Education of Youth in the Creative Arts* (Garden City, N.Y.: Doubleday, 1935).

[11] Rhoda Kellogg, *Analyzing Children's Art* (Palo Alto, Calif.: National Press Books, 1970).

It is an uphill battle, but I feel that some of us gained ground on a mountain in New York State in April 1976. The Symposium on Child-Made Films brought over sixty people to Lake Minnewaska for four days of looking at youth films and talking about them.[12] Almost a hundred films were shown and were taken very seriously. At the screenings, the feeling was very far from the scorn that Mearns and Kellogg had described. In fact, a kind of reverential respect prevailed. The tone of the discussions varied from excitement to desperation. The excitement was realizing for the first time just how good, in all its many forms, this body of work was. The desperation came from the fear that this just might be "The Last Picture Show," an end of an era.[13] Funds are hard to come by these days. The rallying cry is now literacy, not visual literacy. Most of the programs reported on were started as pilot projects with funds from foundations. The pilot period was over, and there was no centralized network of support. Arts councils in the South and Midwest were still in the initial phases of delight with the novelty of it all. But the word from old-timers from New York and Massachusetts was pretty grim: schools trimming their budgets, media work considered a frill. Out-of-school workshops were being closed as community arts funding had slowed to a trickle. Art with a capital "A" just doesn't include kids, as Rhoda Kellogg well knows.

Until this meeting, we had never shared with each other, never learned from each other. Part of the reason was the very nature of the projects and the instabilities of funding. Part of it was the daily exigencies of getting the film to laboratories, getting the equipment repaired, getting all the details together, or shooting the next scene. The complexity of the process demands an almost complete immersion in these details. We could only get through by forging blindly ahead—the Gary Cooper syndrome.

---

[12] The symposium was sponsored by the Children's Film Theater, with grants from New York State Council on the Arts and the National Endowment for the Arts Public Media Program.

[13] There was another way in which film making with kids ended: video. With the inventions of cassette camcorders and VCRs, video became the tool of choice for media work with kids and had many advantages, foremost of which is the immediate feedback.

The symposium didn't end with final rites; it wasn't a post mortem. We could all agree on the importance of the work. The films proved it. How do we see that this kind of work continues? How can these films be seen? How can the filmmaking experience help children to become empowered?

We didn't come to any conclusions. We did, however, begin to see that learning by doing isn't enough. We have to think about what we are doing. We need to become more aware of the social and historical contexts of our work. We need to see each other's work and talk together about our experiences and our goals so that we aren't so vulnerable to the fickleness of educational fashion. Maybe we'll have to make a few demands. Even Gary Cooper went to Washington.[14] What about the American Film Institute? In Canada the National Film Board has been instrumental in preserving, distributing, and encouraging youth filmmaking. Couldn't the American Film Institute take on the same role here? Youth are one-third of the population. How about proportional air time and production monies?

Marie Winn's book *The Plug-In Drug* documents the psychic damage that passive viewing does to kids. Not all kids have been passive with the media. Before we unplug the set, let's give kids their own time and see what they have to say.

---

[14] *Mr. Deeds Goes to Washington.*

# A Homeopath Abroad: An International Perspective on Youth and Media

## February 1977

*When someone suggested that kids should make their own films as self-defense against the aggression of the mass media, M. de Vulpillieres, French Secretary of State for Youth and Sports, told the International Congress: "It sounds to me like a homeopathic remedy."*

EUROPE HAS PAID more attention to children's films than we have—both films for children and by children. Two institutions that perpetuate interest in this area are the International Center for Films for Children and Young People in Paris and the Ludwigshafen Conference on Youth and Film in West Germany. In 1977 I attended both of their yearly rites.

LUGWIGSHAFEN

Since 1960 a youth and film conference has been held in this town each year. Herr Reiner Keller was the founder and in 1977 still served as director of the program. It occurs in the week preceding the Mannheim Film Festival, just across the Rhine from Ludwigshafen. I was the first American to ever attend this conference. I went to show films from my classes at Otisville School for Boys, and to give a report on the Symposium on Child-Made Films, which was held at Minnewaska, New York.

Ludwigshafen is an ugly city. Almost totally destroyed during World War II, it was rebuilt into a giant nightmare shopping mall, surrounded by high-rise apartments. The air stinks. Just outside of town is the BASF plant: the reason the town was hit so hard during the war. That was the chemical plant that among other wartime products made the gas used in the Holocaust. Now it is busy churning out petrochemicals for the booming West German economy. The gas that emanates from its chimneys is now killing the Germans. I was told that Ludwigshafen has the highest infant mortality rate and the highest genetic birth defect rate in Western Europe. As a compensation to the youth, however, the town fathers (the mothers are not much in evidence in the hierarchy of this town) offer this festival once a year.

There were two basic parts to the conference. One was the afternoon and evening screenings of current releases of feature films for children. The other was a series of morning sessions on a variety of topics all relating to media and children—some reports of film work by kids (my Otisville work was in this category); some academic reports by sociologists, anthropologists, and/or semiologists on the effects of media on kids; and a demonstration of work in the area of screen education. The features presented were from England, Scandinavia, Holland, France, and almost all of the Eastern European countries. Every socialist country spends a lot of money on films for children. In East Germany, for example, the money spent for children equals and often exceeds that spent on "adult" films, making an average of five features a year for kids. The Soviet Union makes twenty-five each year. These aren't low-budget "B" pictures, either, but elaborate productions, many in wide-screen format. Both East and West have their share of dreck, replete with the kinds of clichés we have come to expect from the genre of children's features. But there are also some good films, dealing with relevant issues in sensitive detail. My favorites were *Stine* from Denmark by Lise Roos; *Special Education* from Yugoslavia by Goran Markovitch; *The Key That Can't Be Put Back* by Dinara Assanova from Russia; and *Ottocar, Who Wants to Save the World,* from East Germany by Hans Kratzert.

A fascinating aspect of the film screenings was the juxtaposition of East/West points of view. On the one hand was Henry Geddes of the British Children's Film Foundation saying, "Entertaining children is my job," declaring an abhorrence of pedagogy in films: "Children never seem to listen to what you are saying to them." It's got to be fun and visual. His foundation, supported by film industry contributions and the British tax on TV sets, does research for scripts by watching children's audiences and recording their reactions on infrared film. At the other end of the spectrum was Dr. Franz Jahrow from East Germany, whose film *Ottocar* was accused of being overly didactic. He took that as a compliment. "You see, we want to be didactic. The education effect is of central importance. But let us try to understand each other. It is not that your films are without lessons. There are many things in your films that appear codified to us. Of course, our films support our social system and criticize elements which jeopardize further developments. We see the same tactics in films from the West."

Both East and West were attacked by Lise Roos, the Danish director. She deplored the fact that the majority of conferees were men, and old men at that. The median age must have been over fifty. Out of sixty participants only ten were women. She felt that contributed to what she felt was a heavy and dead atmosphere. "All you serious men leave your cozy homes and cozy wives and come here to talk very seriously about films for children. What about life?" Her wild gestures were a refreshing contrast to the German reserve of the chairman. "What kind of life do we have for our children when we let these serious men make all our decisions? They are giving us their television and their films as a substitute for life. They are talking, talking, talking, here for five or six days, then they go back home where their wives are waiting. We must manage to bring our life to our work, and our work has to be about our lives. These men with their ties and their suits and their serious talk: they are not alive!"

INTERNATIONAL CONGRESS

The male-female proportions were more equal at the International Congress which met in Paris the following week. There were many of the same people as at the Ludwigshafen gathering, with a healthy addition of some lively women. The talk this time, however, was still serious, but now couched in redundantly ornate diplomatic language that matched in character the baroque decorations of the hotel suite where we met. The congress has representatives from each European country and has received funding from UNESCO. The official sanctions on the organizations make it into a sort of polite United Nations—without the Third World to ruffle any feathers. This organization started in 1955 with a meeting in Edinburgh. In 1957 an organization was established in Brussels, which helped to plan and coordinate a big meeting sponsored by UNESCO in Oslo in 1962. I know about that meeting, because my film *Children Make Movies* had been shown there. The yearly meetings are an exchange of information on activity in this field, with occasional money from UNESCO going toward a publication on some aspects of the work. The group also sponsors a film festival which shows prize-winning films by children from all over Europe. Features for children are screened each year at the Congress, and collections of these films are circulated to participating countries. There were presentations about film-teaching projects with children in Canada, Finland, and Spain.[15] There was much discussion of ways to encourage media activity in "the developing countries." The feeling seemed to be that the Congress should open up to more participation by the Third World. There was somewhat of a missionary zeal present as the talk focused on how to bring "our expertise" in this area to the "uninitiated." Some even talked about the necessity to start slow with pinhole cameras because Super 8 cameras might be too complicated for "primitive" cultures. No one ever thinks you have to practice Morse code before you turn on a transistor radio. The whole discussion was rather patronizing, I thought, especially

---

[15] One was by Fred Rainsberry, a Professor of Education in Toronto, Canada. He reported on the "Green Door Project," an intensive film-making experiment with 144 children ages 10 to 14 led by Doug Eliuk and Arlene Moscovitch. Also there was a presentation by Rodriguez Gordillo, President of the Institute for Film and Children in Spain.

in view of some of the recent accomplished films coming from Africa and South America.

Most European countries have national centers on youth and media which produce and distribute films and sponsor educational projects. Since in the United States the market system obviates any sort of subsidy, the U.S. representation at these international conferences is sporadic and unfocused. The East subsidizes this sort of work. It's similar to the Olympics: how to support amateurs. The teachers and those doing research in this field should be subsidized properly, perhaps by the American Film Institute. Why not?

Roger Larsen, the author, and Yvonne Anderson at Child Made Film Symposium, Minnewaska, New York, in 1976. Larsen was the founder of Young Filmmakers Foundation, which evolved into Film/ Video Arts. Anderson taught animation to young people in the suburbs of Boston in the 1960s. *(C. Westwood)*

# 3

# Many Voices, One World:
# A New Information Order
# Begins at Home

# Introduction

My trip to Europe for the youth film conferences made me think more about international communication issues. In the late seventies there was a growing movement among developing countries to demand "information parity." UNESCO set up a commission to research policy in this regard. "Travel Notes" looks at the notion of "market" for information: what is the role of producer in a world where images are commodities? How can "developing" countries find appropriate communication technology? This article, written as a report to the members of the Association of Film and Videomakers while I was president of that organization, is a free-form meditation/travel diary on global media. It includes a description of *Western Union*, an odd film by Fritz Lang, a communications cowboys and Indians romp in which the Indians try to stop the stretching of telegraph lines by Western Union. The movie is based on the actual indigenous resistance to "progress" which took place in the nineteenth century. Using this resistance as a metaphor, this essay looks at the attempts by the nonaligned countries to halt the spread of cultural imperialism, attempts some call "delaying progress."

"Otherwise" is a look at the potential for the other voices to be heard in this world—beginning with the reaction to the "one-way flow of information" that marked UNESCO's deliberations on communication equity and progressing to several examples of successful alternative media practice.

"The Willow Declaration" was written in response to press attacks on the UNESCO MacBride Commission, whose report, *Many Voices, One World,* called for a more egalitarian communication infrastructure. This report was the excuse the United States used not to pay their U.N. dues. The Willow Declaration was written by a group of artists and researchers who met at my house in Willow, New York, in 1981 to declare

North American support for the goals of MacBride in solidarity with Third World aspirations. The Willow Declaration points out that those of us in the so-called "developed" world also need our own new information order. The declaration was reprinted in many newsletters and translated into many languages. It was adopted as part of the platform of the Writers Congress, sponsored by *The Nation*.

The struggle for information parity raised the question of how media democracy might be implemented. One effort to create local media democracy in the United States has been the public access movement. Although in the mass media this project has been portrayed as a joke, denigrated, and ridiculed, as I point out in "The Experience of Citizens' Television," this movement has been a unique experiment in creating an infrastructure for open access to communication technology.

# Travel Notes: The Marketing of Information

## April 1980

> We've got to get some of that old entrepreneurial spirit; we've got to get some of that marketplace mentality.
>
> John Jay Iselin, President of WNET,
> at a recent board meeting

PUBLIC TELEVISION is abandoning its liberal rhetoric. Terms like "noncommercial," "diverse," and "democratic" are being erased from their copy these days. Rhetoric like that is OK, as long as it stays quietly ensconced in a grant application or a report to the members. It's quite another matter when it turns up on a poster being picketed around the station offices. So forget diversity. What PBS wants is "quality."

THIS LITTLE PIG WENT TO MARKET . . .

Go to a board meeting of your local public television station. They are by law open to the public.[1] The discussions will center on the new "direction." Let's call it Neo-Public Television. For instance:

- KQED in San Francisco has applied to the FCC for a waiver of their "noncommercial" status. They want to start scram-

---

[1] There is now an organization to address issues of democracy within public television, Citizens for Independent Public Broadcasting, started by Jerry Starr.

bling the signals on their UHF station and sell it to cable stations.

- WNET in New York: They set up whole floors of their huge
  office complex for development to sell their product (Beverly
  Sills?) to cable, HBO, and European television. Caveat
  Indies: New contracts give PBS rights to nonbroadcast technologies—that is, cable, videodisc, schools, libraries, and international broadcast. Independents should get a lawyer and
  negotiate.
- WQLN in Erie, Pennsylvania: They're talking about selling
  stuff to syndication on the networks.
- WETA, WNET, WTTW, and KCET are not only selling air and
  rights, they're selling print. They've pooled some capital to
  make a magazine, one that would announce the local programming in addition to featuring a few trendy articles for
  the presumed high-end viewers of public television. The ob-
  ject is to sell ads and make money. It looks like an airlines
  magazine.

"PROBABLY ANOTHER CULTURAL EMBARRASSMENT"—SCOTT
JACOBS, INDEPENDENT PRODUCER

The Carnegie Commission on Public Television gave out a
dying wheeze: PACE (Performing Arts, Culture and Entertainment). It's a proposal for another PTV bureaucracy, a high-
end pay television channel for public television to sell to cable.
The sample programming in their proposal scarcely mentions
U.S. independents, but sells the lure of the "New Wave." Beth
B? Amos Poe? Eric Mitchell? Nope. They mean the *Old* New
Wave: Goddard, Truffaut, Louis Malle. When questioned
about the lack of indy representation, chief defender Nick De-
Martino says that there will be funds left over. After the galas
at Lincoln Center have been paid for, there will be spare
change for independents and minorities. Crumbs again. Poor
Artists Can't Eat trickle-down theories.

It's Sunday afternoon. I have a few hours before my plane
to Chicago to speak at the Chicago Editing Center, and I
switch on the tube. I haven't watched it for weeks. Months.
Not even the news. Having a tiny baby around (my daughter

Molly is five months old) makes you more careful about the cultural environment. Have you ever noticed how sometimes people will light a cigarette and then notice a baby is present and put it out? Television has some of the same health threats. Mental health.

But now my travel anxiety is overcoming my maternal instinct. Molly is asleep in the other room. Just a toke. Anyway I'd better check out what's going on, seeing as how I am billed as a media expert.

SINGING WIRES

Ugha, ugha. On the hotel set is a movie: *Western Union*, directed by Fritz Lang in 1941. The Indians are restless. The white men start to take cover. Too late. The attack is on. War cries, tomahawks, rifles, and stampeding ponies. They easily overpower the small band of engineers. Engineers??!! This is no cattle ranch battle. These pioneers are *communicators!*

The dumb Indians peer through the surveying glass. They take axes to the telephone poles. They wallow in the jumbled wire. They bite it. Randolph Scott closes the circuit. ZAP! "Ugh. White man has powerful medicine!"

Robert Young warns: "Let's get out of here before they have time to think it over!"

Later, safe in town, they bury their dead and call in help: a colonel and an entire U.S. regiment. "We have orders from Washington to help you all we can. The lines must go through." What's bad for Western Union is bad for the country.

After several battles, the army goes back to the fort. A fiddle sounds. Engineers dancing. The company workers, a jolly bunch, are celebrating the last pole, now that the Injuns have been taken care of. The boss comes out. They all cheer. "I've got good news for you, boys. The job is done." (Hurrah!) "You all get two months bonus and a double feed tonight." (Hurrah, hurrah!) Shots of drunken, happy workers scarfing down the grub.

Cut to wistful Indian. Randolph Scott puts his arm on the

Chief's shoulder: "Chief, you can't fight something as big and as important as Western Union."

Shots of the graves of the company heroes: pan up to the gleaming backlit telephone pole; pan to the luminous sky. Fade.


## FREE TO CHOOSE

The cable rush is on in Chicago's suburbia. Nineteen systems are vying for Evanston. The towns are offered mobile vans for shooting the football games, color cameras for the PTA. Anything short of a percentage of the gross. A local journalist reveals that three major stockholders in one of the companies are Hugh Hefner, of Playboy, Milton Friedman, principal architect of neo-Keynesian economics and consultant to Pinochet's Chile, and Newton Minow, who as FCC commissioner coined the term "vast wasteland." Minow has also served as President of PBS. White man has powerful medicine.


## EXPORTING THE WASTELAND: THE FREEDOM OF INFORMATION BOYS VERSUS THE NEW WORLD INFORMATION ORDER BOYS

> "Give us twenty-two minutes, we'll give you the world.
>
> WINS News Radio

Boys it is. Out of 104 speakers at the World Communications Conference, only eleven are women, which is probably a favorable ratio compared to the status quo in broadcasting. Thumb through one of the trade magazines, say, *Broadcasting*, and count the number of women pictured. I mean the ones in the suits, not the Dallas cheerleaders in the network ads or the Japanese women in kimonos on the Trinitrons. The window-dressing is on the set, not in the board rooms.

This is a conference sponsored by the International Communication Association and the Annenberg School of Communications (funded largely through the profits of *TV Guide*,

Walter Annenberg's cash cow). Over 600 delegates have come to Philadelphia from all over the world. There is quite a controversy stirring here. You won't hear it discussed on Atlantic Richfield's McNeil-Lehrer NewsHour. The Indians are restless. This time they're not buying that strong medicine line. The U.S. and the transnational corporations are saying, "Trust us. Give us your airwaves. We will bring you the modern world." Data. Transborder data. Credit cards. Digital money. Mork and Mindy. The California primary, in color, with Ronald Reagan. Beverly Sills to explain culture to you.

They don't want it. They want their own transponders. They want their own currency with pictures of their own palm trees and national heroes. They want to do their own instructional television. They don't even like *Sesame Street*. They want to do their own cultural magazine shows without Beverly Sills. In short, what they want is a "new world information order." They want to regulate the international communication infrastructure "to ensure a balance of information."

Wait a minute, the U.S. State Department counters. Didn't you guys read *Animal Farm* in the eighth grade? That's totalitarianism! You're trying to censor us. There must be a free flow. No holds barred. No borders shut. Go ahead, regulate your own broadcasting transmitters. We've got satellites. They can bring you color television from space right into your own hut. All you need is this little dish. Then you can get *Ryan's Hope*, brought to you by Nestlé. Sure, we understand human rights: you have a right to get what we're selling.

ELECTRONIC INFORMATION TIGER

The Third World is beginning to recognize that the radio spectrum is the key to economic and military power. All of the industrialized nations' economic and military machines depend for their effectiveness on the use of radio-telecommunications. This makes the spectrum the soft underbelly of aggressor nations. It makes the spectrum the Electronic Information Tiger. . . . The advanced systems of both the U.S. and the industrialized socialist countries are vulnerable to the collective pressure from the small countries, which can, simply by jamming the use of the airwaves, stop aggressors.

Dallas Smythe, Professor, Simon Frazier University

COSTA RICA HAS NO ARMY

Liliana Garcia de Davis is president of the Costa Rican delegation to WARC, the World Administrative Radio Conference, where the allocation of spectrum was discussed last fall and where it will be decided in future meetings.

We chat about the paltry female representation in communications at the policy level, and I express surprise that a Latin American delegation has a woman leader. "You have many stereotypes about us that are false," she replies. "The Spanish culture has a deep respect for women. For instance, I never give up my own name. I am Liliana Garcia. No matter how many times I marry, I will always be Liliana Garcia. Here in the U.S. I see many women who call themselves by their husband's name. I will never do that. I will die Liliana Garcia."

I comment that it is good that her country deems it sufficiently important to send a substantial delegation to WARC. "These issues are the key to our development economically and culturally. Costa Rica has no army. We are the only country in the world without a military, but we do have a communications office."

She is perturbed that the Annenberg conference does not have simultaneous translations. English is the assumed language. This seems rather arrogant, in view of the title: World Communications Conference. Is this a conscious decision that English is the only language of importance? She is also amazed at the ignorance of many of the U.S. delegates. "So many people don't even know where all these countries are. I think they should put a big map up and have everyone identify where all these places are. Someone asked me if Costa Rica is in Africa or Asia!" she sighed.

PRAISE THE LORD AND PASS THE COTTAGE CHEESE

The dining room is full. I'm late. There are a few empty seats.
Clink. Clink. A chorus of clinks. Six hundred communicators
eating Del Monte fruit compote in small glass dishes. There is
an empty place next to a young man whose neck twists un-
comfortably in his starched collar. His short hair and gangly
look would be punk in Soho, if his shirt were more rumpled
and his demeanor more at ease. But there's a slyness about
him and a quizzical expression that soon identifies him as a
"techie."

What do you do? I ask. "Build radio and television stations." Oh. Where? "Right now, in the Andes." For whom?
"Religious organizations." Which ones? "Right now, my own,
which is Baha'i. But I've built quite a few for other groups—
Pentecostals, Methodists, and not just religious groups. In Ec-
uador I worked for revolutionaries, but they got shot, so we
never got the transmitter up." How much does it cost to put
up a transmitter?

> It depends on what they want. I can put up a good strong radio
> signal for about $2,000. A TV station costs more. But I can do
> it real cheap. Sometimes I lose a job because I bid too low, and
> no one can believe the price. Lots of big companies come
> around and tell them that they need to have a lot of fancy stuff—
> things they don't really need. It breaks down in a couple
> months, and then they have to wait for years for parts and re-
> pairs. I build it real simple and teach them how to run it right
> and how to fix it when it breaks down. Except for that one in
> Ecuador, all my stations are running fine, as far as I know.
> South America, Central America, Africa, even Southeast Asia.
> I've been around.

The waiter brings him his special order. A vegetarian plate.


THIS LITTLE PIGGY WENT WEE WEE WEE ALL THE WAY HOME

> (In the U.S.) society's cultural process, its deepest concern has
> remained largely removed from general consideration and pub-
> lic decision making. Television, the most educative force in ex-

istence has been left almost entirely to private considerations and the vagaries of the marketplace. . . . The fetters that bind American talent and limit its national engagement are essentially the same as those which are hobbling the social utilization of global communications. . . . The prospect for a genuinely international space communications system which operates to satisfy global educational and cultural aspirations is heavily dependent on the degree to which American domestic communications are utilized for the social benefit of its own population.[2]

---

[2] Herbert I. Schiller, *Mass Communication and American Empire* (Boston: Beacon Press, 1969).

# Otherwise (If You Live in a House of Babel, Learn How to Sling Stones)[3]

## April 1989

*This is dedicated to Jaime Barrios (1942–89), one of the found-ers of Young Filmmakers Foundation who worked unceasingly as a teacher, a filmmaker, and an interpreter and presenter of "other" voices. In remembrance of an evening at the Min-newaska Conference on Child-Made Films during which Jaime Barrios, Susan Zeig, Pedro Rivera, and I watched Chris Mark-er's film* The Train Rolls On, *an account of the cinetrains in the early years of the Soviet Union through the eyes of the director of that effort, Medvedkin.*

I HAVE SPENT a lot of time trying to help others make their own images. My first work was at Henry Street Settlement on the Lower East Side in New York City. Nowadays social agencies that serve inner cities are called "community centers," but the Henry Street Settlement was founded by Lillian Wald, an associate of Jane Adams and a member of the Settlement House Movement at the turn of the century. The term "settle-ment" indicates the manner in which these social workers came to inner-city communities: they "settled" there, living and working with "others." They were missionaries, and their attitude toward the "others" was patronizing, or, rather, "ma-tronizing." The leaders of this movement were, for the most

[3] Thanks to John Hanhardt and Steve Lavine for proposing that I write this paper for the Bellaggio Conference "High Culture/Popular Culture: Media Representations of the Other," held in February 1989.

part, women, and mostly upper-class women—bringing "civilization" to the "downtrodden." My misgivings about charitable missions have been a bit tempered in recent years by stark confrontation with the brutality of Reaganism in which even this sort of activity has all but disappeared. However, I must own up to my own missionary past: my experience with media began as a workshop teacher in what was left of the settlement movement. I started film workshops at both the Lillian Wald Settlement (1961) and Henry Street Settlement (1963). Most of this work was with young people, ages eight to eighteen. With the exception of the connection with the settlement movement, these workshops were not associated with any social activism (the sixties had hardly begun) and were without any theoretical base or trajectory.

There were other media workshops in those years. Roger Larsen had workshops at University Settlement and later with Jaime Barrios and Lynne Hofer at the Young Filmmakers' Foundation. Yvonne Anderson taught young people from mostly middle-class backgrounds at the Yellowball Workshop in Lexington, Massachusetts. There was occasional funding for this activity from federal educational grants, the funds pushed though Congress by the equipment manufacturers. The work of Marshall McLuhan as interpreted by his disciple at Fordham University, John Culkin, gave a flurry of theoretical rationalization and provided the optimism necessary for some schools to increase their media budgets. Culkin and McLuhan convened a few meetings of media educators, mostly English teachers who liked to show *An Incident at Owl Creek* in class. However, for the hands-on workshop teachers, there was little exchange or collaboration.

In my own case, there was another formative experience, which called into question some of the assumptions of Henry Street Settlement. During my high school years in Chattanooga, Tennessee, I participated in several weekend workshops at Highlander Folk School, an adult education center which was at that time in the hills of Grundy County, Tennessee.[4] Miles Horton, a labor organizer and educator, had stud-

---

[4] This school was documented in a film called *People of the Cumberland* (Frontier Films, 1938).

ied the "folk school" tradition in Scandinavia and adapted
this form of adult education to the Cumberland Mountains.
When formed in the 1930s the goal was to help organize mine-
workers; later (1950s) the school emphasized training grassroots civil rights leaders. Making the pivotal gesture that has
been described as the beginning of the civil rights movement,
Rosa Parks, having been trained at Highlander only a few
weeks before, took a seat in the white section of the city bus in
Montgomery, Alabama. The role that Highlander played in the
civil rights work in the South is not widely known, except
among movement veterans. A hint of its impact may be
gleaned from the fact that the song "We Shall Overcome" was
written (based on an old hymn) by Horton's wife and Highlander teacher, Zilphia Horton.[5]

The essential lesson of Highlander was empowerment of
"the other." Henry Street and the other settlements were
missions. They were colonizers, often benign, but colonizers
nevertheless. Helen Hall was director of Henry Street during
my tenure there. She was an elderly matron who maintained
a formal parlor and a dining room where selected members
of the settlement community were occasionally asked to dine.
These were formal dinners served with uptown elegance. Lessons in etiquette were part of the settlement tradition. The lessons taught more than how to hold a fork and graciously
receive the food the servants (recruited and trained from the
neighborhood) offered. The lesson was one of proper cultural
hierarchy and how accommodation and deference can help
one become an accepted guest and a "good example" for the
rest of the community. In contrast with decorum at Henry
Street, dinners at Highlander were informal and lively with
heated discussions and arguments. The Henry Street parlor
had formal Victorian sofas and chairs. The sitting room at
Highlander was for workshop discussions and filled with simply crafted mountain rocking chairs. Rocking back and forth,
people from all over the South would talk about how to overcome inhibiting feelings of servitude and unworthiness and to

---

[5] George Stoney and Jim Brown produced a film that traces the evolution
of this song through various movements around the world.

appreciate their own communities and lifestyles. The concentration was on formulating opposition to the status quo in order to empower disenfranciosed people. The emphasis was not learning proper manners, but gaining the courage to take principled stands.

My teaching media on the Lower East Side was an unconscious move in a direction indicated by Highlander's work. I had a vaguely perceived sense that young people needed a way of defending themselves against mass culture. I believed that active participation in media production could be a method to empower "others." Of course, the sides are a bit uneven, but it was clear to me that the "problem of representing the other" is, first and foremost, a problem of power—or, rather, overcoming powerlessness so that people can represent themselves.[6] The notion of teaching kids to make media was ridiculed by a cynical French journalist[7] who said that teaching children filmmaking was at best a homeopathic remedy. I am not an advocate of homeopathic medical cures, but I believe that the best defense against mass culture is an offense.

A research commission initiated by UNESCO, the United Nations Educational, Scientific, and Cultural Organization, resulted in calls for a "new world information order" in the 1970s. The published results of that project looking at inequalities in image production around the globe became perhaps the most maliciously attacked volume (pre-Rushdie's *Satanic Verses*) in the twentieth century. The MacBride Report, *Many Voices, One World*,[8] is named for the chairman of the commission, Sean MacBride, founder of Amnesty International, great Irish patriot, son of Maude Gonne, and the only person to win both the Lenin Peace Price and the Nobel Peace Prize, whose tireless efforts for justice in the world were stopped only with his death at the age of ninety-two. The MacBride Report summarizes over a hundred studies made during a period of four years by dozens of scholars from many countries. It dared to

---

[6] See John Gaventa (who was active at Highlander), *Power and Powerlessness: Quiescence and Rebellion in an Appalachian Valley* (Urbana: University of Illinois Press, 1980).

[7] See Section 2, "A Homeopath Abroad."

[8] This report was published by UNESCO's Unipub in 1980.

propose ways in which *other* voices could be heard. It contained suggestions for making media production accessible throughout the world. It saw the essentially "one-way" flow of information as a problem to be reckoned with and addressed. Contrary to the claims of a rather extensive disinformation campaign, the report did not call for censorship of the press. In fact, it clearly articulated the need for more voices, more freedom of expression, and the protection of journalists' rights.[9] But it problematized the extent to which forms of Western commercial media were dominating the entire world. The expression of this concern so threatened Western media corporations that the U.S. representatives at the United Nations screamed excessive regulation and control. This research, clearly within the mandate of the UNESCO charter, was just as clearly a problem for the corporate culture industry. In retaliation, payment of U.S. dues not only to UNESCO but to the entire United Nations was all but stopped. Ultimately the tightening screws did their job, and UNESCO was reorganized, restructured, and restricted—so cleanly swept that even the residue of this research effort is all but gone. Copies of the MacBride Report can no longer be studied, for it is not available on the list of books that UNESCO distributes.

What was so dangerous about this report? Surely not the style. In language replete with diplomatic eschewal and delicate phrasing, the MacBride Report cautiously and modestly proposed ways of thinking about how communication policies might be changed to create structures to encourage media that do not make people into "others." In other words, the "others" are encouraged to speak for themselves, with suggestions for projects to give people equipment and training and some sample regulatory policies that might encourage broad participation in media.

---

[9] For a report on the campaign of disinformation that was orchestrated against UNESCO because of this work, see William Preston, Edward Herman, and Herbert Schiller, *Hope and Folly: The United States and UNESCO* (Minneapolis: University of Minnesota Press, 1989). There is also a Paper Tiger program on this subject: *Dou Dou Dienne and Claude Robinson on The New World Information Order* (1986). Dou Dou Dienne was the chief UNESCO delegate to the United Nations in New York.

The fate of UNESCO's MacBride Commission shows how hard it is to give "others" voice. This massive effort, supported by over a hundred countries, was severely punished for even expressing the *need* for additional sources of information and images.[10] The suppression of this work has discouraged further struggles around these issues, certainly at the United Nations.[11] However, despite the machinations at the international governmental level and the retreat by UNESCO, some distinct advances have been made at a more local level. These examples allow us glimpses of image making that do not divide into "us" and "them" or "some" and "others."

COLLABORATIVE EQUIPMENT SHARING AND NETWORKING

With the mass marketing of electronic technology, groups traditionally excluded from technological power now find themselves able to speak. The home video recorder and the personal computer, while designed for individual use in the "First World," are easily adapted for use by cooperative organizations in less affluent communities.[12] Even in the First World, the need to share the costs of technology in computer work and video has increased the incidence of collaborative work among researchers, artists, community activists, and educators. The organization and administration of video production and editing centers have encouraged collaboration and

---

[10] See Preston et al.'s *Hope and Folly* for a look at the sheer vituperation of the attacks on this commission.

[11] The current president of UNESCO has distanced himself from this sort of work.

[12] This would be an interesting area for further research: the collective possibilities gained from individual targeted consumer products. Let your fingers do the dialectic! How the need to mass market powerful tools to individuals offers opportunities for collective work. This was certainly operating in the formation of groups by artists to do video work in the early days of the technology. It continues with the sharing of resources such as editing and production equipment in media centers around the country, such as the Boston Film and Video Foundation, the Bay Area Video Coalition, the Downtown Community Television in New York City, and the Media Alliance. The role these institutions play within the alternative media scene is a clear one of empowerment.

helped to form mini-communities in rural areas and within large urban centers. When the technology is shared, the cost per image and the expense per bit of information go down to affordable rates. One does not have to be a big corporation or a right-wing lobby to have a computerized mailing list. One does not have to be CBS or Reuters to make news reports.[13]

MEDIA CRITIQUE

One of the most interesting aspects of contemporary alternative media is the critique of mass media. Many empowered video production groups start off with a critique of the culture industry. The British *Miners Tapes* is a clear example. During the protracted coal strike in the United Kingdom several years ago, Channel Four sponsored facilitating workshops with the miners. The first tape they made was one not on labor issues or on the dreadful working conditions in the mines, or the problems of the coal board's relentless closing of the mines. The first tape they did was called *The Lie Machine*,[14] and it is a carefully articulated critique of how miners, the strike, and strike leaders were being represented in the press and TV news.

Another of the Channel Four–initiated video workshops, the Women's Collective in Derry, Northern Ireland, also has completed a work that addresses misrepresentation: *Mother Ireland*,[15] which looks at how Ireland has often been portrayed as a pathetic and weeping woman in contrast to the robust figures of England as John Bull or a regal lion. This tape traces the images back to the seventeenth-century popular press, nineteenth-century sheet music covers, and gravestone imag-

---

[13] Examples of Internet grassroots news providers are the Central American Resource Network (CARNET), which provided information on Contra attacks in Nicaragua, church initiatives for peace by the Witness for Peace Organizations, and details on labor organizing activities in San Salvador, and Peacenet. This sort of collaborative news organization gained momentum with the Independent Media Center during the WTO protests in Seattle in 1999. See Section 9, "Teamsters and Turtles."

[14] *The Lie Machine* is available through Paper Tiger Television.

[15] *Mother Ireland* is available through Women Make Movies.

ery. Contemporary television scenes of weeping mothers of IRA and Protestant martyrs is part of this tradition.

In New York City, the Gay Men's Health Crisis set up a complete video production facility to make weekly programs for public access called *Living with AIDS*. The first project of their new video facility was a program entitled *Doctors, Liars and Women* by Jean Carlamusto and Maria Maggenti, a critique of a misleading article in *Cosmopolitan* magazine in which an arrogant doctor reassures women that AIDS is a rare, if not impossible, disease for heterosexual women to catch. Carlamusto and Maggenti's tape unmasks this poorly conducted research and questionable conclusions. Critiquing "scientific experts" who are often presented with unquestioned authority in newspapers, magazines, and on television has implications beyond this specific case. AIDS discussions have been ambushed by instant experts who mask their homophobia, class bias, and racism behind manipulated statistics. *Doctors, Liars and Women* was made by two women who have been working for five years on a daily basis with AIDS victims, activists, and researchers. The activism energizing the AIDS support communities in New York and San Francisco has generated a dedicated group of authentic experts. Unfortunately they are rarely contacted for information or presented as legitimate authorities in the mainstream press and on commercial television, but the alternative TV work they are producing has an important role in informing activist communities around the country and in providing "other" sources of information on the current health crisis.

> So the fight is for, let us say, representation, but in new forms; forms that are bound up more with participation than delegation, dependent on significant associations of people rather than recorded majorities, moving towards the development of a non-representative representation: the achievement of modes of presentation and imaging and entertainment and argument that are realizations of collective desires, group aspirations, common projects, shared experience.[16]

---

[16] Stephen Heath, "Representing Television," in *The Logics of Television: Essays in Cultural Criticism*, ed. Pat Mellencamp (Bloomington: Indiana University Press, 1990).

The public access movement has developed citizens production centers in over 1,700 cities across the country—production facilities and public access channels: delegated space and time on television for use by citizens. Although many programs are hollow attempts at reproducing network fare, there is a growing amount of access work that is fresh and creative. This work is vitally important to local communities, covering such issues as homelessness, AIDS, the environment, and racism. There are many documented cases in which access programs have had a direct impact on local policies.[17]

There have been sporadic attempts to organize the public around issues in telecommunications: the Consumer Federation, National Organization for Women, United Church of Christ, AFL-CIO National Council, Action for Children's Television, and others have found it particularly difficult to organize viewers, whose relationship to the medium is essentially passive, despite the proclamations of many culture studies apologists about the "alternative readings" of various audiences. Critical viewing of a program that someone else has made is not equivalent to making your own program. The alienation that passive viewing breeds is practically impossible to overcome. In contrast, the public access movement is made up of activists. It is a grassroots media movement with tremendous potential. The activists who have created and maintained their local channels have had to fight in their city councils and planning boardrooms. They have learned to battle the cable corporations with resourceful persistence. They are struggling to create a public sphere for those otherwise excluded from discourse.

> The interest of workers can, since they are unrealized, be organized only if they enter into a life context, in other words, into a proletarian public sphere. Only then do they have the chance

---

[17] Diana Agosta, Abigail Norman, and Caryn Rogoff, *Participate Directory of Public Access in New York State* (New York: Media Network and New York Cable Commission, 1988). This detailed survey of public access use in one state is one of the most complete research projects on the subject of access. The authors go county by county and examine how access works in each community: how the facilities are structured, who the users are, and what sorts of programs are being made and played.

to develop as interests, instead of remaining mere possibilities.[18]

Alexander Kluge has written eloquently of television as a public sphere and is devoting his work to developing alternative television in Germany. He was the prime organizer of the 1962 Oberhausen Manifesto, which was able to wrest resources for the New German Cinema from state bureaucratic structures. "I don't believe in revolutions from above. . . . But I cannot begin to revolutionize society on the basis of film. Therefore I must accept this contradiction. The strategy from below will first of all not work for the mass media. Not everyone is a cameraman or a scriptwriter, or is talented or has the time or the air time."[19]

Not everyone has time, but on access in the United States, there is airtime to spare and community television centers where video technology is being used to present (as opposed to re-present) people otherwise excluded from any public sphere. These are not "settlements" descended from above to teach the downtrodden higher forms or culture or politics. These are grassrooted workplaces, built with the efforts of local organized cultural and political resistance. They will not go away any time soon.

These examples are small birds in an immense and polluted sky. They are, however, not homeopathic remedies. They are not fighting poison with poison. They are fighting poison with truth. And to steal a metaphor from Fernando Birri, sometimes truth has very large wings.[20]

---

[18] Oskar Negt and Alexander Kluge, *The Public Sphere and Experience* (Minneapolis: University of Minnesota Press, 1989).

[19] Interview with Kluge, New York, N.Y., 1989.

[20] A reference to Argentinian filmmaker Fernando Birri"s film *Small Bird with Enormous Wings.*

# The Willow Declaration: United in Support of Democratic Communication

## August 1981

In 1979, the United Nations Educational, Scientific, and Cultural Organization (UNESCO) released the final report of the International Commission for the Study of Communication Problems. For over three years, the Commission's sixteen international communication experts and their Chairman, Nobel and Lenin Peace Laureate Sean MacBride, had been investigating the present inequitable world information infrastructure. When the report first appeared, its recommendations—to decolonize and to democratize world communication—were greeted with enthusiasm by most of the world's media. But scarcely a peep was heard from the U.S. press. Since then, there has been open hostility toward UNESCO itself and a movement in the U.S. Congress to cut funds to that body. The elite media, the academic establishment, the Department of State, and such organizations as Freedom House and the World Press Freedom Committee have portrayed the MacBride Report as a conspiracy by the Third World to limit democracy, to gag Western reporters, to destroy the free exchange of ideas, and to stifle news.

What is the reality here? The roots of the MacBride Commission's inquiry lie in the growing movement of countries in the less developed world to redress the economic and social imbalances that are a legacy of colonial rule. In the early

1960s, leaders in the Third World began to call for a "new world information order" to redress information inequities as well. The predominantly one-way flow of information from the nations of Europe and North America tended to perpetuate economic dependency, to distort local news, and to contaminate local cultural values. Some of the concrete demands for a new world information order include a more equitable distribution of the world's radio frequencies, termination of unauthorized remote sensing satellite surveillance of crops and mineral resources, and increased coverage of Third World affairs in the press of the developed world.

These and other demands are based on fears that technology in general, and communication technology in particular, has been advancing at such a rate that its capital-intensive character put its control into the hands of large monopolistic interests (both capitalistic and communist). Information is defined by the powerful as wealth, and the powerful act accordingly to control that wealth. More and more, the movement and the production of real goods is dictated by information flows. To have no access to information is to have no access to wealth and is one of the causes of the world's imbalances—resulting in real hunger and real inflation in real time. The question before the entire world is whether an advanced electronic information environment of broadcasting and cable television, computers, satellites, digital data streams, fiber optics, and videotext publishing can be responsive to human needs. Can this technology lead to more decentralized and democratic forms of self-reliance and interdependence? Can information be shared with greater justice and equity?

The MacBride Commission addressed these matters in its report. The U.S. press chose to ignore the substance of this work. Information needs and disparities in all parts of the world, including the industrialized countries, were cataloged in great detail by the Commission, but the substance of the research was not mentioned in the U.S. media. The many recommendations for increased public access and participation were overlooked. Suggestions for strengthening democratic information structures were ignored. Instead, an issue (which appears not in the report itself but in one of the dozens of studies commissioned after the publication of the MacBride Report) has been singled out by the so-called "free press" in the West. This item, a call to protect journalists by issuing them licenses, was seized upon as the only "newsworthy" element of these important deliberations. Even the National News Agency in a study of the coverage of these discussions found the U.S. press sorely lacking in objectivity. Such distortions are precisely what developing countries have found intolerable and what the MacBride Report is all about: imbalance of information and the need for re-ordering of priorities. This kind of sensationalized, one-dimensional view is often the perspective from which many international events are reported in our media. Our national and local information is often just as biased. As much as the U.S. media have penetrated the cultural life of most of the world, they fail to reflect the authentic diversity and depth of our own political and cultural life. Western media have called for what is tantamount to a global First Amendment while monopolizing and restricting the right and means to communicate domestically.

In recognition of this and in solidarity with all information-poor people of the world, we offer the following declaration in support of continued inquiry into communication problems.


DECLARATION

We are a group of artists, educators, researchers, film and video producers, electronic technicians, social scientists, and writers united in our support for democratic communications. The economic, cultural, and spiritual welfare of humanity is increasingly tied to the structure for production and distribution of information. Most communications today is one-way, from the centers of power to passive audiences of consumers. We need a new information order here in the United States to give the power of voice to the unheard and the disenfranchised. We strongly support freedom of the press, but we see that in our own country, this freedom now exists mainly for huge corporations to make profits, to promote socially useless consumption, and to impose corporate ideology and agendas. As workers who produce, study, and transmit information, we pledge to change this reality. We will work to preserve and encourage face-to-face communication: people can speak best for themselves without the intervention of professionalism or technological mediation. We support that technology which enhances human power and which is designed and controlled by the communities which use it. We support the participation of workers and nonprofessionals in media production and the use of media for trade union and community organizing. We support the development of community channels for programs, news flow, and data exchange. We support popular access to and control of media and communications systems. We support the internationally guaranteed right to reply and criticize and deplore the fact that this right is being attacked now in the United States by efforts in Congress to eliminate the Fairness Doctrine and public inter-

Media co-conspirators on retreat in Willow, New York, circa 1983. Back row, from left: Mark Dion, Marissa Bowe, Martha Wallner, Shulea Cheung, Helen Granger, Guy Robinson. Front row, from left: Cathy Scott, the author, Robin Andersen, Nancy Bermon, Chuck Singleton. *(Joel Kovel)*

est broadcast regulations. While these laws have been under-utilized and difficult to apply, they have been the principal tools for forcing even token public debate. We who live and work in the United States pledge ourselves to struggle for de-mocratization of communications within our communities, our places of work, and our political institutions. We support the further inquiry by international organizations such as UNESCO into the social relations of the electronic environ-ment. As the Foreword to the MacBride Report states: "It is essential that all men and women, in all social and cultural environments should be given the opportunity of joining in the process of collective thinking thus initiated, for new ideas must be developed and more positive measures must be taken to shake off the prevailing inertia. We hope that these discus-sions will continue and will resonate among and between na-tions and peoples."[21]

---

[21] Willow participants: Stanley Aronowitz, Liza Bear, Eddie Becker, Nancy Cain, Tobe Carey, Carol Clements, Donna Cooper, Ariel Doughtery, Howard Fredericks, Bart Freidman, Bertram Gross, DeeDee Halleck, Julie Haynes, Joel Kovel, Margaret Leo, Michael McClard, Paul McIssac, Karen Paulsell, Andrew Phillips, Karen Ranucci, Anthony Rutkowski (via teleconference), Kusum Singh, Michael Wallace, Marc Weiss, Brian Winston, Sol Yurick.

# The Experience of Citizens' Television in the United States: Public Access/Public Sphere

## *December 1992*

FOR OVER TWENTY YEARS, the United States has been the location of a unique community media experiment: the use of television channels and television equipment on an open "first come, first serve" basis. This experiment has evolved in over a thousand cities and towns to varying degrees of engagement by the public, and with varying degrees of cooperation from the cable corporations that are required to provide the opportunity.

The notion of access as implementation of a democratic project is neither recognized by the public nor acknowledged by most communication theorists. Even though there were a few brief appearances of a mainstream TV "sitcom" (situation comedy) with public access as the plot base,[22] in general, public access does not figure positively in the American consciousness. This is largely due to the scorn and derision that is heaped upon it on network news shows and in the mass-marketed periodicals. The "kinky" sex programs and the use of the medium by skinhead racists are the two areas of public access programming that are regularly discussed to a broad public. There is little mention of the city council meetings, the welfare rights advocacy programs, or the homework helper shows that teens and teachers have organized. There are no reviews of the radical television experiments by video and per-

---

[22] GTG Entertainment, *Room 101* (1988). Later there was the feature film *Wayne's World* to ridicule access.

formance artists, no coverage of the community ecological watchdog programs. Understanding public access television from the vantage point of mass media is like understanding the city from the banner headlines in the tabloid newspapers. Communications specialists have not taken the public access phenomenon seriously. There has been very little appreciation of public access from academics in communication.[23] One could do a data search and come up with only a small amount of information on what is the central most extensive and innovative use of communication technology for open public exchange in the world.[24]

PROBLEMATIC IMAGE

The sensationalist distortion by mass media and the neglect by academia of this important subject is no accident. The media conglomerates that own magazines and newspapers do not write about public access. Most cable companies are themselves owned by the same media conglomerates. The media corporations would rather the popular image of public access be the kinky sex shows and the Nazis. If the cable companies promote public channels, they are lessening their chance to retake those channels. No matter how many channels the cable companies have, they always need more for profit-driven services, from commercial programming such as the Weather Channel, or from Pay-Per-View services that host extra fee movies and sports events. Public access is an obligation cable corporations would rather not have, so they do everything they can to diminish and denigrate the phenomenon.

---

[23] Exceptions are Ralph Engelman, "The Origins of Public Access Cable TV, 1966–1972," *Journalism Monographs* no. 123 (1992), and Doug Kellner, *Television and the Crisis of Democracy* (Boulder: Westview Press, 1990), pp. 207–24. There was also a special issue of the *Journal of Film and Television* on public access. See also Engelman's *Public Radio and Television in America: A Political History* (Thousand Oaks, Calif.: Sage, 1996).

[24] One of the best articles on public access cable was commissioned by the United Church of Christ Communication Office in New York: Jennifer Stearns's *Short Course in Cable* remains a classic overview of the access possibilities. For information on obtaining the booklet write: Office of Communication, United Church of Christ, 105 Madison Avenue, New York, N.Y. 10016.

The popular image of access that has been constructed by mass culture contributes to the indifference of academics to this experiment in communication democracy. The movement is associated with a lowly form of art (sleazy pornography) and an irrational and frightening politic (neo-Nazis). Those who study or promote democratic structures of regulation and rights of expression are ashamed to be associated with them. Both the sex shows and the skinheads are too marginal to inspire any interest from the "pop" culture theorists. All of this has left public access with few enthusiasts except for the several thousand activists who maintain the movement, and tens of thousands who have been trained at local stations and who have made hundreds of thousands of hours of programming.

OPEN TO SCRUTINY

One of the premises behind promoting the images of kinky sex and Nazis as the "symbols" for public access is that they denote the failure of the idea.[25] Instead of castigating the movement for these examples, instead of "killing the messenger," one might think about the fact that these very real elements of U.S. life are indeed available for public scrutiny on television. One can make a strong case for the fact that public access brings issues of racism and religious prejudice out in the open. Pocatello, Idaho, is a case in point. Idaho is a state that has harbored many extreme right-wing groups, and the access system in Pocatello was required to run a weekly program by neo-Nazi Tom Metzger. However, a group of local high school teens were so upset by the programming that they formed the "Pocatello Human Rights Club" and started producing a weekly call-in show to respond to the racist series. In addition, they held forums on prejudice at their high school and worked to build a community of people to take positive steps to address the situation of racism in Idaho. Public access did not invent racism in Idaho, but it did bring this issue to a public forum and inspired the formation of a community group to fight racism.

---

[25] Wallace Turner, "Cable TV Access Rules Give Extremists a Forum," *New York Times*, October 7, 1986.

## PUBLIC SPHERE

In our society of privately owned suburban malls and individualized apartments in housing complexes without communal space, we have very few public forums. Public access makes television a community forum. However, there are always criticisms of access channels: that very few people watch, that they are a waste of time, that the space is so much fallow land that should be producing market crops. While it may be true that in many cities public access is not viewed by many, those loyal viewers may be deeply involved in the programs they do watch. Public access is narrowcasting: producers often are aiming for very specific, often very small, communities of viewers. There are, however, other programs on public access that are watched by large numbers of viewers. Viewership is a function of how active the access center is in promoting the programming within the community, and how important the issues covered are. As Doug Kellner has noted, "A survey by the ELRA Group of East Lansing, Michigan, indicates that access is rated the fifth most popular category of television programming (ahead of sports, women's programming and children's programs, religious programs, etc.); and that 63 percent of those surveyed had an interest in access programming. Local surveys in Austin (Texas) have confirmed that access programs have a large audience."[26]

## EMERGENCY NETWORK

Even if public access were not watched much in normal times, it is there in case of an emergency. In the town where I live, Woodstock, New York, access was used extensively during a water crisis: asbestos was discovered in the town water supply, dropping in big clots from cement-asbestos pipes and coming out in such large amounts that drains were getting clogged with it, not to mention what it was doing to stomachs and lungs (when residents took a shower or used a humidifier). There was a general panic and many weeks of town hearings with reports from construction workers, lung specialists,

---

[26] Kellner, *Television and the Crisis of Democracy*, p. 224.

and ecologists. During those weeks the entire town was glued to the local access channel for a steady stream of water-specific information. The local water may have been cloudy, but public access provided a local well of clear, however contradictory, testimony, undiluted facts, and first-hand reports that were immediate and pertinent to the well-being of the community. The mainstream network channels in New York and Albany gave the issue only a sixty-second news brief. The fact that Woodstock had its own local channel ensured that when an emergency came, residents were able to exchange information and "news" that was essential to their lives.[27]

PUBLIC ACCESS: CREATIVE REGULATION[28]

Public access television is a form of telecommunications regulation. There are four levels on which this regulation is justified:

First is the fact that cable contracts are granting what is essentially a monopoly to a communications corporation to enable them to reach a particular market. Therefore this benefit needs to be compensated by a public component.

The second reason is that in order to construct the physical infrastructure (hanging the wires, sharing the telephone poles, having access to city sewer and tunnels) a cable company needs the cooperation and "right-of-way" from the municipality involved.

Beyond these two legal justifications, there is the third philosophical argument that citizens have an essential right to information exchange. The assumption here is that if the First Amendment protects free speech in an age of face-to-face argument and print media, these rights are automatically extended into more complicated forms of technology as they are developed.

There is also an argument that the distribution of most cable

---

[27] Local channels were used extensively for reactions to the Gulf War and the Seattle anti-WTO protests in those "national emergencies." See Sections 4 and 9 of this book.

[28] An early article about access regulation was by Neil Goldstein and Nick DeMartino, "FCC Weighing Crucial Access, Origination Regs," *Community Video Report* 2, no. 1 (1974).

programming is via the extensive satellite systems which were developed with a heavy investment of public funds and therefore mandates a "payback" in the form of public benefits.

As technology develops with greater emphasis on direct broadcast satellites, delivery by telephone companies ("telcos"), and "wireless" cable systems, the last two arguments become more pertinent. All of these new technologies, cable television, telco-delivered video/infoservices, and satellite television, owe their research and development to the enormous public expenditures by the U.S. space and military programs. A few corporations have become very wealthy by using that research as the basis for their business. Critics of commercial media have pointed out that after the initial outlay of monies for cable-telephone infrastructure (or transponder launch), program distributors have little to do but rake in profits from the public.[29]

Most countries have some form of telecommunications regulation, although many of these have been eroded with the increasing expansion of market-oriented systems. These regulations vary from country to country, but the basic need is to ensure that the public benefits. Public access is a creative response to the need to regulate video distribution, and many studies have shown that not only the public benefits, but the cable corporations as well.[30]

PUBLIC ACCESS: STRUCTURES AND SYSTEMS

The way public access is implemented varies greatly. A public access center might be located at a library, or at a junior high school, or in a church basement. It could be set up in an abandoned firehouse or in a new shopping center. Each municipality works with media organizers and non-profit rep-

---

[29] A lobby campaign by the Instructional Telecommunications Foundation, together with the Consumer Federation, in the late nineties pushed for noncommercial access to all DBS satellites: now 4 to 7 percent of broadcasts must be informational programming.

[30] "Does Penetration Rate Vary for Cable Systems with Access?" in Diana Agosta et al., *The Participate Report*, p. 20. This informative study of the use of cable in one state shows that systems (of the same size in equal type markets) that have public access have more subscribers.

resentatives to find a home for the center. The organization of the space and outreach can be quite different from system to system or even within a given system. Dallas, Texas, started with a plan to create centers in many different parts of the city, but some of the centers flourished and others languished. They eventually shut those centers that were not active and increased the ones that worked well.

It is important to place the center in a location where people feel safe and welcome, and where there is ample public transportation even at night. Since most cities are divided into neighborhoods of class and ethnic groups, the location of an access center in one specific neighborhood can be seen to favor one or another group. The building of a broad base of community contacts and relationships is essential to the success of access. The location in many ways defines future use.

The administration of public access centers can vary from appointed boards (usually appointed by the mayor and/or the city council) to elected boards (via ballot at the center, or to producers and users). Some access centers are administered by the cable corporations themselves. In general, the centers that have autonomy from the cable corporations seem to be the most successful and creative. There is an inherent conflict of interest between the cable companies (who want the channels for their own purposes) and the access community (especially the community of producers, who are in general an independent sort and are antagonistic to intrusion or control).

FRANCHISE CONTRACTS

The franchise is the contract that the city makes with the cable corporation. Many franchises are extremely detailed. Cities have found that they need to spell out in tiny minutiae the terms of the agreement. For example, the public access contract between the cable company and Rochester, New York, has in it that the corporation must provide a certain amount of cameras and recording decks that are up to date (not more than a few years old). It also states that they must be kept in good order and that should they break down, they must be fixed within two weeks or replaced with new equipment.

Cities learned the hard way that they needed to account for upgrading and maintenance. In the early days of cable franchising, many cities were flattered with offers from cable companies for multi-camera mobile trucks with switchers and effects generators.[31] Because there were no provisions for repair or engineering staff, the trucks and their fancy cameras soon broke down and would often sit in the company's parking lot for years. To ensure funds for ongoing maintenance of the access organization and the equipment, many cities have opted for detailed contracts and for a percentage of the subscriber fee (often up to five cents a month per subscriber).[32]

PUBLIC ACCESS: NON-PROFIT ORGANIZATIONS

Many access centers train and promote use of the center by community organizations. The groups vary from animal rights groups to the Boy Scouts. Community organizations have found access useful to promote their projects, to encourage new members, and to interface with the public.[33]

Marge Nicholson gives several reasons why access can be useful for community groups: "The most unusual aspect of public access is that it enables your organization to speak for itself without an intermediary. On public access, you control the program content—not the commercial broadcaster, an investigative reporter, the local government, or the access channel manager. . . . Access can be an effective communications tool for your organization and should be considered as part of your organization's overall media plan."[34]

---

[31] "The Gold Rush of 1980: Prospecting for Cable Franchises," *Broadcasting*, March 31, 1980, pp. 35–58.

[32] Vermont has a state law that requires that a cable corporation give 10 percent of everything: channels, bandwidth, percentage of gross.

[33] One group that has made use of public access are retired persons. The AARP has published a guide for public access: Institute of Lifelong Learning, *Community Television: A Handbook for Production* (American Association of Retired Persons, 1986).

[34] Margie Nicholson, *Cable Access: A Community Communications Resource for Nonprofits, Benton Foundation Bulletin* no. 3 (April) (Washington, D.C.: Benton Foundation, 1990).

ARTISTS AND ACCESS

For many young media artists, performance on public access is a unique opportunity to address a TV audience. Many cable studios have the ability to "go live," which gives the artists an opportunity to experiment with audience feedback. Most television today is tightly controlled, corporately produced. Making live television in a local situation without commercial sponsors can be a new venue for artists. A good example is "A Day without Art," a live program about AIDS. Each year, artists and museums have closed galleries in commemoration of those within the art community who have died of AIDS. Performers and visual artists coordinated a program that was transmitted via satellite to art museums, community centers, and public access stations. The program contained segments from many regions, produced at media centers and public access studios. This was a coming together of a specific community for a national event. The public access stations across the country enabled the production to be seen by a nationwide audience.

PUBLIC ACCESS: PUBLIC DISSENT

Public access has been a public forum for dissent. For the past six years, the Deep Dish Television Network[35] has been building up a base of community producers, graphic artists, and performers ready to contribute to a common project, channels willing to run these often radical shows, and activists who promote and distribute the programs in their communities. The value of a collaborative infrastructure was demonstrated in the days preceding the Gulf War. Video activists in the United States predicted the position of mainstream media, having seen the sort of news censorship and uncritical portrayal of military actions that were exerted during the invasions of Granada and Panama. Since the Vietnam War, in which the media was blamed for "prolonging the war" by providing space for the peace movement, there has been a con-

---

[35] See Section 4, "From Public Access to Geostationary Orbit."

certed effort to ridicule and minimize any pacifist options or critical evaluation of war. Alternative views have remained localized at rallies and teach-ins, rarely heard in national forums. However, this time, with the infrastructure of an alternative network of public access stations, activists, and video producers in place, the Gulf Crisis TV Project (organized by Paper Tiger Television and Deep Dish) was able to distribute their antiwar programs to hundreds of channels in a very short time. With massive organizing by local peace groups with phone campaigns and in some cases picketing of local stations, this national series was also seen on many of the channels of the more restricted PBS network, the government-supported public television.

With the Gulf Crisis TV Project, this community found voice through an alternative communication system. These were not news reports by correspondents sent into separate communities, but work contributed by the communities themselves, collected and compiled by volunteers who identified with the concerns and issues presented. The national initiatives that the Gulf Crisis TV Project and Deep Dish represent are a way of linking local producers and access persons into a production community that gives support and encouragement to public access producers and organizers.[36] In general, access producers are often isolated and unappreciated, often in constant arbitration with the cable company or the local municipality over this or that issue of transmission and budget.

PUBLIC ACCESS: PROBLEMS OF IMPLEMENTATION

A major problem at public access facilities is staff burnout. A lively public access center is an exciting place to work and demands energy and dedication from the staff. Often the staff is young and enthusiastic, but unable to organize their time and delegate authority. Administration of a center that is truly functioning to the needs of the community can be very stressful. Access becomes the place where grievances are heard, where anger is vented, where activism originates, and where

---

[36] This sort of ad hoc network has been the basis for antiglobalization media. See Section 9.

hope is ignited. This is all exciting, but exhausting for those who must play host to a diverse range of community personalities. The best remedy is an experienced community board that can assist in crises, spotting potential staff burnout before it's too late and protecting the overall organization from problematic individual and organizational producers.

There is a "Catch 22" of public access: publicity can ensure local support from city councils and the local public access boards of directors, but each item of publicity brings in new users and more demands on what are usually already stretched equipment budgets and studio time. Public access has the same problem that many non-profit agencies have: constantly increasing needs and a decreasing budget. Successful access centers coordinate outreach publicity with a push for increased budgets from city councils and state arts funds.

## PUBLIC ACCESS AS AN INTERNATIONAL MODEL

The beginnings of implementation of public access in the United States came at a unique and very special time: the early and mid-seventies. The sixties were over, but many community organizers were still active. Portable video equipment sparked interest in media for community activism. The cable companies were eager to please the cities, and the cities were eager to implement cable in a way that did not look monopolistic. All of these came together to enable this unique process to begin. I am not sure it is replicable in other places, but there are important lessons to be gained from studying public access in the United States:

- For a relatively low cost, a community television system can be developed in neighborhoods and towns.
- Communities benefit greatly from open and unrestricted access to telecommunications equipment and channels for exchange.
- The viewing public responds actively to programs that meet their local needs for information and local documentation of entertainment.
- Creative media people and visual and performance artists find access to equipment and channels useful and inspiring.

- Local access programming on local issues becomes extremely useful during crises.[37]
- The expression of even repugnant points of view is important for initiating public dialogue on sensitive subjects.

However, perhaps the most significant development of the public access movement has been the informed practice of thousands of individuals who have taken an active role not only in the production of their own television, but in the implementation, the nurturing, and the defending of local telecommunications structures. The process of organizing public access in the United States has created a diverse and significant group of media activists who are now knowledgeable and vigilant on issues of technology and communication policy.

Image Union, 1976. Skip Blumberg, the author, and Tom Weinberg at the Mock Turtle Soup election night coverage.

---

[37] Following the destruction of the World Trade Center, the four public access channels became a forum for grief, anger, and informed discussion. Deep Dish, Free Speech TV, and Downtown Community Television Center collaborated in making a daily two-hour newscast, "The War and Peace Report."

# 4

# Smashing the Myths of the Information Industry: Creating Alternatives

(Above): First Paper Tiger Crew. Herb Schiller reads *The New York Times*, 1981. From left: Vicki Gholson, Mary Feaster, Esti Marpet, Herb Schiller, Diana Agosta, Martin Lucas, Pennee Bender, Paul Zaloom. Set by Ron Kelly. *(Author)* (Below): Cast and crew for *Ellen Stein Reads Vanity Fair*, 1985. *(Diane Neumaier)*

# Introduction

IT'S ONE THING to critique the mass media and rail against their abuses. It's quite another to create viable alternatives. This section looks at some attempts to create a different kind of television. In 1979 I began to make programs for an access series entitled *Communications Update,* which had been founded by Liza Bear on Manhattan Cable. I organized a production group to tape Herbert Schiller reading and commenting on *The New York Times.* Sitting in front of a subway backdrop, he held forth on the evils of, in his words, "the steering mechanism of the ruling class," that is, *The Times.* It was a perfect fit: Herb's Brooklyn accent and a painted subway; his acerbic humor and the august publication itself; Herb's dignified decorum and our ragtag scruffy production chaos. Herb told it like it is. He was not afraid of words like imperialism and hegemony. When he wrote *The Mind Managers* in the early seventies, he foresaw the media moguls and mergers which now dominate the headlines and our lives. Around the world this book was welcomed (and is still in print in many languages) for its insights into systems of cultural control. Many felt that power, but until Herb, no one had clearly articulated the problem.

Herb read *The Times* every Wednesday night for six weeks. The format seemed to work, the crew liked working together, and it evolved into a collective which became Paper Tiger. By the year 2001, Paper Tiger had produced almost 400 programs, presented hundreds of workshops, and trained generations of videomakers. "Paper Tiger Television" is a history of this collective, with excerpts from the first programs. "Tiger Dreams: Midwest Museum Intervention" is a recipe for a Paper Tiger installation, this one at the Wexner Museum in Columbus, Ohio.

With the coming to power of Ronald Reagan and the Chris-

tian Right, free speech and the First Amendment were embattled during the 1980s. Public access, where free speech reigns
supreme, became not only the butt of stand-up jokes, but a
target for repression by liberals who squirmed when the pro-
Aryan skinheads got time slots.[1] "The Wild Things on the
Banks of the Free Flow" looks at issues of censorship in media
and how public access became the place where wild media is
contained.

"Access for Others" was written for a special edition of the
*Visual Anthropology Review* on indigenous media. The essay
looks back at the early experiment with Navajo filmmaking
(*Through Navajo Eyes*, by Adair and Worth), the work of Terence Turner with the Kayapo Indians of Brazil, and more contemporary examples of media by "others": a discussion of two
areas of "indigenous" urban media makers, the black/Latino
collective called Not Channel Zero and the work of AIDS activists.

"From Public Access to Geostationary Orbit" reviews the
history of Deep Dish Television and the use of satellite transponders to disseminate local programming on a national
scale. Consumer electronic tools, in combination with satellite
delivery systems, offer an opportunity for wide distribution of
grassroots media. During the Gulf War, peace activists and
independent video producers pooled energy and resources to
create a ten-part series on issues that were not being covered
by mainstream networks including such topics as the history
of the Middle East, resistance to the war, and the effect of
military expenditures on the domestic economy. "The Camcorder Goes to War" was a report on the Gulf Crisis TV Project. The Chronology plots the experience of making that series
about the war and looks at some of the problems in working
in collaborative groups on a large scale with stressful deadlines and minimal budgets.

---

[1] Peter Franck, "First Amendment: Friend or Foe," *Propaganda Review*
(San Francisco) 3 (1988).

Celebration of one hundredth Paper Tiger show, 1986. From left: Diana Agosta, Joel Kovel, Tuli Kupferberg. Molly (the Tiger) Kovel. *(Diane Neumaier)*

# Paper Tiger Television: Smashing the Myths of the Information Industry Every Week on Public Access Cable

*June 1983*

*Do You Know Where Your Brains Are?*

THE PUBLIC ACCESS movement took root at a moment of maximum disillusionment with network television. Residual political optimism from the sixties combined with infatuation with small-format video to generate hope that cable would offer a genuine alternative to the vast television wasteland. With few exceptions the U.S. Left has ignored the cable potential—an indication of the media mystification that exists at all levels of this society.[2]

PAPER TIGER

Paper Tiger is one of the nearly 200 weekly series transmitted on access channels to subscribers of Manhattan Cable in New York City.[3] These regularly scheduled programs range from

[2] The longest running exception is the series *Alternative Views*, which appears on public access in Austin, Texas. The series makes use of facilities at the University of Texas and includes a wide variety of interviews, film excerpts, and slide shows. Over three hundred weekly shows have been produced by Doug Kellner and Frank Morrow.

[3] By the year 2000 Manhattan Neighborhood Network was host to over six hundred programs a week, for the most part produced in well-equipped studios in their new headquarters on 59th Street.

astrology call-ins to film reviews by thirteen-year-olds. Many immigrant groups have programs of music and dancing—Bulgarian, Greek, Spanish Flamenco. Several religious cults have weekly slots—Rajaneesh, Krishnamurti, Scientology. The Boy Scouts, the League of Women Voters, and the National Organization for Women of New York all have done series. *Potato Wolf, Communications Update,* and *Artists Television Network* are program series produced by progressive artists using a wide variety of styles and formats.

Paper Tiger began as a special series on *Communications Update* with Herbert Schiller reading *The New York Times,* a task he had habitually done with students as a warm-up exercise in his communication theory classes. I had visited Schiller's classes at Hunter College and had been amazed at both the insight and humor Herb was able to glean from those venerable pages. "Herb," I said, "that would make a great TV show." It could join a sparse but memorable tradition of "readings": New York City Mayor Fiorello LaGuardia reading the funny papers on the radio in the thirties; Julius Lester's sardonic readings of *The Times* on WBAI morning radio during the sixties; Mattelart and Dorfman's analysis of Disney's role in the ideological penetration of the Third World in *How to Read Donald Duck.*[4]

Schiller began with an explanation of how *The Times* serves as the "steering mechanism of the ruling class" and went on for five other programs to cover the "Washington Talk" page, the annual search for the hundred neediest cases, the conflict of interest in the way *The Times* covers communications issues, and how the Sunday Book Review section serves as a gatekeeper of Western ideas.

> Herb Schiller Reads *The New York Times,* #4. Foreign Correspondents in Consumer Capitals:
> Information about the world as we glean it from our daily and Sunday *New York Times* is minimal, trivial, and diverting. It is loaded with views of ruling cliques with whom the foreign correspondents have their daily contact. It would be nice if we

---

[4] Armand Mattelart and Ariel Dorfman, *How to Read Donald Duck* (1975), available from International General, Box 350, New York, N.Y. 10013.

could say that we had a window on the world. In reality what we have is a window to a very special portion of a very special privileged group. All the news that's fit to print, indeed.

The shows were very popular especially with the group that had assembled to make them, and we realized that this was a format that could be used for other programs. The programs that followed went from *Teresa Costa Reads "Biker Lifestyle"* to *Archie Singham Reads "Foreign Policy."*

Murray Bookchin on *Time* magazine:

*Time* makes time disappear. Everything is the same. There is no history—the essence of *Time* is that it destroys the present, the past, and the future. Just like the hands of a clock keep turning around and around and give you no message, no perspective, no coordinates, no sense of direction. What *Time* does is relax you in time.

CONTENT

Each week Paper Tiger offers a critical reading of one publication. In addition to looking at the content and language of specific articles, the program includes basic information on the economic structure of the corporation that produces the publication. Many programs also look at the demographics: who the readers are, what products they consume (for example, *U.S. News and World Report* readers buy wine by the *case*), and how much a full-page color ad costs. Sometimes we examine the board of directors or the background of the editors and reporters. Although the specific focus each week is on one publication, it is the intention of the series to provide an accumulative view of the culture industry as a whole. With the expansion of all sectors of the economy into the information business, it is important to keep track of how this is played out in the vehicles of mass culture. More and more of the Manhattan population works either directly or peripherally in the information industry. Paper Tiger gives them some economic and historical perspective with which to view their own participation in the cultural apparatus. Employees of the featured publication make up the best audience for each show. During the Schiller series, we leafleted *The Times* building during the shift change, so we would be able to catch both the editorial staff leaving and the printing crew entering.


FORMAL STRATEGIES

The programs begin with the words: "It's eight-thirty. Do you know where your brains are?"—a nice joke from a Tuli Kupferberg cartoon that serves several functions. First of all, it implants the time slot in people's minds. Second, it is a stock opening, which can vary in innumerable ways but always has a familiarity about it. Finally, it inverts a familiar phrase used by Group W News in New York—"It's 10:00 P.M. Do you know where your children are?"—to tweak up the anxiety levels of parents in the audience, so that they will continue to watch the news. By using Tuli's inversion, we hope to tweak up the level of critical consciousness with our own anxiety-producing question, which we hope can raise both the consciousness and the interest of the viewer. Although most people are cynical about the media and are aware of being manipulated, most are unaware of how this manipulation is played out issue by issue, ad by ad. Many people think of the media as a form of journalism, distinct from other areas of economic life. By going over a publication in detail, by examining how it is enmeshed in the transnational corporate world and by pointing out exactly how and why certain information appears, a good critical reading can invert the media so that they work against themselves. The next time a viewer reads a publication that was covered on Paper Tiger, each ad and each article becomes a reinforcement of the critical reading.

> Joan Braderman Reads *The National Enquirer:*
> Welcome to the world of the *National Enquirer*. This is it. The contemporary eighties locus of the Great American Contradiction. It's a fucking vale of tears for most of us folks, but the *Enquirer*, like the *Reader's Digest*, is upbeat.

There are certain practical requirements for public access programming, the first of which is that it has to be regular.

Since there is little hope of access programs being included in *TV Guide*'s schedule, or being listed in local papers, the main way of building an audience it to make it a habit: the show must be on every week at the same time. Most TV viewing is habitual: that is, people are home on certain nights and turn on the tube at certain times. However, if they switch the dial around during the breaks between shows, they might linger on something that looks different. Ergo, another strategy is to look different, to have an immediately discernible distinctive quality, without being intimidating or alienating. Paper Tiger uses brightly painted sets to help leaven the heavy subject matter. There are no pompous "director" chairs, no stuffed couches, no glittery curtains. It looks homey, but very colorful, like the funny papers on Sunday. The guest, sitting on a yellow kitchen chair, is projected into the foreground with pizzazz. We sometimes use actors to provide nonverbal translations of the text. For instance, during the discussion of *TV Guide* by Brian Winston, we placed a young woman in the corner of the frame.[5] She was watching television (the actual shows being aired at that time). As Winston points out the lack of real choice on network and cable, she switches channels, pores over a copy of *TV Guide*, and eventually falls asleep in her easy chair. On the *Sports Illustrated* show, a bubble-gum-chewing fan leafs through a collection of baseball cards, while Tuli Kupferberg points out the connections between sports and the military.

If there is a specific look to the series, it is handmade, a comfortable nontechnocratic look that says friendly and low budget. The seams show: we often use overview wide-angle shots to give the viewers a sense of the people who are making the show and the types of consumer-grade equipment we use. On-air dialogue with the control room is amplified. "Cue Herb, Daniel!" gets mixed into the overall sound track. We often use charts and graphics, but they are hand-lettered or cut and pasted rather than created by elaborate computer pro-

---

[5] The Paper Tiger person who took on this role eventually ended up as an actress in network television: Melissa Leo, who was featured for several years in the soap *All My Children* and later was lead actress on *Homocide*.

grams. Sometimes we even make them with magic markers and scissors during the show.[6] The graphics are not fed into a mechanical graphic holder, but are held in place so that the fingers show. At the end of the program, along with the credits, we usually disclose the budget—including everything from magic markers to studio rental. The total can vary from $19 for one show with a black-and-white camera to $150 for a two-camera color setup that includes a switcher, audio mixer, and two studio recording decks. The Paper Tiger aesthetic expanded from paints and crayons to include crude but inspired chroma key effects, such as Joan Braderman sliding down the Carrington banister in *Joan Does Dynasty* and John Walden's hugging of Ted Koppel in *From Woodstock to Tiananmen Square*. By showing the seams and the price tags, we hope to demystify the process of live television and to prove that making programs isn't all that prohibitively expensive.

ORGANIZATION

The group that works on Paper Tiger is a loose affiliation of interested, committed, and talented people. Since they don't get paid for producing the shows, most teach or hold full-time jobs in the media industry. These jobs are often high-pressure and draining. That we can pull a show together after a long day of work is some kind of miracle. We meet in a coffee shop for half an hour and do some rough planning, then run to the studio where we have only thirty minutes to hang the set, test the mikes, adjust the lights, cue up the tape for the breaks, put the graphics cards in order, reassure and cue our guest, and maybe, just maybe, have a minute to do a quick run-through

---

[6] The live shows often had international visitors as makers. On one occasion a young Tiger who wanted to make a list for the hand-drawn credits went around asking the crew what their names were. When he asked a tall guy in a leather jacket what his name was, the guy responded, Volker Schlöndorf. "Oh yeah?" said the credit compiler, who was a film student at NYU. "And my name is Steven Spielberg." But it really was Volker Schlöndorf, who had been brought to the studio in an entourage organized by a Paper Tiger fan, another German filmmaker, Alexander Kluge.

of the opening transition. It can be rough. Equipment problems often account for missed cues and ragged taping. We sometimes spend the breaks madly repairing a set mike or replacing an audio cassette deck that has malfunctioned. "For eighty-five dollars, what do you expect?" is the oft-repeated answer to our many complaints to the studio owner. The shows are done without run-throughs and often with new crew members who need to be briefed during the precious setup time. When the beginning works well, we're off and running, and the show is spontaneous and fresh. When we flub the opening, it sets everything askew, and the momentum is hard to regain.

One of our hardest challenges is to maintain the spontaneous excitement of the first programs, while at the same time improving the "tech." The goal is to make the shows not slick and polished but at least snappy and fast moving. "Clean," as John Lennon said. Many of the people who work on the show do so because it is one of the few places to gain hands-on experience with live television. There is something about going out to audiences live that sets the adrenaline pumping. However, it's hard to put together a show on short notice, using a large crew. Most television is not made with a collaborative, nonauthoritarian structure. Achieving unity and strength while maintaining maximum participation, imagination, and humanism is a basic problem for any group. To try to make a TV show in a nonauthoritarian structure is formidable. Subtlety and tolerance are difficult to achieve in the supercharged tension of a television studio, about to go on the air in three-and-a-half minutes.

Alex Cockburn Reads *The Washington Post:*
*The Washington Post* covers very little of the business of government. . . . Their editorials are unvaryingly reactionary, buttressed by columns that are equally reactionary. They use the word "pragmatist" a lot. That's a terrific word for journalists. It usually means someone who has no principles at all. . . . *The Washington Post* is part of the Iron Triangle. You have the political correspondents who order the discussion, the consultants who run the campaign, and the pollsters who ask the questions that people like David Broder (*Washington Post* col-

umnist) want asked. Thus is the political discourse of the nation's capital order.


## SPONTANEITY ASIDE

This is not to say that the shows are instantaneous slapdash
affairs that are easily replicable. Every show requires many
hours of research on the political economy of the various publications. In addition, each one reflects years of commitment,
often a lifetime of work and reflection, on the part of the guest
speaker. The budget of the program is also deceptive, because
one major expense is missing: salaries. The level of talent, experience, and expertise donated to the series would be hard to
match anywhere.

The live shows are taped for distribution, and this enables
us to clean up things like missed close-ups of articles and
tardy music for sound cues, and reference material as super-
imposed text. This post-production phase greatly increases
both the out-of-pocket costs and the time demands on the
group. Meeting once a week to do live shows is one thing;
reconvening the next day to clean up the tape is another.


## DISTRIBUTION

For better or for worse, after fifty shows[7] the studio organization has remained loose and receptive to spontaneous input
(and mistakes). The interest and demand for the taped shows,
however, is forcing a more organized structure. We have tried
to make Paper Tiger a model for cheap, imaginative access
programming. As such, it is important that the programs be
distributed to other access systems and to schools and community groups. At the present time, they are being cablecast
in Madison, Wisconsin; Woodstock, New York; and on both

---

[7] There are now over 400 Paper Tiger programs, and the organization has
grown to include setting up training workshops in community centers and
curating series at libraries and other venues.

cable systems in Manhattan. Individual programs have been shown on occasion in Austin, Texas; Fairfield, Connecticut; St. Louis, Missouri; and Buffalo, New York. Requests for shows have come from many other communities, but our limited resources for making dupes and buying postage have not allowed broader distribution.[8]

SEIZE THE TIME

Perhaps the only auspicious aspect of the relentless technological developments in the communications industries is the fact that the cost per image has plummeted. Lightweight, high-quality, portable equipment can produce programming for a cost that is within the reach of individuals and groups in the "developed" world. Many of these new images are produced outside the traditional networks of media concentration. However, the bulk of this production is being used to increase repression (surveillance systems, for example) or to reinforce cultural penetration (cassette distribution of Hollywood films and old TV programs). But no historical development is one-sided. The last decade has seen the growth of small-format media as organizing tools for progressive change. The alternative media community has created networks that have greatly increased the production, distribution, and use of media products from sources other than the transnational corporations. Certainly the many films, tapes, and radio programs on the situation in Central America have given U.S. citizens a level of information more profound than that which leaked through the cracks of network news during the Vietnam War. Early cable access rarely was a forum for these alternative views. Organizational work in cable tended to focus on increasing the availability of channels and making access centers responsive to community needs. Very little attention was paid to the

---

[8] It was the hunger for Paper Tiger programs from many community TV stations that lead us to develop the Deep Dish Network. See "From Public Access to Geostationary Orbit" later in this section.

programs themselves or to the possible use of access channels for distribution. The opportunity that public access provides for wide dissemination of progressive issue-oriented media is an emancipatory moment yet to be realized.[9]

The author, Joan Braderman, and Manual DeLanda, 1982. *(Diane Neumaier)*

---

[9] Paper Tiger is a mostly live public access television show. The founders were Diana Agosta, Fusun Atesar, Pennee Bender, Skip Blumberg, William Bodde, Daniel Brooks, Dominique Chausse, Shu Lea Cheang, Linda Cranor, Daniel Del Solar, Mary Feaster, DeeDee Halleck, Ezra Halleck, Hilery Kipnis, Melissa Leo, Martin Lopez, Barry Malitzer, Esti Marpet, Leann Mella, Adam Merims, Alison Morse, Roger Politzer, Preacher, Caryn Rogoff, David Shulman, Alan Steinheimer, Martha Wallner, Roy Wilson, Ellen Windmuth, and many others. It continues to exist as a media-training, production, and distribution collective at 339 Lafayette St., New York, N.Y. 10012. It is supported through contributions, distribution fees, and small grants from the New York State Council on the Arts and a few foundations.

# Tiger Dreams:
# Midwest Museum Intervention

*Paper Tiger has always been an eclectic mix of art and politics,
defiantly homemade in terms of both aesthetic and ideology.
The collective grew out of the fertile soil of the seventies New
York art scene: conceptual, anti-establishment, and raucous.
Despite our iconoclasm, or rather because of it, we have had
several installation exhibitions in prestigious museums and
galleries. This is a summary of an installation which Paper
Tiger created in Columbus, Ohio, at the Wexner Center for the
Arts.*[10]

THE PROBLEM: in a glass and steel building with long corridors
and tall ceilings, how to make an installation that best conveys
the intimacy and homespun aesthetic of the Paper Tiger Collective. Or . . . how to be bad and messy in a clean and well-
lighted place.

PAPER TIGER RECIPE FOR THE WEXNER INSTALLATION

A Paper Tiger Dream House with a cluttered kitchen, a dilapi-
dated but cozy living room, a comic-strewn bunk-bedroom,
and a twilight-lit porch with a barbecue and cricket sounds: a
cozy setting from which to speak hard truths like media imperialism.

*Ingredients*

*The Lobby:* In the pristine museum lobby place a ragtag, exu-
berant newsstand filled to overflowing with (among others)

---

[10] Other exhibitions include the Whitney Museum, San Francisco Art Institute Gallery, Austrian Triennial of Photography, Rotterdam Film Festival
Gallery, Art in General, and the Berkeley Art Museum.

lesbian comics, *Covert Action Information Quarterly,* old Soviet magazines, Native American newspapers, *Organic Gardening,* the Fortune Society newsletter, and Tuli Kupferberg cartoon books.

*The Hall:* two Sunday papers, *The New York Times* and the *Columbus Dispatch,* stapled to the wall, page by page: floor to ceiling. Felt-tip pens for feedback and interactivity.

Hand-drawn scrolls (used for Paper Tiger credits) forming a giant rolling credit machine (ingeniously constructed by John Walden) that turns the loops in a sort of Rube Goldberg crankie.

*The Corridor Ramp:* a timeline of media history, from Marconi's transmissions to the launching of Deep Dish TV.[11]

*The House:* A roof of sound blankets to dampen the booming sound (of the many tapes we show). The unexpected result of this was a patchwork of all the colors of the contiguous blankets, looking like a hillbilly shack that has a roof made up of used leftover asphalt shingles of several colors. A fireplace with a rolling (like an old-fashioned roller towel) fire, in which rotate the heads of mega-media corporations.

*A real kitchen* with a well-stocked refrigerator (with real messages on the door under tiger magnets), snack-filled shelves, and a kitchen table with plastic padded chairs with chrome legs. Thanksgiving was celebrated with museum-goers Norman Rockwell/Paper Tiger style on the long kitchen table. Tiny multicolored Xmas lights twinkle on the verandah/porch, lighting the painted backdrop landscape by Mary Feaster of Midwest Indian mounds and interstates. On the grill skewers with the heads of the networks and media corporations. On the billboard of the painted backdrop, a slide show of "doctored" billboards, guerrilla actions against corporate mes-

---

[11] This work by Michael Eisenmenger and Linda Iannacone form the base for the timeline Appendix of this book.

sages. Porch furniture allows the visitors to hang out and listen to the cricket tape and watch the slide shows.

*TV sets* in the kitchen and the bedroom and by the fireplace. Choose a channel! Forty varieties of Paper Tiger programs are available, or tune into Columbus public access. The tapes dissect *The New York Times, TV Guide, The National Enquirer, Ebony* magazine, and many others, with statistics about the growing concentration of media and the functional censorship that exists even within the "information society." Change the channel, and you get yet another media analysis. This is a Paper Tiger Dream House and corporate networks aren't on the set, but skewered on the verandah and in the fireplace.

*Things to read/do/take home:* a co-ed calendar made at OSU with sexist bathing suit–posed students is remade with collaged reality check photos and terse penned-in messages. A grandmother-type tinted glass candy dish on the coffee table provides a variety of condoms. Collections of corporate reports are available for annotation and stamps (one says LIES!, another says Whose profit?). Computer terminals to do e-mail (this was before the days of the WWW). Snacks to prepare from the refrigerator. Interactive Cooking Instructions: A teacher-training workshop early on, so that many of participating teachers return with their classes in tow. The sixth graders especially like the multicolored fruit-flavored condoms in the candy dish (provided by the Columbus AIDS coalition).

*Productions* made in the studio/set live in front of the museum audience: Luis Beltran, Visiting Professor in the Communication Department talks about Bolivian Miners' Radio. Judith Mayne brings a giggling bunch to watch and discuss soap operas, and John Higgins dissects the Columbus Press.

Make yourself at home. Grab a skewer. Roast your enemies. Have a condom. Open the fridge. Make yourself a cheese sandwich. Relax with some cool comics on the bunk bed. The Paper Tiger Dream House is your home sweet home. The Wexner Museum can be a cozy place. With some scary information.

Melissa Leo reads *Rolling Stone,* Tuli Kupferberg is in the background. *(Diane Neumaier)*

# The Wild Things On the Banks of the Free Flow

## August 1988

*And we danced our terrible dance . . .*

THERE IS AN old saying that freedom of the press belongs to those fortunate enough to own one. In this age of digital cameras and cheap condenser mikes, the number of those with the electronic equivalent of printing presses has grown exponentially. No, it's not the "global village" utopia envisioned by sixties media gurus, particularly in the so-called Third World, where *Miami Vice* and Coke ads appear on TV sets from Thailand to Venezuela and from Nepal to Ghana. It is a sad irony that many of those who nightly watch the glories of consumer life portrayed in the electronic effluence that floods their air waves are living in countries increasingly burdened with debt, the interest payments of which go into supporting the lifestyle of a "First" World whose affluence is farther away than ever. A relentlessly increasing poverty has accompanied the transnationalization of world economies as the products of exploited resources and labor are exported to consumer centers in the North. The destruction of the tropical rain forest is perhaps the most lamented of these grabs, but it's the tip of the iceberg, to use a metaphor that may soon be an anachronism.

The increased availability of electronic transmission and recording has contradictions beyond the sad irony of Haitian slum dwellers watching *Dynasty* reruns. One of them is that here in the First World, despite the increased poverty for many during the Reagan years, electronic recording has entered a populist phase. The advent of affordable camcorders and the increasing use of community video through public access and local media centers have, indeed, increased public expression. Every block has a camcorder somewhere, as evidenced by the growing number of incidents in which neighborhoods have documented occasions of police brutality. Clayton Patterson happened to have a camcorder and let it roll for almost four hours during the police riot in New York City's Tomkins Square Park in August 1988. His tape has been used in litigation against the police stemming from the injuries to over a hundred people.[12] Other incidents where tape was used as a defense by besieged neighborhoods have occurred in Los Angeles and San Diego. Larry Sapadin, director of the Association of Independent Video and Filmmakers, was quoted in *The New York Times* as saying, "It's the democratization of surveillance." Video has been a tool of police departments for years. Is this the beginning of a new era of empowerment for victimized neighborhoods?

This is not to suggest that the activism of popular video use can in itself counter police power that years of abuse have consolidated, nor can it battle with equal valence the onslaught of corporate media that bombard us daily. But there is indeed a widening use of video by community-based individuals and groups. The level of decentralized media activity in the hundreds of cities and towns in the United States is perhaps more sophisticated and democratic than any of the earlier "global village" scenarios.

GLOBAL VILLAGES WITH SEWERS

The sixties dreams of a wired future were always sort of vague as to what the content of the global transmissions would be. Some early video art was aimed at providing beautiful visions

---

[12] Video evidence is not enough to balance a justice system tipped in favor of police authorities, however. Despite clear pictures of specific officers kicking and beating defenseless spectators, in the court proceeding following the Tomkins Square events there were no indictments against the police and little departmental follow-up.

of natural images, as in the work of Davidson Gigliotti, Mary
Lucier, Paul Ryan, and Frank Gillette. Others concentrated on
computer-generated video graphics, such as in the work of
Stan Vanderbeek, Nam June Paik, Ed Emshwiller, and Steina
and Woody Vasulkas. While the most ubiquitous result of
image "enhancement" has been to enhance the network logos
and Olympic graphics, much of early video art had grandiose
aspirations to create "universal" art images that could bring
aesthetic experiences, if not peace and contentment, across
borders and time zones, if not class and race.[13]

Few would have guessed that the true democratization of
video would end up in endless discussions of sewage runoff,
Little League fields, and parking ramps. The tapes of these
discussions, which blossom on every public access channel,
may not make it to the Whitney Biennial, but they are the stuff
of which a genuine public sphere is created. True community
video is hard work and often boring. Media democracy, like
most forms of democracy, is a slow process. To paraphrase
Susan Sontag, if you want fascination, try fascism.[14]

The community use of video has raised certain problems for
the state, the regulatory agencies, and the corporations that
own and control the several thousand cable systems in this
country. Community video and, in particular, local public
access channels have been the center of debates about censorship and the scope of the First Amendment in the "information age." These debates are taking place in a situation of
increasing restrictions on access to government information.

Q. Why is a microchip like the First Amendment?
A. Because GE/NBC knows how to use it better than you.

As information has become a profitable commodity, access
to it for free has become more and more difficult. Donna

---

[13] Ira Schneider did an installation with a monitor for each time zone,
each playing his travel movies. He called it *Time Zone*, a sort of "Accidental
Tourist" video. A documentation of this installation is available from the
Video Data Bank, 37 S. Wabash, Chicago, Ill. 60603.

[14] Susan Sontag, "Fascinasting Fascism," *New York Review of Books*, February 6, 1975. This essay on Leni Riefenstahl was reprinted in *Women and
the Cinema: A Critical Anthology*, ed. Karyn Kay and Gerald Peary (New
York: Dutton, 1977).

Demac has documented how corporations, supported by the Reagan administration, have taken public databases and made them into private archives, for sale at a cost.[15] One of the ways this has occurred has been by using laws and regulations that were set up to protect individual rights, but interpreting them so that they defend, not you and me and the citizen's right to know, but mega-corporations like IBM and General Electric (which owns NBC). These transnational corporations gain access to information that was publicly gathered from publicly funded research and package it for resale. The catch is that only other corporations can afford to buy entrance to these data systems, not your local library or state university, both of which are reeling from budget cuts and escalating expenses.

FIRST AMENDMENT ON THE WIRE

Likewise, the cable corporations have attempted to use First Amendment *individual* rights as a means of protecting their *corporate* profits. They have said that they are denied the right to freedom of expression by having to put programs on public access channels that they don't editorially choose. What their public relations pamphlets leave out is the fact that except for public access channels, these cable corporations usually control as a monopoly the electronic information that enters your home. Public access was devised to be an alternative to that monopoly—to allow individual citizens the right to electronic expression. To equate the expressive rights of, for instance, the Times Mirror Corporation and Jane Doe from down the block is absurd.

Cable corporations have tried many ruses to roll back the regulations that enforce public access. The channels that are

---

[15] Donna Demac, *Liberty Denied: The Current Use of Censorship in America* (New York: American PEN Center, 1988). This excellent text is a useful overview of censorship in many areas, including the music industry, the news media, and scientific research. See also Herbert Schiller, *Who Knows: Information in the Age of the Fortune 500* (Norwood, N.J.: Ablex Publishing, 1981).

used by access are wanted for profitable ventures. When the systems were first established, there were few cable services available. Now there are dozens, all competing for channels in community systems. Many of these cable services, like the Disney Channel or the Weather Channel, bring profits to the systems that offer them, either in direct payments or in donated local advertising time. Public access doesn't take ads and can't bring in bucks for the systems. However, public access is widely supported. Although there has been little actual research, preliminary studies suggest that access is widely watched as well.[16] The corporations that own the large multisystem chains of cable franchises have promoted an image of access as being full of cocaine-snorting decadents and sexist idiots, which is why Ugly George's series on Manhattan cable (he lured naive young women into his studio to disrobe) was for many years the most frequently given example of programming in mainstream articles on public access. Time (now AOL Time Warner), the corporation, is the largest cable system owner. It stands to reason that *Time*, the magazine, will not print an article that in any way is favorable to public access. The attempt to give access a "loose morals" charge fits in with calls for repression of sexual information and a rollback of mores and morals to pre-1960s standards.

FREE FLOW

For decades our society has boasted of its lack of censorship. The "free flow of information" has been the stated principle of U.S. foreign and domestic policy.[17] Countries that practice censorship are condemned as authoritarian, if not downright totalitarian. There is one area, however, in which many liberals and moderates are calling for censorship. This is surround-

---

[16] Diana Agosta, Abigail Norman, and Caryn Rogoff, *Participate Directory of Public Access in New York State* (New York: Media Network, 1988). This detailed report of how public access is used in one state is an excellent study of the institutions and organizations that coordinate the access centers and the community groups and individuals that make use of the channels.

[17] See the discussion of the contradictions of "free flow" in Section 3.

ing a public access program called *Race and Reason.* The most difficult issue involving public access and censorship is the use of public access channels by neo-Nazis. *Race and Reason* has replaced Ugly George as the prime example of community access. In magazines and newspaper articles and on such national programs as *Nightline,* issues surrounding use of public access channels have become collapsed into a struggle for the noble aspirations of the cable executives and city officials (the good) to protect the public from offensive language and evil influences of public access (the bad). In discussions of cable regulations, "free flow of the cable company's information" becomes the standard under which the notion of the First Amendment is interpreted to mean the First Amendment for those with a cable system of their own. And the Nazis become the excuse for eliminating *all* forms of access.

It is true that neo-Nazis have taken advantage of the cable access policies in many cities and towns. The program *Race and Reason* is a despicable mixture of florid racism, homophobia, and anti-Semitism, broadcast weekly on dozens of public access stations in major cities.[18] The journalists who cover media have leapt on the issue of the Nazi programming as an example of public access at its worse. To read the press about public access, one would think that this program is the only show on the channels. They forget to cover public access at its best and never mention the other groups who regularly use cable in many cities: the League of Women Voters, the Boy Scouts, the high school news programs, the welfare rights organizations, the Gay Men's Health Collective, and so forth. Nor does the press address the way in which the racist programs have initiated panels and programs in direct *response* to *Race and Reason.* In cities where racism can simmer under the surface for twenty years before boiling over into angry manifestation, the series has made racism an *overt* issue in many communities. Several communities have formed anti-bias groups, stimulated by the need to answer the types of charges and irrationalities that pervade the racist series. In

---

[18] National Institute against Prejudice, "Bigotry and Cable TV: Legal Issues and Community Responses," Institute Report no. 3, 1988.

Pocatello, Idaho, a human relations committee was formed to look at issues of local racism.[19]

Racism continues to be the most compelling unresolved issue of our country. The *Race and Reason* series did not invent racism, nor does the popularity of Bill Cosby mean that it has disappeared. The vehemence around the discussions of *Race and Reason* proves that this issue needs to be confronted and discussed, and public access channels have provided an important arena for these discussions. The programs and the counter-programs bring the issue into the light to be tested and confronted. That this has happened on public access channels is a tribute to the currency of the access community.

There are no simple solutions to the problem of racism in the United States, just as there are no simple solutions to the censorship issue. Tom Metzger, the producer of *Race and Reason*, is parading around supporting the First Amendment, while, at the same time, many of his colleagues on the Right are trying to clean up school libraries, in some cases literally burning books. There have been persistent rampages of the extreme right wing (and in particular the Religious Right) to "cleanse" the school libraries and textbooks of "secular humanism." They have even gone so far as to say that Maurice Sendak is an agent of the devil and that his book *Where the Wild Things Are*, perhaps the most popular children's book of the last forty years, is designed to lure children into Satanism. Fundamentalists have pressured textbook publishers to eliminate passages of history texts and to rewrite sections to give equal time to defenders of segregation and to advocates of "creation science."[20]

These vigilantes of school libraries are fringe groups that are easily identified and confronted, but most forms of censorship in our society are embedded in our traditional institu-

---

[19] Copies of the Pocatello human relations programs that were made in response to *Race and Reason* may be obtained by writing to Pocatello Vision 12, 812 E. Clark St., Pocatello, Ida. 83201.

[20] Chip Berlet has put together a useful book called *Eyes Right: Challenging the Right Wing Backlash* (Boston: South End Press, 1995), which looks at the Right in the country and how they have utilized the local media.

tions and are not readily perceived. The instruments of censorship are wrapped in many layers of ideology and custom that not only shape and restrict the information we receive but also determine the scope of what we are willing to express. There are economic forms of censorship for all who work in commercial media.

Television journalists know very well the parameters of acceptable "stories." They know what they have to say to keep their jobs. At *The New York Times*, even Pulitzer Prize–winning journalist Sidney Schanberg was not immune.[21] He tried to report on corruption in New York City real estate and the West Way project. In his *New York Times* column, he had the effrontery to ask why *The New York Times* wasn't investigating these issues. He was summarily laid off, after a brilliant and prestigious career at the newspaper. Schanberg's fate was actually well covered (he has just been portrayed as the principal protagonist of the Hollywood blockbuster *The Killing Fields*). Usually the punishments for breach of corporate censorship aren't so well documented or so clear-cut. Punishments are often more subtle. Media corporations don't stoop to jail or exile, they merely change assignments, accept fewer stories from problem journalists, downgrade one's office space, or deny raises.

DOWN, ROVER

Independent video producers and video "artists" are also victims of these less overt forms of censorship. The term *self-censorship* is often used, but it smacks of "blaming the victim" when placed against the economic realities of funding and distribution. *Prior censorship* is another term for survival: it comes from the knowledge of what is acceptable to power. Censorship begins with the very choice of subject and style at the grant application stage. Ricky Leacock, one of the found-

---

[21] See Joseph Gouldner, *Fit to Print* (New York: Lyle Stuart Publishers, 1988), pp. 243–48.

ers of the cinema verité movement, once said that writing a grant was basically sitting down at a typewriter and wagging your tail.[22] Grant applications are tailored to certain agencies and certain foundation personnel. Certain subjects are currently fashionable; certain styles are more acceptable than others. Even if we do get funding, we know what we have to do to get projects distributed. We know what gets shown at certain venues, we know that there are more and less acceptable themes and formats for the Public Broadcasting System, the Whitney, the Museum of Modern Art, and so forth. Even the off-off network venues like the Los Angeles Contemporary Exhibits gallery or Boston's Institute of Contemporary Art have their acceptable styles and topics. Like familiar household pets, we know how and when to wag, and, more important, what is off-limits. We don't beg at the table.

These forms of censorship are invisible. But when censorship does become the focus of attention, it usually arises when the censors and the censored are enmeshed in other areas of contention. Censorship is often the foil behind more problematic issues. Both racism and homophobia have contributed to increasingly overt censorship in recent years. A videotape by the Gay Men's Health Collective examines the controversy surrounding the publication by the group of a comic book on AIDS. This book so inflamed the passions and fears of the U.S. Congress that a law was passed against it.[23] While the Helms Amendment does not directly *censor* the comic book, it attempts to ensure that the normal channels of *economic* censorship are operating. The law would deny any federal funds for AIDS counseling, information, or community work to any entity that would publish such a work. To Helms, the comic did one thing wrong: it accepted the *fact* of a homosexual community and designed the AIDS information material to

---

[22] Richard Leacock, in a presentation at the annual Robert Flaherty Seminar, Boston, August 1976.

[23] Although the Helms Amendment passed with only two nays, it did not become law, because the bill to which it had been attached did not pass. I use it as an interesting example of the homophobia present in our elected representatives.

address the needs and practices of that community. That the comic is informative was never at issue. That it is realistic and effective was also never questioned. That it recognizes a community that the entire U.S. Congress (with two exceptions) would rather forget about is the crime of this booklet.

It is appalling that this form of economic censorship is so enthusiastically endorsed by our official representatives. However, by becoming a *censorship* issue, the case deflects the authentic source of the controversy: the homophobia and AIDS phobia that abound in our society.

A videotape about the amendment and the struggle to publish the comic book was part of a package of programs about AIDS curated by John Greyson for a 1988 Deep Dish series. Many access directors received complaints about one scene in the AIDS compilation: it was a close-up detail from the educational comic book. Of the 200 tapes used in the Deep Dish series, this one segment elicited the most calls for censorship: the only tape that had as its theme a debate in the U.S. Congress. Although a few stations did refuse to air it, most ran it. Many received positive feedback on the program, and in particular on the fact that they ran it. Public access is the one venue where this tape could be transmitted. Many network news programs did stories on the Helms–AIDS education debate. Such is the state of censorship in this society that only on public access could the actual drawings that were at the center of the controversy be shown.

The difficulties of simplistic solutions to censorship questions are particularly evident in the turbulence surrounding a painting that was confiscated by the Chicago Board of Aldermen from a student gallery at the Art Institute of Chicago. One of the painting students had painted a grotesque portrait of the late Mayor Harold Washington: naked except for a bra and a garter belt. Washington is a revered and much missed man in the political life of Chicago, especially within the African American community. Outraged city council representatives took it upon themselves to rescue his memory by forcibly "arresting" the painting. Mindy Faber and Kate Horsfield have collected some of the off-air TV material of this incident

together with some street interviews with the art students.[24]
What is sadly missing is any discussion of the isolation and
racial segregation of the School of the Art Institute from the
rest of Chicago—an isolation so complete that it allows a student to be so distant from the local community that he does
not realize the extent to which this painting would create pain
and agony for a very large segment of Chicago's population.[25]
That this controversial painting is probably the closest any Art
Institute students have come to the political process in Chicago is a tragic comment on the level of engagement of students in our society. The visit by the council members to
confiscate the painting is probably the first time they have ever
attended a student exhibition at the school. Were they ever
invited? Meanwhile the issue of censorship pits the outraged
authoritarians (black) against the free-spirited defenders of
the First Amendment (white). Both sides are depicted in the
TV news footage as fringe elements: the uncool and obviously
furious council members and the kooky, anarchistic art students. The discussion is painful, the participants offensive and
untidy, and the whole thing is neatly wrapped up with a couple of raised eyebrows as the reporter closes the news with:
"And now for a word from our sponsor."

In the Maurice Sendak book, a little boy sails to a nightmare
land where he dances with wild monsters. It ends with the
little boy coming back home to a clean room and a warm supper, having purged the Wild Things in his dream. For most of
us, censorship exists in the realm of the Wild Things: the Nazis,

---

[24] The collected news footage of this incident can be obtained from the
Video Data Bank (see n. 13).

[25] An analogy might be drawn with two pieces that were made in connection with the Kennedy assassination: Paul Krassner's article about Lyndon
Johnson fucking the bullet wounds on the president's body (*The Realist*,
1965) and Ant Farm's *The Eternal Frame* (1976), with Doug Hall playing
the president as Artist on his last ride. While both of these obviously played
on the sentiment of millions of Americans for whom Kennedy was next to
the pope on the wall, there was, in both works, a sense that the media were
the real target. One wonders who the target was in the Washington painting
lampoon. Incidentally, a new book brings convincing evidence that there
was more to the Kennedy affair than press sentiment: a cover-up of astounding proportions is recounted in Jim Garrison's book *On the Trail of the Assassins* (New York: Sheridan Square Press, 1989).

the gays, the radical right, the crazy artists, and the crazed-with-anger black council members. Censors and the censored cohabit a distant world: one easily shut away. We are left in our tidy bedrooms, our post-modern board rooms, our neat offices, where the limits of our public sphere are measured and drawn. And our supper is waiting.[26]

Annie Goldson, Ann Crenovitch, Roy Wilson, Caryn Rogoff, and Daniel Brooks from Youth and Media: *Escape from Tom and Jerry*, live at the Whitney Museum, 1985. *(Diane Neumaier)*

---

[26] This article had its inception as an introductory essay to a series of video tapes which I curated for the American Film Institute Video Festival in 1988. I am indebted to the late Ken Kirby, who first proposed the series and the article.

# Access for Others:
# Alter (Native) Media Practice

## *Written in Collaboration with*
## *Nathalie Magnan*

## *Spring 1993*

The perils of turning over the news-gathering process to parti-
sans have only begun to be understood. . . . In the near future,
amateur video won't look like amateur video anymore. It will
look professional. Then anyone could call himself [*sic*] a TV
journalist, but what would that mean anymore?[27]

(The use of video by the Kayapo), as described by Turner, is
rather forlorn. It is almost as if, now, they are equal partners
with news photographers and photojournalists. (But they are
not because they) enter (the global village) already situated by
a West which gives them little room to be anything more than
what the West will allow.[28]

The more power any group has to create and wield representation, the less it is required to be representative.[29]

WHEN "nonprofessionals" point their cameras beyond the
confines of family pictures, hackles are raised. This is true for
ethnographic media making and art exhibition. Women and
"multicultural" artists can be safely curated into programs
about the family, the body, or ethnic identity, but if the work

---

[27] *Newsweek*, July 22, 1991, "Video Vigilantes," cover story.
[28] James Faris, "Anthropological Transparency: Film Interpretation and
Politics," in *Filmography*, ed. Peter Crawford and David Turton (Manchester: Manchester University Press, 1992).
[29] Judith Williamson, Review, *New Statesman*, December 5, 1986, p. 6.

takes a larger perspective, the uproar starts. The work is branded as "political," "agitprop," and "lacking in aesthetic qualities." The outcries in the mainstream press over the "politization" of contemporary art at the 1993 Whitney Biennial provides an example. In this case an exhibit marked by its inclusion of "other" artists (in which even the amateur video of Rodney King's beating is screened) is branded "Killed by Good Intentions," " Fade from White," "A Showcase for Political Correctness."[30] The heated discussions over the "authenticity" of indigenous media are a similar phenomenon and have raised questions about "science" and "objectivity" (Faris 1992; Ginsburg 1991; Moore 1992; Turner 1992a, 1992b).

At the center of much of the attention is the Kayapo video project which Terence Turner has described. For many, images of feathered and painted Kayapo natives with cameras have come to signify "other" media. The work of indigenous video producers is not unlike the work of community video activists in North America. They both may be regarded as subjugated subjects taking charge of their own images. As Turner has said, those representations are not focusing "on an idealized version of pre-contact culture, but on the process of identity construction in the cultural present."[31] Representation is therefore not one of recovering some purity, but rather one of hybridization—as Stuart Hall puts it[32]—which combines aspects of mass culture and technology with more traditional elements. As alternative media workers and teachers, we see a new convergence of dissenting voices with technologies such as the camcorder and the satellite. The notion of horizontal communication using networks of allegiances between subcultures which bypass established power is no longer in

---

[30] Peter Plagens, "Fade from White: The Whitney Biennial Gives Center Stage to Women, Gays and Artists of Color," *Newsweek*, March 10, 1993; Deborah Solomon, "A Showcase for Political Correctness: The Whitney Biennial Easily Qualifies as the Most Disturbing Deborah Solomon Museum Show in Living Memory," *Wall Street Journal*, March 5, 1993.

[31] Terence Turner, "Defiant Images, the Kayapo Appropriation of Video," *Anthropology Today* 9, no. 6 (1992).

[32] In Stuart Hall and Bram Gieben, eds., *The Foundations of Modernity* (New York: Polity Press, 1992).

the domain of utopia, but tends to take place more and more often. Many of these projects are part of social struggle at the grassroots. Activism within "alter" media can be problematic for social scientists and post-modern academics.

Attention to media, representation, and the politics of identity was a major feature of the eighties in the United States. In the context of the Reagan-Bush era and the repressive morality that came with it, those issues became the focus of bitter cultural battles. Within the mainstream press this interest and concern has been projected back onto the public with a campaign of fear of "Video Vigilantes." Especially after the Rodney King incident in Los Angeles, attention was directed to the potential for a sort of "mob" media. A *Newsweek* cover headline in 1991 stated that "No One Is Safe from the Camera's Eye." By this presumably they mean the eye of George Holliday, whose camcorder caught the Los Angeles police in their vicious attack. At the other end of the spectrum is home video as fun (albeit sadistic fun). Networks have organized weekly series around "America's home videos," from the funniest to the "most wanted." What this presence of amateur video leaves out is any discussion of the formidable networking of community media that exists in the United States, much of it a direct result of public access—cable television channels chartered for public use. Although virtually ignored by the mainstream press, and rarely noticed by communication academics, the arena of public access television represents a practice of "nonprofessional" media making that deserves to be noted by visual anthropologists and others interested in the significance of representation of self. The public access equipment centers, studios, and channels that have proliferated in the past twenty years hold a strong potential for a "citizens' " television. The combination of community studios and the ubiquity of camcorders has given many the option of television in the active mode.

This article is a look at media made by and for "others." By "others" we mean those who traditionally have not had a speaking voice in Western culture, except when mediated by "experts." We use the term "alter" media as a reference to

Rachel Moore's 1992 article "Marketing Alterity" in *Visual Anthropology Review.*

CITIZEN'S TELEVISION

In the years since disciples of McLuhan predicted explosions of popular expression in the global village, access to electronic tools has grown exponentially. Although marketed as a home appliance to record family rituals, consumer video has stretched beyond weddings and graduations. There are lively collaborations between home camcordists and non-profit organizations from the Girl Scouts to Greenpeace. In addition, the alternative media spaces which exist in many cities, supported by local arts councils and artists cooperatives, serve as resource centers for post-production of video projects made with consumer cameras. At public access studios in over a thousand locations in the United States, citizens use their own cameras or free loaned equipment to create their public media sphere. Although conditions vary from city to city, most access channels operate on an open scheduling process: whoever applies first gets either the equipment or the studio or both. Channel time is also up for grabs. Public access is the First Amendment made manifest: the "first come, first serve" access rule means that on most access channels even the Nazis have equal opportunity.[33]

It may not be the revolution some hoped for, and it is not possible to make a simple equation that access equals democracy, but there are thousands of people all over the United States who on a weekly basis make their own television. Andrew Blau estimates that there are approximately 2,000 public access stations broadcasting about 15,000 original hours a week.[34] The services at the different stations vary greatly. The

---

[33] More dangerous than the Nazis to the organization of first-come, first-serve access may be the two-bit entrepreneurs, such as astrologists, therapists, and masseurs, who use public access in a thinly disguised bid for business. See George Stoney's article "On Censorship" on the subject in the fall 1992 issue of *Community Television Review.*

[34] Andrew Blau, "The Promise of Public Access," *The Independent* 15, no. 3 (1992), p. 22.

studios can be prohibitively pristine or slovenly dysfunctional. Programs are often poorly shot using formal structures that inadequately attempt to replicate network talk shows. But as a younger generation gets their hands on camcorders, the energy of rock and rap finds its way into access, along with a new consciousness about identity. There are for most, moreover, no content restrictions, and the producers are a diverse assortment whose ethnic and gender categories are far more varied than the producers on any commercial channel.

The media democracy in the basements downtown has not had a major impact on the huge mainstream network affiliates uptown. In fact, the corporate message is even more limited and hegemonic than ever.[35] As electronic tools have proliferated, the variety of views has lessened in mainstream media. The global village *has* come to pass: Coca-Cola says they need not make commercials for specific national markets anymore: everyone likes the same music, understands the same images, and, yes, everyone drinks Coca-Cola. "I'd like to teach the world to sing in perfect harmony. . . ."[36] But perfect harmony doesn't always reign, and on access channels at least people sing different songs.

FACILITATION

The notion of giving cameras to people who might not otherwise have them has been documented in a variety of anthropo-

---

[35] The organization Fairness and Accuracy in Reporting has tallied the numbers of "experts" on talk shows from Nightline to McNeil-Lehrer—overwhelmingly white, mostly male, and mostly government or corporate spokesmen (*Extra*, 1991). Dan Hallin has counted the duration of sound bites, which have fallen from a high of forty-three seconds in 1968 to eight seconds in 1988 ("Sound Bite News: Television Coverage of Elections, 1968–1988," *Journal of Communication* 42, no. 2 [1992]). These statistics give graphic evidence of the predictable paucity of opinion and views in the organs of mass media. As Herbert Schiller has pointed out, the trend is toward increased commercialization and privatization of information on many levels in the United States, Europe, and the developing world. See Herbert Schiller, George Gerbner, and Hamid Mowhana, *Triumph of the Image: The Media War in the Persian Gulf, a Global Perspective* (Boulder: Westview Press, 1992).

[36] Roger Cohen, "For Coke, World Is Its Oyster," *New York Times*, November 21, 1991, p. C3.

logical projects, the best known being *Through Navajo Eyes* by Sol Worth and John Adair (1972). In this study native people were given lessons in 16 mm film use, and several native people made their own films, which were shown as examples of authentic media expression. The films have been cited as evidence that people from a different culture, if given instruction with minimal reference to existing Western dominant media forms (hardly possible then and certainly more difficult now), would evolve an authentic visual language rooted in their own culture, one that privileges cultural details not readily understood or even perceived by outsiders.

Whether the Navajo experiment is replicable is moot in these days of satellite delivery of CNN and Michael Jackson. The Navajo project was carried out before the hogans got their dish antennas. The global popularity of U.S. transnational culture has made it impossible to get a tabula rasa, if there ever was one. However, Adair and Worth give convincing analysis of the visual cues in the films that the Navajo made. Whatever questions one might have about the romanticization of native culture in this project, one cannot ignore the question that this study brings up for teachers of media: how to teach media in a way that allows for culture-specific expression?

Indigenous media projects in the past were either experiments carried out by ethnographers or social service–type workshops led by committed activists. There usually was a separation between the world of the project organizers and the "community" producers. However, as consumer electronic tools have become more "user friendly," there is a growing tradition of media production in many "other" communities. As a result of decades of public access, there are traditions of training and evolution of shared technical and genre forms that are the result of the access/camcorder situation. Much of grassroots video work takes an activist stance. A look at media projects of several activist subcultures that have evolved in the context of public access may further illuminate this rarely studied phenomenon.

The video activists we are considering, and we count ourselves among them, are situated between video art, sociology, and ethnography. Since it provides alternative voices to an

overriding transnational media culture, the work of activist
video is in many senses by and for "others," acknowledging
that the other side of difference is always sameness, and both
of these terms can only be spoken simultaneously. In that
sense, to take Rafael Roncaglio's words, alternative media
isn't what is marginal, but what alters.[37] Video activists remain outside the power of mainstream media but often appropriate popular media strategies (and off-air footage!) for use
by disenfranchised communities of lesbians, gays, AIDS activists, anti-militarists, radical feminists, ecology crusaders, animal rights activists, et al. The mode of representation used
in the activist camcorder movement has connections with the
critical movements within the art world, such as *L'Internatio-
nale Situationiste* and their critique of the society of spectacle
(Debord 1995). Activist videos defy any notions of easy classi-
fication, but most constitute a radical shift from the "run of
the mill" in terms of formal structure, in terms of content,
but moreover in terms of point of view. It is not just that the
microphone is in the frame in our videos, but more important,
that much of the work is directly engaged in deconstructing
the language that is spoken to us, and in the reorganization of
representation in which the tape itself is a participant. If much
of the work was at first about counter-information, this work
more and more tends to be "about processes of identity construction."[38]

The notion of electronic media as articulation of social
struggle was manifest in the late sixties in the Challenge
for Change program in Canada,[39] which encouraged community use of video for social change.[40] The product of this pro-

---

[37] Rafael Roncaglio, "Notes on the 'Alternative,' " in Nancy Thede and
Alain Ambrosi, eds., *Video: The Changing World* (Montreal: Black Rose
Books, 1991).

[38] Allen Ginsberg in narration for David Shulman's video *Turn It on, Tune
It in, Take It over.*

[39] Dorothy Hénaut, "A Report from Canada: Television as Town Meeting,"
*Radical Software* 1, no. 1 (1970).

[40] Jay Ruby's discussion of Challenge for Change questions the efficacy of
this type of activism (as well as the effectiveness of documentaries such as
*Harvest of Shame)* on the grounds that the conditions documented did not
change. While many of the social struggles which were documented are
still ongoing, it seems crudely cynical to dismiss this work as "ineffective"

ject was the process: there were few actual programs made, but the video was used as an interactive tool for widening community discussion. The most significant effect of these efforts was not any specific social change for the community involved, but the training and developing of the project staff, many of whom continue to inspire work in the arena of video empowerment (Stoney 1971–72; Gaventa 1980).

In the United States one veteran from the Challenge for Change project, George Stoney, began and has continued to lead the struggle for access to media. He was a major force in the initial movement for community television regulations within cable agreements. Stoney focused on the franchises which cable corporations draw up with cities. He organized people to insist that these contracts include provisions and space for community equipment and studios and non-profit, educational, governmental, and "access" channels. The access movement has been rather successful in developing an infrastructure of studios, equipment banks, and open channels on cable systems. Although those who fought to promote access were not operating under any specific theoretical mandate, they instinctively saw some contradictions present in the development of electronic tools. They were embodying what Hans Magnus Enzensburger has noted: "The contradiction between producers and consumers is not inherent in the electronic media; on the contrary, it has to be artificially reinforced by economic and administrative measures."[41]

In the early days of the portable video recorder (the Sony portapak was the popular model) groups such as Videofreex and Raindance pooled equipment and talents in video collectives. The work of these avant garde video groups has been described by Martha Rosler:

---

because radical change didn't occur. This criteria implies a rather idealist notion of social change. Although migrant conditions are still gruesome, *Harvest of Shame* informed a generation and spurred widespread support for the organizing work of the United Farm Workers and their campaigns such as the grape boycott. See Ruby's "Speaking for, Speaking about, Speaking with, or Speaking alongside: An Anthropological and Documentary Dilemma," *Visual Anthropology Review* 7, no. 2 (1991), pp. 56–58.

[41] Hans Magnus Enzensberger, "Constituents of a Theory of Media," in John Hanhardt, Gibbs M. Smith, and Peregrine Smith, eds., *Video Culture: A Critical Investigation* (Layton, Utah: Peregrine Smith Books), p. 105.

Video posed a challenge to the sites of art production in society, to the forms and "channels" of delivery and to the passivity of reception built into them. Not only a systematic but also a utopian critique was implicit in video's early use, for the effort was not to enter the system, but to transform every aspect of it and—a legacy of the revolutionary avant-garde project—to redefine the system out of existence by merging art with social life and making audience and producer interchangeable.[42]

Avoiding a reductive conceptualization of the relation between technology and its potential, or technological determinism, Rosler insists instead on the social relations in which this technology is used. The political dimension of low-tech video lies in its practice, not in its "low techness." It is not because cameras are accessible that we have producers—what those cameras create, at best, are photo amateurs (Enzensberger 1987). Certainly the way the apparatus is marketed is for home (in a nuclear family at that!) use.[43] It is not because the new machines are accessible that we have "radical" productions. However, the crucial element is to have access to those machines without a *technician*, or for that matter an anthropologist or other expert, most often a white male and aligned with structures of power, in between the producer and the machine. To undermine the mythical expertise of specialized technicians, to believe in the possibility of the popular acquisition of production skills, is a radical difference from previous practices in the media. The attempts of early independent video groups to share the tools with the people was often

---

[42] Martha Rosler, "Video Shedding the Utopian Moment," in Doug Hall and Sally Jo Fifer, eds., *Illuminating Video* (New York: Aperture, 1990), p. 31. For an interesting discussion of the interchangeability of "audience" and "producer" in the early days of radio in the United States, see Susan Douglass, *Inventing American Broadcasting, 1899–1922* (Baltimore: John Hopkins University Press, 1987). Douglass looks at radio's "pre-history" when amateurs transcended individual tinkering and began to form lively networks of exchange and support. She quotes an article from *Popular Mechanics* to the effect that wireless telegraphy had "made it possible for the private citizen to communicate across great distances without the aid of either the government or a corporation." The formation of the American Radio Relay League in 1914 was a "grassroots, coast-to-coast communications network" (p. 206).

[43] See Section 8, "Watch Out, Dick Tracy!"

somewhat of a deception, because those tools were actually still ultimately in the hands of the video technicians themselves, no matter how long the hair of the facilitators or how sensitive their attitude. However, once video becomes a consumer tool, this relation changes. The camera is obtainable direct from the mall, the catalog, or the trading post, not the outsider/technician. Media education, however, is not simply about turning on the camera and pressing the right buttons for the edit. It is also about the production of meaning with images. Images have histories bound to culture in a specific sense. The very reason that images are made is to engage in the struggle over meaning. The power relations of images are unbalanced: Western consumer culture projects pictures to the entire world. However, with the development of "alter" media, there is, on a small scale, a body of work that is exchanged on a horizontal level. The connections between Inuit television and Australian aboriginal television are clear. One of Vidéazimut's projects is to link indigenous and activist media from all over the world. Even such "low power" exchanges are a threat to some in the West, to some who are straight, white, and male, and to whom the status quo of the current imagery balance is not a problem.

When a videotape incites action in the real world, the audience and the producers merge. The insistence on praxis rather than a specific technology implies a different structure of production and allows one to pose the project as "counter-representation" and affirmation of identity. This displaces the production/consumption relation. The way in which power is worked out around the tools of representation greatly varies in different situations.[44] Obviously it is not "everyone" who holds the camera. If some alternative practices replicate the traditional hierarchical power structure, just as some replicate the static forms of network television in their programs, there are also many who work collectively, experiment formally, and offer camera lessons to everybody who wants them.

---

[44] Terence Turner, "Visual Media, Cultural Politics and Anthropological Practice: Recent Uses of Film and Video among the Kayapo of Brazil." *The Independent* (New York) 14, no. 1 (1992).

"Collective" here need not be as a literal collective organization of a political group, but rather as a dialogue between
practices and productions within a "community" that shares
political or cultural positions.


## COMMUNITY VIDEO: EXAMPLES OF ALTER (NATIVE) VIDEO

Within the works under consideration here there is an ac-
knowledgment that each tape is not a finished oeuvre, but part
of a continuum of practice, a self-consciousness of the collective process and an understanding of the need for communication *within* the group. The creation of video "documents" is
only part of these projects: distribution and dissemination and
the evolution of further video production are integral. The
communities constructed by these videos are not bound by
territorial borders, but are communities of interest that are
connected, and in a sense *produced*, by telecommunications
channels and satellite transmissions. The *group* empowerment
is primary, superseding any notion that this is a reflection of
a group of "others" to the "world," although this may be a
secondary and quite important result.

With satellites circumnavigating the ether over the equator,
there is no simple "outside" for anyone anymore. Neither for
the ethnographer, nor the "other," nor the activist. What
these examples represent is citizens taking responsibility for
their own images. These images may be appropriated or envisioned, but they are informed, if not through academic knowledge, at least by a developing sense of community history and
an understanding that history is a convergence of many traditions from a wide range of cultural influences.


## NOT CHANNEL ZERO: INDIGENOUS URBAN VIDEO

A group of young African Americans and Latinos from New
York have formed a collective called Not Channel Zero. This
group is indigenous not to the Amazon, but to a contemporary
urban landscape in which they actively appropriate television

space, which is claimed and "tagged" with the same audacity that a wall or a subway car is spray-painted. They articulate a position which is at once inside and outside the dominant culture: culling language and style from popular culture and inverting it with new meaning and associations.

For three years they produced a series of tapes for a cable access slot. In their words, "We want to do work quickly, inexpensively and guarantee that it will be seen by at least three more people other than the members of our immediate families" (interview in *Felix* magazine 1992, p. 54). Public access was the perfect answer. Their aim is at "regular folks that never seem to make it on the network news except when there's a chalk outline of some dead brother or sister focused in the foreground" (p. 57). They cover community events: the birthday of Malcolm X, Harlem protests against the Gulf War, interviews with local personalities such as the first black airline hostess who is still fighting for women's rights. In the aftermath of the rebellion in reaction to the Rodney King verdict, they began taping local reactions to this issue. They collected material from around the country and put together a collaborative program entitled *The Nation Erupts.*

Taking as a starting point media coverage of the reaction to the Simi Valley verdict of not guilty, the tape begins with shots rescanned from TV news coverage. The images are much the same in each—flaming buildings, angry crowds, phalanxes of police. However, the NCZ camera does not show the entire frame. It just grabs the text of the location I.D. and enough of the image for the viewer to know what it is: a corner of the TV frame, zoomed in so close that the image is broken/striped at regular intervals by the scan lines. It is a montage of close-ups of the names of other cities where protests occurred. The barrage of places reminds us that if Los Angeles was the front line, the battle was being played out in many other locations, and the jarring images of the TV close-ups proclaim the fact that the war is also on and *about t*elevision.

The tape proceeds to dissolve the "legitimizing" glue that holds the network images together, as those images, sometimes distorted, are interrupted by clips of community activists, demonstration images, and clips belonging to the realm of video art. A montage of images characteristic of the L.A. upheaval—looters in parking lots, buildings burning, phalanxes of National Guard troops—unwinds with a list of other ethnic riots that have occurred in the United States since the beginning of the century. This is followed by an analysis by video artist Tony Coke of the relationship between looting and consumer society. Not Channel Zero provides the frame for us to review the network images of the rebellion. History is constantly invoked, either by rolling chronology linking the present to past events, by excerpts from civil rights footage, or by quotes from other "amateur" videos that were used as evidence for years of police brutality, scenes that give the eighty seconds of Rodney King a precedent.

A radical break occurs as a blue screen descends and numbers flash up. "It is time for Not Channel Zero's fourteen reasons to Loot and Riot." Constructed in the manner of an educational documentary, this ironic section constitutes an appropriation by people of color of the type of anxiety-ridden questions that the networks use to frame "disturbances." The use of the didactic form of instruction films works as a radical rupture in the flow which up until now could hardly be characterized as smooth. In their words, "We try to mesh hip hop aesthetic with grassroots journalism." Like the Navajo in the Adair-Worth experiment, these young people were never initiated into a formal documentary film tradition. Their training did not take the academic trajectory of Eisenstein, Vertov, Flaherty, Grierson, Leacock, or Wiseman. As Tom Poole, NCZ member, has stated, "Sure, some of us went to film class, but I guess we fell asleep a lot." Their filmic language is culled from Soul Train, MTV, CNN, Spike Lee, or perhaps even the cautionary films from the Health Department on AIDS and drugs. Their cultural influences are as rich and diverse as African and Latin art and music. This is literally hybridization at work.

Even on a subject that is blatantly unjust, we are not in a simple denunciating mode, though there is a hint of a threat that this might appear at any moment. Rather, the second half of *The Nation Erupts* is a careful analysis of the different elements that constitute reality/perception for the media, in a manner similar to that of a cultural critic. In the words of Tony Bennet, he or she examines cultural practices from the point of view of their implication with and within relations of power.[45] This section is steered by an NCZ commentator. He first appears from behind an African mask, which visually clarifies his point of view. This is no interchangeable commentator. Instead of the sleek anchor/interpreter[46] whose appearance meshes in the flow of images, the NCZ commentator contradicts the flow by insisting on his presence: "And now for a Not Channel Zero commentary . . ." Just in case we haven't noticed him, his face is so close to the camera that it literally bursts the confines of the screen. He speaks, he analyzes, he questions, he denounces, with a quiet strength which conveys the power of his anger: "What really surprised me about the verdict was that I was surprised by the verdict. I mean, what was I thinking about? What did I expect?" Or a little later: "Remember the jury was multicultural: ten whites, one Asian, one Latino. Multicultural."

His intervention at once replaces what counts as objectivity on television and allows NCZ to take a stand just as any commentator always does. He organizes the images: testimony from a Rasta businessman surrounds images of the "looting." Footage from the civil rights struggles of the sixties is intercut with testimony of Asians denouncing the media's divisive coverage of Korean/black tensions. The coherence of the commentator doesn't come from the unity of film genre, the origins, or the mode of production, but from the usage the producers make of those images which are already loaded with their own meanings. More than quotes, the clips work as arguments, a hip-hop counterpoint. Not Channel Zero uses disarticulation to reorient the meaning of the images while critiquing their original usage.

Such a meditative work on the L.A. uprising couldn't end without at least a glimpse of the possible solutions, which is what Not Channel Zero does. However, simple solutions are

---

[45] Tony Bennett, *Outside Literature* (New York: Routledge, 1990).

[46] As Eddie Becker, a Washington, D.C.–based camcordist, has noted, the network journalists and correspondents are basically mike stands and are called such in the trade.

not allowed for too long. The utopian vision is shown through the images and voices of children, a sixties civil rights worker, and an older middle-class white woman who, like Rodney King, all want to know, Why can't everybody get along? These positions can be seen as innocence, despair, or naiveté, depending on the speaker's (and/or viewer's) point of view. Of course, it is the wish of everyone that "everybody would just get along." But they don't. We don't. So the tape does not let this happen either. The edit that closes this section and opens the conclusion of the tape is "I'm not going to talk with some old clichés that people from all races should come together." The discussion is now about difference and the common struggle against racism.

Not content to give us information we couldn't get on the regular channels, this program gives us the tools to "read" what the regular channels have given us at the time. Not Channel Zero reinterprets the Los Angeles events, which themselves cannot be separated from their mass mediation. The tape radically alters the meaning given by television to this situation by denaturalizing its image, shifting the points of view, while affirming an interpretation specifically localized in time, culture, and race. To paraphrase Terence Turner,[47] the work of the tape is not to reconstruct a utopic version of the African American culture "but (to show) the processes of identity construction in the cultural present." The main work of the tape is to construct an African American subject in relation to the L.A. upheaval that is radically different from what the networks allowed us to see. Like a crowbar taken to the security gates of a TV showroom, they are opening a cultural space initiated by the violence in the streets.

Even in this case, however, the "subjected" subject speaking for him- or herself can be made exotic. Pat Aufderheide (1993) speaks of the difference in presentation between the indigenous filmmakers at a Manchester film festival and the ones at a conference in Peru. In both cases the Kayapo are the icons with the greatest "exchange" value. When we presented the NCZ tape in France as "a tape made by a young

---

[47] Turner, "Visual Media, Cultural Politics and Anthropological Practice."

black collective from Harlem," it got attention that no wom-
en's tape would have. This is because of the symbolic strength
that Harlem represents in France. The exotic is given credibility—"permission." However, as screenings have made clear,
the precise power of the tape make its reappropriation by any
status quo difficult. The risk is worth it. If there is one thing
the events in L.A. make clear, it is that the West is not homogenous. Official recognition by the majority is not a prerequisite
for horizontal networking by others. The impact is not always
as strong as one might hope for, but the goal is not to be in a
missionary position for a cause, but in search for allies around
a cause.

## VIDEO AND AIDS

*Doctors, Liars and Women* is a documentation of the direct
action of a women's group of ACT UP against *Cosmopolitan*
magazine after the publication of an article on AIDS in which
a doctor stated that "there is almost no danger for women of
contracting AIDS through ordinary unprotected sexual inter-
course." This tape had a significant influence on tapes subsequently made by ACT UP videomakers and DIVA (Damned
Interfering Video Activists) and in the developing of media for
the Gay Men's Health Crisis in Manhattan.

Some of the political strategies of ACT UP were discussed
by Douglas Crimp in a special issue of the journal *October* on
AIDS:

- AIDS does not exist apart from the practices that conceptual-
  ize it, represent it, and respond to it.
- If we recognize that AIDS exists only in and through these
  constructions, then hopefully, we can also recognize the im-
  perative to know them, to analyze them, and to wrest control
  of them.
- Activist art therefore involves questions not only of the nature
  of cultural production, but also the location, or the means
  of distribution, of that production. Until a cure for AIDS is
  developed, only information and mobilization (and access to
  medication) can save lives.

The women who decided to take action against the misleading *Cosmo* article are all white, most of them lesbians, and all active members of ACT UP. They are women in a predominantly male group, struggling with the process of coalition building. The tape offers basic information about women and AIDS, as well as documenting the political process involved in direct action used by ACT UP in 1988. This chronicle is treated in a classic documentary style, with talking heads representing the positions of the women: as AIDS activists in a predominantly men's group, as reporters of their own actions. This documentation is not simply a memory of these women's actions, but also a "how to" teaching tape for use of direct action. The actions documented include a demonstration in front of the *Cosmo* office building, a confrontation/interview with the doctor in his office, and TV clips of news and talk shows about the *Cosmo* article. The tape creates an address that constructs a specific audience and a particular "me"; it is constructing a subject historically and culturally bound. The tape is to be distributed across the country to specific groups of people with a specific identity. The movement of identification calls for an "othering" of the norm, a centering of what is normally "other." As Gayatri Spivak has said, "The opposition is thus not merely reversed; it is displaced. . . . Displacing the opposition that it initially apparently questions, it is always different from itself, always deters itself. It is neither a constitutive nor, of course, a regulative norm."[48]

Videotaping the everyday of the collective in action constructs a sense of affinity and produces networking, a necessary tool against political isolation. ACT UP videos call for other activists to act and to document their own actions, as a means to establish a memory of AIDS activism, and as an inspiration for further action. The strategy for distribution is low tech and hybrid: on access cable, on low-power broadcast, in museum and artists' spaces, in schools and universities, in group meetings at homes and offices. As Flo Kennedy put it in her appearance in *Born in Flames:* "Sometimes hun-

---

[48] Gayatri Chakravorty Spivak, *In Other Worlds* (New York: Methuen, 1987), p. 103.

dreds of little mice in a room can make more damage than a lion."[49] It is this understanding of politics—conceptually close to the European Autonomy movement of the early seventies—in which the politics of distribution should be understood.

The cultural codes deployed in the video are multiple—both those of independent video (irregularity in the quality of filming, vernacular language, faces that we are not used to seeing appearing on the airwaves) and those of a very different type of representation: television (talk shows and news formats). The weight of these codes are not the same. One is legitimated, the other struggling to be heard, grassroots, resistant. However, there is a third type of representation: the appearance of the AIDS activists on a talk show, clips of which are included in the tape. It is "direct action," the "break-in" of protest into the space of normalization, the forced encounter between two worlds that do not usually coincide. The TV talk show is here a desired space, since it permits access to a desired audience and offers the possibility of the (self-) representation by the other. The activists in this context are both "other" and, by the presence in the studio audience in this show, potentially "same." By being present on the show, the activists acknowledge and "appropriate" a segment of the mass audience, previously unacknowledged. However, the spectacle of television accommodates victims testifying better than activists, who "read" as marginal outsiders without much of a legitimate ground. The difficulties of appropriating space on mainstream media, however, is discussed in an auto-critique segment on the tape. Jean Carlamusto says, "When we were in control, things went well . . . when the media got control of the event, we lost our representation. Till then, we had been representing ourselves. I was in the organizing, I was documenting it too, we had control of our image. The next day (on television) it was exactly the opposite." Maria Magenti says, "Though we broke the story that women can be killed from this kind of story, we were made invisible and the only thing left was a debate about epidemiological truth, whether or not so and so

---

[49] *Born in Flames,* directed by Lizzie Borden.

was a doctor, whether or not this was a proof of hetero transmission."

These statements do not take into account the complicated
nexus of determining factors at work in such an action, some
of whose meanings they do not have control over, even in their
own "image production." As the tape indicates, television producers, even network executives, are unable to fully control
the representations they "produce."

*Doctors, Liars and Women* returns the gaze on the TV screen
itself and interrupts the endless televisual flow. A viewer zap-
ping through the channels encounters a reflexive confrontation not only with irresponsible views of AIDS, but with the
representation of those views. This tape is an example of AIDS
activist media practice that inscribes new identities in cultural
production, reshaping discourse that produces identity, in an
active struggle with meaning.

Paul Garrin, a video artist who made a tape about police,
video, and the struggle around Tomkins Square Park in Lower
Manhattan, has said, " 'Big Brother' used to be the state looking at the people, now it's also the people looking at the state.
. . . Use your camera intelligently." One use of that camera is
to look at the media itself. In the examples cited, the viewer is
given some tools with which to look at television intelligently,
to question the way reality is constructed and the way we react
to events as reported on mainstream television. As Not Channel Zero's Art Jones says in *The Nation Erupts*, aren't you surprised that you were surprised?

## ALTER (NATIVE) MEDIA

Ethnography is that rare discipline that does not hold a universal centralized discourse on the "other" precisely because
it has been forced to think of cultural specificity. As hybridization of cultures, language, and media becomes the rule, notions of purity have disappeared. If ordinary television is
implicated in the interests of multinational corporations,
"alter" media is made by and for the public, or rather the
publics: it is television that has the possibility of media speci-

ficity. "Alter" media in the United States makes use of the latest possibilities for image making, speaks a language that is at once the same and different, on channels that a generation of media activists have opened for public use. What "alter" media opens is the destabilization of the relation between observer and observed. This is not an easy reversal of the traditional relation: the cameras are not "given" by the ethnographers, grants are scarce, facilities are crowded. Creating and maintaining this space is difficult work. "Alter" media does not pretend to "represent" any fixed position, but it occupies a much needed space in a small, but crucial, segment of our lives: media. Struggle around television representation is a struggle to have a public existence, a materiality. Those who name become the actors in history. Representation is therefore the construction of an "alter" reality, the production of subjectivity.

The "alter" media experience allows to us to see the media horizon open not on an Orwellian vision, a normative global village wired in, transmitted to, from a central source, but a composite television which would allow what technological determinists have always promised, but never delivered: a vision of democracy which would enable all of us to take charge of our own images.

An oft-repeated anecdote from *Through Navajo Eyes* is when a Navajo elder, Sam Yazzie, asks the ethnographers if the film project will hurt the sheep. He is confidently told that it will not hurt them. Then he asks if it will help them. When told it won't do that either, he asks, "Then why do it?" (Adair and Worth 1972). The ethnographers didn't have an answer to that. Many of us are operating on the principle that it is important to defend the sheep of this world. If becoming visually literate and media-active can help empower those who are the shepherds, as well as those would save shepherd practice, small-scale agriculture, and the balance of life on this earth, then, yes, Sam Yazzie, it is good for the sheep.

# From Public Access to Geostationary Orbit: The Personal Is Political

## *February 1993*

IT SEEMS HARD to believe that scarcely two decades ago computers were limited to the province of large corporations and cumbersome state bureaucracies. The advent of the "personal" computer has changed forever the way we artists and intellectuals in the industrialized areas of the world organize our work and document and disseminate our ideas. Although the specific construction and structural elaboration of the technology remain mystified as magical entities, the notion that the machines are "friendly" and accessible is widespread, and the logic of cyberlife is clearly accepted. The early Mac ads made them seem like videogames, highlighting MacPaint and other graphics programs. Later campaigns promoted the notion that PCs can keep the family intact: Dad could spend more time at home with his "mini-office" or calculate the family's taxes to save accountant's fees. PCs are marketed as home appliances, as cozy as a toaster, which is the trade name for a low-priced computer graphics tool.

One of the contradictions of consumer electronics is that technology developed for individuals is also usable by groups. The demand for Macs on many jobs was a challenge IBM did not expect, but "friendly" systems are popular in the workplace as well as at home. What was marketed for home consumption soon became ensconced in office systems. Corporate offices are not the only group settings in which "personal" computers have made sense. Thousands of community

organizations, from rape counseling centers to ecology research teams, have adapted what are marketed as individual
consumer commodities into organizing tools. Desktop publishing has blossomed with individualized formatting and lay-
out programs. Pagemaker has been touted as the equivalent
of the penny press of the seventeenth century. The advantages
of these technologies in organizing and distributing alternative information is taken for granted now even though it was
unknown twenty years ago.

In video we have seen the rapid deployment of the camcorder during this same time period. This machine has been
marketed to individuals much like the Kodak Brownie was in
the twenties: for documenting family rituals, from graduation
to birthdays to the Christmas tree. It has, however, outflanked
its marketing agenda and is a useful tool for labor unions,
peace activists, and those keeping an eye out for police abuses.
In the arts there is wide use of video as documentation of performance and for interactive installations.

The confluence of individual consumer technology and art
is one of those fertile areas of contradiction in a society dominated by multinational corporations. There are works of art in
this era of electronic reproduction that dance to the dialectic
of these contradictions. One cannot deny the brilliant and inspiring work of the many artists who have appropriated
the machines of bureaucrats: the offset reproduction collages
of Barbara Kruger, Juan Sanchez, David Thorn, Steve
Kroninger, and others; the literally penetrating surveillance
installations of Julia Scher; and the remarkable sculptural
combinations using museum-store reproduction technology
that Fred Wilson has created. Experiments such as these are
a reminder of the radical potential inherent in a mediated
world.

The karaoke boom has enabled bar customers to interject
themselves into music videos.[50] Camcorder images surpass
what most TV stations had for studio cameras ten years ago.

---

[50] Karaoke manufacturers are planning interactive networks of karaoke
users: Tokyo drunks can carouse live with drunken Osakans. See Michael
Schrage, "Karaoke Battles a Case of Laryngitis," *Los Angeles Times*, March
25, 1993.

Video effects that were the domain of people like Paik and the Vasulkas are now available at a flick of a toaster button.[51]

The demands of the consumer market have engendered a wide selection of high-quality images at an ever descending cost. The low price for good video duplication is a challenge to traditions of scarcity in art. Video reproduction is "truer" than the reproductions of paintings that Benjamin wrote about.[52] A copy from a dub-master of a Nam June Paik tape is almost identical to VHS copies that might be made for home distribution.[53] Certainly the notion of "limited editions" of artists' tapes is an idea justifiably jettisoned from gallery and art dealer strategies. The fact that the camcorder and video toasters are now available at the local mall has made some of the rhetoric surrounding video art look a bit pretentious.

WE CAN GET IT FOR YOU WHOLESALE

If the camcorder can be seen as a retail item, the satellite transponder is perhaps a wholesale distributor. This "wholesale" level of electronic technology, beyond the personal consumer arena, has points of possible appropriation for artists and alternative voices. Electronic technology of distribution on a "wholesale" level is now available for a relatively low price.

The changes in the television landscape are quantitative, not qualitative: the strongest presence is still the domination by the commercial networks, now expanded, thanks to satellite distribution, from the big three (ABC, NBC, and CBS) to include Fox and CNN. Other users of satellite transmission capacity have been in three main categories. One is the entrepreneurs who aim at specific markets: narrowcasting. Besides

---

[51] One of the key developers of the video synthesizers is interviewed by Wes Thomas in *Mondo 2000*, no. 9 (1994): "Four Arguments for the Redemption of Television: Video Pioneer Stephen Beck." Beck's techno-optimism bridges the sixties with the nineties: "Video art was one art form that started in museums instead of ending in them. . . . We are turning the television into a computer, and the next generation of kids into their own producers."

[52] Benjamin, "The Work of Art in the Age of Mechanical Reproduction."

[53] With digital film the copies are virtually identical to the original.

the Weather Channel, there is the Science Fiction Channel, the Comedy Channel, and several home shopping channels. Even the truckers of America have their own channel that is distributed to truck stops.[54] The second class of users are the conservative religious organizations such as Trinity Broadcasting and idiosyncratic preachers such as Dr. Gene Scott. These groups have made impressive use of technological resources (direct mail, automatic phone banks, radio and television transmissions) to spread their extremely reactionary ideology. The third class are business and science researchers and experts. From medical schools to social engineers, technocrats have made themselves at home on the satellite transponders. The arts and the humanities have not been as aggressive in this arena.

BIRDLAND

At any given time there are dozens of satellites (nicknamed "birds" by news organizations) encircling the equator. Each of them has a number of channels, or transponders. The majority of satellites are military based, but many are commercial and are owned by aerospace corporations. Transponders can be rented either at an hourly rate, or by multiyear leases. Many satellites have twenty-four of these channels. In the coming years this number will increase dramatically, as new methods of signal compression are developed. In the future there will be as many as six signals where there is now one. For the most part these signals are the "wholesale" distributors of programming. The Disney Corporation uses one transponder for their East Coast feed and another for their West Coast feed. By having these two options, they can program prime time on both coasts with the same program sequences. NASA uses satellites to transmit the feeds from inside the shuttle capsules and the mission control press conferences. All of the networks use satellites to uplink feeds to their news organizations. A compilation feature film utilized raw footage from

---

[54] *Los Angeles Times*, March 25, 1993, p. C1.

these transmissions. *Feed* by Kevin Rafferty was largely based on footage that Brian Springer retrieved by downlinking uncensored 1992 presidential election program material from his satellite dishes in Buffalo, New York. The sometimes embarrassing "verité" moments were the beginning of feeds meant for cuing retransmission or for in-house use.

Some transponder uses are specifically aimed at satellite audiences. There are a number of channels dedicated to technology information and dish component sales. These are aimed at dish owners, who constitute a "retail" audience. At the current time there are over five million C band dishes in use in the United States and Canada. Counting over twenty satellites, each with twenty-four channels, there are about 500 channels available at any given time.[55]

DEEP DISH NETWORK

Deep Dish Television began in 1986 as a collective of video producers and community activists interested in utilizing satellite technology for program distribution. The Deep Dish project started with the production collective Paper Tiger in 1981, a model for low-budget television production that proudly flaunts the "cheap art" of its graphics and its production "values."

Public access has been underutilized by artists and community activists, and Paper Tiger is a conscious attempt to encourage grassroots use of these community channels. Deep Dish was founded to bring together the energies and imaginations of the many community television producers across the country. In this sense it is a reconstructionist solution to the deconstruction of Paper Tiger. Both of these entities encourage the use of a combination (as in a deep dish pie) of technological, art, and activist resources such as

- The work of the thousands of videomakers, individuals, and groups throughout the United States and the world

---

[55] Since this article was written there has been a rise in the number of people using direct broadcast satellite dishes (the smaller ones), now around 15 million.

- The activists from a broad spectrum of constituencies who utilize and promote programs on such agendas as peace, ecology, diversity, and women's rights
- The public access cable channels in many communities in the United States
- Commercial transponders (satellite channels) that are available for rental.

Deep Dish collects material from a wide variety of producers and packages it into seasonal series. Satellite time is rented, and local groups are informed for the "downlinking" of these programs. Most commercial satellites in the U.S. have what is called "geostationary orbits," which means that their orbit is above the equator. When boosted into the correct position, and traveling at the correct speed, they stay at the same relative position to the earth. They revolve with the earth, and their signal is beamed down in a predictable and relatively stable "footprint." For the satellites aimed at North America, this means to the continental U.S. and large parts of Canada, Mexico, and the Caribbean.

## DEEP DISH DOWNLINKS

Deep Dish has focused on "wholesale" distribution: getting the programs out to cable programmers at access centers who can downlink them (with any consumer satellite dish), tape the programs, and find space for them on local channels. These channels could be regular public access, or they could be municipal channels or educational channels that are reserved in the municipal franchises (the agreements that cities make with cable corporations) for public use. For most series Deep Dish rents two hours a week. There is an initial uplink, then a repeat, on a second day, at a different time slot. This means that Deep Dish must work very hard to promote the programming, to ensure that the many downlinkers remember to tweak the satellite dish in time. It means getting people to schedule the work of tuning and taping into their regular weekly chores. Think of a radio station being on for only two hours a week! Much of the work of Deep Dish is this promotional effort: sending schedules, calling to promote, sending reminder postcards, and calling to follow up and to determine the extent of carriage. Although it varies from series to series, several hundred cable systems regularly schedule Deep Dish series on the local cable access channels.

DON'T JUST WATCH TV, MAKE IT[56]

This downlinking, however, is not a passive activity. Most centers who play Deep Dish also participate actively in the network. Perhaps producers from that center have submitted programming to one of the series. Perhaps someone on staff has coordinated a compilation program that has been one of the episodes of a series. Perhaps a local producer acts as local sponsor and produces "wrap-around" segments that augment Deep Dish programming with a local focus. Deep Dish encourages an active engagement with television: for people to become part of a community of interest that engages with issues and reacts to events. By compiling *local* reactions to specific issues, Deep Dish demonstrates how *national* the issues are. The programs begin to do the opposite of what decontextualized fragments of mainstream network news does: on Deep Dish the issues are contextualized and the issue made coherent. In addition, by working with activist organizations, the participation is extended into the community. AIDS tapes list sources for information and exchange. A Cuba Teach-in promotes visits to Cuba and enlists support for material aid brigades. A housing tape describes the steps needed for tenants to organize a rent strike. A war toys teach-in is transmitted live to affiliates of the War Resisters League, and their activists in eight locations give hints of how their community organized: picketing a Toys R Us Store, decorating the windows of a local alternative toy store with games that promote peace and cooperation, visiting schools to discuss the militarism inherent in "GI Joe."

---

[56] Deep Dish bumper sticker, available from Deep Dish TV, 339 Lafayette St., New York, N.Y. 10012.

THE SKY'S THE LIMIT[57]

Deep Dish has proved that distribution on satellite is a powerful organizing tool. Uplinking programs can strengthen a sense of community across wide geographical regions. Deep Dish serves as a catalyst for creative activism and cultural exchange. Deep Dish hopes to develop an international series with an organization called Videazimut, which consists of community producers from over a dozen countries. Corporations and governments have been networking for decades. The use of camcorders, computers, and satellites make possible global exchange between grassroots organizations. In the future there might be a twenty-four-hour program service that can link artists, community leaders, union members, ecologists, intellectuals, and counter-culture consumers.[58]

This sort of technology has been cleverly utilized by right-wing fundamentalists in the United States. They have leased transponders on satellites for over fifteen years and are building maverick infrastructures of channels on commercial, public access, and educational outlets. It is ironic that despite their calls for censorship, for repressive restraints on sexual preference, for restrictive bans on immigration and international exchange, the right-wing fundamentalists have been extremely creative and rather eclectic in their use of video technology. What has prevented a progressive response by the community of artists and defenders of human rights? Perhaps it has been obsession with individualism and notions of elitist art and media practice. Perhaps it is the arts funders who steadfastly refuse to consider collective art projects in favor of "auteurs" and superstars. Perhaps it is the short-sighted priorities of the progressive funding community, where band-aids win out over long-range infrastructure building.

---

[57] This phrase was the name of a short-lived journal published by Lorenzo Milam, pioneer of community broadcasting and early enthusiast of satellite technology for alternative media use. Milam's book *Sex and Broadcasting*, published by Mho and Mho Works (San Diego, 1972), remains the classic account of the joys and problems of do-it-yourself broadcasting.

[58] The Free Speech TV Network is now a twenty-four-hour service on DBS that programs independent and experimental work including Deep Dish programs.

Perhaps we fear the power we could mobilize if we do collaborate.[59] The technology we have at our fingertips is powerful. The sky's the limit.

Deep Dish board meeting. Front row, from left: Daniel Brooks, Bob Hercules, Debra Lubbold. Second row, from left: Iannis Mookis, the author, Ann Bennett, Ron Davis. Back row, from left: unknown, Caryn Rogoff, Safiya Bukhari, Graciela Sanchez, Nolan Bowie. *(Deep Dish)*

---

[59] The impressive reach of the Indymedia centers proves that collaboration can indeed be powerful. See their web site at www.indymedia.org. See also Section 9 ("The Gathering Storm").

# The Camcorder Goes to War: Making Outrage Contagious— A Chronology of the Gulf Crisis TV Project with Texts and Testimonies

*March 1992*
*Written in collaboration with Simone Farkhondeh, Cathy Scott, and Marty Lucas*[60]

> Abbie Hoffman once said his job was to make outrage contagious.

## August 1991: Iraqi Military Invades Kuwait
## United States Begins Troop Buildup in the Middle East
*Paper Tiger Television Starts Planning to Counter Media Disinformation*

SF: In August, when Iraq moved into Kuwait, the United States and Iraq were rattling swords. The way that the mass media portrayed the situation first of all was limited. There was very little information about Iraq, or about the history of the Iraq/U.S. relationship. There was no information about the colonial past of the region. We felt that there was a gearing up toward a bigger confrontation, a war possibly, and we realized very quickly that we would have to move immediately to counter the lack of real information.

---

[60] Thanks to Paul Wong of the Video In in Vancouver for inspiring and publishing this dialogue.

### September: United States Mobilizes National Guard for "Operation Desert Shield"

*Anti-war Teach-ins and Demonstrations Are Held in Many Cities*

DDH: It is hard to say at what point we knew that there would be a war. Everyone from Jimmy Swaggart to Jesse Jackson had said that the most likely place for World War III was the Middle East. After so many years of Armageddon warnings, it was hard to know how to react when the real thing began. There were those who did see it coming: for example, the veterans. In early September my hometown of Woodstock, N.Y., held a rally for peace in the Gulf—organized by Vietnam vets. I heard about it late and hurried to the rally. I came running across the field clutching my Hi-8 camera and my tripod, trying to screw on the "handy snap mount" for the tripod as I ran, eager to catch the last poem by a pair of vet poets who were reciting to the beat of congas. In Woodstock you can always count on pretty good music at rallies. As I got up to the stage, close enough to use the in-camera mike, I was surprised to find that there was already a camcorder taping: one of the vets had set up his own. In 1970 I had helped cut the negative for a collective-made film about Vietnam called *Wintersoldier.* The Vietnam Vets against the War worked with the film collective to document atrocities which they themselves had committed. *Hmm . . . I thought . . . this time around the vets are covering* their own *resistance.* The camcorder war had begun.

Late one night in September I got a call from Margaret Brenman Gibson, an associate of Daniel Ellsberg (the former Defense Department analyst who had leaked the Pentagon Papers, in protest against the Vietnam War). She was in tears: she had just been to Washington with Ellsberg. From their contacts at the Pentagon and in Congress, they had both deduced that the United States was absolutely going to go to war. "How much does an hour of satellite time cost?" she asked. I tried to explain that the $250 for a transponder rental for one hour does not include the costs of the office, the making of the tape, or the promotional work that needs to be done to let people know it's coming. "OK," she said determinedly ignoring the implications of my accounting. "I'm putting a check in the mail for $300."

That was the first funding for the *Gulf Crisis TV Project,* which was officially organized at one of the weekly meetings of Paper Tiger the next week. It was a tense meeting. There were many members of the collective who felt that a war project would eat what scarce resources we had left for the year in a time when our state arts funding was being drastically reduced. Deep Dish staff had serious reservations about the problems that a last-minute, labor-intensive program could bring to what was supposed to be the lull after the fall series and before the spring series storm. However, so many had volunteered to do something to stop the mad rush to war that we did not have the heart to turn back.

Paper Tiger had some minimal production equipment and an off-line editing space. Deep Dish Television had a network of several hundred cable access stations who were willing and able to downlink programming that we sent. We knew that many cable access stations would run peace programming. We got a call from John Schwartz, who pledged that eight full-time cable channels would play alternative material in major urban centers—Baltimore, Los Angeles, Denver, etc. He sent us $5,000 for the rights to air and distribute any programs we would make over his mini-network. Having that first money meant that we could begin to cover some of the costs. So it was full steam ahead.

### October: Peace Talks Fail; U.S. Troop Strength Increased
*Paper Tiger Produces Two Programs on the Gulf Situation*

DDH: By early October the war fever that gripped the country energized the activist communities. People started calling Deep Dish about teach-ins, demonstrations, sit-ins, and draft resisters. I talked with Marty Lucas about all the tapes, like the one of the vets' rally in Woodstock, that were being made across the country. He knew some freelancers who also had footage—one worked in and around the United Nations press corps. She was gathering footage of interviews about negotiations to stop the war: footage that she knew no U.S. network would use, footage that discussed the arm-twisting going on behind the scenes at the United Nations. The Ninth Street Theater was working on performances about the war buildup. The Paper Tiger office in San Francisco was already talking about doing coverage of the anti-war activities there. We started making lists of possible segments for an anti-war program.

SF: A coalition working out of former Attorney General Ramsey Clark's office taped a teach-in at Cooper Union. We edited it into a half hour and transmitted it on cable locally, and sent it to San Francisco, Los Angeles, Chicago, Springfield, Washington, and several other cities as a teaching-activist tool, but once we did that, people started sending us material back. Our circle was circulating many tapes. By this time we were working with the Vietnam Vets against the War, the Coalition to End U.S. Intervention in the Middle East, the War Resisters League, and Hands Off.

DDH: The offices of both Paper Tiger and Deep Dish are in the same building as the War Resisters League. WRL, while a cordial neighbor for over five years, had scarcely taken notice of our media work, as it did not fall within the standard Left classifications of "organizing." However, with the coming of the war, we began to collaborate on many aspects of the anti-war activities, exchanging information and resources on a daily basis. We helped to promote their activities, and we were listed in their mailings. We designed promos for their campaign to help soldiers who wanted to become conscientious objectors, and we agreed to place in our programs a public service announcement calling for anti-war tax resistance. The WRL finally understood that our media work was a form of organizing and that we could work together very constructively.

## November: Bush Doubles the Number of U.S. Troops in the Gulf
*Gulf Crisis TV Project Officially Formed, Sends Out Call for Tapes*

SF: When I put together the list of all the footage we had, it was easy to see that we could mobilize support for a national project about the crisis in the Gulf. DeeDee, Cathy, Marty, and

I came together with the idea for a collaborative series. We needed a call for tapes that would go out across the country to let people know that they could send material to us, to transmit on the Deep Dish TV Satellite Network.

DDH: Cathy Scott designed the call for tapes and with Martha Wallner wrote several proposals for funding. Marty and Cathy organized teams of producers for four programs: Chris Hoover and Simone Farkhondeh to work on the media distortions, Jen and Cathy to focus on veterans and military resistance, Ilona and I to give an overview of the history and current situation, and Marty and Cathy to work on the connection to oil. We saw our roles as coordinating producers— putting together material from others around the country. Within two weeks we received over 130 tapes from as many locations.

CS: It was clear that Paper Tiger was speaking back to the mainstream media—which was ignoring war resistance. It was obvious that we needed a national organizing media effort to make the opposition to the war plans a visible thing. We wanted to empower the people who were already out there working to stop the war, to show them that there were many other people around the country who shared their thinking.

ML: In 1982 during the Israeli invasion of Lebanon, I had the experience of going to the Middle East with video producer Ilan Ziv to work on an independent documentary. On our return we put together a tape about the war which we made available to PBS stations, announcing it on the PBS internal DACS (electronic mail) system and uplinking on public TV's satellite system. We followed up with more DACS publicity and calls to stations around the country. We got several stations to run the show. So I knew that PBS had this "soft feed" option (a "hard feed" comes from a station) for independent producers to get access to the PBS system.

## December: Bush Gives Iraq an Ultimatum of January 15
*Gulf Crisis TV Project Links Up with National Anti-war Organizing Efforts; J. Roderick MacArthur Foundation Gives $20,000 to GCTVP; FBI Starts File*

ML: We had been working since September in a corner of the Paper Tiger office. With funding we would be able to pay people to organize, send out the massive outreach mailings, book satellite time, and buy videotape for our one camera and our edit system.

CS: On December 1 there was a national meeting of hundreds of organizers from around the country held at Riverside Church. We were put on the agenda of the plenary session to explain what we were going to do with our national media project. We made "activist guides" to "take control of your TV set," which explained three different things: how people could get the GCTVP shows in their local communities, how they could contribute to the shows, and how they could use camcorders to make their own programs. Our project was endorsed by both the Coalition to Stop U.S. Intervention in the Middle East and the Campaign for Peace in the Middle East. It was one of the tragedies of the anti-war mobilization that a bitter rift developed in the Left. Two separate groups had been formed, and two demonstrations were held later as a result of this squabbling. The GCTVP office became the one organization with good relations with *both* of the peace movements, on occasion acting as a liaison between them.

DDH: In 1982 at the June 12 peace demonstration (the largest in U.S. history) I was part of a group that uplinked the rally live to those PBS stations brave enough to take it (over fifty did). However, the June 12 mobilization committee would rather give press passes to NBC than to a group of peacenik Videofreex. In those days it was hard to get alternative media taken seriously. We were never invited to any of the organizational meetings nor allowed to make suggestions about press coverage. During the rally our sound lines were cut by rally personnel. There was a total lack of support for or even interest in our project of building an alternative network for the movement. Since 1990, however, there has been a discovery of the potential of activist video. In this case the coordinators for the anti-war actions felt that our effort was important enough to warrant full participation in the initial stages of organization.

SF: At the PTTV office the phone lines were ringing off the hook. The FedEx person was bringing in bags of tapes. We found out about actions all over . . . there was an incredible energy in the office. While the tapes were coming in, we had to log them and begin the editing and at the same time do outreach to make sure people knew how to get the programs, and to make sure that the cable stations would downlink them.

DDH: Because we were in the War Resisters League building, we were in close contact with military resisters. Every day National Guard members, enlisted men, and draft-age youth came by the building for information and counseling. On several occasions crews from GCTVP taped counseling sessions for inclusion in the series, but also to document these important meetings for circulation within the organization.

Peace activists were working directly with videomakers and public access coordinators, realizing, many for the first time, the potential of this collaboration. In the past the recalcitrant attitudes toward technology of many movement organizers have fostered a deep distrust of all media. This time they began to understand the importance of collaboration with activist videomakers. They found that we could work together very effectively: we were exchanging information and resources on a daily basis. We helped to promote their activities, and we were listed in their mailings. We designed promos for their 800 numbers for those interested in getting out of the military, and we made a public service announcement for tax resistance to military expenditures as a break between half-hour segments on the programs.

Another aspect of the project was the outreach to PBS. Both Marty and I had had experience in uplinking to public television. I had worked with *The 90's*, which began in 1988 as a "maverick" feed to the PBS satellites. *The 90's* office in Chicago furnished us the list of those first seventy channels that had taken a chance and agreed to program *The 90's* for the first season. We worked closely with the new alternative PBS station in Philadelphia, WYBE. Program Director John Vernile and Station Manager Aaron Ezekiel agreed to sponsor GCTVP to the PBS system, and together with Deep Dish and Louise Gluck in Willow, New York, did heavy outreach to program directors, through cajoling phone calls, creative fax blitzing, and instigating local pressure groups in a successful assault on the PBS fortress. This resulted in over forty PBS stations carrying the series. These included major stations such as WNET in New York and KCET in Los Angeles, and others in Virginia, Florida, Texas, and Alaska. In addition many of them gave it multiple air plays: New York ran the series four times in very good time slots.

Jen Lion, a young producer who had studied with Sherry Milner at Hampshire College, had received the call for tapes while taping military resistance in Hawaii. She brought us excellent footage of Honolulu demonstrations and also brought herself and her new Sony 5000 camera for the duration of the war. She was one of many people over the course of the project who literally gave their all to the project. At times there would be three or four of us asleep on the floor of the office in the morning. By late December we had collected several Hi-8 cameras, a Super VHS or two, and an M3. In the coming months, with that base of equipment, we recorded literally hundreds of hours of teach-ins, interviews, and guerrilla theater in and around New York. This was a camcorder war all right.

When peace activists would call and ask us to tape their demonstration in Fort Wayne, for example, we'd say, call your local cable access organization, and if you can't get help there, borrow a camcorder from your aunt or cousin and tape it anyway. Many of the tapes we received were documents of town meetings, teach-ins, or demonstrations that were shot by participants who did not consider themselves video producers. We received material in every possible format: VHS, Super VHS, Betamax, Beta-Cam, 3/4, 3/4 SP, even 16 mm film.

ML: We divided into four groups of two producers; each pair would be responsible for one half hour. The shows were *War, Oil and Power, Operation Dissidence, Getting Out of the Sand Trap,* and *Bring the Troops Home.* In addition to the four of us, the group included Ilona Merber, Ramin Ashraf, Chris Hoover, and Jen Lion. The Deep Dish staff, Dolores Perez, Steve Pierce, and Lorna Johnson, helped with the up- and downlinks while Martha Wallner worked on funding and outreach. The Paper Tiger staff, Linda Ianconne and

May Ying Welsh, fielded calls and helped with local production.

### January 1–7, 1991: The United Nations Endorses Bush's Ultimatum
*GCTVP Programs Uplinked*

CS: We called more than 300 cable stations as well as hundreds of activist groups to tell them to encourage both the public access and the PBS stations in their communities to show the series. When a student in Greensboro, North Carolina, wanted to get the program, we explained about calling up the local cable station. The next day he went to a demonstration with fliers he'd made, telling people how to call the cable station and request the Gulf Crisis TV Project. The station received fifty calls and played the programs.

DDH: Our transmission date for the first two shows was January 7. We worked around the clock to prepare for the on-line edits. Fiona Boneham (who was on-line editor of most of the series) stayed through the night with more than one GCTVP producer to get the one-inch masters finished. Downtown Community Television and the Stand-By Project provided facilities at cost.

*The First Programs Were Completed and the Deep Dish Network Brought the Show to Hundreds of Cable Stations on January 7, 1991*

The first series aired on January 7—eight days before Bush's deadline of January 15. The response was beyond anything we expected: hundreds of grateful telephone calls and letters. The War Resisters League had to put more people on their phone lines. We could tell where the programs were running by the location of the calls: Austin, Fort Lauderdale, Kansas, Boston, Portland . . . But the success swamped the Deep Dish office, whose phone number was the tag line at the end of the programs. Key staff members were forced to stop important work just to answer the ever-ringing phone. It was impossible to get a line out: a new call would come in on the heels of the last.

The four lines were busy all the time. Requests for additional information, for dubs of tapes, for interviews taxed an already overworked and underpaid staff. The office became a nightmare of short tempers and long faces. Worst of all: the war seemed inevitable.

### January 7–10: Troops Mass on Iraq Border
*GCTVP Storms PBS Fortress*

ML: The largest PBS station, WNET in New York, repeated the series three times in the days just before the war began.

DDH: Mark Sugg, who produces a weekly program called *America's Defense Monitor* for the Center for Defense Information, shared his downlink list (and by sending us interviews and military footage). By building a database from *The 90's* and the Defense Monitor list, we were able to have a clear idea of which PBS stations would take risks and play controversial programming. It was the last week before the air war started. PBS had very little Gulf-related programming ready. There was a vacuum into which we leapt.

ML: The programs were on the air—all over the country. Many stations gave us multiple air plays. There was such a dearth of material, and such a high level of interest—or rather desperation—that the programs were received with a great deal of enthusiasm.

DDH: There was a snowball effect. The more the programming was shown, the more people wanted it. The fact that it was on WNET New York helped us with other PBS stations.

### January 10–15: U.S. Pushes for International
### Support for War
*GCTVP Reaches Japan, France, Canada, Australia, and Brazil*

DDH: We express mailed VHS copies to several key people around the world. There was an immediate response. In Japan activists made several hundred dubs and showed the programs in many large and small meetings. The tapes served as an organizing focus for anti-war activity.[61] The text of the

---

[61] "Interview with Tetsuo Kogawa," in Schiller et al., *Triumph of the Image.*

four programs was translated into Japanese and typed into the two biggest computer networks. This information went to thousands via electronic mail and became a base for organizing resistance to the war in Japan.

ML: Our outreach was successful in Canada, where peace movement people told a local producer for the Vision Network about the series. This ecumenical religious satellite network reaches 3.2 million households. They preempted two hours of their regular programming on January 15 to present the GCTVP programs back to back. Vision Director of Programming Peter Flemington said, "In light of concerns about the role played by the media in the unfolding of the entire crisis, it's the kind of programming we feel strongly compelled to present." In France Nathalie Magnan and others translated the tapes and organized screenings in Paris and several universities throughout the country.

DDH: The organizational liaison aspects of the project were highly successful. Over fifty stations worked with local peace activists around the country to produce their own local introductions to the GCTVP shows. These local programs, from Santa Barbara, California, to Somerville, Massachusetts, included panels with community peace organizers, camcorder activists, local draft resisters, and high school counselors. Many of these had interactive aspects—some took telephone calls, some showed camcorder footage of local demonstrations and teach-ins. Some groups, like townspeople in Doylestown, Pennsylvania, set up "soap-box" forums: participatory structures to be sure local opinions could be aired. San Francisco camcordists, led by Paper Tigers Jesse Drew and Carla Leshne, started a weekly program just to deal with the Bay area anti-war activities. Rob Danielson and others in Milwaukee did *nightly* programs.

## January 15 Midnight–January 30: WAR!
## U.S. Allies Pledge Millions for War Costs
*GCTVP Masses Troops for Second Series; Channel Four Pledges Thousands*

DDH: January 15 and the midnight deadline rolled in and with it the bombing sorties over Baghdad. The office became even more frantic. What would we do next? When are the next programs coming? everyone seemed to be asking. We had not planned to do any additional programs, but more field tapes came in, unsolicited. Great tapes. Interviews with Chomsky. Demonstrations of 10,000 in San Diego, of thousands in Minneapolis. In the midst of our discussions of what to do next, we got a call from Channel Four in London. They wanted to buy rights to the first series for around $30,000. We had said in our initial contract with producers that any income would be spent on making more programs or more distribution. With the Channel Four money, we could go on. We decided to make six more programs and to try to get even more distribution of the four programs we had already made. We ordered 200 copies on VHS to satisfy all the hundreds of requests we were getting. We had the capital to bulk order so that we could sell them at home video prices.

ML: On Channel Four the four shows were condensed to one hour and shown back to back with a half hour about anti-war activism in Great Britain. The program had the highest ratings of the month, was reviewed in many major dailies, and inspired extensive viewer response. It even got Channel Four sued by a right-wing think tank (later dismissed). Acquisitions Director Alan Fountain suggested that it changed the tenor of debate around the war in England.

DDH: For the second series we tried to set up a structure that would take the heat off of the Deep Dish office. We were lucky to get a large space at cut-rate rent from Deborah Shaeffer and Larry Bogdanow. We hired additional office personnel and outreach staff. We borrowed desks, file cabinets, and shelves and set up an instant office.

In assessing the first series, we all agreed that we had not done enough "affirmative action" in putting the production team together. We decided to try to bring more producers of color into the production for the second series. We brought on eight producers, many of whom were very young and had had little experience with the kind of compilation programming seen in our first series. Several of these new producers were familiar with the facilitating role of Deep Dish producers; some were new to group/collective work: they had only had experience with highly structured production organizations, and the anarchy and open-ended quality of the office structure was perceived as a problem.

The goals were even bigger this time around, and the situation of the real war going on added tremendous stress to everyone involved in the project. For the first series we had been motivated with the urgent need to *stop* the war from happening. Once it had started with its inexorable pattern of destruction and violence, it was hard to feel any power to effect the outcome. Many people were feeling this way and had needed the first series because of the hope it projected by bearing witness to the vital resistance that many in this country had maintained. The mainstream coverage was getting worse and worse. People urged us to keep providing an alternative.

In the first series we were able to use a number of short video art pieces: in the second series most of the segments submitted were in standard documentary format. (Was it that people felt that with a real war going on they had to be more serious?) Most of the experimental pieces that we used in the second series were initiated in New York by the coordinating producers themselves.

SF: One of the things that was encouraging was talking to people all over the country who were active in their communities, knowing that we were sending shows that they were going to use. Meanwhile, just watching television, the disinformation at the time was so angering and oppressive that we had to keep going.

DDH: The contrast between the kind of information that we were able to provide and what was on the tube every night became more and more apparent. The networks' coverage alternated between close-ups from the nose of the bombs and bravura strategy sessions among retired generals. While the polls showed that a wide majority supported the war, often there were polls that showed people distrusting the media. For many on the Left, the rage at the war turned to rage against the media. Cathy Scott, May Ying Welsh, and other Paper Tiger people along with Fairness and Accuracy in Reporting became involved in organizing a huge demonstration on January 28: *Operation Storm the Media*. This historic confrontation with the information industry brought thousands to the streets in front of the network offices in New York in the largest outpouring of anger against the media in U.S. history. It was similar to the scenes in the film *Network* when crowds chant "We're not going to take it anymore!" That demonstration was the largest ever organized in the United States with the media as a focus. It gave us hope that the public could be mobilized around information issues.

One of the themes of the demonstration was the camcorder. Ellen Spiro, Martha Wallner, May Ying, and others made camcorder commando vests from neon camouflage fabric with stenciled slogans: Make Video Not War! Camcorder Commandos! Take Control of Your TV Set!

### February: Air War Intensifies; Bombs Hit Shelter, Killing Hundreds of Women and Children
*GCTVP Suffers Information Overload; Tension and Stress Exhaust Staff*

DDH: The GCTVP office became a sort of clearing house for both media activities and activist actions in general. Hundreds of tapes were sent in, even though we never did a general tape solicitation for the second series. Dozens of volunteers who had heard vaguely about the project and wanted to do something against the war signed up to log tapes or work in the office. The production staff became so large that it was difficult to keep the communication lines open. There was wasted effort on many levels. People would log a tape that was perfect for one of the programs, but the program producers would not have the time to read the logs or check the incoming stacks. Research was requested and done by highly qualified and talented volunteers whose work still languishes in countless files of statistics, dates, and clippings at a storage space in Manhattan. Information was gathered but not retrieved. Producers in other cities were asked to shoot certain sequences. Many of those who worked hard in compliance with those requests were never acknowledged, and their tapes only scanned in fast forward and never used. It was an overload of information. The kind of overload and production panic that we experienced was probably inevitable given the stress, the urgency, and the absence of hierarchical structure.

CS: Paper Tiger and Deep Dish have been working for years to democratize the media and to talk about issues like the "war at home." We had a core group who knew each other and had worked together, and matched their effort with the work of people all around the country.

DDH: We were invited to show the first series at Mediumoperatif at the Berlin Film Festival. By opting for discount tickets we were able to juggle the fares to allow both Panamanian producer CheChé Martinez and me to go. CheChé toured many of the U.S. bases in Germany interviewing dissident soldiers and volunteers in the extensive AWOL support structure set up by peace organizations in Europe for the *Just Say No!* program. One of the AWOL soldiers hung out with us in Berlin. He was just a scared kid from the area around San Diego, trying to get to college with an ROTC scholarship. Getting to know him certainly brought the war home to us.

ML: We hoped that press coverage would help with extending the network for the second series. Maggie Smith put together an aggressive publicity campaign designed to give the project recognition as the first satellite anti-war organizing effort. The major press organizations were as reluctant to cover the TV project as they were to cover the resistance to the war. Ultimately the strong popular response to PBS and cable showings did inspire widespread press coverage. In the initial stages of the second series we tried to set up a structure to produce six half-hour segments in six weeks starting with a feed on February 19. We had nine additional producers: Fusun Ateser, Tony Avalos, Ludger Balant, Yanni Damianos, Indu Krishnan, Victoria Maldonado, CheChé Martinez, Amy Melnick, and Dawn Suggs. We also had Abdul Wahid Cush and Claudia de Megret doing full-time outreach.

DDH: The office had aspirations of being nonhierarchical, but there were obvious differences at work: between those with steady jobs or income sources and those desperate for a place to sleep at night; between those with families and other responsibilities and those who could literally give their all to the project; between those from a highly educated film school background and those with a nitty-gritty rough-and-ready Paper Tiger approach. There were differences of age: those with thirty years experience in independent production and those who had had their hands on a camera for a few months. There was the group that had made the first series and those who were brought in later. The funding was insecure so the material basis of the project was always at risk. People never knew if they would be paid. However one tried to "equalize" the situation, those who initiated the project and who were writing the proposals for the continued funding had a vested interest in determining the conclusion, and an obvious background of experience and confidence. Because of a host of tensions and contradictions, many of the new producers felt less like collaborators and less empowered in the larger project structure. It was tense.

Despite, or perhaps because of, the difficult circumstances, there was a healthy autonomy given to the individual shows, which turned out very strong, often brilliant. More difficult were the personnel relations between show producers and among the larger group. It had been naive at best to assume that twelve headstrong creative people could be almost randomly paired to make a television series in a very short time. It was even more naive to expect difficult racial and national tensions to be erased easily in a common project.

ML: For the second series we developed topics which we felt were being ignored by the mass media and divided into groups to produce the shows. We had moved without fully realizing it into a situation of producing shows as individual producers without creating a framework for collective discussion of the editorial content or direction of the shows. The combination of the deadline pressure and the distance between producers' expectations and the reality of resources created real problems. Nevertheless, one by one the deadlines were met and the programs uplinked to the Deep Dish network as the ground war came and went.

DDH: The first program of the second series, *Manufacturing the Enemy*, looked at the violence and racism that was being aimed at Arab Americans. Testimonies from Arab students, store owners, and dishwashers were compared with memories of the Second World War experiences of Japanese Americans. The final program, *Global Dissent*, contained footage from over a dozen countries, documenting demonstrations of reaction to the war in such places as Taiwan, the Philippines, Spain, Korea, and France. Nathalie Magnan, who coordinated screenings of both series in France, remarked that the second series was much stronger, more angry, more defiant. She said the message was, "OK guys, we tried to be polite the first time around, and you went to war anyway; well, now we're going to let you have it!"

ML: Although the level of the demand for tapes was unexpected, we produced 500 copies of the first series immediately and started sending them out to callers for $20. The growing publicity brought new demands for copies, and we began distributing from San Francisco as well as New York. We estimate that 2,000 copies of the first series were distributed in the United States and Japan. Vision TV in Canada transmitted them to the continent. Since the war's end the ten shows have continued to go out to festivals, universities, media centers, and activists around the country.[62]

DDH: Other distribution strategies included showing tapes in a sixties-type "media bus" in shopping mall parking lots, and even projecting them on the wall of KQED, the public television station in San Francisco, that had refused to air it. I think the GCTVP tapes were seen by more people in a shorter time than any other independently produced and distributed video work in the history of the medium. The series contained the work of over a hundred producers, from dozens of locations. The work ranged from rallies, to comedians, to guerrilla theater, to intimate interviews, to didactic charts and history texts. Artists such as Seth Tobanken and Mary Feaster made graphics for the series. Performance artists Paul Zaloom and Papoleto Melendez created performance pieces. Norman Cowie, Joel Katz, Tony Avalos, and Karen Ranucci made short video art pieces. The programs bristle with anger and outrage, but also have humor, music, and dramatic mo-

---

[62] The programs are now often used in conjunction with the anniversary of the war.

ments. They have testimony from such experts as Edward
Said, Noam Chomsky, Dessima Williams, Daniel Ellsberg,
and Grace Paley and heart-felt testimonies of GIs who were
willing to go to jail rather than fight. The War Resisters
League began a whole new campaign for resistance within the
military based on the calls that they received in response to
the series.

It was the special circumstances of the rush to stop the war
that energized the production. I'm not sure how applicable
our experiences are for future projects. Despite the admirable
solidarity of literally hundreds of producers, despite the often
glorious feats of editing and the astounding pace of distribution, many of us were left with a sense of failure. So much
energy was directed at making the series and the external
process of distribution that the internal group languished.
This is evident in the fact that there was no integration of the
talented corps of new producers into either Paper Tiger or
Deep Dish, nor any follow-up collaborative work among them.
And then there was the war. We hadn't stopped it. We hadn't
even made a dent in the U.S. war machine. The Left in general
in the U.S. is still reeling from the events of that winter.

The yellow ribbons are now faded. For supporters of the
military, the war was supposed to have been a glorious answer
to the Vietnam syndrome. But maybe the Iraq syndrome will
be the ultimate questioning of the U.S. military. The fact that
the war was summarily dismissed from the organs of the consciousness industry may be because the American people are
beginning to sense the reality of the war. The image of its effect on Iraq has been seared into their brains with undeniably
horrifying photojournalism of dying children and ecological
devastation.[63]

---

[63] The war came and went, but it wasn't without a response. We responded, and our response is often rebroadcast on many cable systems
around the country each January on the anniversary of the war. Meanwhile
the price of camcorders is dropping. We're still here. And needless to say,
the experience of GCTVP informed the world nine years later in the days of
protest against the WTO in Seattle (see Section 9, "Gathering Storm").
Many of the people who had participated in the Gulf Crisis TV Project also
worked in Seattle and elsewhere, setting up the independent media centers
and the corresponding www.indymedia.org.

(Above): "We're Mad As Hell, and We're Not Going to Take It Anymore": The Media Demonstration against Operation Desert Storm, Time Square, 1991. (Below): Gulf Crisis TV Project: Anti-war hotline, 1991.

# 5
# Public Space/Public Sphere: Infrastructures for Resistance

Blue Mountain Retreat. Front row, from left: Lynn Chadwick, Jeremy Smith, John Schwarz, Omar Wassau, Patrice O'Neill, Christine Triano, Alan Hunter. Second row, from left: Rory O'connor, Janine Jackson, Loretta Ross, Mark Weiss, unknown, unknown. Third row, from left: Mona Jimenez, Don Hazen, David Mendoza, Danny Schecter, May Ying Welsh. Back row, from left: David Jenson, Jay Harris, Brian Drolet, unknown, Jeff Cohen, Patty Walter, Ron Williams, unknown. *(Author)*

# Introduction

IN THIS AGE of what is euphemistically called globalization, there is little space that is not commercialized, scarce time that is not metered, few venues that are not defined by profit. Even the floor of the supermarket now has huge plastic ad-mats. In order to have alternative voices, some sort of public infrastructure and support is necessary. The essays in this section look at ways in which alternative public media are initiated, constructed, and sustained.

In the mid-1970s there was an attempt to create a series addressing women's issues on U.S. public television: *Woman Alive*, co-produced by Joan Shigekawa and Ronnie Eldridge. After making a successful pilot and securing initial planning money, the series floundered, unable to get the needed corporate "matching funds." Corporate America viewed "women's programming" as too controversial. Even when the producers did get an offer, PBS made them turn it down. The offered funding was from Ortho Pharmaceuticals, makers of birth control pills.[1] That sort of funding was deemed a "conflict of interest," and the administrators suggested that the producers approach Revlon (which was not thought of as a conflict of interest.) Apparently the notion of a program that might liberate women was not considered the right stuff to get women to buy more cosmetics. The series was scrapped. Years later women have still had short shrift from PBS. Ken Burns was chosen to tell the story of the women's suffrage movement.

"Quilted and Patched in the New World Order" was written for a conference on women in Mexico, Canada, and the United States at UNAM in Mexico City. It looks at the status of women in the independent film community in the United States. "Re-

---

[1] This episode was revealed in "Woman Cooking, Woman Spending, but Not 'Woman Alive': Corporate Underwriters Buy an Image on PBS," by Rebecca Moore in *Televisions* 4, no. 1 (1976).

wiring: Women's Activism in the Age of Electronic Repression" looks at the potential and the difficulties for women in the struggle for public space in a "rewired" world.

One of the truisms of the MacBride research (see Section 3) was that the market cannot provide egalitarian communication venues. *Many Voices, One World*[2] suggests setting up training programs and access facilities for underserved groups. This has been the agenda of many non-profits in the independent media community, funded through private foundations and state and national arts councils. "Green Grow the Rushes, O" compares public funding for alternative media to the creation of community gardens. It was written in recognition of twenty-five years of the media program at the New York State Council on the Arts. "When You're Alone and Life Is Makin' You Sad" looks at one of the institutions which has provided sustenance for alternative media. Downtown Community Television has provided long-term sustained assistance to thousands of producers.

"A Public Response to the 'Confidential Questionnaire' from a Foundation" is about foundation support for media arts. I had received a questionnaire which I feared meant the end of a unique and useful program of grants to independent producers. It is a manifesto of sorts directed to progressive foundations.

The hard work of selfless administrators in media centers and funding organizations at access stations was the inspiration for "Finding Strength in Community," a keynote address I made to a gathering of Northeast cable access producers and staff in Burlington, Vermont. On the way to the meeting, I drove by several prisons. I contrast the readiness of politicians to fund prisons and the hardware of repression with the lack of support and the difficult struggles of those who create and maintain spaces and equipment for public media—that is, the local cable access companies whose administrators were at that conference. I was struck by the energy and dedication of those attending, and the authentic community that can thrive in community media centers.

---

[2] See Section 3, "The Willow Declaration."

"Whittling Away at the Public Sphere" is a look at the Whittle Company and their introduction of commercially sponsored daily TV viewing to public schools. Oil corporations have saturated schools with sponsored films and greenwashing propaganda such as Exxon's coloring book on wildlife in Alaska, or the Long Island Lighting Company, builder of the Shoreham Nuclear Power Plant, comic book about how great nuclear power is. Commercial messages have made their way into public education for many years, but the imposition of required watching of sneaker commercials is a new level of egregious profiteering off children and public education.

# Quilted and Patched in the New World Order: Women and Media in the United States

## October 1996

IN THE EARLY SEVENTIES a series of conferences and seminars in Chicago, the Women's Building in Los Angeles, a festival in New York, and a myriad of events initiated an era of appreciation and interest in films by women. Since that time the historical and critical arenas of feminist film have developed, even if the actual production credits remain paltry. Women are more aware of the contributions of such pioneers as Alice Guy Blanche, who in the 1910s was the most powerful and prolific of U.S. filmmakers from her studio in Fort Lee, New Jersey. The work of Ida Lupino, actress/director, has been considered in detail. There was a retrospective of the work of Shirley Clarke, whose films *The Cool World, The Connection*, and *Portrait of Jason* broke new ground in the docudrama.[3]

There is a booming business in feminist film criticism. Volumes have been written about the portrayal of women in film and television. At the annual conference of Consoling Passions, an organization dedicated explicitly to a feminist critique of television, one might hear, for example, four scholarly papers about themes of resistance in *Rosanne,* or panels on implied lesbian attractions in the glances of soap opera heroines.

In Hollywood and feature production in New York, there are more women directors now and certainly more women producers, and women in powerful positions at the studios.

---

[3] See Section 1, "Remembering Shirley."

However, I wonder if these roles do not also reflect the changing power shifts in feature production and the television industry. Perhaps women are useful in negotiating the deals between the banks, the corporations, and the agencies that form the true nexus of production. In the past the power was with the studios and through them the producers. In the current situation, the producers function more as midwives for the investors. And we all know what good midwives women are. If we trace the positions of women up the actual power hierarchy, we soon notice fewer women at the level of management in the banks and multinational corporations who control production. The actual number of women who direct TV episodes and feature films is still a tiny fraction.

There is a sort of film that is consciously aimed at the women's market: the secret to success seems to be including many scenes of food preparation and lots of intergenerational hugging. Certainly including food or crafts in the title doesn't hurt. *Fried Green Tomatoes* and *American Quilt* were ones that did well. The Mexican film *Like Water for Chocolate* broke the record for Mexican imports at U.S. box offices and around the world. Films from popular books written by women have also had success: *The Joy Luck Club* and *Waiting to Exhale* are "women's films" that boomed at the cineplexes. However, it is noteworthy that both of these films, though taken from popular books written by accomplished women authors, were directed by men, albeit men within the "multicultural" framework: a Chinese man and a gay black actor. Actually, the Terry McMillan novel had been promised to Julie Dash, whose *Daughters of the Dust* is a visionary and poetic re-creation of those popular hugs and culinary feasts. Dash, however, transcends that limited genre and was obviously deemed too risky to trust with such a popular novel.

Several women who started out as risk-takers such as Martha Coolidge and Lizzie Borden have made it in Hollywood by conforming to given genres. Lizzie moved from her precise and startling look at prostitution in *Working Girls* to a sleazy murder mystery, à la *Blow-Up*. *Love Crimes* is as full of gratuitous violence and breast displays as any drive-in double feature. Is it really so liberating that in this case the woman has the magnifying glass? Martha Coolidge does cineplex teen films about valley girls, malls, and computer whizzes, in stark contrast to her interesting first film, *Not a Pretty Picture*, an autobiographical piece about date rape.

Yvonne Rainer, a dancer who began filmmaking about the time that Lizzie Borden made her brilliant independent feature *Born in Flames*, is still taking risks. Her film *MURDER and murder* is about industrial and corporate murder in the form of toxic waste, through the story of a lesbian couple, one of whom has a mastectomy. Her 1993 film *Privilege* looked at menopause, racism, and violence against women. Her films are elaborately conceived and exquisitely choreographed intellectual gambits. They weave in and out of au courant theory with a wry twisted thread. Despite their dependency on language (text on screen, text as track, and text as formalized dialogue), they are beautifully composed and shot, and postmodern in the good sense of that term: self-conscious, witty, and eclectic. Shulea Cheang's film *Fresh Kill* (why do many of these women's films use violence in titles?) is a post-postmodern punk romp through a neon industrial landscape where sushi chefs log on to a computer revolution while guerrilla videomakers take over network television to warn of radioactive California rolls. Neither Yvonne's nor Shulea's films are played in the plexes. They are, however, shown in universities, at women's conferences, and at film festivals. They are not on television, except on Channel Four in Britain, which has helped to subsidize both of their work. Yvonne has also received funding from German television.

As for television in the United States, women are in relatively equal positions of power in one arena: in public access, where many women are directing local access centers, making community programs, and teaching young and old how to create media: truly "midwife"-type roles. Though ridiculed in the multinational corporate press, public access is growing stronger and more important. Women all over the country do weekly programs on health, on survival skills against rape and brutality, and on women's history. Dyke TV is one of the most successful weekly programs; it is distributed to public access and a few public television stations, a grassroots network with a lively following. Local sponsors do local fundraising and local reports.

Experimental videomakers such as Sherry Millner often use "family" subjects such as her daughter Nadja's attempt to learn the alphabet. In *Out of the Mouths of Babes*, Millner connects her own domestic scenes to the larger world by juxtaposing a scene from an old war movie of Ronald Reagan learning the proper targets for air combat with text about his war against Nicaragua.

Women have taken an active role in political documentaries. Barbara Kopple and Barbara Trent have both earned Academy Awards for their hard-hitting work: Kopple on striking workers (*Harlan County* and *American Dream*), and Trent, with the assistance of Panamanian producer CheChé Martinez, on the U.S. invasion of Panama and the firebombing of the civilian barrio of El Chorillo (*The Panama Deception*). They also pioneered bringing their work to mainstream theaters and video stores through dogged persistence and sleepless nights of mailings and press releases.

The role of women in pushing for alternative distribution has been crucial. New Day Films and Women Make Movies have both enabled hundreds of thousands of high school and university students to watch media by women. These distribution companies have continued to seek out mailing lists of the women's movement, women's studies classes, and activist organizations. Their strategies have assisted not only U.S. media makers, but also women from around the world whose films and videos they now also distribute. Karen Ranucci has been doing a similar job with films from Latin America. Her LAVA (Latin American Video Archives) provide alternative viewing for many schools and groups, and a small but significant stream of income for Latin American media groups.

Though dominated by white guys in their twenties, the Internet "revolution" includes many women's web pages, chat rooms, and news groups. Reactionaries are also on the Internet, and much of their rhetoric is aimed at women. The

Promise Keepers, a men's organization, proposes putting women back in the kitchen and nursery. Some of their propaganda openly promotes spousal abuse: "You need to tell her who is boss!"

Less explicitly, but as misogynist and ubiquitous, is the hardware culture of the Internet and the world of "new technology." Looking beyond the bright cheer of the neon graphics, we can see that the past covers of *Wired Magazine* and the articles contained therein are almost 100 percent male oriented. This "hardware" publication depends on ads from the corporations who design and build the uranium bullets and personnel bombs of the Gulf War and El Chorillo—the same U.S. corporations that are now selling weaponry and attack helicopters to the Mexican and Colombian military, some of it made in the NAFTA factories along the border. More and more highly complex technology is made in those *maquila* factories,[4] where women are the chosen workforce: more docile, less likely to unionize, and with proven small muscle skills for careful work. Like quilting. The *maquiladora* women do not have access to the World Wide Web, nor are they privy to the negotiations of the International Monetary Fund, the World Bank, and the World Trade Organization, where their wages and work are quartered and drawn.

---

[4] The *maquila* factories have sprung up along the U.S.-Mexican border, especially in Tijuana and El Paso.

Flo Kennedy reads the U.S. press on South Africa at the Whitney Museum's live Paper Tiger show, 1985. *(Diane Neumaier)*

# Rewiring: Women's Activism in the Age of Electronic Repression—Ruminations on Utopia/Dystopia

## Presentation to a Conference on Women and Art Held at Yerba Buena Cultural Center

> Your body is a battleground.
>
> Barbara Kruger Poster

My MOTHER was an architect. She had a problematic career: polio struck when she was in her twenties, leaving her back weak and little strength in her arms. Sitting at a drafting table was hell. Beyond her physical problems, there were the difficulties she had as a woman working in what was pretty much a man's profession. She suffered a lot but kept up her work until well into her seventies, taking remodeling jobs and offering advice and assistance to small business people wishing to expand their offices.

My legacy from her sometimes manifests as a preoccupation with space and spatial relationships. They count, she always said. The physical place of a conference is quite important, and the configuration of its locus is as strong a determinant as the intellectual content. The Yerba Buena Center is a difficult space for creating a sense of community. While it is obviously a useful hall for dance or music performances, it is somewhat problematic for an exchange of ideas. The mammoth stage calls for stage lights, which are designed to separate performers from the audience. At the conference microphones were conveniently placed in the audience, but from the cavernous tiers audience comments seemed like coughs at a concert—a bit out of place. The lighting and the configuration of the stage worked against a true dialogue, but there were many lively moments in which the passion and intensity of the participants (both those on the stage and those in the audience) transcended the architectural and technical difficulties.

The location had a sense of grandiosity and importance. The large crowd of enthusiastic women was so close to the center of power in San Francisco that there were moments in the sunny lobby when it seemed that we owned the city. But the reality is that women are not in power. Affirmative action is being dismantled. Because much of the public's attention has addressed the impact of this on persons of color, no one mentions the degree to which women will be impacted by these cutbacks. Head Start programs are being cut. An all-out attack is being launched against abortions. This is a difficult time for women. In this age of Rush Limbaugh and Newt Gingrich, women must come together. The battleground, as Kruger has asserted, is our bodies. It is generally assumed that the main targets for the radical Right are gays and abortion clinics, as those are the groups that have vocally fought back. However, listening to right-wing talk radio or to the tapes of militia meetings, one quickly realizes that women are by and large the primary target for the armies of the Right. And women have not reacted as a group to this assault.

We all know that there is a core of racism and jingoism in the conservative agenda. Rush Limbaugh's racism is couched in all kinds of covers: he is against immigrants, non-English speakers, welfare mothers, even basketball players. We all know what color those categories are, at least in his mind. Although he doesn't come out directly against dark races, African American activists have challenged his tirades. Women have not responded quickly enough.[5] He can nightly ridicule

---

[5] Eric Morgenthaler, " 'Dittoheads' All Over Make Rush Limbaugh Superstar of the Right," *Wall Street Journal*, June 28, 1993.

mothers-in-law, strong women, intellectual women, women rock musicians. He doesn't need to hide their gender. He only has to say "women's lib" to make his dittoed audience chuckle. He refers to feminists as "Feminazis." He would not dare to heap such approbation on a race. However, it is open season on women.

> *Harriet Dodge is a bearded lady. Her Bearded Lady Café is a community center. At the Yerba Buena Center she has a crowd of admirers in the audience. Like rock fans, they are close up to the stage at almost arm's length—just close enough to grab the sledgehammers she passes out to the crowd. Like Limbaugh's fans, they are primed to respond: they laugh at her every gesture. They are already giggling when she picks up a chair. They scream with peals of laughter as she throws it down and begins to smash it with a sledgehammer, a brilliant send-up of a macho rock concert. Harriet nourishes a community of young women artists at her dynamic restaurant with her down-home cooking. And she can use a sledgehammer when necessary.*

The photos of Nicole Simpson's[6] bleeding body are not directly shown on the courtroom cameras, but the image of her bruised face stares up from the tabloid racks in the supermarket. The defeated woman is a recurring image in the media. Even in sports, a predominant female image is Monica Seles slumped on her knees, her back bleeding from a knife attack. Behind these victim images persists an implicit question: What did they do to provoke it? Is Seles "genetically" linked into "ethnic" strife? The implication of the defense is that Nicole was too promiscuous for her own good. Somehow it is all our fault. Even the Oklahoma bombing was an event that was used against women. Two days after the "Heartland" explosion I was watching a morning talk show. The ads for PMS tonics meant that women were the show's target audience. On the program were two psychologists discussing workplace day-care centers. Dozens of children died in the one at the federal building. For these "experts," workplace day care is a dangerous concept. "See what can happen?" The TV show

---

[6] Murdered wife of O. J. Simpson, whose trial had been completed shortly before the conference.

audience went "Tsk, tsk." Somehow the Oklahoma City episode became an excuse for closing workplace day-care centers. The psychologists talked about the importance of keeping
small children at home. With Mom. The implication is that
women who have careers (and/or jobs to pay the rent) are
selfish and ignorant of the real needs of children. Whatever
happens, there are "experts" who will point out the problem:
women.

> Toni Lane talks about working in San Francisco housing proj-
> ects. Many of the young people who live there die before their
> time. Toni initiated a project of videotaping the funerals of crack
> violence victims. She projects slides—paintings of jail scenes.
> Jails are on the increase in California. More money is spent on
> incarceration than on education. Toni is an African American
> with a degree from the San Francisco Art Institute. Rather than
> teach in an art school or a university, she gives art lessons to kids
> from the projects. She has a storefront gallery for their paintings
> and sculpture.

While in San Francisco for the conference, I take a trip
down to the Mission District. This lively heart of the city has a
Latino population, now interspersed with the recent arrival of
artists and students. Tropical fruits and nopal, the edible cac-
tus, are available in the markets. Salsa and Tex-Mex music
mix with San Francisco heavy metal. Tourist that I am, I take
snapshots of two buildings: one is the new police station/de-
tention center, a heavy presence in the Mission community,
the other is the Women's Building, located just a few blocks
away.

On the corner opposite the police station is El Toro Ta-
queria. This place was "multicultural" before the term became a panel subject: a rare public center where one can
always see a mix not only of races, but of classes and gender
preferences. It now stands in direct confrontation with its
huge neighbor. The San Francisco police have staked out several acres of prime Mission real estate for a fort. Like the
Alamo, or Fort Apache in the Bronx, this place evokes John
Ford, or at least Clint Eastwood, and the cops of San Francisco have no trouble reenacting the frontier myth. This new

structure changes the mood of this part of Valencia Street. The bookstores and botanicas are still there; they just seem outsized. The "post-modern" architecture of the new station attempts a friendly visage, with a nod to Southwestern style and even a Native American prayer circle in the patio. But trying to make a police fort look cozy is like trying to soften the image of a jackbooted highway patrolman with a short-sleeve shirt. The power relations cannot be changed by a pastel rendering. Like some monster from a fifties Japanese horror movie, this guy has big feet. It doesn't fit in. Or maybe it does. The money and focus of the public sector is in law enforcement. Will there be a time when the resources of the city and state create a junior college in the Mission, or a day-care center, on the scale of this institution?

*Aida Mancillas worked on an Internet project in collaboration with Lynn Susholtz. They set up an intergenerational community history project with children from a San Diego public school. The young people write about their grandmothers and about the moon. Their words are shared with other communities hooked into Arts Wire and the Internet. San Diego has an active artists-in-residence program in the public schools. It is just this sort of program that will be eliminated in the current NEA cuts: the opportunities for kids to write about their dreams. To remember their grandmothers. But don't worry. Private industry will fill the gap. Instead of Aida and her poetry projects, they can have Sea-World and the Whittle's Channel One and the other corporations that penetrate our nation's schools to hawk their wares. Why have a poet-in-residence when you can have a cop from the fort up the street to tell the kids to just say no?*

Unlike the police station, the Women's Building did not require the demolition of a row of buildings to exist. And it presents an entirely different edifice. The individuality and quirkiness of the building's facade provide a complicated canvas for a mural that animates a colorful international community of women and children. The Women's Building mural creeps into the crevices of the intricate brick and curls around the columns, like wisteria vines, an organic thread that binds the building to the community. The building is in stark contrast to the police station/detention center a few blocks away.

The business of the detention center is to keep the neighborhood in check. The business of the Women's Building is to keep alive many of the women's organizations functioning throughout the Bay Area. The work done inside is the labor-intensive grind of the non-profit office: mailings, reports, meetings, and seminars. The women who work there form support committees and attend to emergencies. In the evening and on weekends there are events: poetry readings, conferences, art exhibits; most are extremely well attended and broadly appreciated.

> When Susan Cervantes—founder of the Precita Eyes Mural Association, where she teaches the history and practice of mural art—is introduced to the conference audience, there is a loud and passionate ovation. Susan worked along with six other women—Juana Alicia, Miranda Bergman, Edythe Boone, Meera Desai, Yvonne Littown, and Irene Perez—to create MaestraPeace, the mural project that adorns the Women's Building. She shows slides of the building to almost continuous applause from the audience. Photographs of the project have circulated worldwide: positive images of a broad range of strong and beautiful women and their children. The obvious popularity of the project is evinced by the resounding applause as the slides click past, each one a brilliant, colorful tribute to womanpower.

The right wing has made a videotape using scenes from Gay and Lesbian Pride Day parades: it shows flamboyant queens prancing around and a leather-decked crowd kissing one another. These images are bracketed with suited psychologists who talk of homosexuality as a "curable" illness. Over a million copies of The Homosexual Agenda have been distributed to parent groups, churches, and every member of the House of Representatives. The right wing has been able to forge a coalition of many groups with many differing factions, but with an overall agenda on which they can all agree: an agenda that is anti-women, anti-gay, anti-art. It is pro-repression and pro-racism. There is no viable movement in opposition that has been able to unify against this power.

Meetings such as the Feminist Activism and Art Conference help to encourage organizational infrastructure such as the Women's Building and a women's community in the Bay

Area. There are similar initiatives in many cities. A national structure for the women's movement seems lacking. The conference provided many useful workshops on organizing and community building, but there was scarcely any discussion of a national agenda for women. NOW is beleaguered, and the Women's Action Coalition seems to have disappeared from the scene. Where is the national leadership and the organizing to counter the attacks from the Right? The Right is more strategic: a comparable meeting of militias or of anti-abortionists would have included specific strategy sessions and a careful assessment of the national picture.

> *Rachel Rosenthal's performance piece was set in an apocalyptic future. The only contact with the outside was a fax machine, slowly and silently spewing out messages in a heap on the floor. E-mail and faxes have taken the place of many face-to-face meetings. Electronic tools are useful and strategic, but they won't solve the problems of alienation and loneliness.*

Allucquere Stone has described the problems of "virtual" realities—the idea that technology in and of itself is going to change the world for the better, as the myths surrounding VR would have it, is merely pernicious. It's just reifying technology as holy grail, turning salvation into hardware, something condensed and made visible through the telling and retellings of the cultural myths particular to us. These myths are extremely powerful because they carry in veiled form the entire cultural force and imagined progresses of our Western societies.[7]

At the campus where I teach stands the Supercomputer Center: a cold, sterile structure whose few mirror-glass windows stare blankly at the surrounding campus. There are satellite dishes on the roof and surveillance cameras on every corner. When I enter, I get the same feeling I had as an adolescent when I blundered into a boys clubhouse. The Supercomputer Center is for boys. Although there are women in the building, they are the receptionists, the secretaries, the stu-

---

[7] Allucquere Rosanne Stone, "Cyberdämmerung at Wellspring Systems," in *Immersed in Technology*, ed. Mary-Anne Moser (Cambridge, Mass.: MIT Press, 1994).

dent interns, or perhaps the graphic artists for the "soft" ware. The "real" users are men paid by huge grants from marketing firms (building perhaps a 3-D virtual supermarket for new interactive shopping channels) and Department of Energy contracts. A similar technology center at MIT is building virtual reality interrogation rooms. Who will be interrogated? Recent newspaper articles document the CIA's involvement in training the Guatemalan Army to interrogate "revolutionary" Indians. Soon the CIA will have something new from MIT to export to the Guatemalan Army or the Colombian or Peruvian military. Peasants are the targets of these designs, and, if past history is any indication, women will suffer a large part of that repression—most of the bodies in the mass graves at El Mazote were women and children. The UCSD Supercomputer

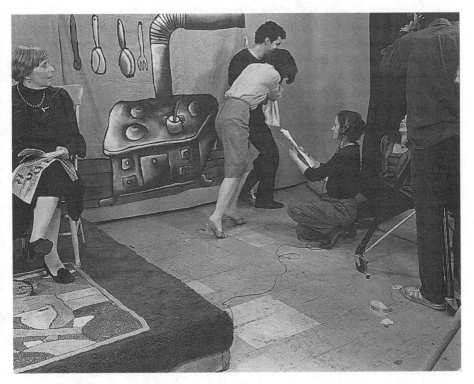

Diana Agosta directs actors for *Jean Franco Reads Mexican Novellas,* 1985. *(Diane Neumaier)*

Center and the MIT lab build serious hardware. This hardware needs soft targets.

I am not a Luddite. I try to use technology to empower my students and my colleagues and my ideas. I am tired of women and peasants being the targets of these machines. I am tired of the way the Right has used television in this country to slam women to the outer walls of the public sphere.

My mother had many setbacks in her life, but she always believed that things would get better for women. She had an abiding faith that the world would eventually be a better place for everyone. I'm not as sure about that as she was. These are hard times. The technology that gave my mother's generation so much faith has helped to make life worse for many people around the world including many here in the United States. That doesn't mean we shouldn't use technology. I'm not as sure as she was that things will inevitably get better, but I do know that things won't change unless we can work together, with paintbrushes and with faxes, with salads from the Bearded Lady Café, with satellites, with e-mail, and with sledgehammers.

# Green Grow the Rushes, O: State Funding for Media Arts[8]

## *December 1996*

WHEN STATE FUNDING for the arts started, lots of people squirmed. Art for money? State-sponsored art? A contradiction in terms! How can something so ephemeral be administered? How can something so inherently anarchistic as art be regulated? How can individualistic egos compete without killing each other?

I was never against it. What better use of public funds? Even bad art is better than guns and nuclear subs. The chaos of clashing egos is better than the corporate order of our heartless malls and offices. For all the fears about paternalism, co-optation, and censorship, the arts programs have demonstrated that goodwill and integrity can make a difference. Financial aid to the arts can be administered wisely with respect for the peer process. State arts programs have made a real difference to artists and their communities. Green grow the rushes, O.

Something has been right. The arts panels were "diverse" before that was a style, most administrators properly humble, the money meted out cautiously, the contracts presented without condescension and always with apologies that the grants were not larger. The media program has helped to sustain a vital independent film and video community: grants for equipment sharing, distribution initiatives, media community fo-

---

[8] Written on the occasion of the 25th anniversary of New York State Council on the Arts Media Program, a program which has been an important source of sustenance for innovative media arts despite threats from the religious reactionaries and suspicious state bureaucrats.

rums. A community of life and ideas in lands of grim asphalt and alienating shopping malls.

Green grow the rushes, O. Media art is a community garden whose lush vegetation belies her sooty soil and grimy light. Here is a place to dance and dream: a canopy whose vines shine with tropic exuberance under which grow nutritious tubers for hungry minds.

Like those who have saved and promoted community gardens, the media arts administrators have cultivated culture. There were regulations to buck, codes to develop, deals to be made in the dull halls of compromise and negotiation. There was an entire assembly to persuade and a public to nudge. There were pests to dodge and heavy boots to fend off. A salute to those gardeners with sharp hoes and green thumbs!

# When You're Alone and Life is Makin' You Sad, You Can Always Go—Downtown, or, 45 Degrees Fahrenheit: A Personal Salute to DCTV from a Dependent User[9]

## *May 1997*

IN THESE DAYS when there are increased pressures pulling cultural institutions into the "marketplace," Downtown Community Television is a bright, shining example of how the market can be subordinated to the larger goal of media justice. Although DCTV has profited from mass media commissions through Jon Alpert's clever use of HBO and NBC to shore up the coffers,[10] DCTV never succumbed to the glamour. The organization never went "Sundance": they never lost sight of their essential mission to empower others, to make changes in the world, to work for a more just and truthful society.

Before Manhattan Neighborhood Network was established and offered free access to equipment and studios, we relied on the slim resources of a few organizations to create material for our weekly public access shows in New York City: Electronic Arts Intermix, Young FilmMakers Foundation (now Film/Video Arts), and upstate there were Media Bus and the Experimental Television Center.

---

[9] Written on the twenty-fifth anniversary of Downtown Community Television, a media center housed in an old firehouse below Canal Street where literally tens of thousands have learned to make their own media.

[10] For many years DCTV founder Jon Alpert sold documentaries to NBC News and HBO, the funds from which contributed to keeping the media center open.

We couldn't have done it without them all, but DCTV was the base of support—the bottom line: always there with a last-minute camera, a microphone when we left ours in a cab, a tripod when the screws were missing from the one we begged off an NYU student, a light kit when ours never even got in the cab and was left on the street after we had loaded everything else.

In 1983 I spent many long nights lengthening into days at DCTV after the U.S. invasion of Grenada (the defeat of whose tiny army Reagan called the U.S. military's finest moment). Fearful of a similar invasion of Central America, Shulea Cheang, Karen Ranucci, Skip Blumberg, Eddie Becker, Joel Kovel, Joan Braderman, and I went to Managua to document the lives of U.S. citizens who lived and worked within the struggling Sandinista Revolution. We did the final edit of *Waiting for the Invasion: U.S. Citizens in Nicaragua* in the bleary hours between commercial users at Electric Films, DCTV's professional editing suite. Our film predicted an invasion of Nicaragua, which happened, though not in the overt way we or they anticipated. One thing I recall after we finished our edit was the painfully apologetic way that Keiko Tsuno, co-director of DCTV, would mention the bill when I booked time for a new project. Even Brownie the dog put his tail between his legs when Keiko got out her calculator. Well, I'm so sorry to mention it but . . . She'd say, "Well, if you don't have it now, don't worry . . ." Of course, she and we both knew that the four hours officially listed on the tab was a tiny fraction of the time we were really logged on. Electric Films was one place where corporate discounts were nonexistent: the few corporate clients they had paid through the nose and subsidized the camcorder commandos who jumped on at night.

During the production of the *Gulf Crisis TV Project* Paper Tiger producers practically lived at DCTV. We were such regulars that Brownie didn't even raise his head when we trudged up the stairs. We had elaborate methods of harassing the commercial customers so they would finish early and a signal system to notify each other when the coast was clear. We were even successful at reprogramming Keiko's calculator so that we could actually finish the on-line of the ten programs on the

Gulf War. Those programs remain an essential record of the strong resistance to the war. They would have been completely inconceivable without the generous assistance of DCTV.

Meanwhile Jon Alpert was fighting his own war at NBC. He had traveled to Iraq with Ramsey Clark. His powerful footage of wounded Iraqi children was just a bit too incriminating for the network's morning news program. It was our turn to feel guilty about our low bill, when we found out that Jon had been "removed" from the *Today* show for trying to bring the reality of that war to U.S. breakfast tables. We worried about DCTV being able to survive without the NBC commissions. We knew times were hard on Lafayette Street. The thermostat was turned down below 45 degrees Fahrenheit, and we borrowed down-filled vests to wear in the control room. It was a long winter. There was a crust of ice on Brownie's water bowl. Fiona, the editor, cut holes in the tips of her gloves for hitting in-points when it was so cold she could see her breath. We brought in hot soup and cocoa for everyone and searched our budget for ways to ante up a more realistic payback for the many hours we were logging on.

By 1989 people all over the world were making video. Shulea put together a series for Deep Dish on the video revolution in Asia. It begins with a demonstration at the Taiwan National TV System, where people literally threw their sets back at the station. Because Shulea was a certified DCTV editor, we were able to on-line it there within our paltry budget. Shulea's series looked at how the struggle for media access was a part of struggles for democracy in China, Hong Kong, the Philippines, Korea, and Taiwan. It was no longer possible to separate the military battles from the media battles.

We were gearing up for our own media wars in Manhattan. For twenty years Manhattan Cable had not provided proper cable access as stipulated by their franchise agreement. The corrupt New York City politicians never pressured the cable giant. However, with the borough presidency of Ruth Messinger, media activists saw an opportunity to draw the line in the sand, so to speak. During the Gulf War the U.S. Army had Norman Schwartzkopf, but we had Cathy Scott, whose strong leadership in the battle for the truth continued after the war, on a local level, with a fight to the finish for a cable access center in Manhattan. Hye Jung, May Ying, Martha Wallner, Simin Farkondeh, and others at DCTV, Paper Tiger, Not Channel Zero, and many media organizations were crucial in forcing the city and the cable corporation to provide the resource that now exists at Manhattan Neighborhood Network. MNN is the largest and best equipped of the media access centers in the United States (probably the world). Within its rosy studios thousands of hours of TV programming are produced each year, by the most diverse of producers: diverse in ethnicity, age, class, ideology, and production style.

That victory and the general (but underreported and unappreciated) success of public access in this country are phenomena which many around the world are now studying. There is a lively interest in the regulations, the process, and the concrete experience of media access in the United States. Brazil recently enacted laws requiring access channels, and throughout Europe countries are pushing the cable corporations for a piece of the public sphere. Every year hundreds of visitors come trooping through, staring in wonder at the media democracy that actually functions at MNN. These visitors go not only to MNN, but to DCTV, EVC, Women Make Movies, Dyke TV, Paper Tiger, and Deep Dish: from Japan, Korea, Germany, South Africa—from many corners of the globe. These visitors recognize that community media centers are the reason public access has been a success. DCTV pioneered community media making with their famous Thursday night classes twenty-five years ago. Each Thursday groups divide into classes of pre-production, camera, sound, and editing, switching the next week for the next class in the circuit. Alpert estimates that over 100,000 people have been certified as video producers in their program. Their faith and trust in their students proved that people can and should be given the means to make their own media. That faith has informed and inspired the many visiting administrators and coordinators of non-profit media centers.

Recent building renovations have revealed that the foundation of DCTV is as wobbly as some of the students' camera pans. Even though its building on Lafayette Street actually floats, bobbing up and down on waves of Wall Street effluent, for all of us videomakers, DCTV has been the rock upon which the independent media movement has been built. Without the strong model of open and dynamic community service that DCTV has provided, the public access movement would be a sterile governmental fortress, ensconced in hollow recitation of bureaucratic regulations.

In many countries videomakers of all ages and cultures are telling the truth of their own situations: stories of strip mining, of child sex industries, of sweatshops, agro-poisons, and police brutality. An example is a group in Guatemala. It is fashionable in academia, where I've hung out now and then, to question the existence of "truth," but Communicarte, a brave group of videomakers, find what they call *The Truth beneath the Earth* (*La Verdad sur la tierra*). They make videos of the exhumations of bodies from the massacres of the 1980s, videos to prove that the atrocities were committed and to know the final fate of the "disappeared." The videos moreover give strength to the living: these bodies must be looked at in the light of day, to prevent that sort of repression from happening ever again. *Nunca Mas!* as they say.

Subcommandante Marcos, leader of the Zapatista rebels, likened activist work to the people in *Fahrenheit 415* (the Ray Bradbury novel so eloquently made into a film by Truffaut).[11] In a repressive world of the future in which books are outlawed and burned, people memorize novels and poems so that they can pass them on. The Zapatistas know a thing or two about passing on the truth, having pioneered the use of the Internet as an activist tool from the time of their first insurrection.

The peasants of Chiapas are under constant pressure from the U.S.-trained and equipped Mexican army. For the indigenous people of Chiapas, "free trade" has meant machine guns, armored helicopters, and infrared heat-seeking bombs and missiles. They have used video to mobilize other Indian

---

[11] See Marcos, *The Word Is Our Weapon: Selected Writings of Subcomandante Marcos*, ed. J. Ponce de Leon (New York: Seven Stories Press, 2000).

communities and to defend themselves against the lies of Mexico's reactionary television. Two of the Zapatista videomakers have been jailed and tortured. Many videomakers in the so-called "developing" world live in constant threat of harassment, physical violence, or death. Here in the United States the main danger we face is having our hard disk crash, or the NEA budget being cut, or not making the short list on ITVS grants. The work of many video-astes in Guatemala, Haiti, Brazil, and Bangladesh is truly a matter of life and death.

One example is the case of a couple, Mario Calderon and Elsa Alvarado, from the DCTV of Bogata called CINEP (Center for Research and Popular Education), a Jesuit-sponsored organization that produces and distributes educational and environmental community video. Members of that group were the targets of a death squad bent on silencing their brave work of exposing the mining exploitation that is desecrating the land and water resources of several indigenous tribes in southern Colombia. Calderon and Alvarado and their parents were murdered in their own home; their child survived by hiding in a closet.

Threats and intimidation are the daily fare for many Third World documentarians. Our support and solidarity can help to shield them from the violence they face on a daily basis. Their brave video documents are often seen in the screening series at DCTV and other alternative media centers. In this age of e-mail and faxes it is important that we extend our hands and our web servers to our brothers and sisters around the world who are speaking truth to power.

# A Public Response to the "Confidential Questionnaire" from a Foundation

*A foundation which had funded one of my films asked me to answer a series of questions. The answers would be collated and summarized by a consultant team. To me, this seemed a way of defusing the ideas and opinions of artist-activists.*

I RECEIVED THE request for information with a bit of anxiety. Does this mean the end of the line for the media fellowships? Another media arts institution to hit the dust? Am I to give a requiem? Are my words a shovel of dirt on the coffin? My nagging fear paralyzes my response. And then there is the way I am approached: evaluation through "confidential questionnaire." It sounds like the sort of "professional assessment" a corporation does when they're about to lay off half the workforce. I have always been instinctively wary of filtering of "anonymous" information by paid consultants. While I appreciate the desire of the foundation to review independent media funding structures, I would rather give my own direct report than to have my opinions folded into any administered "overview." I am not ashamed of, nor am I intimidated by, having my name on my review. I understand that there are many artists who have been involved and that foundation personnel are probably too busy to read individual reports. I would like to be on record, at least, as an individual, not just part of a "summary," and to voice my, however appreciative, instinctively suspicious reactions to this process.

One way of assessing the media arts grants might have been public discussions. I am curious as to whether that was ever considered. While I understand that private foundations are not required to open their processes to public scrutiny, isn't open process at the root of democracy and justice? I also think that a frank and rational discussion of the dire state of the media arts field is long overdue.[12]

THE PANEL

One thing that I most appreciated about being on the selection panel was that it was an exchange between practicing artists/ arts curators/administrators and academics. Because of my position in an academic department (and my department is officially a social science department, not a visual arts or a media production department) I do get the opportunity to interact with intellectuals and researchers. Many of my peers in media production do not. Likewise, many academics, although they may use independent film and video in their classes, do not get many opportunities to meet with real live artists/producers.

I remember with pleasure and excitement the discussions that took place on my panel between, for example, Bruce Jenkins, film curator at the Walker Art Center in Minneapolis, and Jean Franco, professor of literature at Columbia University. Rather than being a dry exercise in theories of aesthetics, this was a lively discussion about a specific tape and a specific community and the relation between the viewer and the viewed. The specifics have faded with my memory, but the lessons about responsible documentation have become part of both my working credo and my teaching curriculum. The venues for these sorts of exchanges are rare. This is what has made the Flaherty International Film Seminars so valuable: a situation in which theory and practice are discussed around very concrete projects. While these discussions can be painful and on occasion emotionally charged, it is this sort of dialogue that "sharpens the contradictions" and our wits. Bravo.

---

[12] An interesting look at the history of media arts funding is Marita Sturken's "Private Money and Personal Influence: Howard Klein and the Rockefeller Foundation's Funding of the Media Arts," *Afterimage* 14, no. 6 (1987).

## THE PROBLEMS

I think that the nomination process has to be very carefully watched so that a sort of cronyism does not occur. This is certainly an ever-present danger. Expanding the sources for nominations is one obvious necessity. The second potential danger with the nomination process is almost the exact opposite of cronyism—let's call it the Protective Mom tendency. This is closely related to the White Guilt tendency. These tendencies are present not only in creating the nomination lists, but in the deliberations of the selection panel as well. The results are that older, tending-toward-middle-aged women nominate younger artists of color and often forget their own peers. As a result I think there are a number of extremely talented important women who have been left out either at the nomination level or at the panel level. This is a gender-specific issue because I think that older women tend to be more nurturing, protective, and "affirmative action–conscious" than successful white male artists. So there is a certain skewing that happens.

The last problem which I detect I will call the Coattails phenomenon. Certain artists will select certain topics not from any inherent interest in multicultural diversity or their stated proposal topic, but as a tactic to garner a grant. This does not necessarily have to be a bad thing. Perhaps even the experience of writing the grant proposal can be an illuminating experience for some of these people. But it sometimes means that once again white males are colonizing "the others," however "multicultural" their grant-writing skills.

## THE CONTEXT

There have been many changes in life in the United States in the past fifteen years, but one cannot say that arts funding has increased. There are a few valiant saplings in the midst of a devastated clear-cut forest. I see this program as a carefully constructed project to encourage diverse voices through providing access to the means of production of images and ideas.

By often providing the first and most difficult chunks of funding, it has been the catalyst for other funding, and the effects of that "ripple" are hard to assess. The projects produced have been important and useful contributions to cultural life in this country. But meanwhile the forest is gone.

ONE ANECDOTE AS TO THE STATE OF THE FIELD

I was talking with Liz Fink, a lawyer who represented the prisoners who were unjustly brutalized following the rebellion at Attica. Largely through her efforts, the Attica survivors are finally, after twenty-five years of court battles, vindicated as to the truth of their claims. As part of a memorial meeting for one of the men who had recently died, the section about Attica from *Eyes on the Prize* was shown. Fink said that as she watched it she realized that the film could not have been made and broadcast in today's climate. She perceived that the two sections of *Nation under Law, Eyes on the Prize II*—the parts about Attica and about Fred Hampton—would be seen as too dangerous in 1997. I think she is correct.

ANOTHER ANECDOTE

Lee Lew Lee, who is half Asian and half African American, recently completed a two-hour feature called *All Power to the People,* which was fully funded by German television and was broadcast on July 4 (to celebrate U.S. Independence Day) during prime time. The program was offered to other European countries through Eurosat, and seventeen countries picked up the feed and broadcast the program on prime time. Meanwhile here at home, he cannot get any TV stations or networks to even *look* at the program. The station executives just say, Don't bother sending it, when he tells them what the subject is: the history of the Black Panther Party.[13] The film recently

---

[13] The film was finally televised on BET (Black Entertainment Television) on their secondary feed in February 2001, four years after its completion.

won a special prize at a festival commemorating Paul Robe-
son in Newark, but it was not even shown in the festival: it
was too controversial.

WHERE DO WE GO FROM HERE?

The right wing in this country has no problem getting their
media funded. One report pointed out that right-wing foundations spend over 50 percent of their funds on media projects.
These projects often have radical implications: from trumped-
up diatribes against ecologists to scathing and false accusations against gays. The implicit racism in much of this work
has been instrumental in dismantling most of the gains of the
civil rights movement and the decimation of many social
agencies and organizations; it has meant the rollback of progressive legislation to a level pre–New Deal. The response
from so-called progressive foundations has been tepid and
completely inadequate. I would doubt if even 10 percent of
their grants go to media. A key problem is the unwillingness
to take a leadership role in providing media that can counter
this barrage of hate and vituperation. Liberal foundations
were instrumental in the development of public television in
the early days. Public television is a shadow of its former ideals, playing old Hollywood movies, British dramas, and cor-
porate-sponsored business advice. Last night we had *Shane*
playing on prime time. Surely there are issues and ideas that
need that precious space on what should be the public air.
There is still, to this day, no regular series on public television
that addresses the needs of women.[14] Do we need a Carnegie
III?[15] I think even that might be seen as "too dangerous" at
this time.

---

[14] One of the more egregious programming decisions was to give Ken
Burns the honor of retelling the history of the women's suffrage movement.

[15] The Carnegie Corporation sponsored two commissions to address the
goals and needs of public media in this country, Carnegie I and Carnegie II.

## THE GOOD NEWS

There are a few rays of hope. There was an enthusiastic response to the Media and Democracy Congress in San Francisco and its follow-up in New York. People from many media worlds (radio, press, television, film) are finally talking together. There is a new level of understanding of the overall problem of corporate media due to the courageous work of Chomsky, Herman, and Schiller and the useful documentation and research by such organizations as Fairness and Accuracy in Reporting (FAIR)[16] and Paper Tiger.

And last but not least is the world of public access, which continues to grow and prosper in cities all over the country, despite well-financed campaigns to undercut it. This movement has had virtually no support from progressive foundations. However, it has grown and developed through the volunteer efforts of thousands of media makers and community leaders. In stark contrast to the rapidly disappearing network of Media Arts Centers, the public access infrastructure is alive and well. As cities are refranchising, many are expanding the access services and air time. The Alliance for Community Media national conferences are authentic grassroots communication gatherings: the participation by people of all ages, colors, and ideologies is both refreshing and stimulating. Yes, democratic media is possible.

## THE GLOBAL SCENE

The lessons of public access in the United States are now used around the world. Brazil recently enacted legislation which requires mandatory public access channels. Japan sent a delegation to New York to visit DCTV, Manhattan Neighborhood Network, and Paper Tiger to begin to create an infrastructure in that country. Korea has enacted access legislation. Catalonia may be the first region in Spain to have access.

---

[16] FAIR publishes *Extra*, a monthly critique of the mass media, and organizes research into the bias and stereotypes in the press and electronic media.

The work of organizations such as Videazimut and the International Media Resource Exchange is of crucial importance in maintaining even the *idea* of democratic communication in an era of expanding global media monopolies. Support for organizations that assist grassroots efforts would increase global exchange and collaboration. There has been foundation support for some international centers of independent film-making that use Sundance as a model. This model may be useful for only a tiny handful of filmmakers, who then get hooked into the multinational co-production industry. The Sundances of the world are out of touch with the realities of local media production, particularly in the Third World. A teacher hired to lead workshops in a Sundance clone in South America came by Deep Dish to borrow tapes for the students. He said, "These tapes are much more realistic for the students than the work of Steven Spielberg." Support that would encourage community media projects and exchanges might be cost effective and ultimately have a profound effect. Rather than give "prizes" which might have the ultimate effect of taking media artists out of their communities, support of community media could enable local producers to stay within the cultural life of their countries and develop venues for popular participation in local media expression. The world of international co-production is fraught with contradictions, not the least of which is the fact that as funding expands across borders, local issues and local talent get cut out in an effort to "globalize" the "product." One of the interesting results of the kind of community media collaboration that has been fostered by groups such as Deep Dish and Vidéazimut has been finding interconnections within *local* production that strengthen local vision, at the same time pointing out global connections, not folding issues into some abstract "universal" subject.

DRUTHERS

If I had my druthers, there would be an artist-in-residence program at media access centers. That's how community television all began—with George Stoney and Red Burns sending out their students to start community media centers around the country. Much of the work now done on access is pretty dreary in terms of aesthetics and could benefit from collaboration with those who experiment and push the boundaries of media arts. I think it is important that foundations and cultural leaders stay aware of the access movement and think of ways of assisting this bold experiment in democracy.

SWEEPSTAKES OR POTLATCH?

We need bold leadership in creating structures to ensure that more than just a handful of capital-A "Artists" can express themselves. With the coming of digital imagery, with the explosion of computer networking, we need to strengthen this technology while preserving democracy and public culture. The Native Americans had the right idea about largess.

Ruben Blades, Panamanian singer and presidential candidate, gives 1985 "Indy" Award from the Association of Independent Video and Filmmakers to the author and Molly Kovel.

# Finding Strength in Community: Wake Up and Smell the Lilacs

## Keynote Address to the Northeast Regional Meeting of the Alliance for Community Media
### May 10, 1996

I WAS ASKED TO speak to rally forth with my customary battle cries, combative rhetoric, brimming with optimism and utopian vision. Sorry. The long winter has dimmed my sunny forecasts. The situation is grim.

Sometimes we have strange allies. Who said this? "Media combinations reduce the diversity of information." That is the Federal Trade Commission Chair, Robert Pitofsky, speaking about the proposed Time Warner-Turner-TCI merger. Surprising as it may seem, it looks like the FTC is trying to put a brake on the galloping merger mania. Or is this a way to up the media contributions to the Democratic Party? The other night a big gala in Washington raised twelve million dollars. How much of that money was from Time Warner and/or Ted Turner or John Malone? Whatever machinations are taking place within the FTC, the FCC, and TCI, we can be sure, despite the sober assessment of Pitofsky, that when the smoke clears, diversity of information won't be the result.

I recall in the late seventies making a program with Liza Bear for *Communications Update* about the New World Information Order. We interviewed several academics and policy people from Costa Rica, from the U.K., from India, and from Africa at a big international conference on global communication at the Annenberg Communication School in Philadelphia.[17] There was a movement for a New World Information

---

[17] See "Travel Notes" in Section 3.

Order, a term which must be clearly distinguished from Bush's rationalization of the Gulf War. The New World Information Order was a call from the non-aligned nations to have parity of information, and an end to what they saw as a one-way flow of information. Their organized resistance caused quite a stir at the ITU (the International Telecommunications Union) and UNESCO—so much so that the United States stopped paying its U.N. bills and has racked up quite a large debt, which exists today and hampers U.N. and especially UNESCO activities. At the conference in Philadelphia there were many dire predictions about information imperialism. They called it like it is. I remember being a bit surprised at the level of gloom and paranoia of these experts at Annenberg. Here in the United States, the mainstream media has an aversion to the word "imperialism." They use the word "globalization."

- Today, as every day, nine new McDonalds franchises will open up somewhere around the world.
- Rupert Murdoch is programming a major portion of TV channels in Brazil, India, and China.
- The local video stores in Vancouver place Canadian films in the "Foreign" section.
- In Carma Hinton and Richard Gordon's film about Tiananmen Square, one of the activists says, "What we were demonstrating for was to have Nikes."

Well, who wouldn't? From Beijing to Detroit, young people are besieged with sneaker ads. And catalogs and billboards. It's so easy to have anything you want. My students at San Diego are deluged with offers for credit cards during freshmen orientation at UCSD. In the past you had to have a job to get a credit card. Now you just have to have a social security number. Computerized records mean no one can be invisible. Like Boston Blackie in the Coasters song, they're gonna find you. Some of my students have five credit cards filled to the max. They have $35,000 in credit debt by their junior year. That's not counting the money they owe the banks for their tuition and books. That's what all those Nikes cost. And the beer and the movies . . . you can buy anything on credit, so why not? While they are in school they have to work three jobs to keep up the minimum payment schedule. They never read my assignments because they have no time to read. In the morning they work at the café spooning froth onto cappuccino. In the afternoon they work at the so-called bookstore helping people try on Nikes with the school logo. In the evening they work at the convenience store ringing up Snapples and gas. Somewhere in between they dash into class at least until attendance is taken. Four of my students confessed to me that they were selling their blood each week. They staggered four donation centers, since you aren't supposed to go to any one center more than once a month. They were good students. They read the assignments. They found selling their blood was the only way they could earn enough and have time to study.

This is a vampire society. Even though the kids work all through school, by the time they graduate, they are completely in debt and indentured to the system or perhaps anemic. They don't have time or energy to volunteer. To go to the Peace Corps. To go to Freedom Summer. To hang out at a public access center. If they do show up at Chittenden County Community TV,[18] it's to quickly learn a new skill to put on their résumé. They have no leisure time. How can they get involved in activist causes? How can they worry about communication legislation?

How can even the administrators of public access have time to worry about legislation? Working at Deep Dish has given me a new appreciation for the thankless tasks of non-profit administration. My life is divided into grant deadlines, interspersed with report deadlines. The details of the office eat my time. Even a noble effort such as recycling means that each week I have to spend time binding up the various paper categories and rinsing out bottles. Not that I begrudge it, but it just means that there is less time on recycle day for everything else. How to see the big picture in the midst of the details? How to have time to plan and delegate? It is hard. And there is the bottom line. I can see how the so-called market mentality creeps in. Even at Deep Dish we start looking at programming

---

[18] The public access center in Burlington, Vermont, where the conference took place.

differently. Hmm, maybe if we get rights to this or that, it could be a tape we could get distribution money from. What sort of co-op deal will bring income? What services that we offer will people be willing to pay for? I have never thought of myself as an entrepreneur. But, hey, what's gonna pay for the phone bill?

Or the information bill? The only information bill I absolutely have to pay is the Internet invoice. For a non-profit organization, that's a whole other area of, on the one hand, debt and, on the other, time use. I spend more time on-line than I do sleeping. Not that I resent it. On the contrary, it is absolutely necessary at this time. But it eats time. And it costs money. Most insidious of all, when I am on-line I am by myself in front of a computer. I find that more and more of my work is taking me out of society—which is why I value the Alliance for Community Media.

And it is why I have reservations about access centers becoming computer centers where everyone is sitting in their cubicle: isolated, alienated from their immediate community. Sure, they may have pen pals in Turkey or Burkina Faso. Sure, they are members of some media pirates' wacky club in cyberspace. But I miss the ragtag interaction as people make a TV show, the exchanges between often very different people, the excitement of a live community show—the kind of event in which the crew and "talent" spontaneously erupt into applause at final cue to fade to black.

Technology can help make community happen. I like to think that Deep Dish has been an experiment in creating that sort of spontaneous, energetic, interactive community from geostationary orbit. I think there are ways we can grow using the Internet. I think that the kinds of activist connections we have made with Deep Dish can and do exist in cyberspace. But I think that one of the reasons Deep Dish has worked is that we have been able to keep the big picture in focus. The issues are the life of the Deep Dish community, not the technology. I recently have been putting together a catalog listing of all of our programs. Looking it over, I am amazed at how often we have been at the right place, at the right time, with the right issue. The issues always transcended the technology. And that's the key.

The issue right now is repression, and it must be addressed. There is an enormous disparity of income in this country. More and more people are confined to service jobs, indentured to their debts. The specter of lynching kept African Americans in place for a century. The lethal injection gurney and the expanding prison industry maintain a similar threat. We sometimes speak of "criminal justice," but the criminal system cannot be called "justice." Every month a dozen people are executed. Every day two hundred new jail cells are created in this country. Ten billion dollars have been allocated recently for new prison construction. Since 1970 the federal and state prison populations have increased ten times—this even though violent crime rates are down. Just as the military-industrial complex kept their profits up with the specter of the communist menace, the military-prison complex has arisen with the specter of "crime." These industries are the fastest-growing sector of the U.S. economy, outstripping even new technology. The ideology that has enabled the creation of this industry does more than construct the vast human cages that loom on our landscapes. It inhibits our initiative and potential for change, just the way that the Cold War cut off progressive potential and ransacked activist organizations and unions.

On the drive to Burlington, I passed two mammoth prison complexes. In the rainy gloom of the early morning the iodine floodlights illuminated these worlds of stark repression. We drive past the prisons on our highways and in our urban centers. Passing these fortresses every day has a major effect on the consciousness of citizens. It forces a denial that creeps into other aspects of our lives. Just as the Poles knew in their hearts what was happening behind the barbed wire at Auschwitz, so we know in our souls the injustice that reigns in U.S. prisons. We drive past and punch the scan button on our car radios to find some upbeat music.

Deep Dish is working on a series on the issue of justice and repression, and in the few months we have been pulling material together we have been overwhelmed with the response.[19] This is the new movement, and as Manning Marable has pointed out, this movement is different from other progressive organizing in the past. This time we are directly confronting fascism. We are looking at the face of fascism. In this struggle we need all the resources we can get. Our community communication centers are essential. Our projects, so very human, so very vital, must be maintained and nurtured.

There is no razor wire here. A purple wall surrounds this college. The heady aroma wafts in as we speak. The lilacs are blooming in spite of the cold rain.

---

[19] The series *America behind Bars* is available from Deep Dish TV, 339 Lafayette St., New York, N.Y. 10012.

# Whittling Away at the Public Sphere: Marketing to School Children

## *August 7, 1992*[20]

NEXT YEAR EIGHT million U.S. students will watch Mountain Dew and Snickers ads in their classrooms each day.[21] The ads are packaged with some "lite" news and upbeat features such as teen fashions and skateboard competitions to make them more palatable for the kids. For the teachers there's a "tough teacher contest," and on the closing segment last May, there was a fast-paced MTV-type montage segment laced with bite-sized quotes from such P.C.-proof white male Western classics as Shakespeare, T. S. Elliot, and Cicero. The programming, however, is clearly secondary, or perhaps supplemental, to the real agenda of Channel One: to make a profit by selling rooms full of sedated youngsters to advertising agencies. As Richard Serra and Carlotta Schoolman said many years ago in an early video art piece, "Television delivers people. You are the product of TV."[22]

The Whittle Corporation has discovered a large and easily harvested product: the school children of the United States. Not only does Whittle sell the kids to the Pop Tarts' and Pepsi's ad agencies, they have set up their own chain of corporate private charter schools, through which they hope to sell the

---

[20] This article was originally published in *Lies of Our Times* (March 1990).

[21] This number is now over 20 million.

[22] Carlotta Schoolman and Richard Serra, *Television Delivers People*, produced by the Kitchen in 1975. Available through the Video Data Bank at the Art Institute of Chicago, 37 S. Wabash, Chicago, Ill. 60603.

kids back to their parents: these schools will be partially subsidized by vouchers from state and federal education funds.

Some of the objections to the Whittle initiative are naive and misguided. There is nothing wrong with television per se in schools. There is nothing wrong with children watching international and national news in classrooms. There is nothing wrong with satellite-delivered media. And there are hard realities which make Whittle attractive to many schools. A beleaguered teacher from a small rural African American community in North Carolina told a colleague of mine not to knock Whittle. Her school had zero budget for equipment and supplies and was still using textbooks from 1955, but by agreeing to show the kids Channel One, the school received a brand-new TV set and a satellite dish that enables them to tape other programs for classroom use. While one can empathize with teachers combating the paucity of education funds, one should be careful about endorsing an enterprise which at this point has a rather large foot in the door of our public school system, however badly in need of repair that door may be.[23]

Channel One did a feature series (one a day for four days) on "the fascinating world of the visual arts," as their cheery correspondent described it from her perch on a stool in William Wegman's studio. After watching Wegman glue leaves to the weimaraner Man Ray's latest reincarnation, the reporter oooohed and aahed at the "collaborative" way in which Wegman worked—that is, with one assistant to hold the dog and another to tilt the quartz light. The segment closed with an art history montage of famous dogs in art. The next day's segment was about Nina Levy, a Chicago sculptor who designs the little plastic animals they give away in cereal boxes. Her segment closed with an ad for Pop Tarts that was set in a gallery in which some Lichtenstein-like paintings join in the chorus for the heavily sugared tarts. The third segment of "Now That's

---

[23] Another corporation which takes advantage of teachers' needs for materials is Anheuser-Busch, which markets Shamu and SeaWorld to millions of schoolchildren daily. A uniquely detailed look at the vertical and horizontal integration of corporate culture is Susan Davis's *Spectacular Nature: Corporate Culture and the SeaWorld Experience* (Berkeley: University of California Press, 1997).

Art!" was on Chuck Close and ended with a historical segment on Seurat and pointillism and a Sprint commercial showing how the "points of light" in their network helped to end Soviet Communism. The last segment was on Rea Tajiri and video art. Rea declares that she is making video with a message, and clips of her moving document on the World War II internment camps are shown. The final clip was a close-up of a Van Gogh painting and a lugubrious voice intoning that this painting sold for over eighty-two million dollars. Then came an ad for Three Musketeers candy bars. So much for message art.

Although the "Now That's Art" series was equally balanced between women and men and carefully inclusive of a person of color, the question of sponsorship remains. One might also question the representation of art as celebrity gossip. There is no question, however, that Channel One is a dangerous presence in the lives of our children. The whole notion of passive "education" is itself a contradiction in terms. Education is active if it is education. The only thing that is active on this channel is the corporate message. But television in schools does not have to be passive indoctrination to corporate hegemony. Looking beyond Channel One's oppressive corporate shadow on the horizon, what are some examples of active and imaginative in-school television?

(a) "Here, Thayer and Everywhere" is a satellite network for progressive public schools begun in Winchester, New Hampshire, where a small high school in the middle of a working-class New England town had enormous success in motivating youth and teachers. Their monthly satellite program looks at innovative ways of dealing with classroom subjects and administrative problems and is lively, made by kids together with their teachers. It pulls together a loose network of over 130 schools that are members of a group called the Coalition for Effective Schools. Their programs are funky, casual, and fun, and the teachers and students are very supportive and enthusiastic. (Elliot Washer, Coalition for Essential Schools, Brown University, Box 1969, Providence, R.I. 02912.)

(b) Strategies for Media Literacy is a San Francisco–based national organization that helps teachers with curricula

around media issues. Director Kathleen Tyner helps to organize workshops in schools that give teachers ideas for critical
viewing in the classroom. They might include a segment from
Channel One in their workshop but would encourage students
to note distortions and assumptions in their news reports and
to look for a hidden agenda in their seductive advertisements.
Tyner publishes a helpful newsletter listing resources and conferences. (SML, Inc., Suite 410, 1095 Market Street, San
Francisco, Calif. 94103.)

(c) The Educational Video Center has trained hundreds of
teachers in creative media work. They have helped to staff
many alternative high schools and junior highs with video
teachers and have set up workshops in many schools around
the country. (Educational Video Center, 60 East 13th Street,
4th Floor, New York, N.Y. 10003.)

(d) Paper Tiger Television distributes over three hundred
video tapes that critique the media in a homemade, down-to-
earth style, many with an emphasis on youth. The subjects
range from a critical look at *TV Guide* to a stinging indictment
of the portrayal of teenagers in the media, made by teenagers
themselves. These programs are good for classroom viewing
and discussion. (Paper Tiger Television, 339 Lafayette Street,
New York, N.Y. 10012.)

# 6

# Independent Producers
# and Public Television

# Introduction

THE LATE SEVENTIES saw a renewed interest in the potential and problems of public broadcasting. In the sixties public broadcasting had been ushered in with a commission appointed by the Carnegie Foundation, called Carnegie I, which advocated a national educational and cultural network. In 1978 a second Carnegie Commission was formed to look into the institution and suggest reform. By 1978 independent producers, frustrated by years of trying to get their work on the public airwaves, were angry at being kept out of both the production funds and the airtime on what was supposed to be public channels. As president of the Association of Independent Video and Filmmakers, I helped organize a series of meetings and forums to address the needs of independent producers. An AIVF public television committee demanded that the Carnegie Commission and PBS administration at both the national and local levels take independents seriously. A Carnegie meeting of over 600 producers at Columbia University was an emotional confrontation between outspoken producers and several members of the Commission, including Commission Chair William McGill and Bill Moyers, already at that time a regular fixture on public broadcasting. The Commission members took copious notes, but it was clear that those notes would be nothing more than small font footnotes in their final report, unless other actions were initiated. So we headed for Washington to speak before the House Subcommittee on Communication. "Mind Power: Collective Action for Media Reform" is a call to arms of the independent community. This section also includes the testimony before Congress, written by the AIVF public television committee, which included Robin Weber, Ralph Arlyck, Mark Levin, and myself. The lobbying effort was actually successful: the PTV legislation for 1979 ultimately included provisions that a "significant amount" of public television's funding had to go to independents. While we tried to find a lawyer to test the language through class action litigation, the PBS establishment scrambled to become "independent" to qualify for the funds. Bill Moyers and McNeil-Lehrer nominally cut their ties to WNET and became "independents."

Independent media producers may have been able to sneak in a few articles of legislative reform during the years of Jimmy Carter's presidency, but the window for alternative information was slammed shut with the ascendancy of the right wing in the 1980s. "Media Makers in Bonzoland" was written after the election victory of Ronald Reagan, in the cold dawn of the moral "majority" era. The battle persisted for years, until Larry Duressa, Larry Hall, Larry Supadin, and AIVF finally were able to form the Independent Television Service (ITVS) to provide funding for independent work with monies from the Corporation for Public Broadcasting. How independent ITVS is at this point is another question. ITVS programs must be offered to public television and the PBS administration, and the local stations are loath to support this rogue entity. So ITVS bends over backwards to please the stations (and Congress), and very little authentic alternative programming gets produced through this organization.

"A Few Arguments for the Appropriation of Television" was commissioned by the magazine *High Performance* as a call for radical television. "Telemanifesto for Collaborative Airwaves" is an appeal for independents to unite and create an alternative network. "Beyond Simi Valley" appeared in *The Independent*, the journal of AIVF. It looks at independent media in the light of the Los Angeles uprising after the Rodney King verdict. It was a challenge to the Independent Television Service to be more accountable to the independent community that had founded and now defended ITVS. "Guerrillas in Our Midst" is a look back at the heady days of video collectives in the 1970s and the ongoing struggles for public television.

# Mind Power: Collective Action for Media Reform

*Presentation to the Conference "Independent Television Makers and Public Communications Policy"*

*June 6, 1979*

HISTORICALLY THE independent media producers' political involvement has consisted of documenting the struggles and confrontations of other groups. Coal miners, autoworkers, anti-war demonstrators, plutonium victims have all had their stories told by committed and supportive filmmakers. There has been relatively little attempt by independents to direct their energies to changing their own material position within the dominant media structures. If these structures were considered at all, it was to make use of them—garnering the airtime on the news with some yippie-type action, or occasionally being allowed access, either a one-time airing on PBS or perhaps served up, smorgasbord-style, with other independents and given a catchy, albeit patronizing, title such as "Flick-Out" or "Up and Coming." There was little attempt to analyze the policies of public television, let alone counter them.

The activity of independents in the late seventies marked somewhat of a departure. Frustrated with the increasingly competitive and unresponsive structures of both PBS and the networks, independents banded together to press their demands. These demands, however, are not just for access or more grant money. They are now addressing the issue of control of the system as a whole. This is a new fight and one that runs counter to a tradition of political impotence in the media field. This impotence has been maintained by a pervasive fog of technological determinism. American media theory has been dominated by a Janus-headed romanticism: two aspects of the same basic credo—the omnipotence of technology. On the one hand we have a McLuhanesque romanticism that continues to permeate our culture: the belief that information, per se, is good, and that an increasingly complex technology always triumphs. This technological Darwinism is evident in Gene Youngblood's[1] utopian prognostications of a transponder future. On the other side, just as romantic, but in a more pessimistic vein are Jerry Mander[2] and the electronic Luddites.[3] Back to nature: reality is pure; it is not transcribed, transmitted, or televised. Electrons are to be exorcised in primal earthy rites. The saint of this sect is the San Diego woman who took out her gun one afternoon and shot her TV set. Their apostle and Sunday school teacher is Marie Winn, bewailing what television does to children and followed by troops of converted parents, saved by pulling the plug on their sets.

While the woman with the gun probably had a better idea than McLuhan, both of these ideologies have the common aspect of seeing the media as all-powerful and something beyond our control or responsibility. In spite of these fatalists, there is a budding hope that media change is possible. Peggy Charin's Action for Children's Television has collaborated with P.T.A.'s around the country in a grassroots movement with wide support and growing clout in Congress. Alliances of blacks and Latinos have challenged license renewals and have forced many stations into affirmative action programs. The Consumer Federation and the United Church of Christ, through their huge constituencies, have applied pressure on Congress and the FCC for major reforms. The AFL-CIO and other labor groups have issued telecommunications policy

---

[1] Gene Youngblood, *Expanded Cinema* (New York: Dutton, 1970).

[2] Jerry Mander, *Four Arguments for the Elimination of Television* (New York: Morrow, 1978).

[3] From a more Left point of view, see George Bradford, "Media: Capital's Global Village," *The Fifth Estate* 19, no. 3 (1984).

statements and have begun to testify on media issues in Congress. The legislative work of the National Task Force on Public Television and the Association of Independent Video and Filmmakers is part of this overall pattern of increased awareness of media policies, and a growing hope that well-directed pressure can accomplish change.

What has been the response of the media establishment in the face of widespread and increasing public demands for media accountability? DEREGULATION. This is no coincidence. While it may not be a well-orchestrated, full-fledged conspiracy, it is part of an overall pattern of government deregulation, justified in rhetorical calls for "freedom of the market." While government regulatory agencies have often been beholden to the very corporations they are supposed to regulate, deregulation is coming at a time when the public's demands for government responsibility (for example, in the consumer and nuclear movements) are forcing the federal commissions to become legitimate. It is harder for these commissions to maintain their positions as handmaidens to the industries they were created to regulate. A post-Watergate vigilance has made that kind of collusion difficult, if not impossible.

The challenge for industry is getting deregulation passed before the vigilant public understands its implications. If the public is asked about regulation versus the free market, what will be their response? What kind of faith does a Pinto driver have in the free market? Or someone who bought Firestone radials?

Dependence on paternalistic goodwill will never change the situation. Independents know that the *fact* (even before any outcome) that there is an Emergency Civil Liberties suit against the networks has had a more profound effect on the airways than any amount of network hype about the "new documentary" or congressional musing about "free flow of ideas." Independents know that the specified proportion for them in the 1979 PTV funding bill means dollars and cents and ultimately airtime, something no rhetoric about "diversity and diverse sources" could ensure. The ranks of independents are growing. The membership of the AIVF doubled in 1978, as the organization revved up their advocacy. Similar organizations of local independents formed in Madison, Atlanta, San Francisco, Boston, Philadelphia, and Minneapolis.

In the 1979 public television funding bill is a provision for open public television board meetings (the so-called Sunshine Rules). It means that independents (and any concerned citizen) can go to their public stations and make themselves known and heard. The drawbridge is down. The fortress that PTV has maintained will never quite be the same. The stations, in particular the larger ones, were aware of the implications of this mandate in their bitter and well-financed opposition to that section of the bill.

No rhetoric would justify excluding public participation. The stations are more wary of independents than of the general public. Independents at an open board meeting are more dangerous than any other consumer/viewer group. They know the business, and they can use that knowledge to form wedges for change. This kind of intrusion into the machinations of the establishment by well-informed professionals is a phenomenon that Columbia University economist Eli Ginzberg noted in an article in the March 1979 *Scientific American.*[4] In his view, the growing cadres of college graduates in all professions and in managerial categories could eventually pose a threat to the entire system: "Clearly their judgment and authority narrows the discretion of top management in the public agencies and business organizations in which they are employed." He advocated the inclusion of these outsiders:

> No establishment can ensure its survival without the recruitment of talent from outside its ranks. If it does not succeed in the full co-optation of the newcomers, however, it may leave itself vulnerable to them as they proceed to advance their own interests and aims and succeed in usurping decision-making power. It remains to be seen whether the demands of the American mandarins can be met without subversion of the risk-taking profit-seeking, efficiency criteria on which the country's business system has long rested.

The establishment can respond either with increased accommodation and co-optation or with exclusionary and re-

---

[4] Eli Ginzberg, "Professionalization of the U.S. Labor Force," *Scientific American* 240, no. 3 (1979).

strictive policies. Either way, the opposition is likely to grow. Either way, the rhetoric contradicts the reality of the situation. For the ever increasing group of outsiders (the independents, the artists, the women, minorities, the public interest and consumer groups), the MARKET itself is inevitably a restrictive and exclusionary structure—one which can only lessen diversity by allowing the already overwhelming and pervasive systems to increase their hegemony. A diverse and publicly responsive media environment can exist only in a protective context of REGULATION in the public interest. Accommodation to the pressures of the public and independent producers will raise expectations and increase the need for even greater participation, which is why the broadcasting industry, which includes public television, is fighting any regulation.

No matter what options are taken by the telecommunications industry and Congress, either toward regulatory/protection or toward unbridled profit-seeking by increasingly larger consortiums of corporate interests, the type of resistance that has developed is not likely to lessen. Mind power is replacing labor power. Information workers will continue to press for control as information systems replace mechanical and industrial production modes.

Independent media producers are important participants in the discussions of telecommunications policies and responsibilities. Imaginative regulatory structures can be responsive to humanity's needs—both for justice and for creativity. These discussions are the cultural aspect of the demands for sustainable ecology and the just allocation and development of the world's resources. The crucial resource at issue here is not the spectrum—it is the human mind.

Paper Tiger crew Alan Steinheimer and Andrea Torrice (on right) shoot Ben Bagdikian, 1986. *(Paper Tiger TV)*

# Statement Before the House Subcommittee on Telecommunications

## *1979*

Ms. HALLECK. Mr. Chairman, there are many thousands of independent American producers working in the 16 mm and small-format video, whose work is shown regularly in museums and colleges here and around the world. Only a small proportion of this work, however, has found its way to broadcast and cable television in this country. Naturally, the Association of Independent Video and Filmmakers, of which I am president, has an interest in increasing that proportion and in expanding that marketplace, which is one of the expressed goals of the proposed act. We feel we could be instrumental in implementing more diverse, responsible, and creative media, but we share the concern of Jack Golodner (union representative, AFL-CIO) that the focus of the bill is on communications as a marketplace. The image of the marketplace connotes a choice between products, things presented, and the best and most useful being chosen. I think it is a sincere desire of the committee to increase the choices available to the American public.

The question is, what is the product? In television, as Les Brown has pointed out,[5] the product is not the programs. It is not even the products being advertised. The product is the audience. The market is the selling of the audience. People are the merchandise, not the shows. The shows are merely the

---

[5] Les Brown, *Television: The Business behind the Box* (New York: Harcourt Brace Jovanovich, 1971), pp. 15–16.

bait. The consumer, whom the custodians of the medium are pledged to serve is, in fact, served up. The new bill even makes reference to this. In contrast to the 1934 act, there is no longer a reference to the interest, convenience, and necessity of the public. The current bill, in fact, refers to the public as a market.

Are we giving up entirely on the public as a part of communications? Whatever happened to the public airways?[6] To trade the rest of the spectrum for a few public television and radio channels is a bad bargain indeed. In spectrum allocation, use of the interstate cable lines, and microwave transmission using satellites, the public must retain regulatory authority as well as active participation through access. We need more public involvement, not less, and we believe that independent media workers with varying talents and concerns are the natural facilitators of public involvement.

The deregulation of cable will inevitably result in the denial of cable access to independent producers and public interest groups. Despite the lack of substantial funds, equipment, and real cooperation from most cable owners, the cable access networks have been a vital showplace for independent talent and initiative. Access centers have served as valuable training grounds for novice producers. This kind of on-the-job-training is impossible in commercial broadcast operations. Small-format video producers on access cable have played crucial roles in many communities, bringing visual evidence of local problems and issues. Many performing artists, writers, and choreographers have worked with independent producers on access stations to try out new works. Where access has been offered, it has been used; where it has been given both moral and financial support, it has flourished.

Minimal, mandatory requirements on a federal level are needed to ensure public participation and local origination. Let us not fool ourselves. The over 300 communities now

---

[6] See William Hoynes, *Public Television for Sale: Media, the Market, and the Public Sphere* (Boulder: Westview Press, 1994), and Ralph Engelman, *Public Radio and Television in America: A Political History* (Thousand Oaks, Calif.: Sage, 1996).

using access are doing so because of federal regulations, not because of the free market.

## SATELLITES AND OTHER TECHNOLOGIES

Technology must implement public involvement, not negate it. A more efficient use of broadcast bands is one way of augmenting diversity. Multiplicity of channels must not be restricted to cable users. The satellite system presents the opportunity to develop a real multi-way communications structure linking geographical areas and cultural and special interest groups. The billions of public dollars that were used to develop these carriers must be repaid in real and constructive public use. Satellites can enable independents to get their work to outlying areas which might not otherwise have the opportunity to view such work. This could encourage a dialogue between station policymakers and independents. Pilot projects could be showcased to foundations, TV stations, exhibitors, and international festivals.

Corporate funding for specific programming has eroded the noncommercial nature of public television. The funds which have come from corporations have by and large not supported our kind of work, because it is often risk-taking and controversial. The fact that it is hard to pinpoint any specific instances of program influence is not the issue.

These underwriters have become entrenched in many of the large stations and have had inordinate influence on the overall tone of programming. Maintaining the proper slick public relations image these guys demand has lessened program moneys and inflated both overhead and production budgets.

Spectrum fees based on audience size would hamper struggling alternative commercial stations in large metropolitan areas.[7] This type of broadcast tax would discourage diversity and force stations into mass market appeal. We suggest a tax

---

[7] H.R. 13015. Sec. 413: b,2,B, calculates the fees for television by number of frequencies assigned to a market and the number of prime-time television households in such markets.

on the profits from commercials and on satellite use by commercial entities. The satellites were designed and implemented with public funds, and a return is due. The imposition of a license fee and the almost complete deregulation of the commercial spectrum would create a dangerous tendency toward polarization, commercial on the one hand and public on the other. It could force all alternative communications to the shelter of public broadcasting and raise the specter of governmental domination of all non-mass-appeal media. It would be like two big brothers: Kojak and Uncle Sam.

We applaud the idea of an endowment, but one that concentrates on programming. Many of our members have had positive, productive relationships with the National Endowment for the Arts. There is very little hard feeling even when our pet projects do not get funded. It has been our experience that the equitable and progressive use of panels of peers has made the NEA decision processes more open, more understandable, more fair, and more productive than what we have seen at CPB,[8] PBS, and most of the public stations. Peer panels with real clout in decision making on all levels in public television, in endowment allocations, PBS decisions, and local station broadcast decisions are a necessary step to a creative public telecommunications endowment. The dependence on British programming that we have seen in the past few years is an insult to the growing numbers of Americans now engaged in some aspect of the arts.

American talent must be identified, supported, and broadcast. Many independent media makers now work in formats that differ from commercial broadcast formats in time, length, esthetic qualities, and subject matter. An imaginative endowment could begin to break the stranglehold the current formats have on airtime.

In many urban centers and at universities all across the country there is a growing audience for the new explorations in the media. The acceptance and availability of new art forms is considerably greater in the major urban centers than in rural America. Public television could really close this gap by

---

[8] The Corporation for Public Broadcasting.

courageously presenting new work in an effort to broaden formats instead of conforming to them. Surely we can provide more variety than Dick Cavett reruns three times on WNET, the largest public television station in the country in one of the most vital, creative art centers in the world.

The endowment would serve not the stations, nor the Congress, but the public. It must have the freedom to see that good programs are made, broadcast, and defended. It would ensure that substantial funds are earmarked for local programming and for programs directed to special and minority audiences. Independent media producers are in a unique position to implement this kind of programming. We have proved that we are a bargain too. Operating outside of the station structures, we are able to work more energetically and efficiently. A substantial portion of total programming funds at both the national and station levels must be allocated directly to large and small independent producers. The endowment must be funded with ample budget.

We question whether a license fee method[9] can be an effective source. Support will be chipped away during negotiations between the powerful broadcasting interests and the Commission. The funds will become leftovers to be fought over by public television and minorities and women interested in station ownership. It pits the least powerful constituents against each other. Dispersal of operating funds to stations must be made by a separate non-programming agency, either the National Telecommunications Administration or a new entity created entirely for this purpose. Community Service Grant (CSG) funding should be set up to reward programming instead of fundraising. At present, many stations have become enmeshed in a fundraising spiral. The more funds they get, the more CSGs they get to raise more funds. Many stations are better at fundraising than they are at programming.

We applaud the inclusion of sunshine laws and public accountability in the new act, but public television will not be public until there are solid mechanisms for open board elections. A new communications act, truly in the interest, conve-

---

[9] This was one of the provisions proposed for funding public television.

nience, and necessity of the public, would begin by making the public a real part of public television. Right now, the audiences of public television should be involved in helping to shape that future.

The discussions of the 1978 funding bill and this rewrite should be aired to the American people. That public television has chosen not to broadcast these hearings is a classic example of their irresponsible attempt to maintain the status quo. The community of American independent media workers welcome these discussions. We are grateful for the opportunity to bring some of these suggestion to the committee. We are excited about the prospects for growth and change.

A public television system working together with the many thousands of independent producers in the stewardship of a responsible and informed public might be able to begin to generate a new kind of communications, one that fosters autonomy over domination and enlightenment over mass deception. Ensuring that diversity flourishes takes foresight and protection. History has shown that meaningful regulation is more dependable than the free market. How many blacks and women got their jobs in broadcasting through laissez-faire?

Congressman Tim Wirth has asked whether it is the right and duty of Congress to intervene in the use of public television's funds. It seems to me that when there are chronic problems within a federally supported system that are not resolved, it is the responsibility of Congress to get involved.

The abusive neglect by public television of women, blacks, and the Hispanic population, the working class, and independent American artists must be addressed, and I would like to say that the written testimony has been endorsed by the following organizations: the Boston Film and Video Foundation; the Chicago Editing Center; Film in the Cities, St. Paul, Minnesota; the Film Arts Association in San Francisco; the Global Village in New York; Independent Media Artists of Georgia; the Millennium Film Workshop in New York; the Northwest Film Study Center in Portland, Oregon; Pittsburgh Filmmakers; the Rocky Mountain Film Center in Boulder, Colorado; and many others.

# Media Makers in Bonzoland: The New Opposition—Independent Media Producers, Media Reformers, and the Culture Industry Rank and File in the Chilly Dawn of a Reagan Presidency[10]

## November 1980

THE ELECTION OF the first American president thoroughly tooled in the consciousness industry throws into sharp relief some of the contradictions of cultural work in this country. The last decade saw a growing collaboration between independent media makers and media reformers. Much of the reform work centered on gaining "access" to "alternative" channels—cable public access and public broadcasting. As these "surplus" sources dry up, the struggle will have to move to an increasing confrontation with the larger mass culture structures: Hollywood, the networks, and the consciousness industry conglomerates.

As far as the New Right is concerned, the so-called "alternative" media is very clearly the opposition, and they are hastily dismantling the institutions that have supported it. Independent film and video producers have been funded by liberal government agencies such as the National Endowment for the

---

[10] This article was commissioned by *Cineaccion*, the French film journal. It was originally published in French.

Arts, the National Endowment for the Humanities, the various state and regional arts and humanities councils, and liberal foundations. Funding has been sporadic at best and extremely competitive, but steady enough to enable a group of self-proclaimed "independent" or "alternative" media producers to receive production funds and even distribution assistance. What was in it for the liberals aside from the glory of seeing agency names roll by on the credits? The Ford Foundation, the Rockefeller Foundation, and the whole system of state and national arts councils (the first one initiated by New York's then governor Nelson Rockefeller) realized early on the advantages of keeping artists happy. The pacification and co-optation of artists was a major function of the Eastern power trusts. These funding groups have made it a policy to shell out enough of a meager but steady dole to keep artists busy with grant applications. Under this system, even people expressing counterviews in the media arts could find enough support and enough audience, isolated and elitist though it might be. This removed most of the incentive for questioning the dominant forms of media expression or launching any attacks on the culture industry or the corporate state.

The institutional patrons of the arts discovered, however, that selection of grants by administrative decree elicited protests and bitterness from the artist community. To maintain credibility they set up broadly representative panels of artists to distribute the money. These "peer panels" diffused the dissatisfactions and disappointments attendant upon the selection process. Maintaining credibility was not without contradictions. The "democratic process" in the arts bureaucracy has funded a growing number of "social change" works. It has also enabled artists to become familiar with the nature and intricacies of the funding process. In fact, centralized art funding has encouraged the development of organizations of artists, with newsletters, publications, and an intense involvement in the legislative process.

As president of the Association of Independent Video and Filmmakers (a trade organization of over a thousand producers) I was involved in forcing the so-called "public" television system (through the Corporation for Public Broadcasting) to support independent producers. In a battle that took several years and numerous trips to Washington, our group tried to use the liberal language of the national Communications Act and the enabling legislation for public broadcasting to demand structural changes, to implement the rhetoric of "diversity" and "public service" that runs through these legislative documents.[11]

We testified at hearings, did extensive research, and put out publications to prove that public television in the United States denies access to producers—often the very producers who receive arts council and endowment funds. Productions from the American alternative media community are screened on German and Scandinavian television and appear in countless European festivals. But they are practically never shown on the tax-funded public channels in the United States.

Instead of showcasing independent producers, public television uses the programs that are approved and supported by oil companies and other multinationals.[12] The "Petroleum Broadcasting System" seems to prefer the brocades of English drawing rooms to the more rugged homespun—and often keenly critical—social documentaries that many young American media artists produce.

We went directly to Congress with our complaints. By exploiting the disdain of the general population (less than 1 percent watch prime-time public television) and by pandering to the frankly chauvinist preference for American-made productions, we were able to establish in law that a "substantial amount" of the available money be spent on independent American productions, selected by peer advisors.[13] This law

---

[11] See Patricia Zimmerman: "Public Television, Independent Documentary Producers and Public Policy," *Journal of the University Film and Video Association* 34, no. 3 (1982).

[12] One can chart the public disgrace of certain corporations by the level of PBS-funded shows they support. During the oil crisis of the 1970s, the oil companies tried to buy goodwill by sponsoring PBS programming. During the savings and loan scandals, banks started sponsoring shows. More recently the flagship news program, McNeil-Lehrer NewsHour, has been sponsored by Archer Daniels Midland, an agro-business company which has been associated with some egregious environmental practices.

[13] For an overview by the then director of the Aspen Institute Program on Communications and Society, see Michael Rice, "Independents and PTV," *Public Telecommunications Review*, 6, no. 5 (1978), p. 19.

signals the first time that independent producers will be involved in the fiscal arrangements of public broadcasting. The law was not lobbied for by independents alone, but by a coalition of groups working on media reform: the labor movement, progressive church organizations, the National Organization for Women, and minority coalitions helped to push for equal opportunity provisions and for the opportunity to make public broadcasting more accountable to their constituents. Of all the provisions included, perhaps the most long lasting is a clause that requires strict measures for making all meetings and financial records of public television stations open to the public. This enables community groups willing to take the initiative to become watchdogs of this mostly publicly funded institution.

The collaboration with labor groups on legislative issues parallels an increasing interest by independents in labor history. Films such as *Union Maids, The Wobblies, Rosie the Riveter,* and *Babies and Banners* have helped to revitalize and renew grassroots rank-and-file union activity with romantic models from past struggles. Humanities Endowment money has, on occasion, funded these histories and their distribution to community groups and schools. This has provoked the ire of the right wing, which has taken aim at the use of NEH funding of film screenings for women office workers. Progressive films on labor issues have sought out working-class audiences, ironically fulfilling the demand for more populist arts by the right wing. That sort of populism wasn't what the conservative critics of the NEH had in mind.

Cable television has been another area of contention for media reform groups. Local activists have taken advantage of contract proceedings to force stringent local access requirements, and local productions are flowering across the country. In Saint Johnsbury, Vermont, for example, local teenagers have produced a regular series of programs on issues of special interest to them: teen pregnancy, military service, alcoholism, police abuse of loitering laws, etc. Their project was initiated by grad students and faculty of nearby Goddard College's Community Media program, funded by town taxes, a jobs-for-youth program, and the local cable company under its franchise agreement. The Saint Johnsbury project is an exception, and the Goddard input was a critical factor, but it serves as a good model for community organizers. As cable gets more lucrative and there are more companies vying for the various franchises, it gets easier to force the cable corporations to include community access provisions. Precedents such as Saint Johnsbury are important models for other groups demanding access.

Activities such as the drafting of city franchises and legislative work in Congress give a practical focus to media reform activities.[14] Political organization around media issues has had to fight the prevailing ideology of the mass media and even communications academics and research projects. Those who might be sympathetic are caught up in a McLuhanist fascination with new technology and a naive faith that "information" per se is liberating. The argument is that with more channels, more satellites, videodiscs, or whatever the next technology is, there will be room for the currently disenfranchised. You'll have your turn when there is room for all. But we are beginning to wake up to the reality that 400 AM radio stations only means 400 stations of the same tired formats. Videodiscs may provide only page referencing and star bios of the latest *Star Wars* episodes, and having more cable channels gives us four episodes of *Gilligan's Island* from which to choose. If there is to be change, it will not be through multiplying the number of channels.

A new source for resistance to the dominant media has come from oppressed communities who have reacted vigorously to media stereotyping. It started when gays and lesbians successfully protested against the movie *Cruising*. The homophobia in this paranoid film deeply offended many in the gay community, and they launched a major campaign against it. Chinese and Asian Americans have likewise protested against the abuses to their images in recent Fu Manchu and Charlie Chan remakes. In the South Bronx, a group of vocal Puerto

---

[14] The research of Robert McChesney in the l990s provides a background of other media reform efforts in the 1930s. At that time there was also a coalition of educators, progressive religious folk, and unions who took on specific media reform issues.

Ricans, lead by Richie Perez, temporarily halted the filming of *Fort Apache, the Bronx,* a Paul Newman vehicle which was attempting to make Western-type heroes out of the local anti-Latino police force. These groups exerted effective pressure, and all three cases resulted in changes in the shooting scripts. But a more important result is the increased awareness which the confrontation with stereotypes provoked. Although the traditional liberal community reacted with trepidation to what they dub "infringement of First Amendment principles," this controversy requires a deeper analysis, for it points out the difficulties of equating individual and corporate rights. Power has to figure into the equation, somehow. What kind of opportunity does the Puerto Rican community in the South Bronx have to tell their own story? Time-Life and Warner Communications, the multinationals who made and distribute *Fort Apache,* have unlimited resources and power. Simple incantation of the First Amendment does not address the realities of corporate expression. Active organizations of mass culture subjects can be formidable media reformers.

Other areas for exchange and cooperation are being developed on the international level: the movement of the non-aligned countries at the World Administrative Radio Conference (WARC) and within UNESCO (the MacBride Commission) toward a New World Information Order. We in the U.S. ("free flow" not withstanding)[15] need our own new information order. We have much to gain by allying ourselves with those members of the Third World who are working to address issues of just development and media equity. By struggling to change the culture industry *here* at the centers of production, we can gnaw at the imperialist infrastructures from within the belly of the corporate media beasts.

As the ultra-Right takes command of the American political process, we contemplate four years of a Hollywood president.

---

[15] For years the United States has advocated a "free flow of information," which sounds good, but basically means that multinationals have access to any markets they want without trade restrictions. UNESCO research questioned whether there wasn't a "one-way flow." It was these UNESCO-sponsored discussions about the need for democratic information exchange that prompted the United States to refuse to pay their U.N. dues.

My community, the alternative producers, are quickly learning that although liberal-dominated government agencies of the Nelson Rockefellers and Jimmy Carters may have found "alternative" and "independent" expression necessary to their co-optive strategies, with the installation of Ronald Reagan and his legions, the very term "alternative" becomes oppositional. The vigilantes of reaction have already taken aim at Pacifica Foundation, the progressive radio network that has often been the sole source of news and public affairs programs that are other than corporate mouthings. On the day after the election, the rightist alliance declared at a Washington news conference that Pacifica would be their next target.

The siege has started. The 1979 strike by the Screen Actors Guild gave actors a share of the profits from the distribution of their work on videodisc and cassette rentals. Future labor disputes in the cultural sector might begin to address increased workers' control over editorial processes. Government and institutional funding for "social change" and "alternative" media will diminish, if not disappear. The coming years will see independent producers get poorer as the grants dry up. They will be lean, hungry, and perhaps dangerous, if their focus shifts from negotiating access for marginal works to challenging the basic structures of corporate culture and the mass media. Media workers—producers, directors, technicians, writers, and actors—those who work independently and those embedded within the commercial apparati—could conceivably exert more control over what they produce and how it is distributed.

# A Few Arguments for the Appropriation of Television

## Summer 1983

SLOWLY, LIKE A sleepy old house cat aroused by the din of a rat convention in her parlor, the Left is waking up to the fact that the Right has preempted the media. "The media" has been a non-issue with progressive organizations. The Left has never had a strategy to deal with media as an issue. Whenever the term *media* was brought up at meetings or conferences, discussions were organized around such petty issues as how to write a good press release, how to get your organization two minutes on the local news, or how to share mailing lists. Media are a vehicle for PR. The overall subject of the *media* was rarely seen as an issue for consideration.

Meanwhile the right wing has leased several dozen transponders. Not too many leftists even know what that means. Transponders are the transmission faces of a satellite. Many of these channels are controlled twenty-four hours a day by the Christian Right, not to mention the mainstream Right of General Electric/RCA, Cap Cities/ABC, et al. The airwaves (and the satellite orbits) are full of propaganda, and it doesn't come from the Left.

Surely the Right has understood for quite a while the need for an overall policy on the media, in terms of both a critique of existing networks (through such concerted attacks as the belligerent campaigns of Accuracy in the Media) and skillful use of a variety of television forms (all the way from the monumental televised spectacles of the Reverend Moon to the hand-held close-ups of real people in intimate community video style of the 700 Club's homey living room set). Right-wing

Christian programs are transmitted on every venue available, from leased commercial channels in large urban "markets" to the most humble public access channels in rural towns with scarcely 2,000 cable subscribers. In contrast, the Left has ceded the airways and is grateful to slip a thirty-second PSA of a toxic waste problem into the 11:30 local news slot once a year.

There has been a fatalism about media discussions by the Left that has made any activism seem futile. The assumption is always that the kinds of networks the Right has set up are way beyond the capacities of the Left's organizations in terms of costs and access to technology. Meanwhile opportunities for media production and activism go begging. And the pessimists are lionized as the only ones who see how really bad it is. It is why a guru of technological fatalism such as Jerry Mander is embraced as a prophet, or why the babblings about left culture by Jesse Lemisch (the Left's version of Hilton Kramer) are published in *The Nation*. The case of *The Nation* is symptomatic of the Left's attitude toward media. They have never recognized alternative media in this country. They will give lengthy reviews to the latest Metropolitan Opera production, but never a paragraph about the community of public access producers.

I remember being invited to what was billed as a high-level discussion at the NYU Humanities Institute, a seminar on media for intellectuals on the Left. Barbara Ehrenrich presided, and one of the leading speakers was a man whose main expertise was how to get on local talk shows. I remember the frustration I felt in that room at the complete unwillingness to discuss *media* as an issue. The discussion never went beyond how do we get *our* issues on *their* media—not what can we do about the larger issue of *media* in America.

But things are changing. At the progressive National Lawyers Guild's regional meeting in San Francisco, there were several signs of change. One was that every panel, literally every one, from one on home-porting of nuke ships by the military to a panel on migrant rights, used video in their presentations.[16] And then there was even an entire panel on media issues, led by Sol Landau, fellow of the Institute for Policy Studies in Washington. He brought up the New World Information Order, the quest of the Third World for parity of information sources. While the Third World rightly needs information, he proclaimed that U.S. citizens are perhaps the most misinformed populace on the globe. There needs to be a new information order here, and the Left has to recognize that need. The meeting was packed, and one sensed that there was at last an understanding of what was at stake.[17]

## ADVOCACY VIDEO: THE WRATH OF GRAPES

For several decades farm workers in the United States have been stricken with more and more work-related health problems, often including genetic damage to their children. Like canaries in the mines, these workers are the first to receive the residue of millions of gallons of pesticide that are sprayed each year on our food. The United Farm Workers launched a campaign to inform the public about the dangers of pesticides. This small, but active and dynamic, union has been able to mobilize a grape boycott of large agribusiness firms in this country. The success of this boycott has been, to a great extent, due to their use of computer technology—mailing lists and data gathering—and their use of video production and distribution. In response to the pesticide problem, the United Farm Workers Union together with independent producer Lorena Parlee made and is distributing a short video on the dangers of pesticide residues for workers and consumers alike. Over one million copies of their tape, *The Wrath of Grapes*, have been sent all over the United States, surely a record for the distribution of a labor union tape.

---

[16] Peter Franck, "The Law, Peace, and the Mass Media: Special Issues and a Working Symposium," *National Lawyers Guild Practitioner* 46, no. 1 (1989).

[17] The National Lawyers' Guild has been quite important in organizing around micro-radio, and pressing for noncommercial channels on Direct Broadcast Satellite (DBS).

*The Wrath of Grapes* is a powerful example of grassroots organizing using high technology to wrest control of imagery. The food corporations have hours of commercials on network television every month in which wholesome, homey foods are temptingly presented. The UFW tape takes those healthy commercial images and shows what is behind them—the workers, the pesticides, and the genetically damaged children. The UFW tape inverts the glossy commercial image of grapes so that it becomes a facade behind which an ugly truth is revealed. Every commercial for grapes becomes a reminder of the untold story, undoing commodity fetishism and returning the laborer to the product. Commercial images of grape-picking "others," the exotic vineyard workers of wine commercials, the Amos 'n Andy–type minstrel line of happily singing grapes/raisins, the beautiful girl on the package with draped open blouse whose fertile belly presents a luxurious basket of grapes—these "other" images created by the corporate growers are collapsed like a folding screen by *The Wrath of Grapes*. After viewing the pesticide helicopters and planes spraying acre after acre of crops, after seeing the heart-rending shots of deformed farm workers' children, the glistening pictures of the moist grapes in seductive commercials have become different signifiers.

ADVOCACY VIDEO: NURSES UNIONS

Tammy Gold, Lynn Goldfarb, and Pennee Bender made a tape for the Hospital Workers Union called "From Bedside to Bargaining Table." Many hundreds of copies have been made as nurses exchange tapes during organizing struggles. It has been suggested that nurses are the population with the highest percentage of VCRs in the country. Many have to work forced-shift rotation and tape their favorite TV programs for viewing later. So they were an ideal group for VCR organizing, a practice that other unions besides the nurses and farm workers are waking up to.

With the diminution of documentary funds at the NEA, NEH, and state arts councils, many film and video producers are finding that unions and organizers in general are beginning to appreciate their skills. There are few foundations on the Left, and they are more likely to fund direct action than media, but progressive organizations with a stable base of support and/member subscribers are beginning to place media as a priority budget item. It is to organizations such as this that media activists and social-issue film and video producers are increasingly looking for support. And the organizations are coming away with their very own piece of video agitprop, tailored to suit and eminently useful, from home and small meeting organizing—you bring the VCR, I'll bring the coffee—to renting a booth at the local county fair and setting up a VCR and TV.

Caryn Rogoff and Abigail Norman made a tape about "home-porting" (the stationing of nukes in harbor cities all up and down both coasts). Before they had even finished, the local committees against home-porting had taken the rough draft of the tape and rented a flatbed truck with a large video monitor to blitz populated street corners to garner signatures for the petition fight to outlaw nuke ships in the local harbor. Adventurous anti-intervention groups have backed station wagons into parking lots at malls and run Central American tapes off the cigarette lighter with the TV propped on the tailgate. Perhaps the most common use is to run tapes as often as possible on the local public access channels.

More and more organizations are using access channels. There is a direct correlation between the tenacious fortitude of the media activists in an area and the quality and quantity of progressive programs that their channel cablecasts.

For the Left it is important to build a sustaining community of media makers and supporters. The Right has done this with the 700 Club, with pledges of support of ten dollars a month from 700 people. While the Left can't offer heavenly salvation or the "rapture" of the Right, we can offer a real alternative to the sop that usually fills TV screens in this country. Because of restrictions against solicitation on public access channels, this kind of access network can't use the tactics of community radio with their marathons and constant plugging for contributions to stay afloat. However, there may be a progressive community out there that is beginning to understand the importance of alternative channels. Perhaps a coalition of media producers, media centers, labor organizations, environmental and peace groups, and art schools and alternative art organizations could form a sustaining base for a regularly scheduled transmission of independent programming. Videofreex of the world, unite!

# Telemanifesto for Collaborative Airwaves: Why Do We Need a New TV Network?

## May 1990

THE AMERICAN CULTURE has quite enough television. Why should we in any way try to increase the amount of television that is available? But does the television we now have fully represent the dreams and ideals, the art and imagination, the wit and wisdom, the cultural pluralism, the concerns and problems that we know exist in our country? As video and satellite technologies have developed, programs and program structures have not fundamentally changed. The "new technologies" are a way of getting a picture more finely defined, a distribution system more widespread. But what about the more creative aspects of television production?

There are four major areas in which visionary ideals and persistent dedication have nourished more creative and responsive television:

- In the early seventies, several experiments were developed to allow artists access to video technologies in public television studios: the TV Labs at WNET and WGBH were important and visionary experiments that were catalysts for a community of media artists.
- Over the last two decades, media centers in many of the major cities of this country have encouraged active participation in video and helped to sustain an audience appreciative of alternative forms and subjects not found in broadcast television.
- The work of the public access advocates for the past twenty years has established popular TV participation at the local

level in most major cities and in hundreds of small towns all over the country.

- Pilot projects of independent program series have served as models for creatively curated television.

Is there a way to utilize the strengths of these initiatives in combination with the technological developments which have flourished recently (growth of home dish reception, expansion of cable channels in local markets, low-power stations) to create an alternative media center in the sky: a place where artists, journalists, community organizations, and public interest groups can create, exchange, exhibit, and experiment? A place where cultural diversity is not an anomaly or an appendage, but the very center and wellspring of the project? Channel Four in Britain began by doing many of those things. We in the United States have a more highly developed infrastructure of alternative media. In addition we can utilize other resources, such as university channels and production facilities. Most educational institutions above junior high schools have media centers for production and some form of distribution capacity: in-house wired networks, cable channels, or broadcast stations. PBS began with the desire of universities to go beyond classroom fare to their community audiences. PBS in its present form has strayed from this early mandate. Substantial needs of both the educational community and public interest organizations aren't being met in the current configuration of educational/cultural program distribution.

Progressive television can be a national resource: a catalyst for creative and responsive production, a reminder of our past, a celebration of our cultural diversities, a critical voice for our problems, a warning system against ecological disaster, an international exchange center for culture and information, a fountain of inspiration, and a beacon of hope for our future. The following developments help:

- Public interest organizations such as Greenpeace, Amnesty International, and the Sierra Club are now making video on a regular basis.
- Computer networks such as Bit Net and Peace Net have easily accessible alternative national and international news and information sources.

- Video hardware has developed to a point that consumer-priced cameras are now broadcastable. *America's Funniest Home Video* is the highest rated program on commercial channels.
- Deep Dish and *The 90's* have proved that alternative TV material combined with alternative TV audiences can begin to create alternative networks.

Is this utopian folly? Or the last escape hatch from eco-cultural disaster? Probably neither, but there *are* powerful reasons for trying to build something that begins to pull some of these elements together.

# Beyond Simi Valley: Camcorders, Television, and Independent Media after L.A.

## *June 1992*

FOR CAMCORDER ACTIVISTS, the judgment in Simi Valley[18] contains a potent lesson: The context is what counts. The camcorder caught it, but it is clear that video is not enough. We need new visions that confront problems head-on and provide fresh and lively solutions for the future. Independent media in this country needs a space in the public sphere that is neither defined in eight-second sound bites nor ghetto-ized into a potpourri series. Independent material should be contextualized in regularly scheduled strands of programming. We need to create our own context.

For almost fifteen years, independent producers and media organizations have fought to gain funding and space on public television. We have lobbied, we have organized, we have written letters and manifestos. We actually have been successful in some of these efforts. The Independent Television Service is a product of that hard work. But the legislation creating ITVS is just half the battle. This victory will mean nothing unless we are willing to be creative and visionary in its implementation. Many producers will remember what happened after our first legislative victory in 1979, when Congress responded to an aggressive lobbying effort by independents with a bill directing the Corporation for Public Broadcasting to promote innovative programming and reserve a "substantial" portion of program dollars, meaning at least 50 percent, for

---

[18] The acquittal of the officers who were videotaped beating Rodney King.

independent producers. But these funds were subsequently whittled away by the "independentization" of such stalwart station cronies as McNeil-Lehrer and Bill Moyer, who created their own production companies to qualify for Program Fund awards. We must make sure this pattern does not repeat itself with ITVS. It is time for us to fully utilize the potential that ITVS represents and take the leadership in defining a new context within public television. This effort must be *pro*-active, not reactive.

ITVS has no constituency. Not even among independent producers—there are only a few "sweepstakes" winners with the huge majority of people holding losing tickets. The political Right is attacking, the CPB is waiting for the end of ITVS or perhaps itself, and Congress wants to see something on TV. ITVS most of all needs support—from the independent community, from media centers, from Congress, and from the many adventurous and innovative program directors at public television stations (who are out there in surprising numbers, though conspicuously absent from the big five status quo PBS stations).

ITVS has the potential to create an alternative programming service fed via satellite to public television stations on a nightly basis. Through such a service, independents could join with those supportive TV programmers in a bold experiment to create a true context for alternative views on public television.

In public radio there are two programming entities: National Public Radio (NPR) and American Public Radio (APR). APR started in Saint Paul, where ITVS is now housed, in order to distribute Garrison Keillor's Prairie Home Companion and other programs to the public radio stations around the country. There is no inherent reason that public television could not have a second programming source. At the present time there are the regional networks such as the Pacific Mountain Network that covers the western states and the Eastern Education Network in the east. There is no alternative network for prime-time programs that is transregion by interest. The interest exists. Many people throughout the system would schedule independent programming. Deep Dish TV, *The 90's,*

The Gulf Crisis TV Project, *America's Defense Monitor,* Satellite University Network, and the *Iraq Aftermath Show* have all been scheduled on public television satellites. These programs have been distributed by what are called "maverick feeds" on the public television satellites. Many have been pulled down by courageous programmers, proving that many PBS stations will run hard-hitting independent programming if given a chance.

By creating a regular identifiable feed, ITVS could help connect with the large audiences of younger and multicultural viewers who are tired of the *Masterpiece Theatre* status quo and who have shown their loyalty and enthusiasm for *The 90's* and *Edge* (both of which have been precipitously eliminated from PBS programming schedules). Though never properly promoted and often poorly scheduled, these shows connected with a new, more diverse audience.

In addition there are the "secondary market stations" in many cities such as WNYC in New York or WYBE in Philadelphia.[19] The old boys of the PBS system have been trying to squeeze these stations by making them pay high penalties for not taking the prime-time feeds whole hog. If the smaller stations don't program exactly what the bigger stations do, they have to ante up high prices for the PBS shows they do take. Because a substantial rebellion is going on about these programming and funding structures, there is a potential to form an alliance between these stations and independents. ITVS could take the initiative to directly work with these entities.

In the early days of ITVS's formation, Britain's Channel Four was the subject of much study, with researchers combing its programming schedules and interviewing administrators. Channel Four has commissioning producers who develop programming ideas and grant production monies for series and individual programs. ITVS instead decided to create a democratic peer review process in contrast to the autocratic and hierarchical structure in London. However, the current

---

[19] Alas, this secondary PBS New York channel (31) was sold to a private corporation in the 1990s. A detailed story of the struggle around a secondary PBS station in Pittsburgh is Jerry Starr's *AIRWARS: The Fight to Reclaim Public Broadcasting* (Boston: Beacon Press, 2000).

setup has retained the notion of commissioning producers by calling the peer panel administrators "producers," although they are not allowed to select programs or series. Combining the notion of production executives with the peer review process does not fit. When grafted on to the peer system, it results in an intervening bureaucratic layer that is viewed with suspicion by grantees. The ITVS bureaucrats are administrator/producers with ill-defined roles and have taken it upon themselves to negotiate co-production deals and have added restrictive clauses to already cumbersome contracts. Producers who have received grants have complained that ITVS can be more prohibitive and complicated than PBS itself. Instead of going with the strengths of either system, ITVS seems to be burdened with the problems of both.

ITVS should be utilizing the democratic and grassroots infrastructures that already exist in our country. What do we have that London doesn't? Media centers. (This is one infrastructure Channel Four never had to begin with, though they tried to create them through their workshop program with varying degrees of success.) Media centers have been dealing with their constituencies for years. Veteran programmers such as Edith Kramer from the Pacific Film Archives, Robin Reidy Oppenheimer at 911 in Seattle, and Chris Hill from Hall Walls in Buffalo have years of successful programming experience. They know how to put programs together—which is what ITVS needs to do and hasn't done yet. Working with media centers would give these facilities and their constituents a real stake in ITVS. It would also be a way for ITVS to decentralize and be democratic beyond its centrally administered peer panels.

Here, for example, is one idea about how ITVS could work in partnership with media centers: Lets call it "The State of the Union": a month of images and ideas from the grassroots. In the wake of the widespread insurrections in the aftermath of the Rodney King trial, this program could serve as a thirty-day forum for individuals and communities who are on the frontlines in the struggle for justice in the United States.

This series would be multicultural, multidimensional, and multitudinous and offer a hard look at the United States: the state of our union from the grassroots point of view. The series would provide thirty programs in January, thirty messages to the new (same old?) president, one each night. It could be offered to PBS with a two-week decision time. They would have to commit and schedule the series on their prime-time regular feed. If they don't want it, however, it would still be possible for public stations to run the shows through maverick feeds by secondary PBS stations.

The programs could be compilations, made at ten media centers chosen by the National Alliance of Media Art Centers (NAMAC). Each center would provide a three-part miniseries reflective of the programming that people in that area are producing—and "area" could mean geography, ethnic group, or subject matter. The centers would then pick a curator (someone who regularly puts together programming for the center, or the local independent series on PTV, or public access) to select and package three hours of programming on subjects that matter.

Each three-part series would have an overriding theme, based on what producers and programmers at the media centers are already doing or want to do—it's up to them. For example, the section from, say, Buffalo could be about women, health and law, gender and choice. The three from the Film Arts Foundation could be about urban issues: jobs and justice in the inner cities. The miniseries from *Chicago Labor Beat* could be about jobs and free trade. The Appalshop series could be on toxic wastes in rural settings. The media centers are already packaging programs for local cable or their local public television.

This would accomplish two things. First, it would help ITVS satisfy the mandate of Congress to expand its geographic diversity. Second, it would be a way to democratize the decision-making process: first to NAMAC, which chooses the media centers; then to the centers, which pick the curators; then to the curators, who select the shows; then to the producers, who choose the topics in the first place.

The entire budget for the series would be $300,000—equivalent to the maximum amount for a single grant from ITVS. This would provide $30,000 to ten media centers, from ten different parts of the country. There is not a media center in this country that couldn't do this in less than a month. Putting programs together is what they're doing already. And there is not a media center that doesn't need $30,000 to do what they're doing already. The sum could be broken down as follows: $3,000 for overhead and outreach, $6,000 per show for producers' fees at $100 a minute, and $1,000 for miscellaneous administrative and promotional costs.

In addition ITVS would put up some money to hire a liaison person for a lively logo and wrap-around for the entire series with composed music (something that's fresh and beautiful), and promote the series to both the stations and the media. The series might also provide some introductory information about independent media and about media centers. At the end of the shows would be the toll-free numbers for purchasing tapes and info on local media centers.

Most media centers have either post-production centers or ongoing relationships with post-production houses. In addition most media centers have major resources in their communities that can be mobilized for this sort of project. This would include contacts with producers, newsletters, and the local press. This also includes relationships with local public television stations. It is assumed that local PBS stations would feel obligated to run a series in which their local media arts center is featured.

The series would amount to a research and development project for ITVS. Not all of the miniseries will be great; organizing programs for exhibition is not the same as putting together TV programs. However, more and more media centers are making TV series. This project would enable ITVS to identify some of the people and resources it could work with in the future. And it would be taking chances: visionary, exciting media work always does. Isn't this supposed to be the difference between PBS and ITVS?

The goals of ITVS and the status quo PBS hierarchy are not necessarily compatible. The larger producing stations have solid reasons for wanting independent series to fail. They see the ITVS funding as reducing the federal programming moneys available to their in-house production budgets. Waiting for

PBS to approve our projects is a futile exercise. We should not let PBS call the shots. We should take the initiative and reach out to the local stations who want to help. This will be a good way to build a constituency within the public television system. It will quickly identify those who are willing not only to schedule independent work, but also to do so in good time slots.

We need to create a strong identity: one that is open-ended and fearless. For this, ITVS needs

- To build a working relationship with independents and their organizations
- To build a constituency with audience and community organizations
- To connect with new, fresh, hip work from many producers from across the country
- To utilize the years of experience and expertise from distributors and knowledgeable programmers at independent exhibitions spaces
- To take advantage of the wisdom and street smarts of veteran media center administrators, many of whom are not making TV series in their local communities
- To work with Deep Dish, Freespeech TV, and other television entities who have already seized the transponders and the airwaves and built grassroots constituencies for alternative programming
- To initiate and create a truly exciting programming service in a bold new television experiment.

# Guerrillas in Our Midst: Experimental Video and Public Television[20]

## April 1998

THAT GUERRILLA VIDEO is now the subject of historical reflection is probably a sign of its demise. There has been a flurry of archival and publishing activity centering on experiments made in the seventies during the early days of video. The Video Data Bank released *Surveying the First Decade,* a compilation of work from that time, and Oxford University Press published Deirdre Boyle's book *Subject to Change: Guerrilla Television Revisited* about the video movements of the early sixties and seventies. This reflection on the utopian impulse in early video is an opportunity to think about the state of media in this country, in particular those movements that have tried to create electronic space for noncommercial views that run counter to the mainstream.

Media studies in this country have been curiously ineffectual in our electronic public sphere. What do we have to show for our myriad studies of media violence, our volumes of feminist readings, and our seemingly endless critical diatribes? Action for Children's Television, the one institution that actually affected policy formation, seems to have collapsed into the V chip. In Britain there has been a closer affinity between those who reflect on television and those who make it. It is possible for theory and praxis to collaborate for structural change. One can draw a line from the work of Stuart Hall, Raymond Wil-

---

[20] A version of this article was published in *Afterimage* (Rochester, N.Y.: Spring 1999).

liams, Peter Wollen, Steven Heath, Laura Mulvey, and other Brits to the inception of Channel Four, which, for all its current shortcomings, is still better than anything in this country. The prolific field of cultural studies in the United States has focused on mass culture, rarely giving even a nod to more marginal and/or experimental manifestations of television. Very little television research actually discusses alternatives to commercial television.

*Subject to Change* brings cultural studies, broadcast history, and critical media scholarship to bear on "guerrilla video." Boyle concentrates on three strands of the video movement of the late sixties and early seventies: Broadside TV of Johnson City, Tennessee, University Community Video (UCV) in Minneapolis, and TVTV, whose trans-geographic crew were from Los Angeles, Chicago, and New York. Broadside was one of the first organizations to regularly produce community programming for cable, though under the aegis of "local origination," not true public access. It was initially set up as an equipment resource center with facilitator/teachers modeled after the Highlander Center in New Market, Tennessee, a leadership training center that had a major impact on the civil rights movement. UCV was a unique collaboration between a university, public television, and local media activists. Community organizations worked with video producers to make programming on important local issues for regional broadcast on public television. TVTV was perhaps the most famous of the video collectives that roamed the land with lens covers dangling from their ever-ready portapaks.

Spunky, restless, and iconoclastic, TVTV's tapes were a breath of fresh air in the seventies, in stark contrast not only to stodgy commercial fare but to the overly earnest tapes from the New/Old Left with their interminable harangues from microphones at demonstrations.[21] Although never willing to spell out a specific ideological stance, TVTV made the *media* their politics, and even their checklist for camera people had a stance of defiance against the standard broadcast mores:

---

[21] Skip Blumberg, " 'The TVTV Show': Behind the Scenes and between the Lines," *Televisions* 3, no. 4 (1977).

"We're not into declarative, explicit action or statements. . . . At best, we want to cover the media covering those actions and cover the people planning for or reflecting on them. The actions themselves are of negligible importance to us."[22]

TVTV was savvy about television and brought together great talent behind and in front of the camera. (On-camera talent included John Belushi, Bill Murray, and Lily Tomlin, and behind the cameras were Skip Blumberg, Nancy Cain, Paul Goldsmith, and others.) They had a way of framing politicians in a context more insightful than the typical network newscasts, interviewing a tipsy politician in a seedy bar, or a dance floor Republican Romeo at a victory party. TVTV always let the camera stay on long enough to see the grimaces behind the smiles. They would watch as the networks interviewed a politician, and when the network camera would stop, and all the lights be turned off, TVTV's cameras would stay on to catch the expletives and surly attitude of the impatient politician or stand-up reporter. Boyle's book is full of these encounters, revealing much about mainstream media as well as providing insight into the style and wit of TVTV's crews.

With the help of people like WNET's David Loxton and the Rockefeller Foundation's Howard Klein,[23] TVTV was able to grab foundation money and occasional channel space from public television for several years for their bold and bright high jinks. There were certain lines even TVTV could not cross, however, as evidenced in the scandal that broke after the screening of *In Hiding: America's Fugitive Underground—An Interview with Abbie Hoffman* (1975). Yippie leader Hoffman had been busted in a cocaine sale setup and was on the lam for several years. TVTV producer Michael Shamburg expressed surprise that Hoffman's interview would cause such a stir. Certainly Shamberg must have realized that fugitive Abbie Hoffman was someone who was not to be given space on the public channels of this country. B. J. Bullert's

---

[22] Deirdre Boyle, *Subject to Change: Guerilla Television Revisited* (New York: Oxford University Press, 1996).

[23] See Marita Sturken: "Private Money and Personal Influence: Howard Klein and the Rockefeller Foundation's Funding of the Media Arts," *Afterimage* 14, no. 6 (1987).

recent book *Public Television: Politics and the Battle over Documentary Film* provides countless examples of PBS gate keeping and the convoluted structures that protect and perpetuate their cautionary stance. Nowadays *Hard Copy* and the other TV tabloids mimic the format of TVTV guerrillas, but their radical content is suppressed.

The eighties became a period of co-optation, or some might call it "sellout." TVTV's Shamburg became a Hollywood producer of the likes of *The Big Chill* and *A Fish Called Wanda*. Allen Rucker is doing network talk shows. Paul Goldsmith took up filming commercials. Not only the people were co-opted. The ideas of the movement often appear in strange convoluted formats, sometimes in direct opposition to the initial impetus. Ideas first sketched by TVTV have found their way to mainstream television on *Saturday Night Live* and other comedy venues. One can easily trace the show *Cops* to some experiments that the video guerrillas did in the early seventies. TVTV's notion of going out with cops on the beat was picked up by Alan and Susan Raymond for the *Police Tapes*, which then evolved into *Hill Street Blues* and eventually into the sort of drug busts *mit* camera that have become familiar network fare. The camcorder is the snare for what Paper Tiger calls *America's Least Wanted*,[24] the heretofore unrepresented black and Latino underclass, now exposed by police searchlights and weekly "hard copy."

For Boyle, the early video experiments (however lopsided in terms of sexual politics and multicultural representation) were visionary and noble but ill-fated attempts to reform a corrupt system. There was an assumption by these video freaks that authentic radical video would alter the vision of the viewing public, in the way that many of their own heads were changed when they smoked their home-grown stashes or gobbled down their 'shrooms. They trumpeted a new "Woodstock" consciousness and believed that people would not put up with the "vast wasteland," as FCC commissioner Newton Minow had pronounced it. There was no doubt in

---

[24] *America's Least Wanted* is a critique of "reality TV" cop shows; it's available from Paper Tiger TV, 339 Lafayette St., New York, N.Y. 10012.

their own expanded minds that sooner or later everyone (or almost everyone) would eventually become conscientized. It was only a matter of time. The early video enthusiasts thought that video would change the world.

It is a sign of their naiveté, their faith in the power of McLuhanesque aphorisms, and/or perhaps their impatience with boring meetings that they did not spend much time thinking about strategies for changing even the policies that were of central interest to them: media policies. The video guerrillas were reluctant to undertake the exhausting and thankless work of infrastructure development, and there was little prospect of funding long-term progressive initiatives. Those few video pioneers who were able to nurture an infrastructure for production, training, and distribution have survived: for example, New York City's Downtown Community Television and Appalshop in Whitesburg, Kentucky.

Access has had a bad rap—belittled and denigrated by the mass media, access was also ridiculed by video cowboy/artists like TVTV, who tended to see the masses not as potential colleagues, but as camp subjects for their extra-wide angle lens. The local origination folks such as Broadside saw pure "first come/first serve" open access as a threat to their own control, and the university/art world savants at media centers such as UCV were embarrassed by the rabble factor. There are those who have focused specifically on promoting and providing authentic public access and who have kept the faith in unfettered media democracy, despite the uneven programming and administrative demands that requires. Perhaps of all the attempts at media "revolution," public access has been the most successful, the most democratic, and the most enduring. As such it is ultimately the most radical, and as such, the most subject to disinformation from the vested interests of corporate information.

The airwaves of this country were initially licensed to commercial entities with the requirement that they broadcast "in the public interest." In much the same way that Ronald Reagan counted catsup as a proper vegetable for school lunches, the FCC counts the Home Shopping Channel as fulfilling the need for "public interest" programming (by pro-

viding consumer information). Robert McChesney, in *Telecommunications, Mass Media and Democracy*,[25] looks back at
"public interest," that much bandied term, focusing on a time
when there was a genuine movement for such a thing in the
late twenties and early thirties. Educators and labor unions
formed a powerful alliance to work for noncommercial broadcasting at that time. McChesney has rescued this fascinating
history from the dustbin of union and congressional archives.
His effort provides a historical case for collaborative work to
create a public media system. That those efforts failed does
not diminish their importance as lessons for today.

In *Public Radio and Television in America: A Political History*, Ralph Engelman traces the promises of "public" broadcasting in this country. PBS has now opened their channels to
advertising as egregious as any spots on commercial networks, in spite of, or perhaps because of, their more upscale
nature. This is not to say that these commercial spots are that
much worse than the "underwriting" of the NewsHour by
such entities as Archer Daniels Midland, one of the giants of
rapacious agro-business, caught in 1995 in a massive price-
fixing scandal. This episode is discussed in James Ledbetter's
useful book *Made Possible by . . . : The Death of Public Broadcasting in the United States* under the telling chapter title
"Buying Silence."[26] The reliance on the contributions by big
players ensures that the one nightly forum for "public" news
is free from any content which might criticize the more brutal
and corrupt aspects of globalization and other forms of corporate profiteering.[27] Pressures from the government funding
agency (the Corporation for Public Broadcasting) have
pushed small nonprofit broadcasting entities into the arms of
larger radio empires (such as that of the acquisitive Allen
Chartok at WAMC, originally limited to Albany, which has
now colonized much of the Northeast's noncommercial

---

[25] Robert McChesney, *Telecommunications, Mass Media and Democracy:
The Battle for the Control of U.S. Broadcasting, 1928–1935* (New York: Oxford University Press, 1995).

[26] James Ledbetter, *Made Possible by . . . : The Death of Public Broadcasting in the United States* (New York: Verso, 1997).

[27] See Hoynes's *Public Television for Sale*.

radio). CPB's pressures have had a devastating effect on the Pacifica Network. This has led to an extreme break between the local, often volunteer, producers and the network's board of directors.[28]

Faced with the dismal prospects for any authentic "public interest" or noncommercial, noncorporate "public" broadcasting, it is useful to look at some of the early courageous experiments to create visionary television and to reflect on the utopian rhetoric that accompanied the origins of public broadcasting. Engelman's book explores the creation of public access and Pacifica in addition to being a detailed overview of the efforts to create a government-supported (but not government-controlled) noncommercial radio and television system. Of particular interest is the role of liberal foundations in these efforts. The Ford and Rockefeller foundations were extensively involved in the early stages of public broadcasting, supporting creative programming initiatives, such as the innovative *Great American Dream Machine* and the TV Lab, and funding research on technology and governance. This historical initiative has been hijacked by the right wing, whose underwriting of programming has given national voice to such ideologues as Ben Wattenburg, Peggy Noonan, Fred Barnes, and others. The only long-term regular commentators on PBS are conservative Republicans, Tony Brown and William F. Buckley (twenty-five years!). Besides underwriting the programs of these pundits, the Heritage, Sciafe, Olin, and Bradley foundations have been profligate in their support of right-wing "think tanks," while tepid "Left" policy institutes such as the Institute for Policy Studies must go begging, competing with the tattered remains of thousands of liberal non-profit public interest and public service organizations. The Right has strategically placed a major share of their grant money into media work and policy development. The money that is spent on media projects by the so-called liberal foundations is a pittance when compared to the well-heeled agenda of the Right through such fronts as the American Enterprise Institute, not

---

[28] Mathew Lazar, *Pacifica Radio: The Rise of an Alternative Network* (Philadelphia: Temple University Press, 2000).

to mention the direct assault against the idea of public television carried on by David Horowitz and Peter Collier.

The wholesale takeover of public broadcasting by reactionary forces includes the intimidation that the Right has been able to foist on the now San Francisco–based ITVS, which is loath to take on anything with the vaguest anti-corporate stance. ITVS even went looking for right-wing filmmakers when so many of their grant requests were from the Left. They sought out right-wing spokespersons on several of their series. Rather than be a vocal champion for independents and a catalyst for change within television in the United States, ITVS is terrified of right-wing criticism and dependent on approval from the public television bureaucracy, which is fundamentally at odds with independent producers. This sorry state of affairs is particularly painful because ITVS was created by the Left-oriented independent community through the rigorous lobbying efforts of local, regional, and national independent media organizations, with the support of trade unions and consumer groups. ITVS has virtually abandoned the field that created it, weakening its constituency for any battles that lie ahead. Because the production funds which are funneled off to ITVS from CPB are seen in the eyes of the PBS power structure as funds that are diverted from their own rightful endowment, PBS is not about to promote ITVS programming and delights in making the ITVS employees squirm and grovel. Meanwhile the infrastructure of the independent community both nationally and locally withers on the vine as one after another media arts organizations close their doors. The organizations that birthed ITVS are abandoned by their profligate child who has gone to live in the gated condo on the hill and shows little interest in its embarrassing activist parents.

In the past, German television has been an important source of funding for independent producers from the United States, such as Yvonne Rainer, Greg Bordowitz, Mark Rappaport, and Su Freiderich. The German model of public service broadcasting was set up by U.S. officials under the Marshall Plan. Sadly, the European noncommercial systems are being whittled away by pressures from global lending institutions. In the United States PBS was never funded adequately and so was inherently corrupt from its inception, depending on annual review by politicians and on programming underwriting by corporations. What little visionary programming has eked out in thirty years of "public" television has been for the most part due to the occasional commitment of a few liberal foundations working in concert with a few state or national arts and/or humanities administrators. Although the headlines are often about obscenity, the well-orchestrated attacks on the cultural endowments, in strategic collaboration with the attacks on public television, are specifically aimed at curtailing visionary and/or critical progressive content in any national forum. It's not really the exposed genitals or the bottles of piss they're after. The Right's strategy, well documented in Heritage Foundation reports, has paid off. Any oppositional voice has been effectively kept from the public debate—except, of course, the extreme Right, whose radical positions serve to "balance" talk shows and to push the so-called center to their side.

The idea of revisiting the original notion of a public interest broadcasting system is intriguing for those of us with deep scars from years of doing battle against that fortress. To hope for any major restructuring might be unrealistic, but any reform movement in media today has a base of research that can provide important grounding for reform. McChesney's work speaks to the potential for a coalition of public interest organizations and the useful role that can be played by foundations who are willing to support visionary projects. Much of the public interest broadcasting movement that coalesced in the early part of this century was supported at crucial moments by the Payne Fund, a small liberal foundation. Strategic generosity at this time in history could have similar importance. As Engelman so eloquently documents, people at the Ford and Rockefeller foundations did try to open up the discourse in the initial stages of educational public television, and their successors could play a similar key role at this juncture. In addition, the United States has a rich history of creative and dynamic video guerrillas, and it is important to nurture and support innovative media work within our national public sphere.

The other grounding for a new reform initiative is the beginning of an authentic media movement in this country. In the last several years, the Institute for Alternative Journalism and others have sponsored two large national meetings to discuss the problems and possibilities of U.S. media. These meetings, Media and Democracy I and II (San Francisco 1996, New York 1997), however problematic (and there have been many criticisms of the plenary programs especially), are nevertheless hopeful signs that the many bright and energetic people who work in media, both mainstream and marginal, can come together to create new structures for collaboration and resistance to commercialism. For the first time since the 1930s, there seems to be a media movement.[29] The conferences have inspired local initiatives in Seattle, Toronto, Los Angeles, Chicago, Philadelphia, and other cities. In St. Louis the Cultural Environment Movement has likewise organized meetings and is conducting research under the direction of George Gerbner. In New York there has been action by the New York Free Media Alliance, moving beyond conference panels and academic studies to organize workshops on pirate radio transmission and internet videocasting. Along with Paper Tiger, New York NABET, the Communications Workers of America, Fairness and Accuracy in Reporting (FAIR), and many other organizations, New York Free Media coordinated a large demonstration outside the headquarters of the media conglomerates, in conjunction with the New York Media and Democracy Congress. The March against the Moguls is documented at a web site (www.papertiger.org) and in two half-hour video tapes that are available from Paper Tiger: *Putting the Demo Back in Democracy,* parts 1 and 2. The Bread and Puppet Theater was there with giant "running dogs of the media," reporter "hounds," and paparazzi wagging their tails. It felt like the scene in the movie *Network* when everyone says, "We're not gonna take it anymore." Only this demonstration was more fun, more culturally diverse, better researched, and well documented—there were camcorders everywhere. Among the speakers was a rap poet named Shank, who took up the title

---

[29] The independent media centers are a bright example of what is now possible. (See "Gathering Storm" in Part 9.)

of Danny Schecter's book *The More You Watch, the Less You Know* and gave it a beat. The glass and steel canyons roared when the crowd chimed in. Tourists in Times Square gave the demo a thumbs up, and even the police who were kept busy adjusting the sawhorses nodded in agreement. As a participant, I have never been in a demonstration in which I felt more sympathy from the passersby. It hopefully indicates that the public isn't gonna take it much longer.

To rally that sentiment into concrete action takes a great deal of work and the kind of careful planning and organizing that the New York Free Media Alliance did for the Mogul demo and that the Institute for Alternative Journalism did for the Media and Democracy Congresses. It also needs the kind of watchdog research that FAIR, Project Censored, Gerbner, and others have done and continue to do. It also takes the serious commitment of historians such as Boyle, McChesney, and Engelman to point out what is *possible*. But to make real change happen, we need the TVTVs, the UCVs, the Broadsides, and, closer to home, the Paper Tigers and the Deep Dishes to point to the *impossible*.

# 7

# Electronic Bandits:
# The Media Wars South
# of the Border

# Introduction

IN 1983, shortly after the invasion of Grenada, I traveled to Nicaragua with a group of videomakers to make a tape about the situation there. In the tense atmosphere of the Reagan presidency, everyone expected an imminent invasion by the United States. While there I met several Nicaraguans who were making their own media of the situation and began an exchange with them. The personnel from Sandinista TV were young enthusiasts with consumer-type camcorders. As an independent producer from the United States, where the networks reject small-format video, it was exciting to be in a country where the camcorder was the official recorder. The cultural events and political demonstrations we attended were all recorded on half-inch tape and broadcast to the entire country. "Nicaraguan Video: Live from the Revolution" is an overview of the video production in that besieged country at the height of the Sandinista years.

My interest in Latin America began in 1952 when I was twelve years old and my father took a job in a U.S.-owned Cuban mine. My family moved to a remote outpost on a Cuban bay, 500 miles from Havana. It was 1952, and Cuba was in the throes of the Batista dictatorship. This experience of seeing firsthand the ravages of corrupt bureaucracy in league with exploitative colonialism left a deep impression on me. I returned there in the 1980s for the first time since I left in 1953. The 1959 Cuban revolution had changed many things, not the least of which was Cuban media. "History in Havana" is a look at the Cuban Film Festival of 1986 and the inauguration of the School of Three Worlds at San Antonio de Los Baños. "Women as Cultural Producers on Cuban TV" is an essay about Cuban television, which I studied for several years in preparation for curating an exhibition series called *Stone's Throw: TV from Cuba, Island in Goliath's Sea*, co-curated by

Monica Melamid. I was especially interested in a comedy series about feuding families and a senior couple who fall in
love.

"Community Media in Brazil" is a description of the *TV
Maxambomba* videomobile that visits the *favelas* of Rio every
evening on a different street corner. "Community Media in
Brazil" traces the route of the mobile video team who produce
and distribute video by and about *favela* residents. This sort of
mobile media is descended from the cinetrains[1] of the early
days of the Soviet Union, when trains equipped with film projectors traveled across the vast expanses to mobilize peasant
and worker support for the revolution. In both situations the
idea was not only to present finished films, but also to make
them: to have the audiences become active participants in
media making. The cinetrains had cameras and lights and
cars with film laboratories for processing. In each town, in
each factory they filmed the workers, processed the film, and
played it back in an interactive loop. Likewise in Brazil, the
*TV Maxambomba* vans project tape but also have a live camera, which is projected on a large screen, where neighborhood
residents comment on a variety of issues, or sing or tell jokes.

The Internet has been hyped as a "revolutionary" tool, but
the Zapatista rebellion in Chiapas was the force that proved
that might actually be true. "Zapatistas On-line" is a look at
the use of computers and the Internet by these clever guerrillas in Chiapas.

---

[1] These trains and their project director Medvedkin have been eloquently
portrayed in two films by Chris Marker: *The Train Rolls On* and *The Last
Bolshevik.*

# Nicaraguan Video:
# Live from the Revolution

## *December 1983*

*The Nicaraguan Revolution occurred in 1979 when almost the entire country applauded the triumphant entry into Managua of the Sandinista rebels, who had been inspired by the memory of Augusto Cesar Sandino, a liberal general in the 1920s who held out against the occupation of the country by U.S. Marines. In the early 1980s hundreds of sympathetic U.S. citizens flocked to Nicaragua to show their solidarity with the aims of the revolution and to assist in the process of rebuilding the country after the damage of both the civil war and the earthquakes of the 1970s. I was part of several delegations to Nicaragua and wrote this overview of how small-format video was being incorporated into the new government. Sadly, local production is practically absent from post-Sandinista Nicaragua. Most programming now relies on imports. This essay is a look at a unique era.*

ANY PUBLIC EVENT in Nicaragua that attracts more than thirty people will also draw a video crew. Not the U.S. network crews who limit their coverage to interviews with irate *La Prensa* editors and impatient consumers in food lines. Not the European crews who work the solidarity brigades from both East and West Germany. Not the independent U.S. and Canadian crews who line up en masse for a Mary Hartman (the nun, not the soap opera dip) tour of La Granja, the model prison farm, or wait for a visit with Ernesto Cardenal at the former Somoza estate, headquarters of the Ministry of Culture. No. The public events: the concerts, the neighborhood meetings, the election rallies, the funerals of martyrs, the marches of mothers, the openings of hospitals, the bombing of hospitals, the openings of schools and likewise attacks on them by the Contras, the school graduations, the theater festivals, the ceremonies for land title distribution to *campesinos*, the Cara Al Pueblo meeting (Face the People)—all these are documented by the video crews of the new Nicaragua.

Portable video has been an essential tool in recent social struggles in the United States, but because the movements of which it has been a part are so marginal, it has been limited to taping organizing meetings here and there and lame discussion programs on public access cable and late nights on public television. In Nicaragua it is a part of a social dynamic that is transforming a country. Video is not just documenting that process. It is very much a part of that process.

The following are notes from two visits to Nicaragua in November 1983 and in August 1984. It is also based on information supplied by my son Ezra, who lived and worked in Managua as a video liaison person for X-Change TV, an organization devoted to cultural exchanges between Central America and the United States.

The first thing one realizes about Nicaraguan media, and the revolution of which it is a part, is that there is no single party line imposed. This is a diverse society, a nation brought together under a broad coalition of groups, with a wide variety of beliefs and styles. This variety is reflected in the various groups producing and distributing video. There is a different feeling in their work spaces and in the tapes they make.

There are five main centers of production in Nicaragua. The largest and best-equipped is the Sistema Sandinista—the national television system. The second is the video workshop that is part of the Agrarian Reform Ministry—Communicaciones Midinra. The third is Taller Popular de Video (People's Video Workshop), which is a part of the Sandinista Workers Union. The fourth is INCINE, under the Ministry of Culture, whose main product is film, but whose work includes video production. The last is Pro-TV, which documents the Cara Al Pueblo meeting and produces programs for the Ministry of Interior.

SISTEMA SANDINISTA

The Sistema programs two channels every day: one from noon
onwards, and the other from 4 P.M. The programming, like
much of Nicaragua, is an amazing assortment of contradictions—from the saccharine novellas from Mexico and Colombia to the dubbed adventures of *Barnaby Jones*. It has ads for
McDonalds (yes, there is one in Managua), Coca-Cola, and Soviet tractors. In November 1983 the station logo was a group
of tiny animated peace doves that flapped their way around a
globe to form the letters SSTV, while an accompanying vertical crawl proclaimed "Toda Las Armas al Pueblo!" (All Arms
to the People!). Despite its revolutionary station breaks, the
Sistema's productions are often reworking of U.S. formats.
Television everywhere has been so completely dominated by
the U.S. model that "professionalism" has come to be defined
as how closely Nicaraguan TV resembles NBC.

The Soviet film that developed in the 1920s was forging new
paths and was able to leap over what few conventions existed
in film at the time. Nicaraguan TV comes forty years into a TV
world in which 180 national television systems look as though
they were all housed on the fortieth floor of Rockefeller
Center.

The most unusual item on an evening's schedule is apt to be
the news, partly because what is happening in Nicaragua is
unusual and interesting, but also because the form in which it
is broadcast is more open-ended and spontaneous than most
of the Sistema offerings. Activities are shot hand-held. This
doesn't mean they are wiggly. Most of the cameramen (in
Nicaragua the Sistema camera people that I saw were men)
are rock-steady and have no real need for tripods. Their stories are often visual essays—not many interviews and no "on-
the-scene" reporters. Information is supplied by the newscast-
ers in voiceover, but often long pieces of visual material run
without comment—in a style that is leisurely and flowing—
more like U.S. public access, where time is free and information isn't sandwiched between commercials. I have the feeling
that this is more from lack of enough tightly edited material
than from any theoretical inspiration of management. One

news show I saw was fifteen minutes of inchoate drunken reveling at the Santo Domingo Festival. Church festivals are always covered. This is a country where the institutional church is in direct opposition to the policies of the government, but where three priests hold cabinet-level positions. All church activities are news—from the Purissima Festival to the bitter pronouncements of anti-Sandinista Archbishop Obando Bravo. Participants in the ongoing church debate are endlessly interviewed in the TV studios. On most nights the church is at least a third of the news.

The segments on the news that are produced in the studio are often awkward and replete with transitional errors and shaky chroma-key edges. The occasional goofs and missed cues have made the administration of the Sistema reluctant to distribute their news programs abroad. X-Change TV has repeatedly tried to get samples of the news for distribution, but Sistema executives would rather lend out their "professional" work—slick entertainment specials—in the "Live from Lincoln Center" genre. These canned and controlled artsy shows are a long way from the "live from the revolution" programs that X-Change has in mind. But the Sistema is probably ashamed of the news. The open informality may charm northern visitors, the transitional goofs may denote self-referential process consciousness to a *Screen* subscriber, but they only give ulcers to the Sistema's producers.

The attraction of X-Change to the more primitive news is an example of the kind of solidarity activity that has been one element of an ongoing debate within the Ministry of Culture and the artistic community in Managua. One of the results of the revolution has been an explosion of creativity among the *campesinos;* native writing and primitive painting have proliferated.[2] This type of art is always popular with solidarity groups. A German art gallery sponsored huge editions of primitive painting posters—reproduced on expensive paper with an elaborate graphic technique. Likewise, editions of

---

[2] For a look at the extraordinary public art of Nicaragua during the Sandinista years, see David Kunzle, *The Murals of Revolutionary Nicaragua 1979–1992* (Berkeley: University of California Press, 1995).

compassionate poetry, produced by internationalists, have been printed and bound and distributed widely. The national folklorico dance movement is doing great, receiving donations from all over the world. But professional artists have asked, Where, in this scheme, is the support for serious artists who may be developing a more complex and probing aesthetic? The attraction of revolutionary tourists for primitive posters leaves out Nicaraguan artists who have spent long careers in the arts. Most of these artists come from middle- and upper-class families, who had the leisure and material wealth to support what in a desperately poor country was viewed as a luxury. In a country where every piece of paper and every pencil is a precious resource, the Ministry of Culture cannot afford to put out editions of their works. Economic concerns are not the only issue, as there are many who believe that the arts should be mass-based and that supporting an elite group of university-trained artists only perpetuates the class differences that still exist from pre-revolutionary times.[3]

While the debate continues, an important role of the Sistema has been to make national performance of both the folklorico and the professional theater and dance groups available to a wide audience. *Sandino: Santo y Sena* (Saint and Symbol), their most elaborate presentation to date, is a dance and music spectacular that was recorded at a live performance in a ruined hotel that has recently become Managua's opera house. The building, hard hit during the 1972 earthquake, is a crumbling shell with an eerie presence that forms a poignant reminder that this is *not* a typical theater in a typical Latin American country, but constitutes an art built on the crumbling remains of resistant traditions. I saw a performance there in which the vigor and enthusiasm of the production burst through the decay of the surroundings. The technical virtuosity of the lighting, the dancing, and the hundred-piece (!) string orchestra was in stark contrast to the extreme poverty of most of the audience and with the decrepit state of the

---

[3] For an interesting discussion of culture in Nicaragua, see David E. Whisnant, *Rascally Signs in Sacred Places: The Politics of Culture in Nicaragua* (Chapel Hill: University of North Carolina Press, 1995).

theater. Imagine that an earthquake has destroyed New York's Plaza Hotel and you are sitting in its ruins watching Ballet Hispanico with an audience of 3,000 unemployed workers from the South Bronx. Needless to say, there are a few differences. For one thing, because of the revolution, the theater is *their* theater. You feel it when you are there with them. That sense of empowerment is a part of the event; it is also a part of the television presentations that record it. The audience cutaways are therefore different. They serve the function of reminding the TV audience of just whose show it is anyway. (Come to think of it, maybe the Lincoln Center cutaways serve the same purpose.)

MIDINRA

Communicaciones Midinra (Ministerio de Desarrollo de Reconstrucción Nacional) is part of the Agrarian Ministry. The offices are a little outside of Managua on the road to Masaya, in what was a rather well-to-do hacienda-type house with a large interior patio surrounded by grandiose archways. The patio is used to store empty VCR boxes. Below the arches, the desks and files are an amazing collection of types—from Danish Modern to Ramada Inn Inquisition style. Their walnut and teak finishes are stenciled in prominent places like subway graffiti tags with huge numbers in bright red and white paint. The numbers designate from which farm the furniture was confiscated. Many of the large farms in Nicaragua were abandoned after the revolution, and the confiscated property from these ranchos gives Midinra a material edge among the video groups. Desks and files they may have, but the office desperately needs more telephones. Over seventy people work there, and their single telephone is the kind of frustrating bottleneck through which any work in Sandinista Nicaragua must eventually pass.

Video isn't the only thing that Midinra does. They have several printing presses and do the work of documenting and explaining the agrarian reform process Their primary aim is making the agrarian reform work understood by and available to the peasants and farm workers in the countryside, and secondarily informing a wider public—city dwellers of Managua, Leon, and Granada, but also other countries and international organizations. Several of their publications are in English.

Arturo Zamora is director of Communicaciones Midinra. It is indicative of his self-effacing style that he has no desk or office but hangs out from work space to work space, jumping up apologetically to give this or that worker back his or her seat. Arturo directs the printing, audiovisual, and video workshops. Audiovisual is a large department with a still-photo darkroom for both color and black and white. They have produced over a dozen slide shows with synchronized tracks. Subjects include "The Benefits of Soy Beans" and "Nutrition for Pregnant Women." Midinra is planning an audio studio and hopes to do a regular radio series in the near future.

The video department consists of four rooms: an editing room, a tape library, an equipment room, and an office. Needless to say, the office is the farthest from the air conditioner. In Nicaragua equipment and tapes are treated with the utmost respect. This is not mystified Third World awe, but a concrete understanding of the hassles involved in part replacement and tape purchase. Augusto Tablada is director of the video department. He likes to tell how he was caught in monsoon-type rains in an open field with their new Sony M3 camera and a 4800 VCR deck. He took off his rain gear and put it as additional protection over the equipment, and spent seven hours in pouring rain trying to hold the equipment out of the mud. "The camera costs dollars," he grins. "I'm only worth cordobas." Exchange dollars are practically impossible to get, and cordobas (the Nicaraguan currency) won't buy equipment. All of the video groups in Nicaragua rely heavily on donated equipment.

Midinra films are available in both 3/4 Umatic and Betamax. Most production is shot and edited on 3/4, then transferred to consumer Betamax for distribution to the countryside. Each regional center has a Beta player and has regular showing of Midinra tapes. They also show work by U.S. independents and even a few Hollywood films.

Miriam Carrero comes to work at Midinra with a shopping

bag full of powdered milk. The boxes have a smiling blond and blue-eyed toddler on the front. The lettering on the box is Cyrillic: the milk is Russian. Powdered milk from the United States is difficult to get here. All U.S. products are harder and harder to get. Miriam has two children: a four-month-old baby and a three-year-old girl. Her mother assists in the childcare, as in many Nicaraguan extended families, but even so, working as a video editor is difficult with two young ones. Miriam gets up at 5 A.M. to go to the market to be sure she can get the week's supply of powdered milk for the baby. Miriam started out in film work at INCINE. She recently changed to work at the agrarian video program, initially because the pay was better. INCINE pays only 3,700 cordobas a month ($130), while Midinra pays 6,000, almost twice as much. Now Miriam is very enthusiastic about video and wants to learn all aspects of production. She runs the editing machines but is very much involved in content decisions. From what I could gather of the post-production process, tapes at Midinra evolve organically (to use an agricultural term) from the material collected. The camera person works with the editor. Input can come from many people at Midinra, and the atmosphere is that of a collective, not a hierarchy. Technical advice is supplied on occasion by agricultural advisors: for example, a cattle geneticist was working closely on a tape on cattle production.[4]

Midinra's work is primarily focused on agrarian topics, but, like Jaime Wheelock, wide-ranging director of the Agrarian Ministry, their interests extend to theoretical and historical issues as well. Midinra completed a memorial tape to commemorate the fiftieth anniversary of Sandino's death, a mixture of archive footage, recent war footage, and agrarian images. It is a passionate experimental tape, using Eisenstein-type montage juxtapositions to rev up emotions. (After an

---

[4] When I walked into the video workshop and saw a tall, Slavic-looking guy, I was initially suspicious that the Russians had arrived to supervise the tiny Nicaraguan video operation. My Cold War paranoia fueled fear that the spontaneity and improvisatory nature that I loved about the Midinra workshops would somehow be suppressed. I breathed a sigh of relief and had to reexamine my own prejudices when I found that he was an expert in cattle breeding, there to help with the text for an instructional tape.

image of a U.S. helicopter being shot down, there is a close-up of a bull being castrated.) The Sandino anniversary was the focus of a series on the Sistema. Each of the *commandantes* had hour-long interviews in which they answered questions posed to them by the Sistema. Midinra took Jaime Wheelock to the countryside, where he discussed the issues with the *campesinos*. They then edited this into an hour program and wanted the Sistema to run that instead of the stuffy studio format interview. The television system refused to air it, saying it did not fit their series. (This type of evasion is a familiar story to independents who try to deal with U.S. public television.) Actually the relationship of Midinra to the Sistema is one of the more baffling issues for an outsider to comprehend. Midinra has to *buy* time on the Sistema: 60,000 cordobas for each hour of program. They do a monthly program, but all the time is paid for, and their programs are subject (as in the interview case) to rejection by the management. This stems from intra-ministry rivalry and is an example of the differences between the various members of the Sandinista coalition.

Midinra has been a haven for foreign independents. Its open atmosphere and friendly workers have made it a place where U.S. independent filmmakers could align their cameras, splice light cables, or just hang out and screen tapes. In a sense Midinra's video grew out of the independent movement in the United States. Prior to 1979 Augusto spent time in the United States and worked with Eddie Becker, an independent producer in Washington. After the revolution Eddie came to Midinra to help train agricultural workers in video skills. The students from his class are still the mainstays of video technicians at Midinra. Eddie found that they picked up camera maneuvers quite easily. What he ended up spending most of his time teaching was how to make a good solder. They have no access to factory service. He brought with him connector parts and several hundred yards of cable from the United States. They made all their own cables. A trouble-shooting manual that he designed for them is the basic handbook of their equipment room.

Most internationalist media people sooner or later find their way out of the Carretera Masaya to Midinra's workshop. Before they leave, they are given a list of missing parts and needed equipment to send back. Video people from Germany (East and West) have been active in their support of Midinra and have raised money from trade unions for essential equipment. A major effort is underway to do a TV series with West Germany; Miriam is co-producing it with a woman from Munich. This show will be a docudrama series on farm life. It is a children's series: the first program shows a young boy visiting his grandfather on a coffee farm. The grandfather explains in detail just how things have changed since the revolution. Another is about the effects of the war on the coffee harvest.

Midinra would like to develop their co-production possibilities. They have been aghast at the enormous sums of money that the visiting U.S. (and Canadian and European) producers spend on equipping a production in Nicaragua. Arturo suggests, "Why not use our equipment and work in co-production with us? That way we can all benefit." Arturo assisted Bianca Jagger on a documentary about ecology in Nicaragua for distribution in the United States. Just as with their printed materials, Midinra sees their audience as including not only Nicaraguans. "We want to do our part to counter the misinformation that the world hears about Nicaragua," Arturo explains. He has embarked on a series called *Alternative Views* (not to be confused with the Austin cable access show of the same name) to begin to counter Western press bias. This type of production could also be done as co-productions, he feels.

Midinra plans a feature film on the history of Sandino. Wilfredo Ortega Mercado, who is currently the tape librarian, has a plan for a program on cultural seduction—how young *compesinos* lose their minds to American consumer goods. Miriam hopes to produce a program on women agricultural workers. And the ongoing work continues—the documentation of land reform, the construction of co-operative dairies, the research into ecological methods of pest control and health care in rural areas. Midinra also serves as a liaison from the producer to the consumer. Of their tapes that have been most popular here in the United States as part of the X-Change TV series, two are on very parochial specific topics: *Que Pasa con el*

*Papel Higienico* and *Que Pasa con las Papas*. The first, "What's Up with the Toilet Paper?" is a sort of point-counterpoint about why there isn't enough toilet paper in the country. Why the shortage? Humorous and catchy interviews with people on the street convey the range of feeling about toilet paper. There *is* a real shortage in Nicaragua, and this lack has become one of the major complaints by the sectors of the population that are most against the revolution. By repeating these complaints and disseminating them, Midinra itself has been criticized. The criticism against the tape only increased its popularity, and the tape became an important element in the ongoing discussions about shortages, hoarding, and rationing. The second tape is about potatoes. Potatoes grow well in Nicaragua, but they were never really part of the Nicaraguan cuisine, and poor farming methods and lack of enthusiasm have slowed production. This is a tape in praise of the potato that includes instructions for successful harvests.

TALLER POPULAR

Memories of the war of insurrection are ever present in Nicaragua.[5] Taller Popular de Video Timoteo Valasquez is a workshop named for a fallen comrade. It is part of the Central Sandinista de Trabajadores, the largest union in Nicaragua. Like Midinra, they also have a regular series on the Sistema and distribute via Betamax to union locals throughout the country. It is housed and shares resources with Tercer Cine, a private production company comprised of Jackie Reiter, Wolf Tirado, and Jan Kees de Rooy. The Taller began as a Super 8 workshop taught by Alfonso Gumucio Dagron in 1981 on a special project sponsored by the United Nations. Later Julia LeSage also taught at the Taller: "We worked mostly on editing techniques and alternatives to sync sound interviews, such as the use of music, other taped verbal material, and background sound.

---

[5] Susan Meiselas's book *Nicaragua* (New York: Pantheon, 1981) is a vivid document of that insurrection. For reflections of the role of the liberation church in that struggle, see Joel Kovel's *In Nicaragua* (London: Free Association Books, 1988).

Super 8 processing soon became too difficult, as Kodak withdrew all trade with Nicaragua. The workshop now works almost entirely in video. Amina Luna, Francisco Sanchez, Oscar Ortiz, and Ileana Estreber are the producers; their work centers on people—close shots of faces alternating with their homes, their land, their work. *Asi Avanzamos* is a tape about a cattle collective, faced with all the problems of building up production, together with the stresses and material losses of the ongoing brutal Contra war. The determination of the people to keep on working (*asi avanzamos*—so we advance) is evident on their hopeful faces. There is a dreamy, romantic quality to many of the Taller productions. This is not the pathetic view of "primitive" life that we sometimes find in the work of Gringo anthropologist/filmmakers. The faces of the people emanate a hope that is reinforced by the real accomplishments they have gained in the face of incredible odds. The ease with which the peasants participate with the video production gives the discourse an intimacy that transcends the interview format.[6] This sharing with the videomakers is what characterizes the work of U.S. independent Skip Blumberg. There is a one-to-one relationship with the camera that is as close as video can get to an authentic human relationship. This intimacy can, on occasion, make the Taller tapes deeply tragic. *Las Mujeres* is about two women who work in reconstruction projects in the northern area. They describe some of the hardships they have encountered in their work, but go on to list the accomplishments of the literacy campaign and the agrarian reform work in the face of the fear and intimidation that the Contras impose. The bravery of these two women included their willingness to talk with the video crew. Shortly after the program appeared on television, both were killed—brutally murdered. One was tortured and raped along with her six children. This type of Contra terror is not unusual; the targets are those who work with the revolution. The Contras rarely attack the army. Instead they go after the schoolteachers, the doctors, the nurses, and the agrarian

---

[6] These tapes are similar to the *testimonio* narratives that have been published in book form by people such as Rigoberto Menchu.

reform workers—and, on occasion, those peasants who share
their hope and dedication with a video crew.


## INCINE

INCINE is the film production unit of the Ministry of Culture.
It was born under fire in the mountains before the revolution.
I talked with Noel Rivera, who was one of the *muchachos* who
formed the mainstay of the army of insurrection. He was only
fifteen years old when he left home to fight against Somoza's
National Guard. In his battalion was a film crew, which
needed someone to run the Nagra, the basic audio recorder
used for film documentaries. He became the sound man after
a few days training and has worked with INCINE ever since.
INCINE has made one feature—*Alcino and the Condor*—and
many documentaries. Their newsreels are often shown before
the feature films in the theaters around the country. Half of
the theaters in Managua are privately owned, and INCINE
has to pay for the time for newsreel projection. The theater
owners refuse to play shorts that are longer than ten minutes.
Noel recounts the story of a newsreel he helped make that was
twelve minutes long. When he saw it at the theater, it was
strangely truncated. The theater owner had just lopped off the
last two minutes of the documentary in midsentence.

Movie theaters in Managua show the same trash films that
we get in Times Square. Kung Fu movies are the most popular, and audiences line up at 7:30 A.M. to see a 9:30 show on
Saturday morning. However, the INCINE Cinemateca is a
state-owned theater that shows a few Eastern European films
(Czech, Hungarian) and occasionally an independent feature
from the United States. Cuban films draw large crowds.

INCINE has a video department directed by Rosanne La-
cayo. The Lacayos are the main force behind INCINE, and
some have accused the organization of being a family affair.
Their most recent tape is a homage to Julio Cortazar, poet
and friend to the Nicaraguan revolution. Within the cultural
debate mentioned earlier, INCINE stands squarely with the

"serious art" contingent. Their main interest lies in producing film versions of Latin American novels.

INCINE has been on the receiving end of lavish gifts of production equipment and production assistance. The successes of ICAIC, the Cuban film institute, after the Cuban revolution led many to hope that Nicaragua's film production would accomplish similar feats. Several factors mitigate against this. The most important is the strain and pressures of the war situation in Nicaragua. Except for the Bay of Pigs fiasco, the attempts on Fidel's life, and the imposed economic constraints, Cuba has not had to withstand the brutal forces of reaction that attack Nicaragua daily. Second, and certainly a part of the first, is the economic situation. Nicaragua is much poorer than Cuba ever was. Film production is expensive, with the price of film and processing in Mexican laboratories rising daily. Third is more internal to INCINE. Their organization seems the most chaotic of the media groups that I visited. INCINE is built on grandiose schemes that get hung up in the simplest of details. While I was there, a group of technicians from Los Angeles were sponsoring technical workshops. The group came with a large donation of lights and equipment. They were surprised at the lack of an electrical interface and were unable to use most of their lights. There was only one circuit capable of running *one* of their lights in the workshop building. These workshops were funded by the Common Sense Foundation. Perhaps they could have had more common sense and have been more utilitarian in the scope. But *quien sabe?* Maybe some nascent cinematographer was energized by the classes and will emerge as a leader of the budding Nicaraguan film industry. In the meantime, the video production unit is becoming more and more important as a center of activity at INCINE.

CARA AL PUEBLO: FACE THE PEOPLE

The other video production unit is the audiovisual department of the Department of the Interior (the ministry headed by the charismatic and original Sandinista Tomas Borge). A unit

from this department produces weekly Cara al Pueblo meetings and does production for the Ministry of Education—both
documentation and tapes for instructional purposes. The Cara
al Pueblos are weekly meetings of the *commandantes* with the
people in the barrios around Managua and in the countryside.
These are perhaps the most characteristic public events of the
revolution; they are to Nicaragua what Fidel's speeches are to
Cuba. It is a significant difference that these are two-way: not
the voice of a single leader, but the questions of the people
directed to a group of their leaders. These may include local
leaders, the directors of the local block associations. The questions range from specifics on the new sewer lines for the
neighborhood to more philosophical questions about the relationship between church and state. When the meetings are
held in Managua, they are broadcast live from a mobile van.
These programs are very popular and would have high ratings
if the Sistema bothered to measure them. There have been
accusations that these meetings are orchestrated by the local
CDSs (neighborhood committees for defense of the revolution), and that only acceptable questions are allowed, but the
shows I saw were spontaneous and often highly critical of the
government. The Cara al Pueblo meetings will become increasingly important as a safety valve, as an effective way for
people to have input into national decision making. The degree to which these meetings express the authentic fears,
angers, and hopes of the people are an important measure
of public accountability. This process is an authentic national
dialogue, and the participation through video is crucial and
given high priority by the government. The Cara al Pueblo has
a well-equipped van which is the envy of the other video producers of Managua.

One of the ironies of the situation there is that, despite the
collaborative attitude at the highest level of government, there
exists among departments a great deal of competition and
possessiveness. There is very little communication among the
various organizations. INCINE has no idea of what Midinra
is doing. Midinra has no way to promote their schedule on the
Sistema, because they are not privy to the Sistema's long-
range planning and do not know month to month where their

slot will be positioned. The Taller has no contact with IN-
CINE. They have only one 4800 portable recording deck. If
that is in the repair shop, they have to cancel all their shoots—
even though there are at least six other decks that could be
loaned from other workshops. There is only one engineer who
works at the Sistema; he has put his job on the line by sometimes sneaking a workshop deck into his shop to repair. There
are healthy aspects to the independence of the various
groups—there is no monolithic look to Nicaraguan video—but
all the groups would benefit more from more sharing of resources.

It is sobering to contemplate the future of Nicaraguan
video. Even if the vicious Contra war stops (which would happen almost immediately if the U.S. stopped funding it), the
economic situation is so difficult that conditions will probably
worsen in the short run. As the dollar pinch gets harder, there
will be increased struggles within the trade unions. Rampant
inflation has hit most workers, even though the prices of sta-
ples are fixed. Midinra, INCINE, the Sistema, and the Cara al

Oscar Ortiz, cameraperson for Taller Popular de Video, the television unit of the labor union C.S.T.-A.T.C.

Pueblo are all part of the government. They are the "voice of the people" only insofar as the government remains true to the ideals and aspirations of the revolution. As a voice of the workers, Taller Popular de Video may play an increasingly important role in articulating their needs and dissatisfactions. The real work of the revolution is in the future, and the video groups can play a constructive role in national media expression if they retain their authenticity and pluralism.

The U.S. independent media community has been an important source for Nicaraguan video— a source for technical assistance, equipment donations, and programming exchange. But perhaps most important has been the inspiration of video use. The kind of personal human community video that has characterized what is marginalized independent video work in the United States has become the standard for a video community in Nicaragua, whose cameras are the eyes of their nation, and whose nation stands at the heart of current human history.

# History in Havana: Notes from the Havana Film Festival

## December 1986

MY FATHER was an engineer with the Nicaro Nickel Company, a U.S.-owned mine in Cuba, and my family lived in a small mining town on the eastern end of the island from 1952 to 1954, before the revolution. In 1986 I went back to Cuba for the first time in thirty-three years to attend the Eighth Annual Latin American Film and Television Festival. The U.S. companies are long gone, and there are no longer beggars in the streets,[7] but in many ways Havana hasn't changed all that much. The peeling stucco buildings are just as beautiful in the yellow light of dusk, and the streets are still chugging with 1950s Chevies and Oldsmobiles.

Havana has almost as many movie houses as it has autos on the streets. Many of these neighborhood houses are the screening locations of the festival, which is scattered about the city. All of the screenings except those at the Cine Charles Chaplin (the theater next to ICAIC, the Cuban Film Institute's home) were open to the Cuban public, as well as the festival hoi polloi. And they were filled. Cubans love film. Many of the films from the festival are shown on television during the two weeks of the festivities. But they are also shown in the many movie theaters in Havana, and Cubans pour into the theaters to see them. There are lots to see. This year there are three special series: one on African films, a series on black Ameri-

---

[7] Sadly, friends have told me that by 1999 beggars had reappeared in Cuba. The burgeoning tourist industry and the disparity between the U.S. dollar and Cuban currency have created class differences that were minimal in 1986. In that year one could exchange the Cuban peso for the U.S. dollar at an even exchange.

can cinema, and an enormous retrospective of Brazilian films. In fact, the Brazilian delegation at the festival was the largest: almost 200 Brazilian directors, distributors, and movie stars were in official residence in one of the four festival hotels. Their presence was felt not only on the screen, but in the poolside parties that raged into the morning also. The samba outplayed the cha cha cha every night.

Since this was my first Cuban film festival, I had nothing with which to compare the selected work. I saw some terrible stuff. I find it hard to evaluate films in festivals—the festival life so outweighs the celluloid at any film celebration, and this is especially true of the Cuban event. The energy of people coming together is unlike anything I have ever encountered. One reason for this is that the festival is defiantly *non*-U.S. and *non*-European. There is energy in that very negation. Another reason is pure desperation: it is harder for peoples of the so-called Third World to communicate in general—poor mail and telecommunications systems, censorship, restricted travel. So when they come together in Havana, there is a lot of action in a short time. But perhaps the most important element is what I can only call history. The Cubans have created a history of the Latin American cinema with their yearly festival, and history is the real energy of the Cuban festival. One has a feeling that the festival itself is, by its very existence, making history. And every year this expectation is fulfilled, in one way or another.

In spite of enormous financial and logistic difficulties and in the face of new domestic cutbacks, Cuba in 1986 embarked on an extension of media/festival-related activities that can only be described as utopian to the point of seeming crazily grandiose. It is precisely through an equally loco flight of reason that the festival (not to mention a socialist Cuba) exists at all. The right wing in the U.S. calls Cuba expansionist. I wonder if they have any conception of the role this island plays in the cultural life of the hemisphere. Expansionist maybe, but in a way entirely foreign to the White House ideologues. Both the Film Festival and the Biennial of Latin Art (that opened a month before the film festival) have fortified hemisphere independence more than any Soviet tanks or anti-aircraft guns.

Ideas, like guns, need to be renewed now and then. With this latest festival, Cuba has moved boldly into new arenas: a conference on women in the media and the expansion of the festival to include video and television and the opening of a school for Third World filmmakers.

## WOMEN IN THE AUDIOVISUAL WORLD

Within the festival three days had been set aside for a conference on women and the media. Because of the enormous interest shown in this schedule, it was expanded to five days. Although many European and U.S. women weren't impressed by the level of theory, the main audience, namely, the Cuban women who work in film and television and the other Latin media professionals, were grateful for the discussions and hopeful for a continuation of the conference as an annual event within the festival.

There was pointed questioning of ICAIC personnel about the role of women in Cuban film. With the exception of the late Sara Gomez, whose film *One Way or Another* (1975) is one of the classics of Cuban cinema, no women have directed dramatic feature films. Perhaps the most incriminating element of ICAIC's obvious problem was the fact that ICAIC women employees jumped to their feet many times during these discussions to defend ICAIC policy. These *buenas hijas* were excessively defensive to the point of pleading that their small stature presented problems with their carrying cameras. Brazilian director Susana Amaral, whose brilliant film *Hour of the Star* based on the novel by Clarice Lespector won a prize, countered passionately, "We carry our children, why can't we carry a camera?" An interesting distinction was soon evident between ICAIC and ICRT (the Institute of TV and Radio), where women hold positions of greater prominence and power. (More about television later.)

There was a lot of rehashing of some tired themes such as the discussions over pornography versus eroticism (the Brazilians were very active in this discussion), and the questions of separatism (with the inherent danger of marginalization) versus mainstreaming. The debate became concrete in the final day's rush to closure when the big question was whether to demand that the festival screen women's films and video as a separate category, or as a regular part of the festival. It ended with a compromise—they asked for greater inclusion in the overall screenings of the festival in general and a special room, centrally located within the festival spaces, for discussion and screenings of more intimate and issue-oriented women's work.

Several British feminists complained that the discussions were naive and vague and formulated on too many different levels of understanding to be of any use, blaming the lack of *savoir* on the Third World status of Cuba and the majority of the participants. This sounded to me like racism. Before leaving for Cuba I had participated in the Viewpoints: Women, Culture, and Public Media Conference in New York City, where many of the same complaints were voiced. The New York conference suffered from similar problems but certainly cannot claim underdevelopment as an excuse. Both conferences pointed out the urgent need for women in media to discuss these issues. The lack of coherence at both convocations points out the need to have some continuing dialogue on these themes. The discussions at both evinced the problems inherent in the preliminary gropings for common language and the difficulties of defining the issues. The Cuban conference recognized the need for ongoing discussions and resolved to meet again next year. They also passed a statement of purpose that, however tepid the explicit demand, was a move forward for women in media in Latin America. The New York conference made no clear-cut resolutions, not even on the matter of whether to meet again.

I felt a more open-ended atmosphere to the Cuban meeting. One never knew where the discussions would land. Here was a double negation: anti-chauvinism and anti-capitalism. The Cuban women's meetings were more genuinely participatory (democratic!) for two reasons: the enormous patience, graciousness, and insight of the discussion leaders, and the physical setup of the conference center, which has both a microphone and translation earphones at every seat—which actually worked. Everyone was a presenter in this two-way conference center.

Although at least four formal papers were read each day over the five days, more than a hundred women from the "audience" were able to testify or respond. One didn't have the feeling that the responses were a kind of tokenism; they were very much integral to the situation at hand. And it all worked. The simultaneous translations into five languages were clear and informed, though it boggled my mind to hear the stiff Russian (male) translator turning into English what was one of the most personal and heartfelt presentations of the conference by a highly emotional Soviet Georgian woman director, Lana Gogoberidze. She spoke openly of the difficulties of juggling her time-consuming career with the demands of her teenage daughters and her somewhat jealous husband.

## VIDEO AND TELEVISION IN LATIN AMERICA

During the last week of the festival a meeting was held for video and television representatives. Video work has rapidly increased all over Latin America. The festival expected under a hundred video entries this year but received over 600 in pre-festival mailings, and an additional 200 were hand-carried by festival participants. Festival organizers were completely overwhelmed with this mass of material. In the past the festival has been open to all submitted films, but the cost of film and processing limited the volume of production in Latin America. It is indicative of the cost efficiency of video that the enormous outpouring of video made a restructuring necessary. In the future the videos will have to be prescreened and selected.[8]

The meeting of video and television producers was a strange one. The head of one of the state-owned Mexican television networks was there, as were video guerrillas from the Zapotec

---

[8] A collection of many of the community videos from Latin America has been translated and edited by Karen Ranucci into a six-hour series called *Democracy in Communication*. It is available from the Latin American Video Archives at 124 Washington Place, New York, N.Y. 10014.

Indians, whose tapes on their collective activities are a direct challenge to state policies on indigenous populations. The director of the Cartajena festival (a government-run organization) and several well-dressed executives from the state-run Colombian cultural television shared the floor with a young woman whose video group represents Colombian guerrilla militants. The meeting was co-chaired by Ismael Gonzalez, president of Cuba's ICRT, and Sergio Corielli, former ICAIC movie star (he played the disaffected bourgeois in *Memories of Underdevelopment,* Cuba's most revered feature), now video enthusiast and the vice president of the ICRT. There were two widely differing points of view in the room. One was from the TV people—those executives from the state systems and those producers who see the state systems as a "market" for their wares: cultural programming with a national and regional emphasis on cultural identity, such as shows on local artisans, music programs, and costume dramas about Simon Bolivar.

The other group could only be called video rebels. The very word "market" is an anathema to them. Their basic work is not to sell programs, but to use video for organizing and community empowerment. Latin American films are bought and sold at the Cuban festival, and the TV execs saw the inclusion of television as a simple extending of the offering of product. The video crowd was more interested in collaboration and exchange than profits. They wanted more time for discussion and space and equipment for technical workshops, focusing on practical issues of low-budget production and non-profit distribution. They even proposed that the lights should be left on at the video screenings as the darkness of the ICAIC screening rooms tended to obviate discussion, the most important product of their work.

The Cuban TV officials were genuinely interested in the guerrilla video work. They took their problems quite seriously, taking notes and on occasion even cutting off the longwinded TV officials to allow more of the grassroots video producers to speak. This interest in community video is, I found, not an anomaly. There is a new wind blowing at Cuban TV, and much has changed since the appointment of Gonzalez. For years visitors to Cuba would complain about the tired dogmatic forms and dull visuals of Cuban TV. Gonzalez brings a fresh approach. He comes not with a broadcasting background, but a background in psychology, of working with group empowerment. Corielli comes from an acting career, but he quit movie acting to work in street theater—forming collectives that worked in communities throughout the island. He brings to Cuban television a spirit of experiment and collaboration. One of the best examples of the new Cuban TV I saw used a highly stylized commedia dell'arte pantomime troupe combined with the spontaneous exuberance of a group of urban children in a highly conscious experimental video work combining guerrilla video, street theater, and conceptual art. If this is a sample of things to come in Cuban TV, this island will have television that will be to UNIVISION (the Spanish-language commercial satellite network) what the New Latin American Cinema is to Hollywood.

The final awards ceremony was held in the Karl Marx Theater, an enormous auditorium with two tiers of balconies, whose stage was dressed with a tacky series of baffles and geometric shapes—an enormous constructivist version of the Academy Award set. The scale conveyed an alienation and a coldness that is very uncharacteristic of Cuba. This year, to the surprise of almost everyone, the first speech was made by Luis Fernando Santoro of Brazil. On the surface, it would make perfect sense. This year's festival is honoring Brazilian cinema, and it would stand to reason that this coveted speaking assignment would go to a Brazilian. However, there is a world of difference between Luis Santoro and the producers of *cine nuovo* who have been Brazil's conspicuous representatives to the festival. Santoro is not a filmmaker, nor does he come from the imperial halls of Brazilian Globo television, second only to the United States in exports to the continent. Santoro is a community videomaker, as alien to the high-rise zone of the Brazilian media establishment as a parish priest espousing liberation theology is to the Pope. His work is with trade unions (the rank-and-file groups and P.T.—the Workers Party). He works with small-format video not to create products, but to facilitate dialogue. The Brazilian video community, informed by the movements of the base community churches and Paolo Freire's literacy campaigns, has grown to an astounding size. Over 350 community video groups exist in Brazil, and they have formed a powerful alternative network. Santoro's speech was no homage to Latin cinema, but a direct challenge to the old guard of Latin American film to recognize the vitality of community video. Santoro's key position in the ceremony was an obvious recognition by the festival committee of that vitality. The presence in Cuba of community video activists from all over the region was a coming together of a movement that is parallel to what the Cuban festival did for Latin film eight years ago. The opportunity to meet and share work was for most an astonishing beginning. Few of the producers knew each other until meeting in Havana. The kinds of exchanges this gathering produced can only strengthen the community video movement in Latin America in the same way the Cuban festival has strengthened Latin film.

## THE INTERNATIONAL FILM AND TELEVISION SCHOOL OF THREE WORLDS

The most ambitious leap of the festival was the new school. A foundation headed by novelist Gabriel Garcia Marquez and made up of representatives from most of the countries in Latin America has created a school for media in Cuba. The announcement sounded like some UNESCO pronouncement—a great idea for the future, but hardly within the realm of reality in the hard-pressed economy of Cuba and the constraining schedules of the celebrities who were named to work on this project. But work they did, and the most dramatic moments of the festival came not at the cold and repetitive ceremony of film awards. Festival attendees were taken in tour buses to San Antonio de los Baños, a small village forty minutes away from Havana to witness the inauguration of a new school for Latin America, Africa, and Asia. Thousands of dollars worth of film and video equipment had been garnered from various parts of the world by Marquez and his committee. A thousand Cuban workers had put in fourteen-hour days to convert a small agricultural school into the impressive modern media campus. A group of 150 students from thirty-seven countries had been chosen from script and essay contests, held in their various countries.

The ceremonies began at five in the glowing Cuban sunset, 2,000 festival goers, 1,000 construction workers, and the 150 students all packed into the stone courtyard at the center of the school. There was a buzz of excitement and anticipation about the whole event. It was a new beginning for Latin American media. The students sat in the front rows, dressed in the school uniform—blue jumpsuits. Around their necks were colorful scarves with the school's emblem: a red circle, a blue square, and a yellow triangle. Behind them in the next rows of honor sat the construction workers dressed in white and also wearing the kerchiefs with the school emblems. Is this a workers state or what?

Each student let go a dove, and on a well-choreographed lighting cue the birds flew aloft to catch the last rays of the sun. Francis Ford Coppola was in attendance, as were Julie Christie, Delphine Seyrig, Gregory Peck, and almost every Latin film director in the hemisphere. It was very festive with colorful flags, and as twilight approached brilliant lights came on. The whole ceremony was broadcast live on Cuban television. Fernando Birri, founder of the New School and who looks like an elf with his twinkly eyes and wispy hair and beard, in his cocky Zorro hat (worn at all times) addressed the crowd, like a magician invoking spirits. He had founded a film school in Santa Fe, Argentina, that was smashed (literally—the thugs axed the moviolas and bulldozed the buildings) by that country's military junta in the seventies. Birri spent most of his speech explaining the scarf design: the yellow is the ray of light, the blue square is the machine that forms the art, the red circle the humanity whom the art serves. Or as levels of the three-year school, the yellow is the spirit of the new student, the blue is the learning of the technology, the red circle is the final year when there is a synthesis between technology and the purpose to society. Birri called for this new school to be "anti-scholastic," critical and unfailing in its search for truth, but declared that in student productions everything was allowed as long as it was for beauty. Against beauty, nothing!

he declared. This was an obvious reference to a famous speech by Fidel Castro to a Congress of Writers in the sixties in which he said that everything *with* the revolution was allowed, but *against* the revolution—nothing. Birri's playfulness and the rich diversity of the student body of this new school are an interesting addition to the future of both Cuba and Third World media.

Birri had been a student at the Centro Sperimentale in Rome, home of the Neo-realists, whose inspiration fired Cuba's first filmmakers. In fact, three of the main Cuban directors had studied in Rome: Gutierez Alea, Santiago Alvarez, and Alfredo Guerera. Garcia Marquez had also been a student in that school, which is one of the reasons for his continuing interest in media. This new school, then, is the grandchild of the Neo-realist Movement, touchingly signified by the presentation to the audience of the elderly Roman teacher of these men. That this man was brought from Italy to consecrate this gathering is an indication of the Cuban sense of history. For the young students from those beleaguered and indebted Third World countries, here was a history lesson: the phoenix-like aspirations of cinema artists from postwar Italy, heralding a new school for the youth of Asia, Africa, and Latin America.

The words of the dedication were in the form of a birth certificate:

> A few days after the beginning of the warm spring of 1986, surrounded by the turquoise blue Caribbean Sea, under a crescent moon, shipwrecked from Utopia, rescued from a world of imperial injustice and atomic madness, the New Latin American Film Foundation decided to create the International Film and Television School of Three Worlds . . . a center that generates creative energy for audiovisual images, a factory of the eye and ear, a laboratory of the eye and ear, an amusement park for the eye and ear. To express what is still unnamed, an image, a style. To express ourselves, to find ourselves a name, to imagine ourselves.
>
> So the site of Utopia, which by definition is nowhere, is located somewhere. For reasons of geographical, political, and poetic chronology, it is in what others call the Third World and

we call Our America, Our Africa, Our Asia, Our World. . . .
In the light of the flashing serpent-like foams of the Caribbean
and the pulsing beams of the spy satellites—false stars of audiovisual penetration that will not preclude the dawning of our
liberation struggles—in this fecund orgasm of collective imagination, let us wish long life to the Utopia of the Eye and Ear
that found its somewhere in San Antonio de los Baños, Cuba,
reunion island of three worlds.[9]

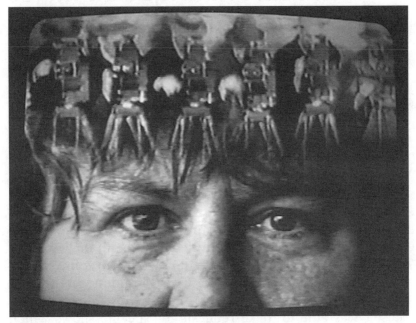

Still from *The Gringo in mañanaland. (Author)*

[9] From Fernando Birri, *Birth Certificate of the School of Three Worlds* (Havana, 1986).

# Women as Cultural Producers on Cuban TV: The Case of Maritza Rodriguez and Los Abuelos Se Rebelan

## June 1992

MONICA MELAMID and I initiated a project of collecting samples of Cuban television for a series of exhibitions in the United States in response to the transmissions of TeleMarti that was begun by the U.S. State Department.[10] It seemed only fair that if the United States was beaming to Cuba programs made in Miami and Hollywood, it was time to see some examples of Cuban TV in this country. I traveled to Cuba in the winter of 1989 and spent two weeks screening (sometimes in fast forward) over a hundred hours of TV programming. Although much of the material I saw was suggested by Cuban TV officials, I was able to make requests for specific shows which would then be supplied by the television archives office. The names of the programs I requested came from street interviews I conducted with a wide variety of people asking them what their favorite programs were. We put together a somewhat eclectic request list, which we constructed from discussions with Cuban friends and from this informal polling of

---

[10] The first exhibition was at Artist Space Gallery in New York City in April 1990. It next was presented in Columbus, Ohio, at the Wexner Center in June 1990, at the Institute for Contemporary Art in Boston in November 1990, and at Hall Walls Gallery in Buffalo in November 1991. In addition, a one-hour edit of the program was transmitted on the Deep Dish Television Network in the spring of 1990 to over 400 cable stations and twelve public television stations.

people on the street. Each day I spent some time walking around Havana, interviewing people about their TV habits and asking the names of their favorite shows. The Cuban TV officials were very helpful in providing the programs if the tapes still existed: one of the problems of television on the island is the terrible shortage of materials, requiring programs to be bulk-erased so that the stock can be used for new efforts. We wanted to get a representative sample, not necessarily the programs most critically acclaimed or the most approved by the television officials.

## CUBAN TELEVISION

Cuban TV does not run commercials. It is run by the state as an instrument of education and propaganda. In the early years of the Cuban revolution there was not much attention paid to television.[11] The Cuban revolution inherited an infrastructure designed more for rebroadcasting U.S. programs than for producing a national television. There was virtually no model of a national television system anywhere in Latin America. The most Latin element in Latin American television in the fifties and sixties was Desi Arnez dubbed into Spanish on export versions of *I Love Lucy*. For many years after the revolution, Cuban TV was used for news, Fidel's speeches, and reruns of old U.S. TV shows. The creative energy in media production was focused on ICAIC, the Cuban Film Institute, with a good deal of success. The films that were made under ICAIC's aegis changed forever the direction of Latin American film. The movement of "New Cinema in Latin America," like the "New Song" movement, became an inspiration for cultural production throughout the continent. Films produced in Cuba such as *Death of a Bureaucrat, The Last Supper,* and *Memories of Underdevelopment* by Tomas Gutierez Alea, *One Way or Another* by Sara Gomez, *The Other Francisco* by Sergio

---

[11] Reynaldo Gonzalez, "New Elements in Cuban Television," *Stone's Throw: TV from Cuba*, catalog from Artists Space Gallery, New York (1990), p. 10.

Giral, and *Portrait of Teresa* by Pastor Vega are included in the pantheon of world cinema. These groundbreaking films date from the sixties and seventies, and although Cuban cinematic form has not developed appreciably since that time, the Cuban cultural infrastructure has continued to nurture media development in Latin America through the Festival of Latin American Cinema held every year in Havana.

Most people in the United States have the perception that Cuban TV consists of wall-to-wall Fidel speeches. Fidel is probably less in evidence than George Bush is on ABC. In reality, Cuban TV is an uneven but often inspiring and creative mixture of standard TV genres: soaps (in this case decidedly not selling soap), game shows, talk shows, music video (with an Afro-Cuban beat), and sitcoms. These programs are made on a yearly budget that is less than a week's shooting tab for a typical U.S. sitcom. In essence, they are programming two national television channels out of thin air. That they are able to come up with dramatic, moving, and often quite imaginative explorations in television is nothing short of a miracle. Miracles, however, seem to abound on the island these days. It is a miracle to get through the day as the blockade continues and stringent economic belt tightening gets even tougher.

So what does Cuban TV look like? It's not glitzy like Univision. There is very little evidence of sequins here. There aren't any auto chases—gas is too expensive. No Home Shopping Network selling veggie slicers and zircon rings. In terms of general impressions, it is closest to the Scandinavian educational television I have seen: slow-paced and earnest children's programming, thoughtful and intelligent discussions, gripping human soap operas that occur in simply furnished homes (this is not *Dynasty* or *Dallas*), experimental music/dance presentations, and detailed instructional programs such as crop diversification and the uses of soy milk. In short, it is noncommercial humanist programming. However, there are fresh influences at work that make it some of the most interesting TV in Latin America.

One of the most felicitous influences on Cuban TV has been the New Latin American Film movement, showcased each year in Havana's continent-wide Latin American Festival of

Cinema, Video, and Television. The creative energies of the continent have always been at home in revolutionary Cuba, especially when repressed elsewhere. During Chile's darkest days, her exiled filmmakers, writers, and musicians were frequent visitors to Cuba. For decades Cuba has been a major source of inspiration for artists of Latin America—not only in film, but in music, literature, and dance as well. Their energy, in return, has had a great influence on Cuban cultural life, including television. Cubans have collaborated with many international artists and have hosted many symposia on art and the humanities. The influence on Cuban TV has resulted concretely in series on Latin American writers and musicians, but moreover has helped to sustain a level of sophistication that belies their economic isolation.

The presence of the school in San Antonio de Los Baños has brought a youthful vision to the island's media. The international students have brought winds of change to Cuban TV: they have encouraged development of the omni-present "video-clip" (MTV style) that attained a uniquely Cuban style with such musicians as Cuba's famous Silvio Rodriguez and have pushed for more controversial content, such as issues of homophobia and censorship in the arts.

A third influence is the creative use of small-format video that the economic difficulties have made a necessity. This resorting to "cheap art" (or as Cuban director Julio Garcia Espinosa put it in a famous essay, "Towards an Imperfect Cinema") has brought a fresh vision to what often was fairly stodgy studio production.

In December 1988 the official name of the annual Cuban festival was changed from only designating cinema to include television and video: the Latin American Festival of Cinema, Video, and Television. This expansion of the name parallels an expanding interest in television and video as a powerful creative medium, not only in Cuba but in all of Latin America. The Cuban Institute of Radio and TV (ICRT) got a boost from the creative leadership of Ismael Gonzalez, a psychologist who has emphasized programs that are popular, less overtly didactic, and use genres of proven effectiveness in television. At this time, also, there was an expansion of the technical po-

tential as portable video equipment, which could function
very well with low light, began to liberate the productions
from cumbersome studios and expensive klieg lights (many of
which had long since lost their bulbs). It is my conjecture that
the experiences of Nicaragua also had an effect. The Sistema
Sandinista made extensive use of portable video, using Betamax and VHS consumer formats for broadcast of news, cultural events, and even telenovellas. Miguel Nicochea at the
Nicaraguan Interior Ministry under the Sandinistas produced
a sort of *Mission Impossible* teleseries about drugs and the
CIA, all shot and edited on consumer and low-end industrial
equipment. This series was very popular in Nicaragua and
was exported to Cuban TV. Another factor in the Cuban TV
renaissance was the appearance on the air of many other
Latin American programs, not only Nicaraguan programs,
but also telenovellas from Venezuela and Brazil as a result of
improved trade with Latin America in the mid-eighties.

Gonzalez's tenure at ICRT brought increased emphasis on
audience research: TV log reports (sort of Nielsen-type dia-
ries) were sent to random samples of viewers in all parts of
the island. This information was collated and analyzed in the
Institute's research center and was used in classes for script-
writers and directors at the training center, which is next door
to the research facility.

In this atmosphere of development and expansion (in spite
of the continued U.S. blockade) creativity was given wide lati-
tude in several areas of Cuban TV. Important experiments in
the use of mass media as an educational vehicle were initiated
using popular TV genres. There are a number of women in
Cuban TV, especially prominent as directors in the areas of
children's programming and teleseries. In the area of children's programming (despite a minimal budget and enormous
problems with equipment and supplies) Cuban TV was able to
produce a number of series that are extremely popular.

Cuba's children's programming has no "My Little Ponies"
or "Power Rangers" for sale. Even with its minuscule budget
Cuban TV does not slight children's programming. It would
be interesting to compare, minute by minute, the Saturday
morning children's programming on NBC (part of the Gen-

eral Electric Corporation, presumably with an interest in selling their war machines and keeping the situation tense between the U.S. and the island) with any episode from the children's shows on Cuban TV. I was struck by one comparison. I had seen a children's program on NBC about Egypt and the hidden treasures in the pyramids. The emphasis was on the gold, details of mummy preservation, and what was known about the individual king. There was no mention of the social relations in the society. On Cuban TV one of the episodes we choose for our curated series included a song describing how the slaves in Egypt built the pyramids. The emphasis was on the unfair treatment accorded slaves at that time and the heroic work they accomplished. The treasures were described as evidence of the class divisions in that society. Propaganda? Commie mind control? At least there aren't any Sugar Smacks[12] commercials on Cuban TV. There is a determined effort to create pedagogic models of television. Especially notable is the work of Iraida Malberti, who specializes in programs for the very young: her target audience is ages two to five. She produces a series called *Cuando Yo Sea Grande* which uses child actors in a variety of situations as if they were grownups. It is a fantasy program, but one which poses possibilities of careers for the child viewers. For example, one episode takes place in an airport, where a child is waiting to say good-bye to his father. He goes into a dream and awakes on the runway boarding the plane as a pilot. Other careers that have been portrayed are teacher, nurse, doctor, and farmer. In each case the child imagines a world run by children, in which he or she is a fully functioning participant. In another episode two children act out several episodes from *Don Quichotte de la Mancha*. The series is intended to empower children—to allow them to see themselves as real participants in productive life. While the kids in the show are cute (sometimes a bit too cute), they are never ridiculed. The perspective is from their point of view: the camera is often about three feet from the ground. We see many table legs and adult

---

[12] The name of this cereal was later changed to downplay the sugar content.

shoes, a view from between park benches and a shot from under the playground slide. It is not a verbal show; the only sound is music and sound effects. If adults ever speak, their voices are speeded up and garbled, as they must sound to infants.

## LOS ABUELOS SE REBELAN

When I was conducting my interviews on the street, the most frequently mentioned favorite show was a Brazilian telenovela that was running at that time; the undisputed second choice was a Cuban series about old age, *Los Abuelos Se Rebelan*. What struck me as unusual was the fact that *Los Abuelos* was recommended by both young and old, both men and women, both intellectuals and street cleaners. When I asked to see the series, the Cuban TV officials smiled apologetically. They would be happy to let me see it, but I should know that it was a very low-budget affair. The series was not originally produced to air in prime time, although after its scheduled run on Sunday afternoons, it proved so popular it was rerun three additional times in prime time. It had been made, however, on an extremely low budget: with single camera shots, very little editing, and without any studio setups. When I saw the programs I was immediately struck by the fresh creativity, the succinct pithy quality of the script, and the brilliant use of single camera takes.

During the 1980s there were resources allocated to producing short dramatic series, in formats very similar to our soap operas or the Mexican and Brazilian soap operas. Similar, but no cigar. The dedication of all of Cuban TV has been to enhancing the revolutionary process. During this creative period many of the programs included more open confrontation with the actual problems, and the programs that dealt more openly resonated with the population. *Los Abuelos Se Rebelan* was directed by Maritza Rodriguez and was shot in 1986 and 1987. I was curious about the director and the circumstances of the production. In 1989 while doing my research in Havana, I tried to contact Rodriguez. Unfortunately she was working on a new series and was unavailable for an interview. However, in 1991 Kelly Anderson, a video producer from New York, traveled to Cuba and was able to videotape an interview with Rodriguez. She explained how the series began:

At the time that we began there was an explosion of interest in problems with aging in this country: issues surrounding old age centers, health care, increasing problems. I wanted to focus not on the big problems, but on the daily life with older people, to address these issues with humor and sensitivity. Many older persons live with their families who deny their humanity—they are people with feelings, with emotions, with worries. They either treat them unjustly or just forget that they are there. They use them: as messengers, as baby sitters, to help with problems with other parts of the family.[13]

The program was originally placed in a time slot on weekends that is occupied by a certain type of slapstick comedy. These comedies are often burlesque buffooneries with old people as subject/victims. I screened several episodes from one such series called *Asi Como Era* which was set in the fifties and had a sort of "Beverly Hillbillies" group of septuagenarians who took many pies in their faces and banana peels under their feet. What Rodriguez was able to do with her series was a quite astounding transformation of this heretofore pathetic genre. Instead of buffoons, the old people in Rodriguez's series become dignified protagonists, surrounded by the sometimes ridiculous younger members of their families, who are always stressed out and preoccupied. As Jean Franco has pointed out, "[The old people in *Los Abuelos*] are the only members of society with time for friendship, gossip, and romance."[14]

The series is set in real houses, shot in real kitchens and patios. The style is snappy, with quick vignettes, shot with a hand-held camera in one take. The overall effect is fresh and spontaneous. Rodriguez attributes this to her experience as an art director and her work with improvisation: "I try to get

---

[13] Maritza Rodriguez, interview, Havana, July 1992, p. 3.
[14] Jean Franco, "Los Abuelos Se Rebelan," in *Stone's Throw: TV from Cuba*, p. 9.

a certain kind of realism. This means we improvise a lot. I encourage my actors to improvise. This is the work that I love: close work with actors to elicit the spirit of the situation lightly; not to have it weighty, heavy. I don't pretend to solve the problem. The solutions are not that close. I just try to present the problem with humanity. This is the goal with all the themes I tackle."[15]

Rodriguez shows considerable skill in constructing the drama. The scenes are particularly well transitioned. The musical bridges are short and punchy, not maudlin and lingering like the transitions in much of U.S. soap opera and Mexican telenovelas. The series confronts difficult problems in Cuban life: shortages of housing, difficulties with transport, conflict between generations, conflict between genders. These problems are presented with a gentle humor and a perceptive almost Renoir-esque (the filmmaker, not the painter!) humanity. The characters of all three generations are presented with carefully etched personalities, whose foibles are the source of affection, not scorn. It is this same treatment that Rodriguez gives the Cuban regime. Daily problems and frustrations become familiar objects of affection. The waiting in line for food is juxtaposed with a daily exercise class for seniors in the opening sequence: the lacy look of a well-used ration book is the cause of several jokes; the shortage of beds is a musical chairs game that becomes a useful map for deciphering the status of the various family members. The dreams of the revolution become the recalled dreams of the middle-aged couple window-shopping at a furniture store, who look back at their youthful hopes with amusement and nostalgia, without bitterness, bravely shouldering the deprivations of today with a good-natured shrug.

One of the main themes in the *Abuelos* series is the lack of housing in Cuba. Two families struggle with the various room arrangements, given the situation of the presence of a grandparent in each of their homes. Director Rodriguez described her goal in making the series: "I wanted to focus not on the big problems, but on the daily life with older people, to ad-

---

[15] Rodriguez interview, p. 2.

dress these issues with humor and sensitivity. Many older persons live with their families who deny their humanity—they are people with feelings, with emotions, with worries. They either treat them unjustly or just forget that they are there. They use them: as messengers, as babysitters, to help with problems with other parts of the family." [16] The series is centered around an elderly couple who are attracted to each other. The story unfolds as each family comes to terms with the fact of the old couple's relationship and the potential this holds for possible room changes. That the dreams so idealistically presented in early Cuban films have not been totally realized is not a reason to give up or become bitter. Rodriguez contextualizes Cuba's problems with those of the rest of Latin America, in which case Cuba makes a fairly positive comparison in many respects. She also points out that the material problems are just part of the situation and that gender relationships do matter, even in a "revolutionary" society.

The men in the series are not without their macho proclamations, but the camera pulls out to reveal that the most pompous of these dinosaurs is quietly washing out his wife's underwear. In her interview, Maritza contextualizes the machismo of Cuba within a macho Latin American context and lays the burden of addressing this issue squarely at the feet of male producers: "We are all part of Latin America: Latin America has tremendous problems. We are underdeveloped mentally more than anything. [Men] need to prove to women that they are without a macho point of view. It's not easy. Things don't change overnight."[17]

Rodriguez does not count herself as primarily a feminist. In fact, she goes to great length to deny a specific feminist purpose in her work. She does recognize, however, that since she is a woman she does bring forward the point of view of women: "I have never been a part of that (feminist) melodrama. For me gender is not an issue. I am not a flag-waving feminist, I don't throw around slogans. But of course my work is part of that same feminism that you are talking about. My

---

[16] Ibid., p. 3.
[17] Ibid., p. 4.

point of view comes out in my work: it is there because I am on the side of women, with the same struggles, the same hopes, with the same objectives."[18] She speaks about the participation of women at ICRT: "In the technical arena there are only a few women. You can count the tape operators on one hand. There is only one camera operator. There are not that many women directors, but the ones that are there are very good and have good positions."[19]

It is my impression that women have more important roles in production at Cuban TV than at ICAIC. ICRT producer Gloria Pedosa has organized conferences and seminars around the issue of women in the media in conjunction with the annual festival. She put together the May 1993 National Conference on Women in Media in Havana. Pedosa counts herself as a feminist and is more critical than Rodriguez of the situation of women in media in Cuba, but she is also one who has been able to maneuver quite a bit within ICRT. She has produced a lengthy series on women and film in Latin America, traveling to several countries to interview producers and filming segments and discussions with women each year at the Havana festival.

I have met several other women producers at ICRT, and I know that their work is some of the best of Cuban TV. Although the director of the ICRT research institute was a woman, the top administrators at ICRT are all men. However, both Pedosa and Rodriguez see Cuban TV as an institution supportive of women producers. Rodriguez speaks of the "myriad of things" she knows are possible on television and looks forward to developing further programs. She produced a twenty-part series about divorce, *SOS Divorcio.* "My work is only a small beginning of what we ultimately aspire to." [20] It is clear that she sees television as an important arena. Her work is dedicated to the vernacular: to expressing complex ideas in a popular form.

*Los Abuelos Se Rebelan* is not only constructed in a popular

---

[18] Ibid., p. 5.
[19] Ibid., p. 6.
[20] Ibid., p. 4.

form, it repeatedly makes allusions to popular songs, to pop stars, and even to Hollywood culture. In one scene the grandmother puts down her daughter by quoting a popular song; in another the psychiatrist compares his rebellious patient to Johnny Weissmuller (Tarzan) screaming from a vine; and there is a child getting ready for school who tries to comb his hair in the latest punk style. The references to mass culture are done from the point of view of daily life, mentioned in a naturalistic style; they are not camp or cynical allusions. These forms of culture are part of life and as such crop up in the dialogue. This is a series set in everyday working-class homes; it does not try to copy the popular U.S. TV series *Dynasty*, with lavish fantasy sets, but neither does it deny *Dynasty*'s existence. There is a "hipness" to the series that tacitly acknowledges the seductions of consumer culture. The characters are participants in current (what might be considered by some to be subversive) cultural trends. The characters are not heroic icons of socialist realism, nor are they romanticized as innocent and pure "correct" citizens. They are conscious and street-smart, but they are never bitter or angry. Their frustrations are annoyances that are not insurmountable. The grandfather takes the children to a restaurant, and although they acknowledge their limited budget and lick their chops as they read the menu fantasizing about the fare that could be ordered if they had enough money, the restaurant vignette closes as they all accept the limitations and with great restraint order what they can afford. These citizens are full of foibles and quirks, they know enough to know what they are missing, but they are ultimately good citizens, bearing the burdens of scarcity with resourceful good cheer.

Cuban TV is a unique example of a television system that is completely cut off from transnational capital, and one that functions solely as a public service. Within the constraints of the Cuban state, it has created notable television fare. Just as Cuban medicine, before the difficulties of the current crisis, has been able to make astonishing progress in the area of community health care without the resources but also without the constraints of a profit-oriented health care system, Cuban TV with tiny material assets but with an extremely creative and resourceful staff has been able to develop some remarkable examples of popular television as a social service: a television whose primary purpose is education, but a television that does not fail to recognize the need for popular media to entertain and to engage.

## CREATING POSITIVE CONSENSUS

Television is a medium of the home, and the directors of Cuban TV understand the importance of the home in mediating the economic constraints that are felt especially by women: the lack of privacy, the shortage of space, the food rationing, the increased work schedules with more pressure on family life. Perhaps one of the most effective strategies of the Cuban television program makers has been to acknowledge the deprivations of the population with humor, sympathy, and goodwill. For this task women producers have been especially effective. Maritza Rodriguez succeeds as a keen observer of the day-to-day details of the deprivations, from the hole in the ration card to the way in which the dinner is arranged to highlight the pathetic presence of only a few *desnudo* squid in a "seafood" salad. It is these details that the audience recognizes and at which they laugh. Like a resourceful mother, Rodriguez "makes do" with a smile, nudging her audience to do the same.

*Los Abuelos* provides the viewers with the semblance of a positive consensus in Cuba; it presents families who are able to transcend daily deprivations. As an example of a successful television production, *Los Abuelos Se Rebelan* is itself a model of transcendence: a cultural gesture against multinational corporate entertainment products, an inexpensive but popular TV series that takes on human problems with respect and humor and never implies that Coca-Cola will make things go better.[21]

[21] I would like to acknowledge the assistance of Monica Melamid, Rafael Andreu, Alfredo Perera, Kelly Anderson, Mickey McGee, Maritza Rodriguez, Iraida Malberti, Juan Hernandez Diaz, and especially José Antonio Jiménez.

# Community Media in Brazil: The Well-Traveled Route of *TV Maxambomba*

## *February 1997*

*Tv MAXAMBOMBA*[22] is a project of CECIP (Centro de Criacão de Imagen Popular), a group that has been in existence for over twenty years working in the *favelas* of the poor, the unemployed, and the squatters, many of whom are immigrants to urban Rio from the northwest parts of Brazil. Every evening, as dusk approaches, a colorful van bumps into a town square in these barrios of Rio de Janeiro. Equipment is unloaded and a projector mounted. A screen is set up on the top of the van as the audience gathers, bringing their folding chairs, their baby strollers, their bicycles. Street vendors set up shop selling colorful shaved-ice cups, snacks, and sodas. The *favelas* visited by the yellow *Maxambomba* van have few TV sets and may not even have electricity. Watching the street TV in this community may be the only TV they have. The crowd swells to several hundred. As the sky darkens, the projections begin: the program is usually a mix of short animations (one by Norman McLaren from the Canadian National Film Board on the night I visited in 1995), local sports reports (street soccer from the *favela* neighborhood, shot and narrated in the same style as the World Cup broadcasts), a music video by one of the local musicians (complete with visual effects à la MTV all shot locally), and a "main event" discussion program, this time about AIDS.

---

[22] There is a French study of *TV Maxambomba*: see Pascal Percq, *Les Caméras des favelas* (Paris: Les Editions de l'Atelier/Editions Ouvrières, 1998).

The night I visited, the discussion feature was a funny, sprightly program of interviews with women from teens to grannies about the problems and strategies they have to get their boyfriends and husbands to wear condoms. This tape doesn't end in any conventional denouement, but cuts to a live image from a camera that is right there, in the town square, and a local interviewer (a sort of "D.J." called the "animator" who is half Oprah Winfrey and half commedia dell'arte buffoon) asking one of the audience/participants, "And you, Maria, what coaxing words do you use when you want him to put on that condom?" He has chosen Maria because he knows her effervescent personality makes her the right person to start off the lively discussion that follows. The images of the interviewer/animator and Maria and the many women and men who follow her in the raucous debate are projected on the large screen on top of the van—on the same screen as the previous tapes. The receptors become the spectacle. The discussion is funny, passionate, and serious often at the same time. It goes on for several hours. Sometimes these discussions are themselves also taped and replayed to assembled groups in other locations to enlarge the dialogue. This sort of video conversation was used in the *Challenge for Change* project in Canada in the early 1970s to resolve conflict.[23] Disseminating and projecting voices from the grassroots in this manner gives dimension and power to the speakers, often those who are powerless and exploited [24] Workers, victims, and local citizens are given the sort of space usually reserved for officials and celebrities. It is, perhaps, similar to some of the intense discussions one can hear on North American radio talk shows, but with a major difference: completely absent is the cynicism and indifference of the Howard Stern–type host, the tidy sentimentality of Winfrey and her imitators, and the patronizing framing of mass talk radio. This is public discus-

---

[23] George Stoney, "The Mirror Machine," *Sight and Sound* 41, no. 1 (1971–72).

[24] A book from the Southern Appalachian region documents how video was used as a catalyst for community development: see John Gavanta, *Power and Powerlessness: Quiescence and Rebellion in an Appalachian Valley* (Urbana: University of Illinois Press, 1980).

sion more like a town meeting from somewhere in New England. In the specific case of the condom/AIDS discussion, the discussion is an evolving community process with a very real goal: the immediate health and safety of the participants. Although the conversation was initiated by a humorous and clever video and a lively comic host, it evolves to a practical look at AIDS in that community, and beyond that to a serious discussion of power within sexual relationships. The audience/participants include everyone from three-year-old tricycle riders to great-grandmothers with walkers.

Each month the van will return to that square on the same day of the month. Tomorrow they go to another street square. They cover thirty locations every month throughout the Nova Iguasu *favela*, with a population of over three million. Each night *Maxambomba* shows local sports, music, and discussion. The meat, or more appropriately, the rice and beans, of the program is the nightly discussion video, which can be about AIDS, about water sanitation, about women's rights, or about the electoral process. The topics are things that are of direct concern to the viewers/participants. Aside from the more elaborately produced, occasionally imported animations, the format in general is low-resolution consumer video. The productions are not ashamed to utilize certain conventions of mass culture: the sports announcer, the music/clip video, the "man on the street" interview. *TV Maxambomba* exuberantly appropriates genres and formats for their own local use, for their own local issues.

*TV Maxambomba* consists of both production teams and projection teams. One of the critiques of many community media projects is that they last as long as their often precarious funding holds out; but many projects with this level of activity quickly burn out. *TV Maxambomba* is hardly a flash on the screen; they have been operating for decades and have influenced several generations of youth in their communities. The producers and exhibitors who now administer the project are youth from the *favelas*, trained and supported by CECIP, which initiated the program.

Another Brazilian group that began with street projections is *TV Viva*. Community video is not without imagination. In one of their tapes politicians are portrayed as donkeys (à la *Mr. Ed,* the talking horse fifties TV show). Their tapes have a raucous sense of humor and a vicious irony. *TV Zero* is now programming on a state-owned channel in northeastern Brazil (a benefit provided by a Left-leaning elected local government), although they still do community screenings on the street.

The Dominican Republic's *TV Machepa* is made in the style of *TV Maxambomba:* a group of media activists create weekly programs which are screened in barrios around Santo Domingo. Here the program consists of the "animator" on occasion wearing a snorkel and mask anticipating a Noah-like flood, since "things are bad, so bad in the country of the Dominican Republic." During one of the programs the electricity goes out on the host, who blithely keeps up the banter with a completely black screen for about twenty minutes. This segment is a good indication of the intentional limitations of this video activity. This is obviously not something that aspires to replicate network glamour and glitz, but is solidly "in the dark" along with the majority of the Dominican populace.

The cinetrains of the Soviet Union required huge outlays of equipment and supplies. Video is cheaper, more portable and accessible. The model of *TV Maxambomba* has inspired groups from Malaysia to Buenas Aires and even New York's Downtown Community Television Center, which in recent years has initiated street projections in conjunction with their video workshops. The train rolls on.

# Zapatistas On-line: The E-Mail Read Round the World

## *June 1994*

WITHIN A FEW HOURS after the takeover of San Christobal de las Casas by the Zapatistas on the morning of January 1, 1994, computer screens around the world came alive with news of the uprising. By January 3 Subcommander Marcos himself was on-line. In Marcos's prose one senses an expertise and familiarity with computer-based text, if not directly with e-mail. For a press corps clutching their modem-connected laptops, Marcos became the first superhero of the Internet. It was as if Lenin, John Reed, Che, and Max Headroom had merged files. The Lacandan jungle address became the locus of a global news agency whose lead dispatches were written by guerrilla combatants themselves.

> January 1, 1994. The first declaration of the Zapatistas:
> We are the inheritors and the true builders of our nation. The dispossessed, we are millions and we thereby call upon our brothers and sisters to join this struggle as the only path, so that we will not die of hunger due to the insatiable ambition of a 70-year dictatorship led by a gang of traitors that represent the most reactionary and sell-out groups.
> To the People of Mexico: We the men and women, full and free, are conscious that the war that we have declared is our last resort, but also a just one. . . . JOIN THE INSURGENT FORCES OF THE ZAPATISTA ARMY OF NATIONAL LIBERATION.

The lyric prose of the declaration, first reproduced nationally in Mexico's daily *La Jornada*, was translated into English within hours (and many other languages within the first week), was downloaded into the files of newspaper and magazine journalists, and was posted on dozens of computer bulletin boards and conferences to be reproduced in hard copy in hundreds of venues. The Chicano student newspaper at the university where I teach (the University of California at San Diego), brought out a special Zapatista edition, reproducing the declaration in large type spread over six pages. Latin American institutes and Spanish departments made instant "wall newspapers" of the declaration with tear-sheet print-outs.

The media images of the initial campaign were created with a clear understanding of what the effect would be. The graffiti painted on the buildings in San Christobal (sometimes in English for CNN cameras) and the smoldering remains of the municipal records were images designed to give maximum media effect with a minimum of war. The timing of the January 1 event was precisely arranged. The bourgeoisie of Mexico were celebrating the New Year and the beginning of NAFTA when rudely awakened from their dreams of an easy transition. Bursting through their TV screens were the new icons of romantic rebellion: the ski-masked Zorro/Zapata *guerrilleros*. Just as the TV audiences thrilled to the sensational news reports of the triumph of the underdogs, the Internet watchers avidly scanned the exciting posts direct from the jungle. The e-mailers reacted with comments and speculation. There are hundreds of screens of discussion over whether or not Marcos was a priest. Even a high-ranking Jesuit official came on-line to deny any connection to his order.

> March 15, 1994:
> Shadows of new rage. Our path protects those who have nothing.
> To the State Council of Indigenous People and Peasants:
> To the Mexican People:
> To the people and governments of the world:
> To the national and international press:
>     The federal government, usurper of popular will, has reverted to lying about what happened during the dialogue in San Cristobal de las Casas, Chiapas. The evil government says that there are "agreements" when there was only dialogue. Do not allow yourself to be taken in by lies. Brothers, the powerful now

usurp the truth and try to deceive us saying that peace is just a question of a signature.

How can there be peace if the causes of the war continue to cry out due to our perpetual misery? The arrogance which resides in the governors' palaces and the homes of the wealthy businessmen and landowners continues to shout war and death for our race. . . .
Respectfully,
From the southeast of Mexico
Clandestine Indigenous Revolutionary Committee General Command of the Zapatista National Liberation Army

March 15, 1994:
To the national and international press:
Sirs:
Were you missing me? Good, well, here I am anew and not so new. . . .
Do they want more war to understand peace? Accept it, locals of San Cristobal, you were happier when our troops were within the walls of your proud city which you now arm with fear. Learn about this struggle which arms itself with shame.
Greetings and good luck in the ides of March.
From the mountains of southeastern Mexico.
Subcommandante Insurgent Marcos
P.S. Of immediate nostalgia.

Yesterday's images of guerrilla warfare.

Lucha sang tangos in the afternoons, hours of tangos and crickets. Food was running out. We knew what was coming. We were already invincible and small. January was still a long way off. . . .
The mad hatter and the March hare song:
Happy, happy not birthday
To you, I give you (twice).
If today is not your birthday
then we will have to celebrate,
etcetera (twice).
Alicia was able to get out. We are still here . . . and we sing . . . still. . . .

Although many journalists have trooped to the mountains to get interviews (the most recent is in the July 1994 *Vanity Fair*), the EZLN does not depend on the likes of Herbert Mathews to get their message out. Until *The New York Times* published Mathews's interview with Fidel, the revolutionary activity in Cuba was virtually unknown to the rest of the world.[25] Since the first week in January 1994, there have been many official EZLN *communiqués* posted. The difference is striking. These rebels do not need to wait for the Western press to come to them. They have the means to disseminate information through a widely based electronic network.

In this day and age those declarations were not delivered on parchment or even bond paper. There is a great deal of speculation about exactly how these messages have been transmitted. The assumption of instant access is a romantic myth. Guerrillas with Power Books attached to cellular phones is a powerful image, but given the reality of cellular reception, the actuality was probably more prosaic: perhaps statements shared with a small newspaper in San Christobal. Word has it that Marcos does have a laptop. The *communiqués* are written on disks which are carried down from the jungle camp. Was Chiapas "the first post-modern rebellion" as some have claimed, or "pre-modem": brought out on diskette and posted to e-mail?

> March 24, 1994 (Just after Colosio's assassination):
> Communication to *Proceso, La Jornada, El Financiero, Tiempos*, the national and international press.
> Sirs:
> Them. . . . Why did they have to do this? Who are they punishing with this crime? If they are trying to justify a military action against us and against our cause, why did not they kill one of us? The country would have bled less than with this infamy which now makes us shudder. Who was this man harming? Who gains from his blood? . . . Let them come. Here we are, where we were born and where we grew up, where there is a great heart which sustains us, where our dead and our history reside. Here we are, in the mountains of southeast Mexico. . . . Come for us. . . . Now nothing is safe, much less the hopes for peace. Farewell.

---

[25] Mathews spread the word not only for Fidel's rebels, but for the Loyalist cause during the Spanish Civil War as well, when he and Ernest Hemingway posted regular dispatches from the cities and countryside besieged by the Fascists.

Subcomandante Insurgente Marcos

P.S. For those that no one sees. Greetings, brother *Zapatista-moles*. We have shown thanks to your patient and obscure work. The black night of infamy comes again. The end of our cycle is near. We promise you that we will shine intensely, so as to outdo the sun, before disappearing forever. Until the last hour we will salute the dark side which supported our brilliance. Interior light which shone through us so as to shed light on this small piece of history. . . . It is the dark side of the moon that makes possible the bright side of the moon. Like us, if we are the dark side of the moon. We are no less for it. It is rather because we are willing to be the dark side that it is possible for all to see the moon (and because in order to see it you have to learn to fly very high). And so it is that few are willing to suffer so that others will not suffer and to die so that others may live. Farewell. . . .

Subcomandante Marcos[26]

What effect the e-mail activity had on actual events is hard to assess. At the very least, it is clear that the direct *communiqués* from the guerilla leadership served to counter disinformation. They were (and still are) a hedge against increased government repression. The firsthand detailed news of the bombing raids on January 5 were widely published, and this almost certainly intensified the solidarity campaign and helped to bring people out for the massive demonstrations in Mexico City and smaller, but significant, rallies throughout the world. The uses of the Internet to present the stance of the Zapatistas during the negotiations forced even Televisa to report the official demands of the guerrillas.

Internet conferences were used to post emergency *communiqués* and circulate information about solidarity actions.[27] A

---

[26] The *communiqués* from the EZLN and Marcos have been published as *Zapatista! The Writings of the EZLN* (New York: Autonomedia, 1994), compiled and with an introduction by Harry Cleaver from the University of Texas.

[27] An e-mail announcement on January 13 of the completion of a video tape report from Chiapas, *A Cry for Freedom and Democracy*, by CheChé Martínez, brought over a hundred orders for the tape within a few weeks. The tape was used by many solidarity groups for community forums on the situation in Mexico. In several instances after using the tape, individuals would re-post the announcement in other conferences, resulting in even more distribution.

survey of the postings shows the hunger for accurate news: requests for information, questions about certain facts, searches for biographical details. Of particular note is the rapidity with which information was translated and retransmitted. English language versions of articles from *La Jornada* and *El Financiero* were posted within a few hours of their appearance. Experts in various areas would often tag on addenda to reposted news. Agronomists and anthropologists who specialize in Chiapas and Central American agriculture jumped in to add details and background.

In the last few years there has been an exponential growth of computer communication in Mexico.[28] Although much of this activity has been concentrated in the *maquila*/industrial sector, most recently spurred on by NAFTA, there is substantial use of e-mail in Mexican universities and surprisingly even in small-scale agriculture. As the *Wall Street Journal* has noted, "Poor farmers can track the prices, in Mexico and internationally, for the apples, limes, papayas and mangos they grow."[29]

One can guess that the Mexican government is scrambling to get their counter-insurgency efforts on-line. Many have speculated that the PRI-controlled government tried to close down the rebels' computer link. For a short period of time, *laneta*, the Mexican server for the Internet, was down, and worried communicators flooded several conferences with accusations of government censorship. Whether or not the PRI was responsible, the messages surrounding this event show how essential the *laneta* connection was, as there was a general panic when it was broken. However, the connection was restored by circuitously rerouting the information, proving to many that it is not so easy to censor the Internet. No one can prove that there was deliberate tampering of the Chiapas connections. Although breakdowns of computer networks are common occurrences, in this case the charges of sabotage seemed credible to many Internet surfers, as the breakdown

---

[28] See Paul B. Carroll, "Foreign Competition Spurs Mexico to Move into High-Tech World," *Wall Street Journal*, July 5, 1994.

[29] Ibid, p. A9.

occurred at the height of the negotiations with the government at which time the Zapatistas were releasing their eloquently stated demands. Considering the widespread support
for the EZLN throughout Mexico, this information was not
the sort of thing the PRI wanted floating around during the
negotiations.

If the closing down of *laneta* was government repression,
the PRI and the Rand Corporation[30] have postulated a power
to computer networking that some might question. Is the audience for these discussions basically limited to university
computer labs? In the United States the "lanic gopher" at the
University of Texas (lanic.utexas.edu) provides a chronologi-
cal history of the modem traffic on Chiapas. In browsing the
thousands of entries, one sees that this conference, like most
computer conferences in the United States, is predominantly
white and male and based squarely in the U.S. academic community. In fact, one of the items with the most responses is a
discussion of John Womack's position on the Zapatistas. As a
major biographer of the first Zapata, Emiliano, Womack obviously carries a great deal of historic (or at least history departmental) weight. His questioning of the authenticity of the
Zapatistas brought on a clatter of keyboards defending the
EZLN and documenting the connections between the Zapatistas of today with their forbearers. This sort of historical debate
has a peculiar urgency when posted next to contemporary descriptions of ongoing state repression and updates of hostage
exchanges. However, it raises certain questions: if we log in
from our comfy offices, are we practicing a kind of academic
voyeurism and/or armchair (or, rather, swivel desk chair)
warfare?

The Chiapas computer conferences, and the publications
that have emanated from them, have allowed many people to
feel closer to a revolutionary process. A vital part of any revolutionary movement is the degree of hope that is mobilized.
Perhaps the most effective outcome of Chiapas on-line has

---

[30] The Rand Corporation published a study of militant activism: see John
Arquilla and David Ronfeldt, *The Advent of Netwar* (Santa Monica, Calif.:
Rand Corp., 1996).

been the boosting of the psychological morale of Latin American activists, anti-GATT cadres, and human rights workers. The January actions were a hit with grassroots organizers worldwide, who daily wage legal and moral battles for many of the same causes that the EZLN champions. However momentary the triumph of the small and barely armed group of peasants who confronted the transnational marketing infrastructure in January, they have brought a measure of hope that has been woefully in short supply during the past few years. There was a sense of direct connection, of an authentic "interactive" movement, as groups and individuals forwarded messages, excerpted passages, pinned up tear sheets, and posted their own comments on-line. The Zapatistas have been exemplary in their mobilization of new technologies to disseminate information and to point out the emancipatory potential in the Internet.

> Now is the time for hope to organize itself and to walk forward in the valleys and in the cities. . . .[31]

And on the computer networks. Connect.

---

[31] EZLN *communiqué*, June 16, 1994.

# 8

# Software for Hard Times:
## Liberatory Uses of
## New Technologies

Cover from Com-Gen-100, an experimental class taught at the University of California, San Diego from 1987 to 1993. *(Design by Molly Kovel)*

# Introduction

"TEACHING ON THE NET: The Dangerous Format of Com Gen 100" is the story of a unique class which began as an experiment to break down the alienation of large lecture classes and to try to activate and motivate students to take charge of their education and their lives. An early attempt to use the Internet in education, it accepted "no hard copy" and led to a uniquely de-centered class.

"Close Comfort: Soft Ware for Hard Times" is a meditation on the commercialization of public education and the plight of students in an alienated context, just south of Disney's Anaheim. "Watch Out, Dick Tracy!" looks at reverse surveillance: can people watch the watchers? This essay was written in the wake of the Rodney King episode, in which a camcorder tracked the violent excesses of the Los Angeles police department.

The United States is now the country with the highest percentage of its populace in prison. Almost 6 million people are either in jail, awaiting punishment, or on parole. For the past five years I have worked with Deep Dish TV on several series looking at this situation. "The Undisciplined and Punishment" grew out of my work against the prison industrial complex. It looks at the use of new technology in the activism of prison families and reform advocates.

# Teaching on the Net:
# The Dangerous Format
# of Com Gen 100

## June 1994

THE ADVERTISING AGENCIES know just how hungry Americans are for community: nothing short of sex sells so well. From the cracker-barrel geezers bathed in a rural golden rim light to the affable urban jocks on heavenly basketball courts, the notion of community suffuses television. And everyone is told what soft drink to guzzle and what shoes they need to wear to get it.

The longing for community is a deep need in my students, and I know that my most important work as a teacher is to somehow, some way, before the quarter is over, create a space and a situation in which they can be part of a community that does not define itself by products or boundaries of race, class, and gender. This is not an easy task on a campus that has an impersonal mall for a student center and acres of parking lots filled with personal automobiles.

The texture of daily education for my students is actually quite close to attending a cineplex at a giant shopping center. First the search for the parking place, then the line for the ticket (registration), the guzzling down of salt and sugar (the predominant ingredients at the campus eateries), the search for the seat, and finally the show. Unfortunately, at the university the rich tones of the arc lamp projector glowing through a finely tuned color print are replaced with florescent glare from Formica desks, vinyl floor tiles, and sterile wallboard. Instead of subtly mixed sounds of a quadraphonic soundtrack, we have the hiss and crackle of the PA system as the professor drones into the microphone for the allotted hour and fifteen minutes. Then the students get back in their cars and chug off to their jobs at the real mall in order to be able to pay the ever increasing fees for this "educational" process, a process which daily drifts further from any notion of community into huge galaxial orbits of administrative and business complexes.

The immense scale and multiplication of bureaucratic layers of the current university entities, instead of promoting efficiency, create a system which grows more and more dysfunctional. The fluorescent lights misfire in blinking arrhythmia; the vinyl floor tiles are dotted with chipped obstructions and yesterday's bubble gum. The notion of a hallowed space for intellectual development is a cruel hoax. The only ivory in these towers is the liquid soap dispenser in the bathroom, which solidified last year and is still clogged.

Is community possible in this situation? Or to turn that around: is it possible to survive in this situation without community? What is the role of technology, and what is the role of art in the creation of community? For several years I taught a course at UCSD that attempted to build a community of students that would transcend geography, architecture, and the bureaucracies of the state educational system. Ironically the community formation I am discussing was dependent on the personal consumer. It also depended on large centrally controlled state and private corporate computer networks. Whatever the success of this project, dependency on a large corporate structure and complicated technology is rather troubling.

COMMUNITY IN THE CORPORATE UNIVERSITY

Despite inherent contradictions, the Internet can be fertile soil for communities of similar interests within large institutions. Computer hackers have always known this: there are communities of computer "freaks" who are on-line daily with each other in most universities and corporations. In the hacker case the computer is the content of their community. The dialogue is most often about the technology itself.

In 1987 I began experimenting with using computer networking within a large class to encourage community formation. E-mail can be a place where all students can exchange with each other and the faculty, and where issues and ideas can become part of community discussion. These exchanges are the beginning of communities within the class and a sense of community in the large class in general. By requiring all students to log on to discuss readings and media, students and faculty are thrust into the electronic space. The assignments for this class accept no "hard copy"—it's on-line or no grade. In addition, students and staff must enter within a dialogic format: their writing must be in response to entries that precede theirs.

The initial "content" is reviews of video tapes that students watch through a library media "reserve" center. They are required to see several tapes a week from a large reserve list. They comment on these tapes (and on the comments of other students) via e-mail in files grouped around the specific tapes. The tapes are often emotional and troubling for many students (*Tongues Untied*, Marlon Riggs's powerful look at being an African American gay person, is a good example). We found that students who would never discuss certain issues in class are able to open up through the perceived anonymity of computer mail. Students who do not speak out in class, who would not ordinarily choose computer communication, who would never define themselves as computer hackers, often become the very ones who are the most passionately involved and the ones whose entries provoke the most response and continuing dialogue.

The engagement is facilitated by and greatly depends on the incorporation of art into the process by the use of challenging and profound video tapes to provoke responses from deep within the experiences and intuition of students and faculty. The work of Yvonne Rainer, Sherry Milner, Jane Cottis, Joan Braderman, Marlon Riggs, and Sadie Benning have been the points of entry for many participants. They connect with the personal visions of these videos, viewing them in semi-privacy, on their own schedules at the library video reserve room. They then can turn from these isolated viewings to the community of the computer terminals (located in the same access room). They respond with comments and critiques and often with their own art: poems, chants, or raps that twist and curl through the electronic mail—organic forms in an inorganic field like blades of grass bursting out from macadam. Sooner or later these buds find others to intertwine with: comrades, soul sisters, like-minds.

Communities of correspondence begin to coalesce around certain issues: gender preference, censorship, suburban upbringing, women's rights and agendas. A sense of rapport among and between communities begins to diffuse through the classroom to encourage a general atmosphere of trust and openness.[1] (Or it can spill over with energy and anger from intense discussions that have on occasion battered raw emotions.) On e-mail each file is read in turn. There is no "head of the class," no privileged space for teachers. It tends to equalize students and faculty (no one is immune from accolades and/or anger). It facilitates the formation of small communities within the class and engenders an overall feeling of understanding and interest in the larger community of the entire class (at times over 250 students). The fact that these students become numbers in a large computer infrastructure does not in itself mean that the students must be atomized and dehumanized. In this case, by allowing equal access, by encouraging self-expression and empathy, computers can be tools of creative community.

*The Ingredients: Notes on Com Gen 100, 1987–1992*

Large enrollment. Large lecture classes. How to make this class a laboratory for communication. What is the form of

---

[1] Students on e-mail are anonymous only in the sense that their faces aren't seen. One of the most startling results of this class has been the various ways that students (and faculty) find to create very specific identities for themselves through this seemingly homogenous venue of computer conferencing. The logons can use nicknames or pseudonyms; they can vary the concrete form of the entries (shape, word spacing, line adjustment) but more uniquely in the various personality indications of the often quite intimate and emotional statements.

communication in a large lecture class? Mass communication. Teacher to masses. One way. Is there another way? Can we restructure the communication of the class itself? How can a large lecture course serve as a vehicle for participatory communication?

## Some Ideas, Some Experiments

First: *remove the teacher* from the front of the class.

For the most part, the *presentations are by the students*, or films, or guest "performers."

*Group work:* Class assignments that force students to come together. *To progress, they have to work together.* They have to rethink their individualistic competitive drives. They have to notice what other students are doing, not so they can beat them, but so they can work together.

*Com Gen is a leveler.* Everyone starts at the same place. This drives the high achievers crazy. "But how can I know what my grade will be?" They whine. They worry. They write memos. For them education has been, up till now, entirely predictable. For the first time they aren't sure how they will do.

*Twenty-six groups*: The number of letters in the alphabet, the number of groups able to make two-minute presentations in one class period.

*Equal access, electronic mail:* E-mail allows all the students equal access to the TAs and to the professor. Get on the computer, you're on the screen. You don't have to depend on setting up an appointment. Working students can log on late at night. You're there. You're as much there as the other 250 students. In addition, every student has a computer account which can then be used for other class work.[2]

*Computer literacy:* All students must use e-mail for all written course work. Hard copy is not accepted. Students who would be fearful are forced to use the tool. Students who tend

---

[2] This course was initiated in 1987 when few students had their own computers and when the computer labs were used almost exclusively by science students and computer geeks.

to emphasize the technology for its own sake (computer hackers, for example) are forced to learn to use it in expressive terms.

*Equal voice:* We use *four microphones* at all times in the class: two up the aisles and two in the front. The microphones are passed from student to student. The TAs sometimes work like Oprah, urging reluctant students to express the thoughts they had articulated in the section, drawing out subtle opinions and contradictions. You don't have to shout. You don't have to have a loud voice. Professors use microphones, why not students? Microphones are the appropriate tools for a room as large as the lecture hall.

*Pragmatic use of technology:* From the first day, when students use the blackboard to divide into groups, to the last group project with rap music amplifiers, the apparatuses of communication are used not for an exercise, but for contact with the instructors and/or with the other students.

*Amplification of the technology:* Video cameras playback live on monitors situated on either side of the class: gestures, performances, presentations, conversations, declarations, denunciations, rebuttals, pleas, and reactions. This is a constant referent. What is seen on the screen? What is seen at the podium? How do these images relate to each other? Which details are chosen for the camera? Which details do the eyes seek out?

*Tools used in the class:* All modes of communication are used: the alphabet, language (written, spoken, sung, transmitted), microphones, chalk, cassette recorders, video cameras, editing decks, still cameras, slide projectors, film projectors, VCRs, monitors, computers.

*Meta-class:* The class becomes the subject of the class. Students become conscious of their education: of their own role in it, of the expectations they have, of the requirements the system makes, of the role of technology as a tool in this process. In this context it is necessary and expected that passionate discussions about the class occur. These discussions occur in class, in sections, on e-mail, in the halls, on video tape, in memos to the chair, even in petition drives to eliminate the grade structure of the class.

*Media and the Third World:* This is another theme of the class and is the *subject* of required videos, of class screenings, of student projects. This serves as an ever-present example to highlight (1) the ways in which forms of power influence communication, (2) the ways in which students have, to a great extent, remained ignorant about a major part of the world, and (3) the ways in which creative use of appropriate technology can counter traditional mass media genres and structures even in situations of "underdevelopment."

*Technology that doesn't increase alienation:* Is technology inherently alienating? Are there tools that can assist communication processes? How have artists, journalists, scientists, community organizations, grassroots leaders, media activists, and others used new technologies to expand consciousness and *develop community?*

*Is it possible even within a large bureaucratic state university to create a community?*

To utilize technology for self-expression, for collaboration, for passion, for feelings, for organizing? To encourage exchange and the freedom to express outrage, confusion, anger, enthusiasm, sympathy?

*Can tools be human?*

Results of the first experiments: The course works. It does what it sets out to do. My worry: it's too predictable. The community appears in about the ninth week. It works every time. Is this calculation? Is this manipulation? My hope: that the class would evolve as different people contribute and develop it. That a petition arose should not be a problem, but a victory. That undergraduates would take their education seriously enough to petition about the grade structure and then to ask that they get out of the grade rat race? Amazing. My reservations: I would want the class to be taught with grades. I think that the students need to see this class in the same light that they do all their required classes. The manifestation of the petition should only make them see the larger problem of grades in general. Com Gen TAs and professors know their students performance. They have plenty of material on which to make judgment: individual film reports and other e-mail submissions, the section and large class discussions, the class and discussion evaluations on e-mail, the group projects, the e-mail conferences, and the myriad presentations, performances, and video work that is the bulk of the course work.

CONCLUSION

The class works. It takes seriously the need to integrate theory and practice. Production should not be ghettoized as a kinky and weird subject, nor treated as a strictly technical problem. Com Gen is not designed as a technical course, or one for self-selected production freaks. It operates on the following premises:

1. It is a required course.
2. It is an important confluence of the many areas of communication research.
3. It is the theoretical grounding for those who will continue with production as a major interest.
4. It is the basis for the practical application of communication tools for all students of communication to understand the constraints, the power, the problems, and the utopian potential for human uses of communication technology.

Com Gen 100 has attempted to come to grips with some of the basic problems of communication in direct *practical* terms. It has been a problem for many students that they are steeped in a rigorous critique of mass media, but are given *no* sense that change is possible.

The goal of Com Gen 100 is to empower students to critique mass media through the creative use of communication tools. That they have seen their own education as part of mass culture, open to critique, is a successful application of the course methods and theory.

# Close Comfort: Soft Ware for Hard Times

*October 1995*

ANOTHER EUCALYPTUS grove has bit the dust. When I first came to teach at this university ten years ago it was a paradise of sweet-smelling trees. For several weeks each year the eucalyptus branches would turn a glimmering orange as thousands of monarch butterflies came through to rest on their flight to Mexico. In those days hummingbirds zipped across the patio, and swallows made nests under the eaves of the Media Center. Now the campus is more like downtown Toronto than Eden. Tall boxes of glass and steel have discouraged the hummingbirds and the monarchs.

Returning this fall to teach yet another quarter, I grimace as I pass the aromatic stumps. They bleed a savory sap that makes trails across the sandy soil. I can't see them from my office. In fact, I can't see anything from my office. As the only member of the faculty who teaches production, I am on the bottom rung of the department hierarchy. My office is at the end of the hall—near the maintenance closet filled with stacks of toilet paper.

On the way from the parking lot I pass the student lunchroom. A large sheet of Plexiglas is bolted to the outside of the stucco wall. Under it is a poster with a wide border of advertisements for candy bars and caffeine tabs surrounding a center of "soft news": the subject of this month's "news" is "Time Management." It's a wall advertisement in the guise of news. The walls of this public university are being sold to the highest bidder. I wonder how much it costs to buy young eyes. I wonder who makes the editorial decisions for this monthly "news" sheet. Someone actually spends time trying to think of subjects so boring that the students will find the advertisements attractive.

I scrounge three quarters from my pocket, ready to get a copy of the *L.A. Times*. But the vending box on the corner near the lunch room has changed. It is now *USA Today* that cheerily beams out from the Plexiglas door. No thanks, I mutter, and trudge to the department mailroom. I thumb through my mail. A bill for the campus parking sticker. The parking fees are up. I have little choice but to pay. The bus from the student/faculty housing complex where I live has been canceled. The new bus stop is over a mile away. Several routes have been combined so that, even when you finally get on the bus, it takes forty-five minutes for what had been only a five-minute ride.

An insistent phone rings as I pass the main office. It's waiting for the voice mail to kick in. The department receptionist/office manager no longer answers the phone. At this moment a dozen students are sitting on the floor in the hall awaiting their turn with her to check their schedules. She now doubles as the undergraduate advisor and has the responsibility for placement and matriculation of 500 students, in addition to the details of the office infrastructure of a large academic department. Although I notice the "Empty Paper" light blinking on the Xerox machine, I decide to put off my photocopying rather than bother her with this supply detail.

There is a tall stack of campus newspapers on a table in the mailroom. I pick up one issue, noting how thick it seems. As I open it, it loses two-thirds of its heft as several dozen slick brochures slip out to the floor. They are glossy ads for credit cards. Students are cordially invited to accumulate credit card debt—in addition to the thousands of dollars they owe for tuition and fee loans. Some have six separate credit card accounts. They are indentured for at least a decade when they graduate.

I bend to pick up the mess of fallen Visa/MasterCard forms and hear behind me the rustle of the recycle bin getting emptied. The man who is tending to this task averts his eyes as I look up. He is recently arrived from Oaxaca, and his face is dark brown from years in the fields. I wonder what happened to Lourdes, the Chicana woman who used to do these chores. She was a union member and an employee for nine years, dismissed when the university maintenance went on a "contract basis." The university now negotiates with "independent contractors" who can employ workers for less than minimum wage, with no benefits and no questions asked about documents. It's one result of moves to privatize the university.

Brrrrrrrrrr. The sound of a leaf blower echoes through the cement building. The grounds crew is also made up of contract workers. A very short man with long black hair has a gas engine strapped to his back and is cleaning the sidewalk of the debris from the eucalyptus trees. Actually he is blowing it from many small piles into one huge pile. It's what we used to do with rakes. Rakes are quieter, in addition to being more efficient. I wonder whatever happened to rakes? The harsh sound of the motor sets off some strange harmonics when combined with the rattling of the aluminum ventilation vents in my office and the buzz of my hard disk. The combination of noises is so penetrating, I cannot work and decide to go to the one place where I have consistently found pleasure on this campus: the open-air swimming pool. A swim in the bright La Jolla sun before succumbing to the fluorescent lights of my office will put me in a better mood. As I lower myself into the tepid water, I notice a shiny rainbow gleam on the surface. The pool has a layer of diesel oil on it: the residue from the exhaust of the heavy equipment that is busily putting up another concrete tower to the west. The edge of the pool's east side has vertical black streaks where the westerly winds have tossed the oil-streaked waves against the turquoise tiles. The sun has baked this scum into a strange hieroglyphic language.

I CAN READ THE WRITING ON THE WALL:
THERE IS NO COMFORT IN PARADISE

This university is a microcosm of what is happening in the world. With the exceptions of the military and the prison industry, public institutions of all sorts are reeling from budget cuts. Although there are some who are profiting on one end of the scale, for the vast majority of people in the United States life is not getting any better. The only glint of a utopian future comes from the software companies. The idea of a better world seems somehow to hinge on having universal access to fast modems. Can technology help us to create communities of resistance to battle the rampant ecocide, the exploitation of labor, the commodification of education, the trivialization of information, the indenturing of our youth, and other horrors of our post-industrial lives?

## @ MARIENBAD . . .[3]

There is a delightful interview with Julio Garcia Espinosa, a director from the Cuban Film Institute (ICAIC), in a Channel Four (UK) program about Latin American Film.[4] He laughingly recounts how during the sixties he and other Cuban filmmakers would read Beckett or watch the films of Resnais and Antonioni: those sixties documents of alienation and distance. (In Spanish he uses the word *incommunicación*.) He and his colleagues would laugh because in Cuba they had a different kind of *incommunicación*—material *incommunicación* in which they couldn't make a telephone call because of mechanical breakdowns, nor could they go anywhere because they didn't have enough gas. They had no film stock, so they couldn't shoot anything and even their typewriters had no ribbons. They were authentically *incommunicados!*

He was expressing what they experienced as a Third World country trying to create, trying to communicate, and he contrasted this with Antonioni's world where communication problems were existential: the angst of an affluent society separated from itself. However, Antonioni's alienation/*incommunicación* resonated as material difficulty from their per-

---

[3] This is a reference to *Last Year at Marienbad* by Alan Resnais (1963), an example of the French "New Wave." The film's image of figures walking isolated from each other through a cold landscape became an icon for an alienated generation.

[4] This series was made by Michael Channan for Channel Four in London.

spective in the Third World. Stories of scarcity and shortages do not seem so far away, even for me here at the once opulent University of California. It seems that what we are experiencing here in the United States is our own structural adjustment.

## RED DESERT

Is the angst felt by Antonioni a luxury now, pushed to the receding distance by very real dread? Or is it that the gestalt of the global situation is such that no matter what one's relative affluence, when compared to the Brazilian *favelas*, for example, one can no longer feel distance? The world is smaller: it is impossible to ignore the problems that "development" has wrought.

We are all under the ozone hole. "We are the world . . ." as the Live Aid/World Aid campaigns so insistently chanted.

Last summer in New York City I watched a group of homeless AIDS victims wash each other's wounds with water dripping from a fire hydrant. The scene reminded me of the tender care among beggars of Satyagit Ray's Bengal. I remember watching images of the poor in the films of Ray many years ago and thinking about how strange and horrible that poverty seemed. I wept at the desperation of postwar Italy as portrayed in neo-realist films like *The Bicycle Thief*. Nowadays that sort of poverty is right down the highway. Even in San Diego ("America's Finest City" as they call it) there are streets lined with homeless families dressed in rags almost as dusty and frayed as those of West Bengal. And fifteen miles from San Diego, just over the border, there are families of NAFTA *maquiladora* workers who live in cardboard shacks more primitive than the adobe homes of rural India.

For those who grew up in the affluent fifties in the United States, with TV images of suburban utopia, and glossy magazines full of ads for middle-class consumption, poverty, which once seemed so distant, is now very close indeed. And it is not comfortable.

Who documents the daily struggle of the urban poor? Where are the Rays of America's urban ghettos? Where is the Flaherty of the empty Georges Bank?[5] Who spins the yarns about the fishermen who have no fish?[6]

Are the would-be chroniclers of our problematic world glued to the screen of computers, busy stacking bits of pixels for a prehistoric special effect? Have they been lured into the roulette rooms of software creation? My students have many opportunities. The young artists of today's media have long résumés. The more imaginative and sharp they are, the more rapidly they are snapped up, even before they graduate. The hungry market for cyber/liberal arts majors is described in an article on the front page of *The New York Times* on October 2, 1995, "From Liberal Arts to Cyber Careers": "You have kids coming out of school who see it as not only a hip thing to do, but also getting reinforcement from their parents that it's a smart business move," said Mr. Ross (an executive at Byron Preiss Multimedia in New York).

### BLAKE NEVER KNEW THESE DARK SATANIC MERGER MILLS

Talented young people are whisked away to design web pages, CD-ROMs, digital editing software, and digital sound systems. In the canyons of lower Broadway, Mercer Street, Silicon Valley, and Wiltshire Boulevard they sit in front of power computers coaxing their software into rotating speeding buses and blasting target bridges with the latest 3-D techniques. As they morph celluloid monsters, their bosses are morphing with each other on the top floor. The creative youth whose brains are the engines of these media machines are deeply cynical about both the world and the corporations that have hired them. Does it matter if they are working for Cap Cities or Dis-

---

[5] A reference to the work of Robert Flaherty, whose *Man of Aran* chronicled the difficulties of eking out a living on the rocky wind-blown land off the shores of Ireland. Although Flaherty has been criticized for over-dramatizing certain aspects of the fishermen's lives, the overall impression is an accurate portrayal of the grim and desperate struggle lived by these (literally) marginal families.

[6] The North Atlantic from Maine to Nova Scotia is facing almost total depletion of the fish populations that have supported local communities for generations.

ney or Westinghouse or Fox, or a murky combination of any
or all of these? They are incapable of talking or thinking ab-
stractly about the system or themselves. After work they go to
the gym, climb their endless Stairmasters and ruminate on
the bottom line on their credit card statements. Like many
developing nations, our youth are indentured to a life of para-
lyzing debt.

SEARCH FOR COMMUNITY

Where are the "independents"? Each year the film schools
spew thousands of graduates out into the media effluent,
where there are enough gigs to keep most of them in pay envelopes—envelopes that are quickly emptied to make school
loan payments and keep their credit cards just under maximum limit.

As someone who has been involved in the "Independent
Media Community" for forty years,[7] I see major changes in
this new electronic age, and those changes aren't just in the
format. Camcorders are more accessible than 16 mm, and the
cost per image and for duplication is down. There are more
venues, more festivals, more organizations. On the one hand,
it may seem that there are more options, more channels, more
"creative" jobs, more "entry-level" positions. But "entry"?
That's about it. Many of these jobs are "entry" into a life of
working for mega-corporations. "Opportunity"? Maybe, but
the opportunity to get a weekly pay check, not to really create
your own media. There are few options for autonomous invention, and scarce space and time for individual vision.

The kids wheezing behind fog machines on elaborate MTV
sets in another age might have defined themselves as independent producers and in between gigs applied for grants,
scrounged equipment, and made their own work. But they
have their loans to repay, their credit card bills to pay up, and

---

[7] In 1962 I joined a ragtag group called Filmmakers' Coop, whose voice
was the journal *Film Culture*, and whose work was shown at Cinema 16,
founded by Amos Vogel, and at the Charles Theater on Avenue B, where
Jonas Mekas and others organized screenings of "underground" films.

in New York and L.A. there is always some kind of job: gaffing a Michael Jackson video here, editing an AT&T infomercial there, compiling lists for web-page tie-ins or digitizing video clips for CD-ROMs. There are lots of jobs around. And it's not just multimedia companies that are hiring. There are video subsidiaries in many marketing concerns. For example, many real estate companies videotape the unique features (bidets in every bathroom!) of the newest and most glamorous condos on the market. These tapes are distributed free from Blockbuster shelves. Someone has to shoot those tapes every month, and edit them and schlep them around to various video outlets. This may have more appeal than carrying around a leaf blower, but it is essentially moving real estate from one pile to another.

The image industry eats our youth in large bites. The bowels of the culture machines churn with unceasing greed, devouring ideas and icons, mysteries and melodies, grinding down passions and pride in the meaningless drudgery of the market. Creativity is what the carnivorous corporate culture needs most. Without it the hardware is cold and boring. Young hearts pump vitality into the media machines. The culture industry demands authentic creativity and human subjectivity, which is extracted as ruthlessly as mahogany is pillaged from the rain forest. The multinational media mills saw and plane away the natural forms, smoothing over any signs of organic life. The requirement is a culture with flashes of creativity, but bland enough and predictable enough to be seamlessly repeated and interchanged, stacked and sold.

THE HANDS OF VICTOR JARA

Are we embedded in our strategic hamlets/malls that we cannot react? Do we watch each other across the Chilean stadium quietly humming the music of our forcibly amputated artists?

The fall of the democratically elected government of Salvador Allende in Chile was instigated by the International Telephone and Telegraph Company. (That fact alone should make us wary of large telecommunications companies.) ITT's coup was engineered by the CIA and the Chilean military. The guitarist Victor Jara was a Chilean folk singer/composer who was one of those who were rounded up as dangerous persons. The military cut off his hands.[8]

The Chilean thugs knew a thing or two about the power of autonomous culture. The power of art is also understood by the current thugs in Washington, who have cut off the hands of our cultural infrastructure. The dismantling of public culture is the unraveling of twenty-five years of small victories and careful knitting. However problematic, the cultural bureaucracies were not built on market principles, and because of this were able, in small but important ways, to nurture what little of a public sphere we have in the United States. But as we see in the endless congressional debates over art, there are times when autonomous culture is indeed dangerous.

ARISE, YE MODEMS OF THE WORLD . . .

The music of resistance is not long silenced by violence, nor can it be forever muffled by the dense web of multinational mergerdom—which is where the Internet comes in.

On the Net we are together underground. The roadside flowers of the information highway are the samizdats of the west. On the Internet we reconnect those dots of color, we can salvage those strands of common history. We search out the flecks of color in the dull fabric of our corporatized world and reweave them on looms of our own making. We connect using their routes for our ideas. We can touch each other, and we know we are not alone.[9]

---

[8] Jara's widow, who saw his body at a morgue, has recently said that although his hands were badly beaten and bruised, they were not actually severed, although this has long persisted as a myth in songs and poetry of resistance in Chile.

[9] A Canadian Security report noted the use of the Internet by activists. "Creating the foundation for dramatic change, the Internet has had a profound impact—in part by enabling organizers to quickly and easily arrange demonstrations and protests, worldwide if necessary. Individuals and groups now are able to establish dates, share experiences, accept responsibilities, arrange logistics, and initiate a myriad of other taskings that would

Are the pathways and connective nodes really ours? It's comfortable and it's close. But it's not secure. A recent set of Internet guidelines published by the University of California warns that university connections may not be used for union organizing. Meanwhile the corporations busily making deals with the university can use it for their own needs, which may or may not include organizing to stifle union activity. The regents, not the unions, make the rules.

The openness and facility of on-line communication, however, make policing of the Net difficult if not impossible. In fact, the inherent structure of the Internet may be so open that even the profiteers may have a hard time. *The New York Times* cited its "weaknesses": the ease of downloading and transference, which "can be traced to the technical underpinnings of the network, which was set up more than a quarter century ago not as a medium for conducting business, but as a way for academic and scientific researchers to exchange information."[10] But then there's the question of who is connected. Whole countries have virtually no access to Internet communication. Many rural villagers have no telephone, let alone a computer. There are too many people left out. We can have a grand time exchanging poetry and Net connections, but it's like trying to eat a candlelit dinner on the subway. The context can't be forgotten.

HARD TIMES

My students grew up watching *Cops*. They were in high school for the Gulf War. They didn't have maps of the world in their

---

have been impossible to manage readily and rapidly in the past. International protests and demonstrations can be organized for the same date and time, so that a series of protests take place in concert. The Internet has breathed new life into the anarchist philosophy, permitting communication and coordination without the need for a central source of command, and facilitating coordinated actions with minimal resources and bureaucracy. It has allowed groups and individuals to cement bonds, file e-mail reports of perceived successes, and recruit members": "Anti-globalization: A Spreading Phenomenon," in *Perspectives*, a Canadian Security Intelligence Service Publication, Report # 2000/08, August 22, 2000.

[10] "Discovery of Internet Flaws Is Setback for On-line Commerce," *The New York Times*, October 11, 1995.

classrooms, but they had free posters of picturesque Alaskan nature distributed by a post-Valdez Exxon. Their schools had to cut out art classes and music, but each child is given a coloring book about the wonders of nuclear power distributed by the local power authority. During lunch they were not allowed to talk while the PA system played the theme from Disney's *Beauty and the Beast*. In junior high they saw films made by SeaWorld, not by Robert Flaherty. They think they know about AIDS because they saw a program on *Oprah*. The closest they get to the Third World is the handicrafts they buy at Pier One to make their dorm rooms exotic. The state where I am teaching is now spending more money on prisons than on higher education.

We in the United States have a higher percentage of our populace in prison than any country on earth. One out of every three African American young men is either in jail or on parole. Half of all the money spent on public housing in the last decade is money spent on jail cells. Our Death Chambers are multiplying, our Death Rows full.

A nation that prioritizes repression is out of balance. A nation that cuts off the hands of culture is a sick society. A nation is woefully wrong to leave victims of the century's most ruthless plague out in the cold. A nation that can condemn its elderly citizens to misery is a nation with a terminal sentence.

We are all on death row. We are all living with AIDS.

When we realize our situation, we reach out to others who also recognize the danger. We grope in the dark, whispering to each other. On the Internet we know how to whisper, but how does one scream on line? Or maybe we need to learn to whistle.

# Watch Out, Dick Tracy! Popular Video in the Wake of the Exxon Valdez

*June 1992*

DICK TRACY used advanced technology. He was the comic hero with the two-way radio wristwatch. He was also a cop, and cops can usually get the technology they need. But in 1948 I, a knobby-kneed eight-year-old girl, had a Dick Tracy watch, which made me the most technologically advanced of my family, not to mention my block. No one in our neighborhood even had a TV set at that time. I got my two-way radio watch by sending in Kix (or was it Shredded Wheat?) box tops with a quarter and a self-addressed, stamped envelope. It was a classic case of military research benefiting the consumer. The cops got their equipment, and we Kix eaters shared in the advancement of science. I was ecstatic. It didn't matter that it didn't work. Neither did the infinitely more frustrating battery-operated walkie-talkie my younger sister got in the late fifties. The Dick Tracy watch had no pretensions. It was pretend. I didn't expect it to work. It was adapted for the home market. It was the idea that counted.

From the cereal box to the TV set, the military is a part of everyday life in the United States, and the merger between General Electric and RCA has only made more obvious the kinds of symbiosis that the military has had from the beginning with the major media corporations.[11] Both GE and RCA

---

[11] Jack O'Dell, Chairman of the Pacifica Board, recently suggested that we should expand the term "military-industrial complex " to read more accurately "military-industrial-media complex," in a paper presented at the

have been two of the biggest military contractors since World
War II. NBC was a subsidiary of RCA and is now a part of the
mega-military corporation the merger created. Collusion of
military and communication technology isn't new. The first
large U.S. corporation was Western Union, which had its
western expansion subsidized by Congress as a wartime expense for the Union during the Civil War. Native Americans
fought this expansion by cutting the wires and on occasion
felling the telegraph poles with axes. Resistance to the relentless advance of corporate communications seems just as futile
today, if not more so. What recourse exists in a world ringed
with satellites and stitched with microwave links?

Western Union told the Indians that they had "singing
wires."[12] It didn't tell them that the wires could be used to call
in troop reinforcements to suppress resistance. Information
from transnational information corporations about information is obviously suspect. The views of IBM on artificial intelligence or of Kodak on the history of images are complicitous
with the profit needs of their corporations, whether these
views are expressed in a public relations handout or more subtly woven into a museum exhibit.[13] However, there are some
notions about communication and technology that are so pervasive that they are accepted as axioms and are not so easily
perceived. One such view of technology is that military research is the source of advanced consumer products. We are
to feel grateful to the Joint Chiefs of Staff for everything from
Tang (the space-age orange juice) to snowmobiles. I recall that
Kubrick's film *Barry Lyndon* was heralded with the news that
certain scenes were shot in actual candlelight due to the mi-
raculous advances in lens technology made by the U.S. Army
(chasing Vietnamese peasants in the dark, no doubt). In more
recent years, news clips have shown how interstate bridge

conference Anti-communism in the U.S.: History and Consequences, Har-
vard University, 1988.

[12] Fritz Lang's first film in Hollywood was *Western Union,* in which Randolph Scott portrays the cowboy who helps subdue the progress-resistant
Indians.

[13] Herb Schiller's *Culture Incorporated: The Corporate Takeover of Public
Expression* (New York: Oxford University Press, 1989) documents how corporations have usurped public space for their messages.

builders are able to use specially designed army helicopters (ideal for machine gunners hovering over banana plantations and coffee terraces).

It's not always the army. Sometimes it's the U.S. space program (a largely military exercise, however) which is our benefactor. The space/military complex has been credited with the development of the video camera and the digital watch. Technocrats like the trickle-down theory of technology to boost military and space budgets. But the image of technology that is developed by and for experts with happy side benefits for the masses ignores the pressures and demands of the mass market in the development of such items as the digital watch and the VCR.[14] The notion that military research is a source of consumer benefits not only helps to boost budgets for General Dynamics, it also serves to mystify both technology and the military and remove both from any connection to popular need except in a remote second-hand way. This trickle-down disinformation serves to increase the sense of alienation and powerlessness of media workers, artists, and activists alike. If communication technology is fortified within the military, it is farther from our reach. This construct obscures some of the contradictions present in technology designed for popular consumption, and in particular those inherent in the mass-marketed apparati of communication.

This is not to infer that a research based on seduction of consumers is more progressive or necessarily better than military research. Tang is a miserable excuse for orange juice whether it is concocted in the labs at Livermore, General Dynamics, or General Foods. But it may be instructive to contemplate what the idea of military research as consumer benefactor does to the way we think about research and the potential for shaping that work. In the fallout from Three Mile

---

[14] The way in which much of consumer product history is attributed to military research is grist for the mills of the conspiracy theorists among us. Or as Michael Parenti put it, "Why is it that everyone is willing to accept the notion that if you're talking about price fixing or contra funding we can recognize a conspiracy, but as soon as we mention the media in terms of ruling class needs we're all of a sudden conspiracy theorists?" From a media panel at the conference Anti-communism in the U.S. (see n. 11).

Island, Bhopal, and Chernobyl there is a distrust and distaste for technology in general. The profound alienation and impotence that most people feel about technology has overshadowed any embryonic thoughts we might have had about the liberatory potential of most machines. But people are more willing to struggle against nuclear power proliferation than the toxic effects of our communication system. The widespread sense of technological impotence is increased by maintaining the myth that the development of communication technology is inherently based in a military arena. It is clear that everyone but the radical right and the corporations have been effectively intimidated. How can we challenge the media if RCA and GE are in charge?

While it is important to understand that telecommunications in this country has been framed and circumscribed by military and consumer research, both are driven almost exclusively by instrumental arrangements of the media/military corporations in their quest for profits. There is perhaps no country in the world in which broadcasting and telecommunications in general have been so devoid of public service directive. The history of how this evolved has been eloquently and exhaustively detailed by Erik Barnouw in his classic three volumes *A History of Broadcasting in the United States*.[15] Barnouw was not optimistic about the possibility of regulatory reform of this system:

> The conflicts of interest built into our broadcast media probably guarantee that present arrangements will continue for some time. The advertising industry will not readily give up its custodianship of our cultural life, which it has purchased with good money. Our clandestine warfare agency will not readily surrender its purse strings over international transmitters. Major military contractors will not readily give up their central position in our principal communication medium. Congressmen will not readily surrender their right to accept benefits from an industry over which they legislate.[16]

---

[15] Erik Barnouw, *A Tower of Babel: A History of Broadcasting in the United States to 1933* (New York: Oxford University Press, 1966).

[16] Barnouw, *The Image Empire: A History of Broadcasting in the United States, from 1953* (New York: Oxford University Press, 1970), pp. 339, 343.

Since Barnouw wrote these lines in the 1960s, there have not been any power shifts to offset his dim view; in fact, the levels of greed and corruption have risen to unpredicted heights. However, developments within cable and consumer technology have made the situation more complex. With the introduction of home video and public access television, there has been a media evolution, if not a video revolution. Video technology is being used by a vast number of people in ways that have begun to challenge the passive consumption model that has dominated electronic communication ever since department stores first began to sponsor radio concerts to sell sofas and radios over the air (for listening to those same concerts in one's own home).

Bertolt Brecht's famous treatise on the emancipatory possibilities of radio drew its inspiration from the inherent "democratic" potential of transmission itself.[17] There is no reason why electronic transmission—broadcasting as opposed to receiving—cannot be a popular-based activity. There is no law of the apparatus which decrees that it is only reception of radio signals that is widespread. Transmission (including radio and television and cable and satellite) always contains the potential of multiple transmitters: multiple sites of transmissions and multiple messages to be transmitted.

One writer who clearly perceived a dialectic in technological development is Lewis Mumford. In his classic exploration *Technics and Civilization,* he noted the contradiction between capitalist development of technologies and their inherent social tendency toward democratization: "If we wish to retain the benefits of the machine, we can no longer afford to deny its chief social implication: namely, basic communism."[18]

Mumford believed that this basic premise could be the source of a redirection of science toward a utopian social sphere whose technology would be at the service of human needs. Mumford's optimistic exhortations were written before

[17] Bertolt Brecht, "Radio as an Apparatus of Communication" (1932), in *Brecht on Theatre*, ed. and trans. John Willett (New York: Hill and Wang, 1964), p. 51.

[18] Lewis Mumford, *Technics and Civilization* (New York: Harcourt Brace, 1934), p. 406.

Auschwitz and the atomic bomb, but his is not the work of a naive dreamer. It was written after the Depression, and the basic formulation stems from a deep comprehension of the social depths to which a profit-driven system could plunge. There are passages that sound like descriptions of Reagan/Bush Amerika:

> Labor has lost both its bargaining power and its capacity to obtain subsistence: the existence of substitute industries some-times postpones the individual but does not avert the collective day of reckoning.[19]
>
> Lacking the power to buy the necessaries of life for them-selves, the plight of the displaced workers reacts upon those who remain at work: presently the whole structure collapses, and even financiers and enterprisers and managers are sucked into the whirlpool that their own cupidity, short-sightedness and folly have created.

Mumford's solution was a rational approach to technology:

> All this is a commonplace: but it rises, not as a result of some obscure uncontrollable law, like the existence of spots on the sun, but as the outcome of our failure to take advantage by ade-quate social provision of the new processes of mechanized pro-duction.[20]

Mumford's vision was typical of the social prescriptions that animated much of the New Deal. This ideology breathes through the films from that period: *The City, The River,* and *Valley Town,*[21] in which an abiding faith in technology (i.e., ar-chitecture, urban planning, and hydroelectric control of river valleys—the TVA) reaches a crescendo like the soaring music of Aaron Copland on the soundtrack. The cynicism of the pres-ent era makes the hyperbolic rhetoric of those films as silly as a tractor-trailer full of Edsels on the deck of the Exxon Valdez.

---

[19] A recent article in *The Nation* describes how Iowa farmwives, caught in the spiral of loss and foreclosure, are jobbing auto parts manufacturing in the evenings on their farms.

[20] Mumford, *Technics and Civilization*, p. 402.

[21] *The City* (1939) by Willard van Dyke and Ralph Steiner, *The River* (1937), by Pare Lorenz (Willard van Dyke, camera) and *Valley Town* (1940) by Willard van Dyke and Irving Lerner.

Progress indeed. TVA evolved into a shoddy nuke proliferator only now confronting the legacy of toxic radioactive wastes they have generated throughout the region. The glorified suburban utopias of that same period are now stifling ghettos of disrepair and desperation, and many of the urban expanses bulldozed for city renewals are weed-choked wastelands that have given up awaiting the scarce capital for housing projects and have become sites, for tin warehouse "free-enterprise zones," where sweatshop foremen can bypass health and safety regulations and pay less than minimum offshore wages.

Against the backdrop of this history, the following question confronts us today: are there essential differences between electronic and mechanical apparati that change the obviously bleak prospects for the popular use of technology? In other words, is it possible to have a populist vision of the processes of electronic production? Mumford's technocratic vision has ominous implications in our post-modern age. His recipe for utopia called for central planning, rational state control of resources, and labor. In an age of computerization, electronic surveillance, and multinational culture industries, the specter of any sort of "central planning" is frightening. The use of computer data and video images to arrest and persecute the Chinese students of Tiananmen Square is as horrifying as the high-tech tanks currently being designed for optimum crowd control in Israel and South Africa.[22] Electronic technology has enabled the notion of central control to be functional to a degree never envisioned by Mumford, Bellamy, or Fritz Lang. Only Kafka had a gloomy enough vision to accurately foresee the grotesque forms we now encounter. However, Mumford's

---

[22] Maria Elena Hurtado and Judith Perera, with Jung-nam Chi and Mary Zajer, "The Science of Suppression," *South Magazine* (November 1988): "A South African riot control vehicle, the Nongkai, was hailed by Pretoria's law and order minister, Adriaan Vlok, as a 'new concept in protection'—in this case protection of apartheid rule from unrest in South Africa's black townships. Equipped with a front-end loader, the Nongkai can remove obstacles like barricades and burning cars. It can also cut wire and even winch itself out of trouble. . . . [For use in riot suppression] various methods of capture have been tested, including launchers that fire nets over the crowd. Tear gas, intended ostensibly to disperse crowds, is often used in confined spaces and in dangerous concentrations. . . . The name Nongkai means peacemaker" (p. 70).

sense of the contradictions inherent in the mass market and the active desires of people encouraged his tremendous faith in the creative needs of humanity (or "mankind" in his pre-feminist language):

> Creative life, in all its manifestations, is necessarily a social product. . . . To treat such activity as egoistic enjoyment or as property is merely to brand it as trivial: for the fact is that creative activity is finally the only important business of mankind, the chief justification and the most durable fruit of its sojourn on the planet. The essential task of all sound economic activity is to produce a state in which creation will be a common fact in all experience.[23]

This is something that Sony well knows. As Ben Keen has pointed out,

> It should be understood that Sony was formed as an engineers' company; as such, it was pervaded by a strong, idealistic belief in the beneficial nature of modern technology. This may have been initially a reaction against the wartime squandering of technical creativity on weapons of destruction, but the fact that even today these ideals still seem to be important to the company suggests that they run somewhat deeper. It appears that the founders of Sony really did (and do) believe that their technological efforts could significantly enrich people's lives. . . . By choosing unique product goals that involve immense engineering challenges (and hence pleasures), Japanese management has continually redefined the meanings of technological progress in its chosen field.[24]

Today Mumford's radical technocratic vision of central state control presents a chilling model of power. The challenge is to develop his insights into emancipated uses of technology in a decentralized and genuinely democratic way. Sony's totally administered and engineered corporate utopia may be even more frightening, but there are many other features of the consumer video phenomenon that are worthy of our attention. In fact, it is evident that pockets of resistance

---

[23] Mumford, *Technics and Civilization*, p. 410.
[24] Ben Keen, " 'Play It Again, Sony': The Double Life of Home Video Technology," *Science as Culture* 4, no. 1.

have arisen which have the potential to evolve into more highly organized and autonomous centers of democratic communications.

Equipment manufacturers have every interest in selling ever increasing numbers of machines, and to guarantee a mass market the machines have to be priced cheap enough for everyone to either have one or feel that one is not entirely out of reach. The level of competition has ensured that the picture quality has developed at increasingly higher levels and at ever lower prices. However, the corporate program suppliers, that is, commercial television and the movie companies, have an obvious interest in maintaining control over the programs that are consumed, distributed, and, more important, whether and how they are duplicated. One of the reasons that U.S. firms lost the initiative in the magnetic duplication field is that they were so bent on pushing the videodisc. Laser discs can be stamped out for mass market consumption and are completely passive: they cannot record cost effectively for home consumption. But these passive play-only machines never gained a foothold in the home market. People may be willing to buy one-way passive digital discs for listening (CDs have completely taken over the audio field—try buying a record these days). However, there is a difference between audio and visual attention; one can listen and do other things. Passive video technology has never made it with consumers.[25] RCA wasted $550 million finding that out.

The masters of video technology have been successful at marketing elements of active control even for hitherto passive viewing. Early Sony ads stressed the "time-shifting" possibilities: one could change the flow of television transmission to selectively watch specific programs at one's convenience. One of the most attractive features of a VCR is the control it gives to viewing: still framing, fast forward, rewind, repeating: these are controls which allow a selective and critical viewing in an active mode. VCR users are unwilling to rest as passive

---

[25] Since this was written, the DVD player seems to be gaining a foothold with consumers tired of the poor quality of VHS movies. DVD recorders are next.

viewers. The consuming public demands that the machines they buy produce and reproduce and have the capacity to time-shift images.

From the beginning of photography, equipment manufacturers have attempted to encourage a certain type of image production. In the early days of consumer photography, equipment was sold to the home market by promoting portraits of family members, family milestones, get-togethers, and memories of travel. This "domestication" of imagery was continuous with the domestic fate of women: safe in the home, the kitchen, and occasionally on vacation. For almost an entire century a certain (usually gender-specific) passivity has been promoted in the imagery of Kodak ads and especially in their instruction books,[26] where almost 100 percent of the subjects for the novice camera users are women.

In their advertising and hobby books Eastman Kodak never suggested that Brownie owners take pictures of their workplace or record their rank-and-file strike. Nor did Kodak promote the use of still photography to document water pollution or industrial waste (especially since they are on the top of the list of industrial polluters).

With the development of the "home movie" camera, the subjects were the same as those in still photography, only now they waved to the camera. Eight millimeter movie cameras and Super 8 rigs were marketed as live-action snapshots. With the introduction of consumer video, home camcorders, like still photography and home movie cameras before them, are pushed as adjuncts of the bourgeois heterosexual family:[27] ads for cameras feature baby's first step, Mom greeting the proud, freckled-face catcher of a string of brown trout, and the tearful hugs of high school graduations. In the TV ads families and friends use camcorders in traditional "home movie" genres. However, there are several areas of difference between video camcorders and snapshot or even home movie cameras: the first difference is the size of investment. Video cameras are more expensive than Brownie cameras, and consumers are

---

[26] Diane Neumaier, "Teach Yourself Photography: 50 Years of Hobby Manuals," paper presented at the Society for Photographic Education Conference, San Diego, Calif., 1987.

[27] Sheila Pinkel, unpublished research on Eastman Kodak.

apt to want to get more use from them than a yearly glimpse of the kid's birthday.

A second difference is in the site of display. Photos fit neatly into special albums piled on the coffee tables and in gilt frames on top of bureaus. In these almost sacred locations for memory and ceremony, homemade photos (and commissioned photos such as wedding pictures) are clearly kept apart from other commercial, documentary, and industrial photography. That type of "professional" picture is in magazines, books, and on billboards, in other words, in public spaces. Home movies and slide shows are family rituals for holidays and milestone events. The projector is taken out of the closet, the chairs moved around, the screen erected, and the room darkened. The viewing is an extended family ceremony. Homemade video, however, has its place not in a separate and ceremonial realm. It is shown on the family TV set, which, although it is located as the "hearth" of the modern home, is the central receiver of external "reality," the window on the world outside: in this respect, it can be defined as a public space.

A third difference between "home" video and "snapshot" photography and home movies is the use of sound. The fact that video has a voice makes it a different medium from most consumer film rigs (whose sync sound provisions never really worked for consumer use). With the introduction of sound there is an increased demand on the subject. It is embarrassing to just stand around waving at the camera if there is a microphone on. One needs something to say. Consequently, home videos tend to have more content, even if this tends to be banal.

There is also a narrowing of the gap between "amateur" images and "professional." With home movies we always knew they weren't MGM. The size of the image, the clarity of registration, the skilful use of lighting all made "the movies" look very different from "home movies." With video that differential is less evident. The new video cameras obviate the use of lights, and the resolution of detail is approaching that of network sitcoms. So, too, the use of a hand-held style, casually zooming in and out, has appeared in IBM commercials and on MTV. All this has brought a meeting of the images that puts in doubt any attempt to hierarchialize "professional" video photography.

Finally, an important difference has been the expansion of the video market beyond individuals to organizations and groups. Video is purchased by businesses and groups in a way that never happened with still photography and home movies. Golf clubs, day-care centers, ballet classes, and biology labs are potential camcorder users. Video has to be "user friendly" so as not to intimidate the untutored; otherwise these groups would never feel comfortable enough with the technology to purchase the equipment. As a result, video handbooks break with the wife-and-kid-posing images that adorn photo textbooks. Video sales pitches include shots of everyone from nuns to Kayapo Indians shooting video. The stereotype of domestic use is broken. Consumer cameras show up at town board meetings, school tax hearings, rent strikes, block parties, and Rotary Club meetings. The camcorders are becoming a fact of civic life not easily dismissed. To be widely sold, video has had to be serious (and fun), public (and private), and accessible across gender and racial boundaries. It has been marketed, in other words, as nothing less than a popular tool.

In many cities where public access television is thriving, there is also a good audience for "homemade video," or rather many audiences, for when access works best, it is "narrow casting"—providing programming for communities of interest, answering specific informational needs. In Milwaukee a group of deaf people was able to produce a weekly "signed" show so successfully that they inspired a group of partially blind persons to also get trained and do a series themselves. They received an oversized monitor through a grant to disabled people and devised a system for using headphones for guests to signal their camera cues, since the normal hand signals weren't readily perceived. Among the thousands of groups using access are welfare rights groups, Latin America solidarity organizations, the United Farm Workers Union, and local affiliates of Amnesty International.[28]

Deep Dish has programmed series which brought together

---

[28] See Diana Agosta, Abigail Norman, and Caryn Rogoff, *Participate Directory of Public Access in New York State* (New York: Media Network and the New York State Cable Commission, 1988). This is a county-by-county survey

communities of interest. For example, one program is called *Home Sweet Homefront*. Produced by Louis Massiah, it combines footage on the struggles for housing from many different communities, from Philadelphia, New York City's Lower East Side, and Minneapolis, among others. The community video footage is ironically framed with Mumfordesque clips from housing films from the New Deal. The program neatly juxtaposes the homeless activists with the liberal rhetoric from a bygone era and paints a vivid picture of a major crisis in locally specific terms. In direct contrast to the decontextualized and atomized way these issues are portrayed on the nightly network news, the local struggles are recontextualized in this program and given an additional historical frame of reference.

Meanwhile on Main Street, popular video has arrived, and it is growing vigorously. While the boards of directors of public interest organizations on the national level are debating whether to buy a computer for the mailroom, the rank and file have seized time and channels and are making television. Video camcorders in the hands of community activists have begun to cause ripples in the sands of the TV wasteland. The creative use of technology that Mumford dreamed of is alive in hundreds of small studios, in trailer parks, in community-controlled mobile TV vans, and in high school rec rooms. It's called public access.

One of the most interesting uses of video is as self-defense against the police. For years African Americans and Latinos have been victimized by excessive police force. Every year several hundred young men die in police custody or in street struggles with undercover cops. Camcorder video has enabled communities to document these incidents. For years police have videotaped demonstrations and community organizations. But as mass sales of video recorders have increased, harassed communities have taken to watching the police. "It's the democratization of surveillance," said Larry Sapadin, director of AIVF (the Association of Independent Video and Filmmakers).

Watch out, Dick Tracy. We've got you covered.

---

of who is using public access and what kinds of programs are being produced throughout New York State.

# The Undisciplined and Punishment: On-line Resistance to the Prison Industrial Complex in the United States

## *February 1999*

IN THE PAST several years a lively list-serve group has evolved that addresses issues of incarceration and justice in the United States. Each night I log on to messages that range from desperate pleadings for someone's life to cautious discussions of what the slogans should be on the posters for the next Free Mumia march. There are technical descriptions of prison architecture and quests for herbal cures to cell block bronchitis epidemics. It is the underside of one of our leading industries: locking people up.

Prisons are a big business: construction of cells, outfitting of facilities, training and equipping guards are some of the expenses of an industry that is sapping state and local funds for education and welfare. In the past seven years California has increased prison spending by 500 percent while scaling back higher education by 25 percent. In the state capital of Sacramento, the prison guard union is the biggest lobby, outflanking tobacco and agribusiness. The prison contractors, law enforcement suppliers (stun guns, barbed wire, restraint suits, etc.), and the guards' union were able to join forces to pass the Three Strikes Law to ensure long terms and full cells. The United States has more people per capita behind bars than anywhere else on earth. At present almost two million people are behind bars: five million are in the system if you include those awaiting sentencing or on parole. Women are the fastest growing sector—and especially women of color. Finally equal justice under the law.

Prisons have become a key source of labor, with many transnational corporations contracting with states to manufacture goods and set up telemarketing stations. TWA and Eddie Bauer sporting goods use prisoners to work their phone reservations and orders. Microsoft Windows 95 was packaged, shrink-wrapped, and shipped by incarcerated workers. The State of California put it this way: "Why go abroad, when you can have a disciplined workforce here at home?" in a video to entice more corporations to join the "Joint Ventureship Program" of placing factories in prisons. As more and more U.S. businesses become entwined in this booming industry, it seems harder and harder to reverse this trend, even though crime rates are low everywhere but on television.

However, in response to these conditions there are a variety of resistance activities that range from grassroots demonstrations to full page ads in *The New York Times* to save Mumia Abu-Jamal, convicted of killing a policeman in a patently unjust trial. Abu Jamal is the first internationally recognized U.S. Death Row prisoner since the Rosenbergs were executed during the Cold War (http://www.mumia.org). For many in the United States, Mumia is "the Voice of the Voiceless" (the title of a radio show which he hosted before his arrest), the symbol of those masses behind bars, and a figurehead for the broad movement of those who are resisting the prison industrial complex.

The counter-prison movement includes ex-prisoners, families of prisoners, Quaker and other religious peace activists, victims for reconciliation, human rights workers, Vietnam vets, the Bruderhof (a Christian communist network of communities numbering several thousand), academics from sociology to geography to cultural studies, philosophers, lawyers, parole officers, and guards. For this diverse crew the Internet has become a major tool.

There are countless web sites for individual prisoners and pages for organizations and coalitions. An organization in Berkeley, the Prison Activist Resource Center, has been a central node (http://www.prisonactivist.org) in much of the activity, maintaining both a list-serve and a web site with numerous links. The center was one of the central organizers of the successful Critical Resistance Conference in Berkeley in September 1998, a gathering of over 4,000 prison activists and spokespersons.

Prisons are usually located in rural areas, far from the urban centers where most of their population comes from. A growing trend in incarceration is to having private corporations contract with states and cities to house prisoners. One of the results of the increased privatization of prisons is the fact that prisoners are moved across state lines. Someone arrested in Missouri could end up in Texas, where the cost of maintenance is lower, and access to legal aid and human rights may be harder to come by. One way that prisoner's families use the Internet is by creating individual prisoners' pages with personal histories, art work, poetry, and addresses. Usually posted by parents or spouses and friends, these sites become a virtual presence of the loved one, who is often far from home. Although many prison families do not have personal computers, they can log in at the local library, school, or cyber cafe. There is an anecdote that a cleaning woman in a large New York law firm logs on in the evening not only to activist sites, but also to on-line law journals and case records to work on legal strategies for her husband's case (http://www.findlaw.com).

A mother's site is at http://www.geocities.com/CapitolHill/1526. A site to browse on high-end machines is http://people-oftheheart.org/index2.htm. (Watch out, it crashed my computer with all its streaming video and graphic arpeggios.) It's an amazing story of an eleven-year-old child who has been sentenced to twenty-five years.

The Internet can also be a way to find out the latest instruments of repression. There are many industry sites where you can order handcuffs and pepper spray (www.counterterrorism.com/copex.html), and there are counter-cop sites such as http://www.prisonactivist.org/copwatch. Hundreds of service organizations are posting sites, like activists against unjust sentencing (http://www.sentencing.org) and the Bruderhof Christian radicals (http://www.bruderhof.org/hold/issues/deathpen/ inmates/index.htm).

There are many artists' web sites addressing these issues. The graphics collective Third World War has posted a series of comic strip–style drawings and texts. David Thorne and others have created a series of posters which are posted on-line (http://www.igc.org/prisons/resistant-strains). Various political prisoners have posted drawings of their cells, and many sites have prisoners' drawings and paintings. There are many prison poems and drawings on the Deep Dish site (http://www.igc.org/deepdish). A web page of the Critical Resistance Conference is archived there. I worked with Gina Todus, Chris Burnett, and members of Paper Tiger San Francisco to stream audio from that conference and post cultural material and statistics from the conference. The site has been accessed by thousands of users and is still being updated.

An overview of prisons in the United States is posted at http://members.tripod.com/~gmoses/prison/plinks.htm, and one on the maximum security isolation units is http://www.igc.org/prisons/cpf/CPFshu.html. Many black nationalists see the U.S. prison system as genocide and compare it to South Africa under apartheid; they have a web site at http://www.amandla.org.

A list-serve with postings of many messages a day is maintained by the Prison Activist Resource Center. The purpose is to provide news alerts and pointers. For some the Listserve is literally a matter of life and death. The most desperate messages are the pleas from mothers or wives or children trying to enlist help to beg for pardons as the execution date nears. There are currently almost 4,000 people on death rows awaiting executions. E-mail campaigns have been used successfully to get medical attention for sick prisoners or to obtain eyeglasses, and there is always hope that a flood of messages will startle a governor or member of the state supreme court to take notice and review a capital case.

The prison list-serve is the center of many controversies. One very active member is Cayenne Bird, who is said to be the wife of an inmate who was killed by guards. She is quite patriotic, and her site has billowing American flags as a background. She has been critical of the fact that former Black Panther and ex-

Communist Party USA member Angela Davis has emerged as one of the main leaders of the prison activist community. Cayenne does not consider herself a radical and spends much of her time trying to register voters; her site is located at http://hometown.aol.com/jumplaw/politics52/index.htm.

Cayenne has many ongoing arguments with other list-serve members. For a very brief period of time, a volunteer working on the site tried to manage the postings by editing the mail. The hue and cry that ensued was deafening and worse than all the ongoing spats. He quickly apologized, and the site continues in its free form and often cantankerous manner.

At its best the list-serve is a true lifeline for the thousands of prison activists and families of prisoners out there waging what have been lonely battles against powerful state and corporate apparati and the peculiar form of state slavery that has evolved in this post–Cold War World. The prison movement for many of us battle-scarred lefties is the final battle: one which looks at the true end stage of "free market" capital. We are looking at the face of fascism in America. We are the enemy.

# 9

# The International Implications of Media Democracy

# Introduction

"THE USES OF COMMUNITY MEDIA" is a global survey of ways in which grassroots organizations make and disseminate media. In it I contrast the community video report on the exhumation of bodies from the years of genocide in Guatemala with the worldwide coverage of the funeral of Princess Di. This paper was initially presented to the MacBride Round Table, a group of communication researchers dedicated to keeping alive the vision of Sean MacBride, who as chair of the UNESCO commission on communication advocated information parity in the world.

"Report from Delhi" is about a conference of video producers which was held in Delhi, India, in 1993, sponsored by Vidéazimut, an international organization of grassroots producers. The fact that it was held at the same time Rupert Murdoch launched Star TV only heightened the contradictions of trying to support alternative media in a transnational world. This impressive gathering of over 400 videomakers and academics was organized by Vidéazimut and the Center for the Development of Information Technology in Delhi. I was co-chair of the "manifesto committee" with Regina Festa, a Brazilian communications professor. Our "New Delhi Declaration" was ratified by the 400 attendees and later by several other international communication organizations.

"Icebergs in the Paths of the Colossus" looks at the difficulties of creating oppositional media in the face of the rapid globalization of the world economy. It offers some strategic examples of successful counter-corporate projects. "Our Right to the Sky" is a statement about the need for grassroots communication that utilizes international satellites under the jurisdiction of the International Telecommunications Union: a utopian demand for mutual exchanges of hand-held visions and views.

"Gathering Storm" is a look at the media collaborations that took on the World Trade Organization in Seattle and the potential for the struggle for public noncommercial airwaves in this country and the world.

# The Uses of Community Media: A Global Survey

## *Presentation to the MacBride Round Table, October 1997*

IN THE EARLY WORK of critical theorists like Lippman, Horkeimer, Adorno, and Schiller media audiences were seen as passive—vulnerable to the engineering of "mind managers." Dallas Smythe described television audiences as a commodity of exchange between advertising agencies and program administrators. Sometimes called "Nielsen families" after the measurement company, the passive audience's only value was as a sum of numbers for calculating fees for the thirty and sixty second spots. There is sometimes confusion over the term "global village." Video enthusiasts of the seventies appropriated Marshall McLuhan's term for their rambunctious activities with portapaks, but McLuhan's villagers were consumers of media, not makers. Chomsky and Herman do a persuasive job of showing the mechanisms of mass media in manufacturing consent from passive viewers. As the years pass, actions on Wall Street only confirm what were sometimes called conspiracy theories of the totality of corporate media. The more channels, the more the content remains the same and the more eyeballs are harvested. The audiences grow larger, swelling to the massive communal sigh at megamedia events like the funeral of Princess Di.

Recent forays in audience studies and reception theory have championed a more active role on the part of mass media audiences, sometimes seen as cultural arbitrators through program selection and as differentiating viewers who decode resistant messages in mass media fare. But it is still mass media made for mass audiences. The viewer may actively sodden an entire box of Kleenex watching Di's cortege, but she is first and foremost passively receiving messages which are made for her, organized and produced in locations apart from her own daily life.

There is another type of electronic visual media which is being made in this world, in a mode of production distinctly different from the mass media model. This is the work created by community media groups and independent producers who have appropriated consumer video equipment. While much of the use of small-format video is documenting family birthdays or graduations in affluent neighborhoods, there are a growing number of people who put together video programs to record community events and to share information and history with others in locations that range from Bangladesh to Brazil. The efforts of community media makers are often ridiculed or dismissed variously as "a flash in the pan" or "a drop in the bucket." They are belittled as pathetic when measured against the power and ubiquity of mass culture. The assumption is always that these local community efforts are in direct competition with the Goliaths, the moguls. When audience size is measured there is, of course, no comparison. Even setting aside the power of well-aimed slingshots, the scope and power of the vertically and horizontally integrated transnational media business is without match in world history. The notion that community groups with a few camcorders, radio mikes, and web sites would effectively challenge these structures is absurd. But the very notion of this sort of wrestling match is not consistent with the goals and practice of most community media. This is media not bent on entertainment or amassing viewer numbers, though on occasion this can be the result. In the alternative media world there is a different operational framework—the relationship between makers and watchers is not at all the same. In fact, the term "watchers" is not descriptive of that relationship. "Users" or "user-participants" is perhaps more appropriate. This is work created to educate, to communicate, and to empower local citizens. It is made by community media groups and independent producers with low-cost and widely available consumer equipment on every continent, in almost every type of situation.[1]

Community media is often part of a larger process of community activities that can include environmental organizing, alternative health care, community self-defense, labor union mobilization, and hundreds of other activist projects. Video, radio, and Internet activities are integrated into the organizing. A widely recognized example is the web site created in conjunction with the defense of the London Greenpeace activists who were sued by the McDonald's Corporation for passing out brochures alleging that Big Macs were bad for everything from service labor to children's health. The web site (www.mcspotlight.org), the videos, and the radio tapes were coordinated to produce an effective campaign that ultimately "won" the case in the court of public opinion, although the civil judge's decision was more ambiguous.

Community media is often treated as historically insignificant, but many groups are actively building an authentic "public sphere" in their communities and deserve serious consideration not only in academic study, but in public service funding and infrastructure assistance as well. They also deserve to be considered as legitimate providers of important global information and accorded recognition in the official discussions of international telecommunications at the International Telecommunication Union and UNESCO.

EXAMPLES

There are useful models all over the world. One of the sequences from a group in Guatemala is a procession of coffins through a small rural town, bringing exhumed remains to the

---

[1] See Alain Ambrosi and Nancy Thede, eds., *Video: The Changing World* (Montreal: Black Rose Books, 1990), which reports on various international projects in community media. Two recent publications provide useful information on community media: see Clemencia Rodriguez, *Fissures in the Mediascape: An International Study of Citizens' Media* (New York: Hampton Press, 2000), and Alfonso Gumucio Dagron, *Making Waves: Stories of Participatory Communication for Social Change* (New York: Rockefeller Foundation, 2001).

research rooms where they will be identified. This is not the casket of Princess Di, which took over television not so long ago. *La Verdad Baja la Tierra*, like Di's televised funeral shared by so many of the world's peoples, is about death. The bodies in this case, however, are not those of fallen royalty, but those of peasants who were massacred during the eighties in Guatemala, victims of the genocide that ravaged Central America, funded for the most part by counter-insurgency funds from the United States. This tape is not for entertainment, though it obviously has a purpose to testify and persuade. The video is made by *Communicarte*, a group originally called the Forensic Video Collective, because their first important task was to video the exhumations of the bodies from several massacre sites—for identification of the relatives, some of whom could not (either for reasons of distance or fear) travel to the sites of exhumation. For Guatemalans who live in continuing fear and intimidation, the tape also has a specific purpose: to look at this terrible history in the face, in a effort to move forward, to confront this horror in the bright light of the video image. The fact that the tape can be made at all proclaims a new-found courage. In the past, circulation of these images would need to have been clandestine. The tapes of *Communicarte* are used by local organizing groups and religious organizations and are not intended for a mass audience, but for the very specific needs of those profoundly concerned with this situation.

Several groups in Brazil and the Dominican Republic are working in their communities with projections in the streets and town squares. *TV Maxambomba* and *TV Machepa* are lively, entertaining production groups which mix commedia dell'arte theater with pop culture political video (see Section 7, "Community Media in Brazil"). In Asia many groups have perfected the use of videocassette sales for alternative diffusion. In much of Asia there is lively commerce on the streets of pirated U.S. films on tape, much as in the United States and the United Kingdom there are audiocassette "mixes" sold at flea markets and in rock concert parking lots. Utilizing this tradition, several video activist groups have set up similar sidewalk stands which display and sell their productions at street corner prices. One group that did this quite effectively in the eighties was the environmental collective *Green Team* in Taiwan. This activist group of environmental radicals used video to expose toxic waste dumps in Taipei and radioactive residue polluting indigenous land on offshore islands. Documentation of their theatrical guerrilla demonstrations served to popularize environmental actions, much the way that Greenpeace's guerrilla theater tactics and "photo ops" have done in the United States and Europe. On one occasion the *Green Team* took aim at the national television network itself with a raucous demonstration in which protesters hurtled their old TV sets at the TV headquarters. They were mad as hell, and they weren't going to take it any more. Broadcasting officials stared in dismay at the mountain of shattered tubes and circuitry at their doorstep.

Independents in Mexico are also using creative distribution of alternative video. Cassette sales have boomed in Mexico in the wake of the Zapatista rebellion. Several groups such as Canal 6 de Julio put out monthly news bulletins on tapes which are available at bookstores and magazine racks for the same price as *Vanidades*.

A community tape which was distributed to practically mass media numbers of viewers was *Matanza en Aguas Blancas*, which is about an incident in which the Mexican army assassinated sixteen peasants on their way to demonstrations in the state of Guerrero. The tape was made from off-air news which used footage made by an army cameraman. The images were broadcast shortly after the incident in one of those curious openings that one can occasionally find on otherwise carefully controlled networks. The story was quickly censored off the airwaves, but Canal 6 reproduced it and amplified it for cassette distribution, surrounding the original "Rodney King"–type surveillance footage of the massacre with a larger discussion of the situation in Guerrero and interviews with peasants who survived. The tape became an expose of both the initial incident and the way in which the official Mexican television leaves out contextualizing information about violent incidents and sweeps brutal actions of the Mexican Army under the rug.

One of the tapes about the Zapatistas, *Viaje al Centro de la*

*Selva*, a lyrical report on the first Zapatista *encuentro* in the midst of the Lacondan jungle, is reported to have sold over a million copies. One of the makers, Javier Eloriaga, however, spent eighteen months in jail for his collaboration with the rebels. As alternative video becomes effective in regional struggles, makers become targets of right-wing attacks. In Colombia recently, two workers with CINEP (the Center for Research and Popular Education), a Jesuit research organization in Bogota, were brutally murdered by a seven-member death squad, with U.S.-supplied armaments so prevalent in Colombia, and indeed the rest of Latin America, under the aegis of the "drug war." Mario Calderon and Elsa Alvarado were working on a video about the land struggles of a group of indigenous people near the Panamanian border, land wanted by transnationals for mining development. They were killed by the death squad in their home in Bogota, in a scene reminiscent of the purges in El Salvador and Guatemala. CINEP has vowed to continue the work begun by the martyrs despite this brutal slaying.

The images of Kayapo Indians of Brazil in full ceremonial headdress armed with video cameras[2] have become the clichéd icons of the use of new technologies by native peoples. Native groups have used video effectively for more than twenty years. Of all the groups around the world making local media, the networks of exchanges that have been promoted by indigenous peoples have been the most successful. At the time that the mass media were celebrating the quincentennial of Columbus, indigenous communities were active in denunciating the colonialization and exploitation that the so-called "discovery" initiated. Radio and video programs were widely exchanged among native groups and provided a clear picture of the unity of indigenous peoples on this issue and on current land rights struggles that are still going on. Deep Dish TV coordinated a seventeen-hour series of native voices speaking about the quincentennial called "Rock the Boat."[3] The native

---

[2] Terence Turner, "Defiant Images: The Kayapo Appropriation of Video," *Anthropology Today* 9, no. 6 (1992).

[3] This series was coordinated by Cynthia Lopez and curated by native filmmaker Beverly Singer of Deep Dish.

point of view was heard on a scale scarcely imagined before the advent of video and audio cassettes. The anti-quintencennial campaign in general was so successful that department stores in the United States who for years used to have "Columbus Day" sales advertised in local newspapers and on television have stopped the practice. *The Wall Street Journal* noted that nowadays the name of Columbus has too negative a connotation.

Although video made by community groups is most often shown in closed-circuit exhibition, and usually not produced specifically for TV transmission, the obvious benefits from program exchange and diffusion have made the issue of TV access a focus for many groups. The search for channel space and cooperative television administrations has become a challenge to local and state broadcasters. Occasionally video groups will garner space on cultural or educational channels, as is the case in Venezuela, Colombia, and Mexico. During the peace negotiations in El Salvador, the right to acquire commercial time on national television was a major demand of the FMLN, the rebel liberation front. A few small local stations in Japan have begun to introduce public space for community members. The evangelical Christian organizations have been very energetic in finding space for their messages against abortion, birth control, and lesbian and gay relationships. They have garnered time not only on leased channels in the United States, but by purchasing channel time in many other countries.[4]

Radio has also been important within indigenous communities for communication and empowerment. Native radio stations have a substantial infrastructure in Canada, Australia, and many parts of Latin America. One videotape that celebrates the kinds of exchanges this programming can do is *Radio Novelas*, made with a group of Canadian Cree Indians. It traces a trip made by Cree radio producers to Bolivia, where indigenous tin miners have effectively used radio to promote their rights for decades.

---

[4] See Steve Bruce, *Pray TV: Televangelism in America* (London: Routledge, 1990).

As global commercial networks reach to more and more corners, there is a danger that traditional public communication spaces—the cafe, the market, the club, and the public square—will be replaced by corporate supermarkets and the reception of messages from far away, eliminating local discourse. Public access can be a local forum for grassroots expression and active participation. In some communities the public access center becomes a hub of community activity, serving as a way of bringing people together. The diffusion over cable of programs interesting to very specific groups becomes a way for people in those groups to find each other. This is especially apparent in the use of access by ethnic or national groups, who often do not know that there are others from their country or region, but find them through weekly telecasts on the local channels.

The activity of making programs can be, in itself, a beginning step in civic engagement. People who take advantage of public access often increase their interest in civic issues. A study by John Higgins, a professor at San Francisco University, shows that those people who became involved in the public access channel in Columbus, Ohio, were very likely to take more initiative in civic activity in their town after having spent time at the access center.[5]

For those who live in areas that do not have cable television, or for those who may not be able to afford it even though it passes by their door, there are other ways in which media regulation could provide benefits. Since most forms of commercial program distribution are sent via satellites which use the public resource of global orbits, the use of these orbits could be "taxed" and the funds used to promote local media production and distribution in ways that are appropriate for local needs. The work of grassroots producers such as Brazil's *TV Maxambomba* of screening development and health videos on the streets is a model which can be replicated in many countries. In South Africa community radio producers have been very active in local program production in remote villages and

---

[5] John Higgins, paper presented at the MacBride Round Table Meeting, Boulder, 1997.

have developed wind-up radios which enable even the poorest citizens without electricity to receive the broadcasts. Poor communities, both in remote rural locations and in urban slums, have very basic information needs which are not met by the programming made by global marketers.

Community media deserves funds and space for local production and infrastructure for global exchange. Internet diffusion is an obvious possibility, but satellite TV transmission is more immediately possible given the current state of the technical infrastructure. The value of this sort of exchange is on many levels: creating communities of interest across borders, exchanging information that has global relevance, providing models for popular organizing, and providing inspiration for creative production. These exchanges can provide information about specific problems that are replicated from community to community, often faced in total isolation. Nongovernmental organizations (NGOs) and activist groups need to be able to share information and to witness the documentation of local problems and solutions across borders and regions.

GLOBAL MOVEMENT FOR COMMUNITY MEDIA

Videazimut, an international organization with offices in Montreal and São Paulo, is a service and advocacy organization for grassroots community producers, such as those who participate with Paper Tiger and Deep Dish. The membership comes from many countries and includes producers, teachers, technicians, workers organizations, and community activists, united in the interest of utilizing new technology for basic human needs. Vidéazimut has sponsored several international symposia, including one on development and new technology in Delhi (see "Report from Delhi" in this section) and one on community television in São Paulo. The goals of the organization are to promote the use of community media through training, exchange of information, and representation in international forums. It also can provide information about the dangers faced by alternative media makers and can be a base of support against abuses such as the murder of the CINEP producers.

More research in this area is needed. Community media is often treated as historically insignificant by communications academics, but many groups are actively building an authentic "public sphere" in their communities and deserve serious consideration not only in academic study, but also in public service funding and infrastructure assistance. Community media organizations deserve to be considered as legitimate providers of important global information, on the forefront of useful experiments in communication development. Grassroots pioneers who utilize electronic tools in humane and imaginative ways need to be accorded recognition in the official discussions of global telecommunications at forums such as the ITU and UNESCO.

Community media makers cannot rival Murdoch's Star TV, but they should have the right to exchange (and gain subsidies for) video and radio projects via satellite and the Internet. The successes of public access in the United States, Germany, Australia, and other countries have proved that "taxing" the profits of the telecommunications infrastructure can provide revenues to initiate and support a public interest communication system. Perhaps similar regulations on a global scale could take a proportion of the profits from global commercial networks to support public interest media exchange. We have the technology to set up a way to share and collaborate around issues and ideas. We are beginning to understand how effective the Internet can be for this sort of exchange. A global community media network could address specific areas of interest and concern.

As the gulf between rich and poor widens throughout the world, having access to tools of mobilization and information becomes more crucial in the struggle for justice and equity. Authentic democratic communication is a threat to the status quo. The rhetoric of democracy and free flow of information can be a straitjacket or a springboard to promote the real possibilities of participatory empowerment. The media are essential in that process.

The idea is not to create a mass audience to weep for princesses, but to tax the mass media corporations that exploit those tears. Those corporations utilize resources that are the provenance of all peoples on earth: the airwaves and geostationary satellite paths, and moreover our eyes and hearts, the access to which is now so readily available to commercial and governmental entities.

# Report from Delhi: The Front Lines of Cultural Survival

## March 1994

*In February 1994 I traveled to India to attend the New Delhi Symposium on New Technologies and the Democratization of Audiovisual Communication. The meeting brought together 400 producers, distributors, researchers, teachers, and activists from twenty-five countries.*

THE AIR IN Delhi is yellow: not the acrid greenish yellow of a bad day in L.A., but a soft brown, almost golden yellow. They say it is from the burning of dung in small stoves. From the airport we drove through streets lined with people: people huddled over the dung stoves, people hanging out newly dyed cloths to dry, people peddling sewing machines in roadside open-air tailor shops, people getting their hair cut sitting in improvised outdoor barbershops. From reports by other travelers, I had expected the lazy cows that meandered through the intersections, but not the energetic monkeys that perched on roofs, fences, and even stop signs, swinging down now and then to grab a snack from their communal keepers. The cows and the monkeys seem to belong to everyone: food scraps are generously shared, and of course the dung is tidily gathered to be dried for fuel.

The symposium was held at an Islamic University, Jamia Hamdard, in an enclosed compound just outside the main center of New Delhi. The university is quite religious, and the mornings begin with prayers that echo from all corners of the compound as the Muslim students greet the dawn. Conference attendees were warned that alcohol is strictly forbidden. My dorm room was small, spare, and clean, sort of like a monk's cell. During the week I grew to value its simplicity, in contrast to the energetic chaos of the surrounding city and the bustling density of the symposium.

The symposium attendees came from Burkina Faso, Bangladesh, Brazil, Peru, Denmark, Korea, Mauritius, and many other countries. They ranged from the business-suited technocratic computer professionals from Australia, New York, and London to colorfully robed puppeteers from the Indian provinces. The plenary sessions tended to be dominated by windy speeches from the suits, and the "workshops" by energetic declarations from the more colorful grassroots practitioners. A workshop on distribution brought camcorder activists together. These included a Japanese group who use video in labor organizing, a Calcutta activist funded by the U.K.'s Channel Four to make tapes about the appropriation of community lands for dubious World Bank projects, a women's group from Delhi that distributes feminist health tapes, and a young pharmacist from Malaysia who organizes women's empowerment workshops using film and video.

The group traded stories of their problems and triumphs. In Malaysia it is against the law to own more than three video tapes of the same program. One can get fined and sent to jail for distribution without a license, which is only given out by one government agency to other government agencies. In Japan video was a key tool used in organizing a successful strike at a large electronics plant. The workers sat in and sent video out to the press and to large solidarity meetings. The Calcutta filmmaker wanted to know why her film on the World Bank project which had won so many worldwide prizes still was not shown on Indian television. One of the program directors from Dardushan, Indian TV, was in the workshop and muttered that they were still considering it. He shuddered as the room burst into outcries of rage as other Indian media producers released their frustrations on the surprised administrator.

The encounter seemed to encapsulate the frustrations many community producers feel. As channels multiply everywhere and camcorders and cheap editing facilities allow production to take root at the local level, there seems almost a diminishing proportion of local programming actually available on television. The plenary sessions extolling the promises of new technology were at odds with the workshops where the practical experiences of community organizers described the problems of penetrating the fortress of mass-produced culture brought about by the transnational media infrastructures. The discussion of the diffusion of community work eventually found its way into the plenary sessions. The conference ended with a declaration that was written by a delegated committee and brought to the entire group for endorsement, after a long and heated exchange.

Rupert Murdoch was in Delhi at the same time as our meeting to inaugurate an additional Indian channel for his satellite network. As commercial channels such as those beamed down on India by Murdoch overtake national television and radio systems worldwide, the minimal local production that has on occasion flowered in regional media systems is being sacrificed for MTV channels especially designed (in New York and London) for the Indian and other national "markets."

The local sponsor of the symposium was CENDIT, the Center for Development of Instructional Technology, an organization founded a quarter century ago with that same burst of optimism and faith in media that fostered the first alternative video groups in the United States. I visited the CENDIT offices and felt quite at home, having spent many years of my working life helping to keep similar non-profit alternative media institutions such as Deep Dish and Paper Tiger afloat. The offices also reminded me of AIVF, the Association of Independent Video and Filmmakers, and the Media Network, as it serves as a national clearing house for independent producers over all of India. It has several databases of both producers and media users. It has a bank of equipment for loan to organizations and individuals and a series of editing and post-production facilities. CENDIT distributes more than 200 programs to organizations all over the Indian subcontinent. There is also an extensive periodical collection and files on grants with sample proposals and lists of past funded projects. The files on festivals and equipment are tended by a helpful and extremely cheerful staff, who do not seem to have fallen victim to the same burnout cynicism that sometimes overcomes our non-profit community. Their frustrations must be great, however, if only in the realm of power (as in current— not to mention politics). Their electricity goes out several times a week, which makes computer use and video dubbing very problematic. The work I screened there, however, belied the "underdevelopment": it was extremely moving and engaging, well shot and edited, and quite interesting formally. It is thus all the more sad that little of their work, like much of the de facto censored independent work here in the United States, is seen on national or even regional television.

The symposium was organized by Vidéazimut together with CENDIT. Videazimut is an international association of grassroots video producers and activists, based in Montreal, which has many different countries represented on its board of directors. I was the only official representative from the United States. Vidéazimut is working to help the many thousands of community video organizations across the world communicate with each other.

So how does one make communication more democratic? Meetings such as the symposium and the planned congress are important beginnings. I think we all came away from Delhi with renewed enthusiasm and dedication. The strength of the experience and talent of the hundreds of producers and researchers was an energy field that transcended both the temporary Delhi power outages and the pathetic ghostly image of Michael Jackson from MTV that flickered nightly on the TV set in a corner of the dorm lounge, but we were all too busy chattering away about the workshops to watch. We eventually commandeered the lounge TV to hook up a VCR and exchange our own programs. My favorite was a lyrical documentary from Bangladesh, made on a VHS camera by Tareeq Shahriar, the poet of the Symposium, who regaled us with live accompaniment of songs and chants. Afterwards he told us of the difficulties of making video in his country. Now when I start to complain about an equipment breakdown in New York, I think of Tareeq's good-natured jokes about keeping dust out of his camcorder in Bangladesh. Or maybe I recall the bravery of Ambiga, who takes on the Malaysian military to distribute feminist video in Penang.

I came away with an overwhelming appreciation for the fine work of media activists in many global villages who confront daily frustrations and threats to document not only environmental horrors, injustice, and war but community music, regional art and poetry, ancient dances, and post-modern performances. They are on the front lines of a war to save our cultural environment. Transmission technology is now cheap and widely available: humankind could share this work, locally, nationally and worldwide—if there can be implemented through international law the kinds of proposals that came forth at this symposium.

# Declaration of New Delhi: International Community Television

## *February 1994*

CONSIDERING:

- That the communication and information sector has become central in establishing the direction of social and political change at a global level
- That information and communications are dominated by corporate and military interests
- That the control of information represents a serious threat to democracy, cultural diversity, and the evolution of civil society
- And that an increasing number of people have come to recognize the considerable potential social and political benefits of the new technologies and are opposing the corporate and state control of information and communications,

We, the participants of the International Symposium on New Technologies and the Democratization of Audiovisual Communication, convened by Vidéazimut and CENDIT in New Delhi on February 12, 1994, being media producers, users, and distributors, communication researchers and teachers and representatives of many community-based and national organizations who have come from Australia, Bangladesh, Brazil, Burkina Faso, Canada, Denmark, France, Hong Kong, India, Italy, Japan, Kenya, Korea, Malaysia, Mauritius, Mozambique, Palestine, the Philippines, Peru, Russia, Singapore, Taiwan, the United Kingdom, and the United States recognize and lend our support to the principles expressed by, among others, the U.N. Declaration on the Right to Development; the U.N. Covenant on Civil and Political Rights; the U.N. Declaration on Human Rights; the declarations of the MacBride Round Table; and the Quito Declaration.

We clearly observe that economic development in Asia and around the world is leading to less equal distribution of resources and wealth and continues to exacerbate the rapid advance of ecological devastation. We are witness to increasing monopolization and commercialization of information and the expansion of a global economy which has led to a subversion of democratic processes and reduced popular participation. The inability of a large part of humankind, particularly women and indigenous cultures, to exercise control has meant their subordination to global corporate and repressive state regimes. In this context it is further apparent that as new technologies are introduced, human dignity is diminished.

We demand global democracy, rather than a global supermarket, and affirm our unity in support of the following:

1. All peoples and individuals shall have the right to communicate freely, to utilize the tools of communication, and to inform themselves and others.

2. Airwaves and satellite paths are a global people's resource to be administered equitably, with a significant portion devoted to serving the public interest and for community use.

3. We oppose the militarization of space and the exploitation of space for corporate interests. Any exploitation of airwaves, transmission channels, and earth orbits should be subject to a public levy to be used to support local community expression, to be used to facilitate non-commercial information exchange, and to contribute to ensure equitable distribution of information technologies.

4. Communication and information technologies must be used to facilitate participatory democracy and the development of civil society, and not to limit democratic rights.

5. Information systems exhibit great potential for real popular participation and should be organized according to the principles of decentralization in order to nurture the rich diversity of human culture.

Individuals are not born consumers; information is not a commodity, but rather a utility to be shared. The symposium brought many people who have been creatively using new technologies from the simple video camera to computer networks and satellite transmissions to enhance democratic participation. Such examples show that it is possible and necessary to appropriate and liberate technology to defend ecological struggles, to empower the disenfranchised, to express cultural diversity, and to strengthen popular participation in genuinely democratic processes.

In this struggle, we align ourselves with the growing movement of local and international organizations who have spoken out in favor of democratic communication and lend our support to the principles expressed by them. They include, among others, Vidéazimut, CENDIT, Asian Media Alternatives (AMA), the Asian Mass Communication Research and Information Centre (AMIC), the World Association of Community Radio Broadcasters (AMARC), the World Association for Christian Communication (WACC), the MacBride Round Table, the Union for Democratic Communications, the Alliance for Community Media, the Telecommunication Policy Round Table, and Computer Professionals for Social Responsibility.

# Active Media Subjects/Observers in a WTO World: Icebergs in the Paths of the Colossus

## November 1998

> Viewers/makers of the world unite . . .
> You might even get rid of your burger chains!

HOW CAN ALTERNATIVE MEDIA survive in the globalized market-driven economies as we approach the next century? What sorts of state regulations are possible and/or desirable? What sorts of support structures are possible on local, regional, national, and global levels? What are some progressive models for participatory use of communication technology that challenge the existing orders?

Many of us have learned to survive in the wake of the colossus. Like scavenging sea gulls we pick up the crumbs. The wasteful competitive production practices of market-driven technology have meant that designed-in obsolescence leaves castoff versions of equipment and software that are affordable and still useful.

Or we hitch a ride. As commercial media stampedes to high-resolution digital formats, production of good quality imagery and sound for community production has had a corresponding improvement. Good images are now cheaper and more portable. All well and good, but we need strategies that take the initiative, that go beyond the flea market, beyond being parasites, beyond cyber-hacking. If we want to stop the Titanic, we need to study iceberg construction.

Communication is now recognized as a focal point for progressive change. The forces of reaction and repression have long understood this. Therefore we need to connect and collaborate and share strategies and successes. We need to seize this moment to grow and thrive. The intersection of microradio, the Internet, and video activism is providing many lively sites of resistance to corporate globalization.

ACCESS

The creation of public access channels and facilities in the United States, Scandinavia, Germany, Australia, and many other countries has proven that "taxing" the profits of the telecommunications infrastructure can provide revenues to initiate and support a public interest communication system. Perhaps similar regulations on a global scale could take a proportion of the profits from global commercial networks to support public interest media exchange. In Korea the labor unions have realized the importance of video documentation and mobilization. Their dramatic use of video in their movement is an inspiration to other rank-and-file labor groups throughout the world.

*Video + Activism + International Exchange = Boycott*

A video on the unhealthy and underpaid work of children in Honduras and El Salvador, *Zoned for Slavery*, became the focus of a tour made by three young women workers featured in the tape to shopping malls and high schools in the United States. After watching the presentation, young people in several communities spontaneously initiated pickets and protests at local malls calling for a boycott of clothes made in sweatshops. The Clean Clothes Campaign is an international effort in this direction that uses the Internet, video, and community organizing.

*Solidarity across Borders*

The Kuna Indians are among the most technologically advanced of the indigenous peoples. We have all seen the images of the Kayapo with their video cameras. But the Kuna are also using the Internet and e-mail and a unique sort of solidarity financing: they made a video which was financed by the casino receipts of a tribe in San Diego.

## Bookstore Distribution

In many bookstores in Mexico one can purchase inexpensive copies of video news, including reports by the Canal 6 de Julio, an activist group making monthly video editions. The wide interest in the Zapatista uprising in Chiapas has sparked an interest in video from the area and from other sites of resistance.

## Street Projections

Pioneering groups in Brazil, such as *TV Viva* and *TV Maxambomba*, have taken street media screenings to a high level of sophistication and artistry. On occasion community video groups such as these are able to sustain themselves by garnering state and municipal funding to provide important information on community health issues such as AIDS and water purification.

## Satellite Diffusion

MED TV, a satellite network which is devoted to programming of interest to the wide diaspora of ethnic Kurds, has been so successful that the country of Turkey has applied international pressure to attempt to shut it down. Despite pressure and harassment, the organization continues to provide programming to Kurdish people in twenty countries, who can access it through direct satellite dishes. The tactic of using satellite time for diffusion by community groups has been the premise of Deep Dish TV. Deep Dish compiles local programming from across the United States (and international programs as well) around specific themes such as health care, housing, militarism, and justice and has rented time on commercial transponders. The principal targets for Deep Dish

transmissions are the receivers (dishes!) at local cable channels, where the programs are then taped and used on local
access and educational channels.

## Reconstructing National Identity

Photojournalist Susan Meiselas and a group of brilliant young
web designers have created www.akakurdistan.org, which
provides a visual record of the Kurdish people. Meiselas traveled throughout Iran, Iraq, and Turkey gathering snapshots
and studio portraits and family anecdotes to create a web map
of the region in which the viewer/reader can travel via geography or time to the sites of cultural struggle of this beleaguered
people.

## The Campaign That Is a Web Site: http://www.mcspotlight.org

When McDonald's sued a pair of humble environmental activists in England, little did they realize the creative forces that
would be unleashed in opposition to the mega-junk food
chain. The McSpotlight web site has been visited by tens of
millions (two million people each month for almost a year).
Like the original brochure which was the target of the libel
suit, this handy site has concrete facts on the environmental
impact of the burger industry, the debased labor involved in
their sales, the seduction of children with unhealthy food habits, and many other greasy sins. On this participatory site you
can print up a brochure for local organizing in a choice of
twenty languages. If the corporation tries to open a shop in
your town, you can print out a report to present to your local
planning board containing a list of urban congestion problems other McDonald's sites have experienced.

From these and other models we can see the practical uses
of alternative media for:

- Community mobilization
- Collaboration with workers' struggles
- Reconstructing popular history
- Creation of sites for access and training

- Building structures for distribution through sales, street screenings, and satellite transmission.

These activities depend on the struggles of informed and dedicated media activists. Their work needs to be supported through international development funding and through the support of those states and international organizations that understand the need for authentic public information systems.

## DANGERS AND PROBLEMS

Success in challenging existing structures can bring brutal reaction. Alternative media which show a potential to mobilize public support are increasingly vulnerable to repression. Med TV is a case in point. If the satellite network was ineffectual and marginal, it would not have sparked the reaction it did. Nowhere is the danger more apparent than in Colombia, where one year ago two videomakers, Elsa Alvarado and Mario Calderon of CINEP, who were working on a video about the land struggles of a group of indigenous people near the Panamanian border, land wanted by transnationals for mining development, were violently murdered. They were killed in front of their young child by a death squad in their home in Bogota, in a scene reminiscent of the purges in El Salvador and Guatemala.

We have the ability to use computers and the Internet to share and utilize vast amounts of data. In many cases, for example, in the environmental arena, activists have been able to assess information and mobilize campaigns that far outstrip the often clumsy corporate reaction in cleverness and strategy, despite heavy funding and fathomless corporate computer power. The McDonald's campaign is obviously a case in point.

Central to any project for constructing alternatives is the necessity of a vigilant opposition to commercial media. There are many initiatives to promote "media literacy," some of which are actually created and promoted by media monopolies themselves. An informed media criticism is essential for democracy. The work of Schiller, Herman, Chomsky, and the organization Fairness and Accuracy in Reporting are useful tools for discussion and analysis. It is time for "a ruthless criticism . . . not afraid of its own conclusions, nor of conflict with the powers that be" (letter from Karl Marx to Arnold Ruge).

The notion of non-commercial accountable media is in direct opposition to the commercial logic that has overtaken the world. There are powerful forces aligned against the principles of true freedom of expression. If alternative media is a threat when it is successful, it is clear that we need global support systems to stave off repression. The violence at CINEP is surely not over. Organizations such as Vidéazimut can serve as early warning systems to organize international solidarity against threats and violence.

It is 150 years after the *Communist Manifesto*, and we see the revolutionary subject in contemporary society swallowed by narcissism and consumerism. A Verso Books prestige edition of the *Manifesto* becomes the window theme for a swank Fifth Avenue bookstore. El Ché adorns a Swatch wristwatch. We are all living in a Banana Republic.

> Workers of the world, unite! You have nothing to loose but your chains!
>
> Marx and Engels, *The Communist Manifesto*

Chains are still with us, in fact, becoming a popular commodity. A recent catalog of police equipment advertises chains of all materials and sizes, some equipped with electronic signal devices that can position the wearer via a geostationary satellite. In the United States not only do we have designer chains, but chain gangs repairing roads in the South and Southwest, and indentured poor under the aegis of "workfare" in the Northern ghettos marked by humiliating vests sweeping the streets for less than minimum wage. Around the globe children are pressed into service creating the booty of First World shopping malls.

> We have a choice . . . We can have a cynical attitude in the face of the media, to say that nothing can be done . . . Or we can simply assume incredulity. . . . But there is a third option that is neither conformity nor disbelief: that is to construct a different way—to

show the world what is really happening—to have a critical world view. . . . It is our only possibility to save the truth, to maintain it and distribute it, little by little.

Subcommandante Marcos, Address to the Meeting of Free the Media, February 1997

# Our Right to the Sky: International Regulation for Local Expression

## January 1995

IN THE 1970s the International Telecommunications Union (ITU) was the forum for a debate about communication equity: many countries in the so-called "developing" world had banded together, as part of the Non-aligned Movement, to demand parity of access to information resources for a "New World Information Order." The ITU debate at the World Administrative Radio Conference of 1978 centered around the reservation of radio frequency spectrum space, especially satellite paths, for the "developing" countries. At that time there were few entities in the world that had the technical ability to utilize this global resource: the United States, Soviet Union, and France were the only countries with a full capacity to launch communication satellites. However, other countries were afraid that if they did not reserve space, they would be hampered as to future development. They were especially concerned about leaving open the possibility of having their satellites in the highly desirable equatorial orbit, called "geostationary," which was needed to have a stable signal for specific regions.

The staid ITU, which had been designating global telecom slots for years without anyone taking notice, was rocked with charged discussions that cut to the real issues: the commercialization and militarization of space resources by large and powerful countries and multinational corporations. This put into question the right to communicate and the need for justice on technological issues. These discussions found a voice in the MacBride Report, *Many Voices, One World*, which resulted from UNESCO research into information distribution. The MacBride Report was so controversial that the United States virtually stopped payment to the United Nations for several years in protest. The result was a shift at UNESCO away from such "controversial" projects.

The debate about information justice took place twenty-five years ago, before many countries had either satellite-launching capability or programs and information to distribute. It is only now, with the implementation of Murdoch's Star TV in India, Latin America, and almost every corner of the world and with the global marketing of GAP and Coca-Cola through MTV that we realize how important those discussions were. Both the ITU debate and the UNESCO/MacBride intervention were the opening salvos in a continuing struggle for information justice that will only grow in importance. Because of increased access to consumer-priced information tools by individuals and groups at the grassroots level, regional producers of small-format video and communicators are beginning to understand the potential for democratic exchange of ideas and culture that is possible with this technology. When the MacBride Commission talked about community communication, they did not have the examples of *TV Maxambomba* from Brazil or the Video Farm in Malaysia, or the use of the Internet by the Zapatistas in Chiapas. In a sense those discussions happened too early, too soon. In the United States in the mid-1970s a group called the Public Interest Satellite Association was formed to work toward having non-commercial space on satellites. At that time satellite services were just beginning, and it was hard to project what the future might bring.[6] It is important, at this time, to rethink that struggle in the light of the impressive evidence of local, non-commercial work that is being produced around the world and here in the United States.

The question is, How can the grassroots use of information

---

[6] Andrew Horowitz and Bert Cowlan, "Should People Fight for Satellites?" *Televisions* 4, no. 1 (1976).

technology be cultivated in the "vast wasteland" of global commercial (and military) hegemony of technological resources? Perhaps it is time to look at the ITU and to reinsert the public into their agenda. The ITU was organized before the United Nations, as a global agency to assign radio frequencies to prevent interference between nations. It has the task of designating both global spectrum and orbiting satellite paths. Both of these resources are essential infrastructure for any telecommunications project. At the current time, most of this supposedly global resource has been assigned to commercial entities and military users. With the collapse of the Eastern Bloc, the demise of the Non-aligned Movement, and the privatization of national telecommunications agencies, there is no organized resistance to the commercialization of the world telecommunications infrastructure. This is why the Murdochs and the MTVs of the world have free access to their target "markets": we are all in the bull's eye.

The deployment of the vast stream of entertainment and advertising needs the physical use of the public airwaves and the global orbital space for dissemination. These paths are resources that belong to all the world's people. At the current time they are used mostly for commercial programming by a few large entertainment corporations and by military and corporate speculators of a very few countries for data collection and surveillance. Regulation of these spaces could include a mandate to ensure that there is a public "payback" for this use of the global resource. Fees for use could provide resources for education and development. A fund could be set up to create facilities and initiate training for local media creation. The fee collection could be regulated by the ITU and the funds administered by a commission made up of representatives of community media NGOs.

An example of how communities can successfully "tax" corporations to reconfigure communication infrastructure is the public access movement in the United States. Begun in the early seventies, community groups and visionary city officials were able to extract from cable corporations provisions that ensure public access to cable channels and equipment. Although this movement has been ridiculed in the popular press in the United States (a press for the most part owned by cable corporations), it has flourished in many cities and provides a model for the rest of the world as to how excess communication profits can be directed into "affirmative action" for information equity.

As community organizations around the world wake up to the importance of communications issues, perhaps we can look to unions and NGOs to become involved in this important struggle. Multinational corporations are exploiting workers across borders, so it is self-preservation that will force workers in these industries to begin to communicate with each other. Several unions now have pilot projects in this area. Workers in Brazil are communicating via pictures of working conditions and workplace safety with Japanese workers in the same corporation. Environmental organizations are realizing that they need the global reach of the Internet to track down such things as rain forest destruction and toxic waste. Environmental and worker organizations need to take up the banners for global non-profit communication resources. They can be important allies in the future information struggle.

We need an international forum to formulate possible structural modes that could address our rights in this area. What better forum than an ITU, charged to oversee the global infrastructure? As nation states have privatized their communication systems, ITU rules on trans-border transmissions have held little consequence, and the corporations have jumped into the vacuum in this international forum. However, it is not too late to reassert the need for an authentic public participation in this crucial forum. What better representatives to these organizations than those of us who daily work at the community level to foster grassroots communication? The local and regional models of collaboration and participation can be reformulated to design a global system of information resources that sees humanity not as markets to be exploited, but as participant citizens. There are global deliberations on such issues as saving the whales and ozone depletion. Can a global standard of participatory communication be addressed by asserting the public nature of global information resources, such as earth orbits and spectrum?

A research project such as the MacBride Commission would have quite a bit to study these days. World communications have expanded so quickly that we have hardly had time to understand what is going on. In this rapidly changing environment we need to think of ways to protect democratic communication. We need to examine these models of participation and think about whether there might be ways of encouraging and subsidizing them by regulations imposed in the global arena such as the ITU, UNESCO, or perhaps even the World Court.

Addendum: Since this piece was written, an international non-profit group of communications academics and practitioners, headquartered in MacBride's homeland of Ireland, has formed the MacBride Round Table, which, under the leadership of Sean O'Siochru, has begun talks with the ITU about having NGOs participate in a formal way in that organization. The ITU is now an official U.N. organization and as such is required by the U.N. charter to have participation by NGOs. How this is formulated is being negotiated, and there are other complications that may limit the powers of the ITU. With the redefinition of information as a commodity, the World Trade Organization is beginning to take over some of the regulatory functions that had been performed by the ITU. The WTO has no democratic, representative basis, such as U.N. organizations are required to have, and will be a difficult forum within which to negotiate democratic communication.

# Gathering Storm: The Cyber Forum of Indymedia

> The Independent Media Center is a network of collectively run media outlets for the creation of radical, objective, and passionate tellings of the truth.
>
> From the manifesto of the Boston IMC, March 2000

> Let's make a network of communication among all our struggles and resistances. An intercontinental network of alternative communication against neo-liberalism . . . (and) for humanity. This intercontinental network of alternative communication will weave the channels so that words may travel all the roads that resist. . . . (It) will be the medium by which distinct resistances communicate with one another. This intercontinental network of alternative communication is not an organizing structure, nor has a central head or decision maker, nor does it have a central command or hierarchies. We are the network, all of us who speak and listen.
>
> Statement from the 1996 *Encuentro* in Chiapas

> TEAMSTERS AND TURTLES, TOGETHER, AT LAST!
>
> Demonstrator's sign, Seattle N30, 1999

IN SEATTLE AND Davos, D.C. and Prague, Calgary and Nice, media activists and environmentalists, labor rank and file and tree huggers have coalesced into a formidable force that not only has had an impact on the international money lenders but has caused major disruptions for agribusiness giants such as Monsanto and fashion outlets at the Mall like GAP and Nike.

One of the notable aspects of the recent activism has been the powerful integration of the movement with the alternative media. This is not an attempt to "get on TV," but a commitment to create new forms of information sharing using new spaces and technologies and new ways of collaboration. This media movement has emerged through the creation of independent media centers (IMCs), where media activists have constructed their own public information spaces, both physical and virtual, by integrating various media formats and technologies: camcorders, web radio, streaming video, microradio, digital photography, community cable access channels, DBS transponders, and laptop journalism. This time the revolution is not only televised, but digitized and streamed.

> [We need] a nimble, plural, international guerrilla strategy to break the corporate grip on democracy.[7]

Years before the worldwide web, Hans Magnus Enzensberger wrote, "The open secret of the electronic media, the decisive political factor, which has been waiting, suppressed or crippled, for its moment to come, is their mobilizing power."[8] He could hardly have predicted the way in which the media themselves were mobilized. Using e-mail and the web, activists have been able to create a community of information gatherers and distributors, which can react quickly to events and build a net of audience/producers at local, regional, and international levels. Enzensberger notes the collaborative potential: "A further characteristic of the most advanced media—probably the decisive one . . . is their collective structure."[9]

The independent media centers and their website, indymedia.org, have emerged as models, not only for new ways of media making, but as practical examples of collective production. Many different streams came together: the video activist

---

[7] Hilary Wainwright, Red Pepper, http://www.redpepper.org.uk/

[8] Hans Magnus Enzensberger, "Constituents of a New Media Theory" (1971), *The Consciousness Industry: On Literature, Politics and the Media* (New York: Seabury Press, 1974), 96.

[9] Ibid., 107.

community, the microradio pirates, the computer hacker/code writers, the 'zine makers, and the punk music world. These multimedia activists were ignited by several gatherings called The Next Five Minutes, organized by Geert Lovink, David Garcia, and others in Amsterdam during the 1990s. These meetings provided a window on the possibilities of collaborative mega-media events. During this period, the global movement for justice and accountability arose to counter corporate globalization. There was also a recognition by progressive groups of the importance of alternative media and the realization of media's key role in producing a passive consumer culture. There is, finally, the recognition that the information/entertainment oligarchy is one of the pillars of global capital. News programs produced by these corporations, though operating under the label of "journalism," cannot address issues that threaten the status quo and are obliged to engineer "consent," as Noam Chomsky and Edward Herman so clearly laid out in *Manufacturing Consent*.[10]

For anticorporate activists, creating new ways of communicating must be part of the solution. Behind the strategic blockades of the radical environmentalists and the lively and passionate videotapes and websites produced by the camcorder commandos and data dancers, the IMCs represent a sea-change in the form of public action and its documentation. By creating a new way of making things happen on a global scale, the IMC movement can be seen as a concrete example of how alternative structures for life and work can be effective and powerful.

The most radical aspect of the antiglobalization movement is its nonhierarchical nature. Decision making is by consensus. All participants are themselves empowered. This is in keeping with the way the anticorporate globalization movement is structured: decentralized, based in affinity groups whose work is by consensus. Developing an authentic consensus is always difficult and time consuming. As an IMC handbook puts it: "There is a tricky trade-off to negotiate: on one

---

[10] Noam Chomsky and Edward Herman, *Manufacturing Consent* (New York: Pantheon, 1988).

hand, you want to let able, willing people with the ability to take action do so without too much hassle about it; on the other hand, you want checks and balances to make sure people's voices are heard and to keep decision making power from centralizing beyond what is functionally necessary."[11]

A key element of the IMCs has been the open process of the entire structure, enabled by the use of the web and list-serves for various interest areas and a discussion group for the process itself. Within the process strand, issues such as representation and parity are continually addressed. The process of each separate IMC (and its website) is worked out within an independent group, taking into consideration the global discussions of other centers. The following is a text that was intended to be included in a "how to" pamphlet for creating independent media centers:

> DECISION-MAKING PROCEDURES: IMCs are collectively organized projects that run on principles of consensus. This organizing structure is inextricably bound to the success of the IMCs. This non-hierarchical process encourages every media maker to contribute his or her best work, and to participate as much as s/he desires. One model which has worked well when an IMC is operating at full capacity is have two meetings a day—one general meeting each evening and one "spokescouncil" meeting each morning.
>
> Each general meeting has been a consensus-based meeting with multiple facilitators for the sake of parity (gender, racial, background, etc.). Each spokescouncil meeting has included team coordinators and/or empowered team representatives. Both meetings had meeting groups that held decision-making power. At the general meetings, consensus has been reached among everyone present, while at the spokescouncil meetings only the empowered reps participated in the consensus (though everyone else in the room took part in the discussion).

A functioning IMC is a beehive of activity. The arrangements can be temporary, such as the leased space in a Los Angeles Veterans Center for the Democratic Convention IMC, or per-

---

[11] First draft of IMC blueprint made by Seattle IMC staff after WTO events.

manent, such as the storefront in Seattle that became a hub of on-going meetings, screenings, and media production after the seminal WTO meeting. The subgroupings of the IMC community are divided by medium: within the physical space of the IMCs, withing specific web groupings, and within e-mail lists that service the various participants. For example, at each IMC there is a photo corner, where photographers have computers and space for scanning, in order to post still pictures to the web. This group will have separate meetings in addition to the general meetings. The photographers are part of a general indymedia-photo list-serve and may even have a separate list-serve for photos within that location, that is, photo-Seattle, photo-DC, etc. In addition to photo exhibits, there are similar groupings for video, radio, print, and tech/web.

CONTRADICTIONS

The movement for an alternative media, with its flexible and open structure, its democratic rendering of the use-values of new technologies, and its continual involvement in interconnecting people in a transnational movement, provides a model of the evolution of a radical opposition, from the spontaneous appearance of individual creative practice, to the collective gathering of small co-operatives with enhancement of practical and technical skill, to the growth of national and international collectives. The IMCs evolved within the larger antiglobalization movement and are not external to, but integrally part of, this movement. This is seen as a problem for traditional journalists, who proclaim themselves as "neutral" and never "taking sides." IMC media makers openly declare their affinity with the antiglobalization movement and counter with the observation that mainstream media is never neutral but solidly behind maintaining the status quo and the corporate bottom line.

Mainstream critics have snidely put down indymedia activity for being contradictory for using corporate tools such as the internet to attack corporate agendas. Indymedia makers have countered that that is a time-honored guerrilla tactic—to turn the tools of the oppressors against them. However, a more considered rejoinder is that the internet was developed in a collaborative process through public funding via educational institutions. Its creation did not spring from a search for profitable products to market. The entire effort was subsidized by public grants and nurtured in an atmosphere of mutual cooperation, not unlike the process of indymedia itself. The early internet researchers were not initially making products that the commercial sector could (and would) develop. As e-commerce takes over much of the bandwidth, it is efforts such as indymedia that are preserving the authentic interactive potential of the internet and, as such, preserving its role as a progressive public resource.

As the anticorporate movement proceeds and the confrontations heat up, the movement and the indymedia that are bound to it increasingly refuse to compromise with the powers that be.[12] One characteristic of this media activity, along with the antiglobalization movement of which it is a part, is the fact that they are forthright in proclaiming the negation of capital.

> One hears the word, "revolution," more frequently these days among those whose engagement in such struggles enhances their own power and radically separates them from the power of capital. At first this is a vague slogan to express radical discontent; however, the logic of things demands also that revolution be given a goal, a content, and an agent. In this way, a spontaneously developing collective evolves into a community of resistance.[13]

The anticorporate stance can sometimes be complicated by the contradictions between the desire for exposure of the issues and the need for material support for the IMC operations. What is the principled stand when profit-driven corporations

---

[12] The delegitimation of the electoral process in Florida will be certain to increase the radical potential of U.S. activists.

[13] Joel Kovel, *The Enemy of Nature* (London: Zed, in press 2002).

who happen to have millions of viewers wish to utilize the footage or information gathered in this nonhierarchical, not-for-profit mode? There are endless discussions on the various IMC list-serves about whether such footage should be given outright to mainstream networks in hopes of maximizing exposure, or whether this sort of archival sale can be a way of supporting and sustaining the IMC movement.

The only requirement to get a press pass at the IMC is that one signs a pledge outlining the expectations of ownership and control:

> The IMC is an all-volunteer, collectively-run media center operating as an alternative to corporate media and corporate institutions. It is a resource for pooling resources and getting the message out—it is not a resource for profit. By presenting my I.D. and signing on to be an IMC affiliate, I confirm that I have read and understand the following and will work within these guidelines in order to make the most efficient use of space and resources to accomplish the IMC's mission (see below). I understand that if I choose to behave outside of these guidelines, I am not acting in agreement with the IMC and my participation will be limited at the discretion of the IMC core team.
>
> I will behave non-violently when in IMC spaces, when covering events as an IMC participant, or in any capacity related to the IMC's functioning. This includes refraining from abusive language and behavior that is racist, homophobic, or sexist.
>
> I will not engage in any illegal activities while in an IMC space.
>
> The IMC is providing these resources freely, at great expense and labor, to broaden access to media production and distribution. In return, I agree to volunteer to cover shifts at the IMC and I will confirm this with the Volunteer Coordinator. . . .[14]

PARTICIPATORY MOBILIZATION

The format of indymedia is appropriate to the diverse and complex networks of activists who have formed these move-

---

[14] From a handout distributed at the Washington, D.C., IMC, April 17, 2000.

ments. However, there have been those who questioned the representation in these organizations. In a challenging essay that has been widely distributed on list-serves and web-sites, Betita Martinez, a Bay Area Chicana activist, has charged that the antiglobalization movement is mostly white,[15] without major participation by people of color, who are often the victims of the sort of restructuring imposed by International Monetary Fund and World Bank "reforms." Within the IMCs there is in fact a dependence on the technical skills of mostly white young males. Since the IMCs are by and large volunteer organizations, often using equipment loaned for the occasion, many working-class youths cannot afford to donate their time and may not have the technical equipment to contribute to this sort of nonprofit work.

A number of people are attempting to address this situation. In a note for planning a tactical meeting on the IMCs someone wrote: "How can we bridge gaps in gender, color, culture, age, access, language, and 'otherness' for capacity building and empowerment?" There are discussions about setting up workshops in working-class communities and perhaps holding special meetings to discuss issues of race and class. Some are wary of having this dynamic movement become a victim of identity politics, but others feel that on a worldwide scale, many of the movement leaders are people of color who can help establish IMCs in countries and regions outside of Western urban centers, IMC Chiapas being one example. The most powerful aspect of the antiglobal struggle is the internationalism at the core.

> I was proposing to think about the possibility of a radical democratic citizenship . . . in which we are going to try to articulate in a common identity this multiplicity of political space.[16]

---

[15] Looking at the videos from Seattle, it is hard to acquiesce to that view, and certainly the actions around the conventions in Philadelphia and Los Angeles were made up of people of color to a great extent. In Prague there was an entire contingent of lesbians and gays.

[16] Chantal Mouffe, interview with Ian Angus, November 6, 1998, Knowledge Network, British Columbia's Public Educational Television Service, http://www.knowtv.com/primetime/conflicting/mouffe.html.

HISTORY IN THE MAKING

The IMC Chiapas was initiated just before the indigenous groups from that beleaguered corner of Mexico set off across the country to Mexico City early in 2001. The IMC was mobile; it occupied one of the buses in the caravan, where activists edited the news on laptops as the group gained momentum and added followers from each village they passed. Each day short videos, audio clips, photos, and text provided testimony of the prior day's adventures. By the time the group arrived in Mexico City, an hour-long program had been edited, which, combined with C-Span style coverage (with simultaneous translations), was uplinked via satellite to the Free Speech network and made available in streamed video on the web. This momentous event was unprecedented in Mexican history. The Zocalo (the central plaza in Mexico City) was filled with its largest crowd ever. This received scant attention in the mainstream U.S. press, but the IMC sites all pointed to the Chiapas posts and hundreds of thousands of visitors from all over the world were able to get firsthand reports of the events.

THE FORMAT OF THE WEB PAGE

Though quite popular and visited by literally millions, the indymedia websites are not about spectacle, but about involvement, engagement, and participation. The home page is divided into columns, the first being links to all the IMC websites from the various locations throughout the world. The center section is a loosely edited, regularly updated news post. The right-hand column is for ongoing continuous posting, open to all who have access to a computer and a modem. The sidebar of the indymedia page is a first-come, first-serve, open bulletin board. This sidebar can be searched for specific media, for example, for all the video posts or radio or photo segments. The software was initially developed in Australia by Matthew Arnison for use by activist organizations on that continent.[17] It has been tweaked and formatted by Manseur

---

[17] For more information, see the interview with Mathew Arnison by Madhava in *Punk Planet* (April 2001).

Jacobi of Freespeech TV, Chris Burnett of Regeneration TV, and others of the IMC tech team. This software enables any browser/reader to easily post their own text, photos, audio, video files, or still photographs. Each location site has archives of pictures, audio-video, and texts. The selections on the center column of the indymedia web site are selected and edited into an ongoing montage of information, drawn from the spontaneous posts, and are collated in the form that was initially posted. These "headline stories" and posts on the open right-hand column are immediately linked to any comments or corrections that are posted unedited in response. This continuous dialogue is clearly different from the simplified news bites that are fed to passive viewers of CNN.com.

In assessing the indymedia site, one has to take into account not only those who visit it to find out the latest news, but the impressive numbers of people who have posted not only their own news stories, but comments and additions to stories, along with those who use the easily managed multimedia posting opportunity to share their own photos, video, and audio files. It has been estimated that more than fifteen thousand still photographs alone are available through IMC sites.[18] An example of the creatively improvisatory nature of the network is what happened after the Seattle indymedia site became inundated by literally millions of hits during the WTO meetings. Technicians browsing the site from various locations were aware that the site was overloaded with visitors. Several mirror servers, including some from other countries, sprang into action, expanding the bandwidth capacity to handle the overflow.

TRANSMISSION

Even though the web audience was in the millions, from the first days of the WTO protests in Seattle an effort was made to disseminate the IMC productions beyond the internet. *The*

---

[18] One hundred fifty of these photos from ten of the sites were exhibited at the Berleley Art Museum in October 2000 and are scheduled for other locations.

*Blind Spot,* the Seattle IMC's daily newspaper, which was composed and available on-line, was also printed in hard copy tabloid editions of several thousand and distributed at the demonstrations and to cafés, universities, and other public locations. The web radio was transmitted on micro- and community radio stations in many locations, often over several channels in the host server. In Seattle a ferryboat on Lake Union hosted one of the radio transmitters, and the video was literally bicycled (the streets were closed to cars) to a satellite uplink. For five days, programs on the WTO and the Seattle actions were transmitted by Deep Dish TV and the Freespeech DBS network. These satellite transmissions were picked up by home dish owners and community stations as well as public access, educational, and governmental channels and retransmitted to their audiences.

This network of collaborating media channels did not just spring up during the WTO protests. Deep Dish Network and Freespeech TV have been collecting independent work for such an ad hoc network for years. Deep Dish pioneered this sort of targeted programming during the 1991 Gulf War, when they produced ten programs before, during, and after the war. At a time when only military press conferences and heroic stories of U.S. troops were presented on the corporate channels (and I include PBS in the corporate list, as much of their programming at this time was funded by General Motors, maker of the tanks used in the war), Deep Dish, working with independent and community producers from around the country, was able to present the many voices of opposition to the Gulf War.

During the 2001 political conventions in Philadelphia and Los Angeles, thirty-five hours of programs were transmitted live, using roll-in tapes from the days' events. Each day, a morning news program, hosted by Amy Goodman and Juan Gonzalez of Pacifica Radio, was presented. In diversity, in depth of content, in exposing the contradictions of the Republican Convention, the IMC programming far surpassed anything either commercial networks or Jim Lehrer could offer.[19]

---

[19] In-studio guests and field interviews for just one two-hour television program from Philadelphia included hosts Goodman and Gonzales; media critic Ed Herman; Frank Sesno, Vice President of CNN News on psyop in-

The entire operation is done with a small grant from Frees-peech TV and money from a few private donors, even though the production is on a scale that would cost mainstream news outlets millions. The IMCs are successful because of the high level of volunteer assistance, especially from the digital tech community. The collaborative nature of the indymedia work is something the mainstream press can't fathom. In covering this media revolution, the corporate press, either unwilling or unable to see the implications of this new form of information sharing, has focused instead on trying to find evidence of "hacking." Hacking is something the mainstream reporters can deal with, while the more complex forms of anti-global cyber activism appear to be beyond their scope. Conventional journalists are stuck with the notion of an individual geek/ maverick computer terrorist, and they have a hard time "get-ting" decentralized, consensus-based media affinity groups.

In Australia, during the demonstrations in Melbourne at the September 11, 2000, meeting of the World Economic Forum, "J.M.G." posted the following:

> The inabilities of the mainstream media to comprehensively document the issues and events surrounding S11 are con-trasted by the growing number of community based, indepen-dent media outlets and individuals granted a forum for interactive dialogue through IndyMedia. The IndyMedia site provides a "channel" for open discourse, free of editorial, as a simple click on the "publish" button enables anyone and every-one to upload their stories. Rather than challenging or infiltrat-ing the mainstream the objective of IndyMedia is to create a system outside of the dominant socio-political culture, empow-ering citizens by providing greater access and opportunity. Under this method of communication the traditional concept

---

terns at CNN; Contragate perpetrator Oliver North; Jimmy Hoffa, Jr., Teamster president; Republican National Committee Chair Jim Nicholson; Newt Gingrich; Nora Callahan, prison activist; former inmate Mary Gaines and her children Rakesha, eighteen, and Ricky, twenty-one; Tamika, whose brother is in jail; two protester-prisoner Jane Does calling in from their "cell" phone; Rick Beltram, a Republican delegate from South Carolina, and Steve Beltram, his son who is a protester; Warren Mowry, Republican delegate from South Carolina; and Michael Franti, lead singer from Spear-head on the Cultural Jam.

of the "audience" is refuted—challenging the reader/writer to come to their own conclusions by wading through the diverse range of stories relating to S11 and other events. The sheer enormity and breadth of information available has lead to a greater level of engagement with both the issues and the other reader/writers. Creating this space for audience control has harnessed the inherent qualities of hypertext—unlike the majority of on-line news services, which remain overwhelmingly one-way in their transmission.

MAINSTREAM COVERAGE OF INDYMEDIA

The distrust of mainstream media has been codified in the "IMC Blueprint" with the following rules:

1. Try to get mainstream media to schedule times to come to the IMC so it is possible to let everyone know they are coming. If possible, we try to clear the scheduled mainstream media visit through a general meeting.
2. All mainstream media doing articles on the IMC should register as mainstream media—it is even possible to give them special passes to wear while they are in the IMC.
3. Someone from the outreach team can accompany mainstream media at all times when they are in the IMC.[20]

Sometimes IMC activities catch the interest of the press and greatly increase the number of visitors to the website. As related by "J.M.G.":

Creative applications of the Internet technology during the S11 protests demonstrated the ability of the Net to not only function as an organizational tool but also as a form of civil disobedience in cyberspace. . . . The old media was important in publicizing and drawing attention to the new, highlighting the fact that, although the Net is an important new tool, activists still largely rely on coverage in the traditional media and cannot rely solely upon the emerging communications networks.[21]

---

[20] Posted on IMC lists as IMC Draft Blueprint by Janet Berkow, October 2000.
[21] "J.M.G.," post to IMC lists, October 2000.

PROBLEMS

The open format of indymedia makes it a vulnerable target for the right wing and agents of the National Security Apparatus. There have been posts that are clearly attempts at disinformation. These have been roundly attacked by counter-postings, but sometimes damage is done. The infiltration of the movements in Philadelphia, D.C., and Los Angeles was troubling, but rather obvious. Specific agitators and infiltrators were identified and cautioned against, but this sort of counter-reaction is also subject to misuse by infiltrators. As the Bush regime takes power in Washington, these efforts to destabilize the movement will surely increase and may become more tricky to fight as police tactics become more subtle and difficult to spot.[22]

Another problem is the use of postings as a sort of chat room. Some of the discussions have become hangouts for particular characters, who regularly visit and post just to rant with their friends. This happens less in times of activist actions (such as in Prague or Genoa) but makes it sometimes tedious to read the posts.

A major problem is sustainability. This effort has been built largely with volunteer work. There are tensions and burnout to contend with. Since the initial work is usually getting coverage of an event, it has been hard to continue the work with the same energy and direction. One exciting way to overcome this is now being explored through the development of a regular daily newscast/summary which could provide an ongoing focus and center for media activities.

DIALOGUE

The process of indymedia is completely open and completely accountable: there is no gate keeping, no selection process (except for what is selected for emphasis on the center news

---

[22] The use of police as undercover "Black Bloc" in Genoa only served to expose the police's role in the ensuing violence.

column). Any statement is immediately available for comment, discussion, and/or correction, and attempts by provocateurs and other agents of state repression can be spotted by watchful browsers and diffused.

This open structure is especially appropriate for the type of movement that has evolved around corporate globalization. As "J.M.G." points out:

> The time limitations of the (mainstream) news format, demanding concision and the production of neat binary oppositions, does not lend itself well to a comprehensive coverage of something as diverse and complex as the S11 protests. Whereas there are clear difficulties in the format of mainstream news, oversimplification of the issues was inappropriate as both the political issues and the protesters themselves were multifaceted and resistant to basic explanations. The Internet technology, as applied by the Indymedia news service, was much more conducive to permitting a proliferation of heterogeneous voices.[23]

The struggle against neoliberalism has many fronts, reflected in the loosely compiled, spontaneous postings, which vary from rant to thoughtful essay. The discussions on the indy sites range from first-person reporting of events to reflection on tactics (how the Prague demonstrators utilized colorful pepper spray–proof costumes), to non-violence (one of the most active discussions are the comment pages with a photo of a Molotov cocktail landing on a line of police in Prague), to cautionary identification of police informants, to detailed information about biogenetic experiments. There are passionate postings about race and inclusion, about effective strategies for facilitating meetings, about securing legal assistance, and documentation procedures for anticipated court trials. Those who are physically present at an IMC are only a fraction of those who participate. Photographers, videomakers, radio people, writers, and web mavens can post from any location, from any continent. During the Genoa uprising, photos from solidarity demonstrations in São Paolo, Rome, London, New York, and many other cities were posted. Each photo, each video, each radio and text post to any of the indymedia sites is

---

[23] "J.M.G.," post to IMC lists, October 2000.

then subject to discussion within the site. There is no single voice, no "party line."

This movement is comprised of eclectic groupings of progressive organizations, from those labeled sects, to those engaged in electoral party building, to those who eschew any formal organizational designation. Indymedia has served an important function in facilitating communication between many of these groups and individuals. For perhaps the first time an open and ongoing global dialogue is evolving about building a different kind of world. People and groups on the Left are talking to each other. Through these discussions and the international coalitions that grow with them, a movement is emerging whose strength and breadth have no need of vanguardism and whose medium is history itself.

Live from the Independent Media Center of Los Angeles, Skip Blumberg focuses on Alicia Littletree and Kevin Danaher on Democracy Now TV, with Amy Goodman and Juan Gonzalez. Also in the photo are Portland anarchist Tim Reams and many IMC staffers. *Author)*

Tom Poole stands by the Deep Dish/Free Speech TV staellite truck outside Patriotic Hall in Los Angeles, where the IMC took place. *(Author)*

# TIMELINE: TECHNOLOGY AND ALTERNATIVE MEDIA[1]

**1922**

"It is inconceivable that we should allow so great a possibility for service to be drowned in advertising chatter!"—President Herbert Hoover on radio advertisements

**1928**

Unions, educators, and progressive religious leaders band together to seek noncommercial broadcasting spectrum space

Philo T. Farnsworth invents the cathode ray tube

**1932**

NBC starts a TV station in the Empire State Building

**1934**

Communications Act signed

**1938**

Orson Welles broadcasts *War of the Worlds* on Mercury Theater of the Air

**1939**

RCA demonstrates TV at the World's Fair

World War II begins

---

[1] Thanks to Michael Eisenmenger, Linda Iannacone, Davidson Gigliotti, John Handhardt, Erik Barnouw, Chris Hill, Lab Guy, Paula Manley, Tim Goodwin, Rika Welsh, and others for their assistance in compiling this timeline.

**1940**

NBC begins to relay telecasts to GE's labs, history's first TV "network"

**1941**

TV becomes commercial broadcast service

FCC initiates FM service

December 7: Japan attacks Pearl Harbor; the next day the United States declares war on Japan

December 11: the United States declares war on Germany and Italy

**1944**

During the war the Office of War Information and the Voice of America broadcast 3,200 live weekly programs of U.S. information and propaganda in forty different languages

**1945**

End of World War II: the United States drops two atomic bombs on Japan

**1946**

The House Committee on Un-American Activities investigates the motion picture industry for Communist infiltration, resulting in widespread blacklisting

Edward R. Murrow, new CBS vice president, starts documentary unit

Color television is demonstrated on CBS and NBC

**1947**

HUAC Hearings in Hollywood sniff out "Red" influence in movies

## 1948

The year begins with 175,000 sets and nineteen operating TV stations in the United States. It ends with nearly one million sets and forty-seven stations.

First cable systems built in Landsford and Manoy, Pennsylvania

## 1949

*The Lone Ranger* and *Hopalong Cassidy* initiate the TV Western series

The Pacifica Foundation pioneers the concept of listener-sponsored radio, providing two of the most fundamental policies in the First Amendment: free speech in broadcast and access to media. This becomes a network of five radio stations in Berkeley, Los Angeles, New York City, Houston, and Washington, D.C.

## 1950

Nielson ratings begin measuring TV viewing habits

NBC launches *Today* show

President Truman orders the Air Force and Navy to Korea, approving ground forces and air strikes

CBS institutes a loyalty oath

## 1951

The first daytime soap opera, *Search for Tomorrow,* begins

*I Love Lucy,* the first successful filmed (rather than live) TV series

Edward R. Murrow and Fred Friendly's radio program *Hear It Now* is brought to TV as *See It Now*

NBC launches the *Today* TV series starring Dave Garroway and J. Fred Muggs, a chimpanzee

Blacklisting institutionalized at networks and agencies

The CIA starts up a propaganda operation to promote U.S. government interests through international media outlets

## 1952

*Dragnet,* the prototype of the documentary-style police detective series, begins

The Supreme Court rules that movies are protected under the First Amendment right of freedom of expression

Ampex makes first recognizable videotape recording

FCC reserves TV channels for education

Cable systems number seventy with 14,000 subscribers

Lucio Fontana identifies TV as a medium for artists in his Television Manifesto of the Spatial Movement, issued in Milan

## 1953

First issue of *TV Guide* is published by the Annenberg family

## 1954

29 million TV sets in use in the United States

Army-McCarthy hearings broadcast, carried live by ABC

Swanson introduces the TV dinner for 95 cents

## 1955

First Sony pocket radio

## 1956

Videotape recording system introduced by Ampex (commercially used in 1957)

John Henry Faulk files suit over Aware attack and blacklist conspiracy

**1957**

Sputnik launch: the Soviet Union sends up the first satellite, combining missile technology with solid-state electronics

First VTR remote trucks appear

**1959**

The Cuban Film Institute, ICAIC, is established by government decree just three months after the victory of the Cuban Revolution

**1960**

Networks ban news documentaries other than their own productions

Cable systems number 640 with 650,000 subscribers

**1961**

"Children Make Movies" workshop at Lillian Wald Settlement, Ave. D, Lower East Side, New York City

Over 90 percent of U.S. homes have one or more TV sets

FCC Chair Newton Minow calls TV a "vast wasteland"

**1962**

Alexander Kluge and others draft a manifesto at the Oberhausen Film Festival, which inaugurates the New German Cinema

Filmmakers Co-op is founded to distribute alternative films. *Children Make Movies* is the first co-op film sold (to the Educational Department of the Ford Foundation).

FCC grants license to Lorenzo Milam for KRAB FM in Seattle, the first of the "Krab Nebula" community radio stations

**1963**

Martin Luther King Jr.'s "I Have a Dream" speech is televised during the Civil Rights March on Washington

The assassination and funeral of President Kennedy and televised murder of Lee Harvey Oswald disrupt all regular programming for four days. Oswald's murder is repeatedly aired, becoming the prototype of instant replay.

Establishment of COMSAT (Communications Satellite Corp.) with U.S. tax dollars although ultimately it benefits only large multinationals

Charlotte Moorman initiates New York Annual Avant-Garde Festival

### 1964

CATV or "community antenna television" begins to be called by the term "cable television." Cable TV serves to bring programs to towns that don't yet have stations of their own.

Paul Baran of the Rand Corporation writes "On Distributed Communications Networks"

Nicholas Johnson, maverick media populist, appointed to the FCC

### 1965

Cable systems number 1,325 with 1,275,000 subscribers

*Understanding Media: The Extensions of Man* by Marshall McLuhan is published, making "the history of mass media central to the history of civilization at large"

Nine Evenings: Theater and Engineering, 69th Regiment Armory, New York City, organized by Billy Kluver of Bell Labs

### 1966

"Down by the Riverside: The USCO Show," Riverside Museum, New York City, curated by Gerd Stern and USCO, Steve Durkee, Jud Yalkut, and others

Challenge for Change, Canadian experiment in grassroots video communication/activism begins

Millennium Film Workshop is founded in New York City

## 1967

Julio Garcia Espinosa of ICAIC publishes the essay "Towards an Imperfect Cinema," a polemical reflection on the whole practice of revolutionary film, one of the major theoretical statements defining the scope of the New Cinema of Latin America

Pacific Film Archives is founded in Berkeley

Canyon Cinema is founded in San Francisco

American Film Institute is founded

Sony introduces the DV-2400, the world's first portapack VTR, a half-inch tape in a helical system. Weighing twenty pounds, the portapak is almost as easy to operate as an audio tape recorder and leads to an explosion in do-it-yourself TV, revolutionizing the medium.

## 1968

Young Filmmakers Foundation (later called Film/Video Arts) is founded

Newsreel (production and distribution of activist 16mm films) is founded

CBS debuts the weekly news show *60 Minutes*

Stanley Kubrick's *2001: A Space Odyssey*, an important science fiction film with the most elaborate use of special effects to date

*How to Talk Back to Your TV Set* by Nick Johnson published

Exhibit: "The Machine, as seen at the End of the Mechanical Age," MOMA, New York City, curated by Pontus Hulton

Images of the Tet Offensive in Vietnam are carried live by satellite to news programs, bringing the grim reality of the Vietnam War directly to U.S. living rooms

First community-operated TV channel begins in Dale City, Virginia

**1969**

ARAPANET (internet initiative) is commissioned by Department of Defense

Appalshop established in Whitesburg, Kentucky, to produce films about Appalachian culture

Visual Studies Workshop is founded in Rochester, N.Y.

Woodstock Festival: Three Days of Peace and Music

*The Medium Is the Medium*, experimental series by WGBH-TV, Boston, produced by Fred Barzyk

Channel One, video screenings in New York City, initiated by Ken Shapiro, Chevy Chase, and Eric Segal

The video collective, Videofreex, begins: Skip Blumberg, Nancy Cain, David Cort, Bart Friedman, Davidson Gigliotti, Chuck Kennedy, Mary Curtis Ratcliff, Parry Teasdale, Carol Vontobel, Ann Woodward

Global Village is founded by John Reilly, Rudi Stern, and Ira Schneider

**1970**

Black Citizens for a Fair Media is founded by Emma Bowen out of concern for the mainstream media's portrayal of African Americans. Each year they hold a community meeting at the Apollo Theater in Harlem, N.Y., with the Chair of the FCC to keep the community informed about developments in the communications industry.

National Public Radio (NPR) is founded

Alternate Media Conference, Goddard College, Plainfield, Vt.

Raindance video collective begins: Frank Gillette, Ira Schneider, Paul Ryan, Beryl Korot, Michael Shamberg, Megan Williams, Louis Jaffé. Publishes *Radical Software*, journal on art and video.

Construction of the Paik Abe Synthesizer: video effects created

**1971**

Everson Museum initiates first museum video program, curated by David Ross

Pentagon Papers are published in *The New York Times* after being photocopied (a recently developed technology) by Daniel Ellsberg

Black Citizens for a Fair Media challenges CBS's license for their negative depictions of African Americans. They succeed in forcing CBS to hire a person of color at the head of community relations. ABC and NBC follow suit.

First designated public access cable channels begin in New York City

The first hacker, John Draper, finds that a cereal box premium whistle is at 2600 mHz and can trigger free phone calls. The magazine *2600* is later named after this tool.

Kitchen Center is founded by the Vasulkas and Shridar Bapat

Downtown Community Television is founded by Jon Alpert

Protests at the Pentagon on May Day inspire a group of video producers to collaborate in one of the first Independent Media Centers

Hans Magnus Enzensberger publishes "Constituents of a New Media Theory"

Alternative Media Center is founded by George Stoney and Red Burns

Videofreex move to Lanesville, N.Y., publish *The Spaghetti City Video Manual*, and begin micro-TV "self-service" broadcasting to neighbors in the mountain hollow

National Endowment for the Arts sets up Public Media program

*Great American Dream Machine*, an innovative series by National Education Television, is launched

## 1972

Pong, the first video arcade game, created

Community activists organized as the Puerto Rican Education and Action Media Council protest negative depictions of Puerto Ricans and advocate for increased employment within the industry. They successfully pressure WNET TV in New York City, by taking over the studio during an evening pledge event, to establish *Realidades,* a local TV program with Latino content.

FCC sets national access standards for cable TV through the efforts of Commissioner Nick Johnson

Collective for Living Cinema is founded

*World's Largest TV Station* and *4 More Years* produced by TVTV (Top Value Television) at the political conventions

*Through Navajo Eyes* published by John Adair and Sol Worth, pioneering study of Navajo filmmaking

Micro-radio stations thrive in Tokyo: over 2,000 initiated, inspired by Tetsuo Kogawa

Nam June Paik with Charlotte Moorman, Concerto for TV Cello/TV Bra, Everson Museum, Syracuse, N.Y.

Teepee Video Space Troup begins at the Chelsea Hotel: Shirley's Clarke's experimental video collective

"Plumbers" invade the Democratic Party Headquarters at the Watergate. This crime leads to the collapse of the Nixon administration in 1974.

Television Laboratory is initiated at WNET, New York City

## 1973

Women's Video Festival, University of Illinois, Circle Campus, Chicago

International Computer Arts Festival, The Kitchen, Mercer Arts Center

**1974**

Nam June Paik, Electronic Art IV, Bonino Gallery (Galeria Bonino), New York City

WGBH New Television Workshop is founded

First national broadcast of half-inch video: *Cuba, the People* by Jon Alpert

Association of Independent Video and Filmmakers is founded by Ed Lynch and others

*Television Delivers People:* text video analyzing TV as people market by Richard Serra and Carlotta Schoolman

**1975**

National Federation of Community Broadcasters (local non-profit radio stations) is founded

Ant Farm, a San Francisco artists collective, builds a tower of TV monitors, sets them on fire, and drives a Cadillac through them in the production *Media Burn*

**1976**

National Federation of Local Cable Programmers (NFLCP) begins, later becomes Alliance for Community Media

Image Union video collective covers the Democratic Convention for five nights on local origination cable; entitled *The Five Day Bicycle Race*, the five-hour broadcast on election night is called *Mock Turtle Soup*

Child-Made Film symposium at Minnewaska Mountain House

Boston Film and Video Foundation is founded

Bay Area Video Coalition is founded

Independent Media Artists of Georgia (IMAGE) is founded in Atlanta

**1977**

The ABC miniseries *Roots* reaches a record 80 million viewers

The first feature films available on video cassette

Christian Broadcasting Network (CBN) begins as a forum for televangelism; by 1981 CBN is aired 24 hours a day

VHS recorders are introduced by JVC

*Send/Receive:* experimental use of satellites by artists Liza Bear and Keith Sonnier

NEA sets up funding program for major media centers

Union for Democratic Communications is founded in Philadelphia

**1978**

PBS announces plan for satellite interconnection of its stations

National Alliance of Media Arts Centers (NAMAC) meets for the first time in Pittsburgh (though not based there)

The Black Filmmakers Foundation, a national nonprofit organization, is founded by Warrington Hadlin and others to develop audiences for the work of black independent video- and filmmakers and to establish a support system for established and emerging media artists

The Association of Independent Video and Filmmakers (AIVF) testifies in Congress and before the Carnegie Commission on the need for independent media on Public TV

**1979**

COMSAT announces plans for satellite programming direct to the home, via rooftop dishes to be marketed by Sears, Roebuck

Communications Update begins on Manhattan Cable, founded by Liza Bear, Michael McClard, Vickie Gholson, and DeeDee Halleck

The Moral Majority and other groups threaten sponsor boycotts over sex and violence on TV

Media Network is founded by Marc Weiss and others

Sandinista victory in Nicaragua

The Second Alternative Media Conference brings together independent producers at Bard College in New York State to discuss film and video as an organizing tool

## 1980

Ted Turner launches the Cable News Network (CNN), a 24-hour news service

1.1 percent of American homes have VCRs

National Alliance for Media Arts and Culture (NAMAC) founded

Solidarity Movement in Poland

Sony introduces first camcorder, combining recording and camera functions

FCC initiates low-power TV

## 1981

Polls show that Walter Cronkite is the most trusted man in America

Private satellite dishes are approved by the FCC. By the end of the decade there will be 2 million in use in the United States.

Paper Tiger Television is founded. Initial producers are Diana Agosta, Fusun Atasar, Pennee Bender, Skip Blumberg, William Bodde, Daniel Brooks, Shu Lea Cheang, Linda Cranor, Karen Einstein, Daniel Del Solar, Mary Feaster, DeeDee Halleck, Ezra Halleck, Melissa Leo, Esti Marpet, Leann Mella, Adam Merims, Alison Morse, Roger Politzer, Preacher, Caryn Rogoff, David Shulman, Alan Steinheimer, Martha Wallner, Roy Wilson, and Ellen Windmuth.

MTV initiates the first rock video cable channel with the music video "Video Killed the Radio Star" by the Buggles

33rd Session of the U.N. General Assembly adopts resolution on the New World Information Order calling for the strengthening of "the capacity of developing countries to achieve improvement of their own situations, notably by providing their own equipment, by training their own personnel, by improving their infrastructures and making their information and communication media suitable to their needs and aspirations." Resolution sets off strong negative reactions in the U.S. press, which unfairly characterizes the intent of the NWIO as an attack on free speech and as promoting Third World government-controlled media.

Computer Professionals for Social Responsibility is founded

## 1982

Cable television experiencing boom period via numerous new satellite program services

Media Network is founded to distribute information on social issue media

March for Disarmament in New York City brings together more than fifty video activists for a live six-hour satellite program

## 1983

The internet begins functioning

World Association of Community Radio Broadcasters (AMARC) is founded in Montreal

United States invades the small Caribbean island of Grenada and increases covert war against Nicaragua

Rupert Murdoch announces plan for Direct Broadcast Satellite Service (DBS)

The Voyager Company (a laserdisc and CD-ROM production company) is founded by Bob Stein

## 1984

Qube, the interactive cable system, troubled by nonrenewals in Columbus, Ohio, pulls back from its plans

The Supreme Court rules that home taping of TV shows does not violate copyright laws

Cable Act passed by Congress deregulating industry; prices soon zoom for cable service

Paper Tiger West is formed by Jesse Drew, Allan Steinheimmer, Karen Einstein, Lisa Rudman, and others

The U.S. government's offensive against the Third World movement for a New World Information Order culminates in the unilateral withdrawal of the United States from UNESCO, drastically undermining their communication development programs

## 1985

Cable systems number 6,600 systems with 32 million subscribers

VCRs now in 30 percent of American homes

45.7 percent of American homes are wired for cable

Average TV viewing peaks at 7 hours and 10 minutes per day per household

Squeaky Wheel/Buffalo Media Resources, Inc., a media arts service organization, is founded in Buffalo, N.Y. They produce a public access show highlighting local and independent producers and publish *Squealer* magazine.

Henry Hampton's *Eyes on the Prize* is broadcast on PBS stations

Apple's *1984* commercial introduces the Macintosh computer

## 1988

Fairness and Accuracy in Reporting (FAIR) is founded

The United States Information Agency (USIA) develops TV Martí, satellite transmissions of U.S. programming and propaganda to Cuba. Congress appropriates $23.3 million to establish it.

Paul Garrin and Clayton Patterson capture police brutality at the Tompkins Square Park riots in New York City on their home video cameras. Their tapes are subsequently shown on network news with the disclaimer "amateur footage."

The Paper Tiger South West Production Collective is formed in San Diego, California, by John Walden, Margaret Dafani, Luana Plunkett, Neil Morrison, Bob Kinney , Jane Cottis, and others.

Congress directs CPB to create a program fund for independent producers as a result of intense lobbying by media arts organizations. This fund later becomes ITVS.

## 1989

ABC debuts *America's Funniest Home Videos*

Time, Inc., merges with Warner Brothers in what will become an era of merger mania

FCC initiates an inquiry on the effect of the Cable Act

Whittle Corp., owned 50 percent by Time Warner, introduces satellite Channel One into the school system, placing news spots and corporate ads before a captive student body

162 million TV sets in the United States in 90 million homes

The Berlin Wall falls

Hi-8 video format is introduced

64.6 percent of homes in the United States have VCRs

*The 90's,* weekly magazine program of camcorder independent segments, begins on many PBS stations

Union Producers and Programmers Network (UPNET) is formed, linking eight labor video activist groups

DIVA (Damned Interfering Video Activists) TV is founded, militantly addressing AIDS issues

## 1990

Cable systems number 9,575 with 50 million subscribers

Not Channel Zero, a collective of African American and Latino videomakers, begins producing for Manhattan public access

Electronic Frontier Foundation is founded

Videazimut, an international nongovernmental coalition promoting audiovisual communication for development and democracy, is founded

Gulf Crisis TV Project is formed by Deep Dish and Paper Tiger to counter mass media saber rattling. Eventually ten programs are produced and transmitted to community channels.

## 1991

The Kayapo people of Brazil begin using video for documentation and confrontation with government authorities

The Gulf War: bombs with TV cameras in them are dropped on Iraq

The brutal beating of Rodney King by Los Angeles Police is documented with a home video camera and aired repeatedly on major network TV, raising awareness not only of racism, but the power and accessibility of video as a weapon and a witness

The Center for Media Education, a Washington organization for media reform, is founded

The Satellite University Network, founded by Jaime Barrios, DeeDee Halleck, Cynthia Lopez, Pedro Rivera, and Susan Zeig, initiates a series of Latino programs through the Center for Puerto Rican Studies

Public access centers around the country produce 10,000 hours of original programming a week, 520,000 hours a year

Marlon Rigg's *Tongues Untied* is scheduled on POV and censored by many PBS stations

## 1992

A series of Cuban Television programs is beamed from satellites to U.S. communities in retaliation for TV Marti: *Stone's*

*Throw, TV from Cuba,* a four-hour series produced by DeeDee Halleck and Monica Melamid

Paper Tigers, artists in residence at Somerville Cable Access, initiate a workshop with Haitian producers

Roberto Arevelo starts the Mirror Project, a model youth production effort in the Somerville/Boston area

Congress requires DBS operators to set aside 4–7 percent of capacity for noncommercial educational use. Free Speech TV utilizes this set-aside to transmit first 24-hour progressive network.

### 1993

U.S. Court of Appeals overturns the 1992 Cable Act provision allowing cable operators to censor access channels, reaffirms that indecent material is legal

### 1994

The Zapatista Rebels take over San Cristobal de las Casas on January 1, the day NAFTA takes effect, posting ongoing communiqués to the internet and list-serves

CD-ROM (voice, video, and text) with Mumia Abu Jamal, death-row inmate in Pennsylvania, is produced by Brian Drolet at Voyager Company

World Trade Organization is ratified in the U.S. Congress

### 1995

DBS satellite programming offered nationwide

### 1996

Media and Democracy Conference, organized by Don Hazen, brings together producers, activists, and researchers in San Francisco

The 1996 Telecommunications Act, under the guise of promoting competition, eliminates media cross ownership and allows phone companies to enter the cable TV business

**1997**

Media and Democracy Conference held in New York City

Manhattan Neighborhood Network programs from new studios: producing 30,000 hours of community programming a year on four channels, the most of any access center in the world

**1998**

PBS announces program development deal with Disney/ABC

Supreme Court upholds free speech on PEG access channels

**1999**

Email surpasses "snail" mail

Next 5 Minutes Conference in Amsterdam brings together internet, microradio, and video for a hybrid media center/hackers lounge/happening

Creation of the first Independent Media Center and indymedia website in Seattle during massive protests against the World Trade Organization

*Show Down in Seattle: 10 Days that Shook the WTO*, documentation of WTO protests, is transmitted to community TV stations

**2000**

FCC issues rulemaking to allow nonprofit microradio stations, which Congress later undercuts due to pressure by the National Association of Broadcasters (NAB)

AOL acquires Time Warner (merger completed in early 2001)

Freespeech TV begins 24-hour transmission on Echo Star's Dish Network

*Democracy Now* and *Crashing the Party* provide 35 hours of live national satellite coverage of the Philadelphia and Los Angeles conventions in collaboration with Independent Media Centers in both cities

Demonstrations at the NAB convention in San Francisco to condemn their actions to suppress microradio

## 2001

Manhattan Neighborhood Network begins 24-hour internet casting of their four access channels, the first full-time streaming of TV channels

# ANNOTATED BIBLIOGRAPHY

Adair, John, and Sol Worth. 1972. *Through Navajo Eyes.* Bloomington: Indiana University Press.

Adilkno (The Foundation for the Advancement of Illegal Knowledge). 1998. *The Media Archive: World Edition.* New York: Autonomedia.

Adorno, T. W., and M. Horkheimer. 1972. *The Dialectic of Enlightenment.* New York: Continuum. Originally published in 1947. This classic critique of mass culture is essential reading.

Agosta, Diana. 1987. "Using TV." *Media Active: The Media Network Newsletter* 1, no. 4. This special issue looks at activist uses of television, including an essay about Deep Dish.

Agosta, Diana, Abigail Norman, and Caryn Rogoff. 1988. *Participate Directory of Public Access in New York State.* New York: Media Network and the New York State Cable Commission. Copies can be obtained from Diana Agosta, 180 Claremont Ave. #32, New York, N.Y. 10027.

Ambrosi, Alain, and Nancy Thede, eds. 1990. *Video: The Changing World.* Montreal: Black Rose Books. Firsthand reports on various international projects in community media.

Andersen, Robin. 1995. *Consumer Culture and TV Programming.* Boulder: Westview Press.

———. 2000. *Critical Studies in Media Commercialism.* New York: Oxford University Press.

Angus, Ian, and Sut Jhally. 1989. *Cultural Politics in Contemporary America.* New York: Routledge.

"Anti-globalization: A Spreading Phenomenon." 2000. *Perspectives.* A Canadian Security Intelligence Service Publication, Report # 2000/08, August 22.

Arquilla, John. and David Ronfeldt. 1996. *The Advent of Netwar.* Santa Monica, Calif.: Rand Corp.

Aufderheide, Pat. 1993. "Ethnographic Film and the Politics of Difference." *Popular Culture.*

———. 1998. *Communications Policy and the Public Interest: The Telecommunications Act of 1996.* New York: Guilford.

Barnouw, Erik. 1966. *A Tower of Babel: A History of Broadcasting in the United States to 1933.* New York: Oxford University Press.

———. 1968. *The Golden Web: A History of Broadcasting in the United States, 1933–53.* New York: Oxford University Press.

———. 1970. *The Image Empire: A History of Broadcasting in the United States, from 1953.* New York: Oxford University Press.

———. *The Tube of Plenty.* 1975. New York: Oxford University Press. This work is a compilation taken from Barnouw's monumental three-part history of broadcasting.

Benjamin, Walter. 1987. "The Work of Art in the Age of Mechanical Reproduction." In John Hanhardt, ed., *Video Culture: A Critical Investigation.* Layton, Utah: Gibbs Smith.

Bennett, Tony. 1990. *Outside Literature.* New York: Routledge.

Berlet, Chip, ed. 1995. *Eyes Right: Challenging the Right Wing Backlash.* Boston: South End Press.

Birri, Fernando. 1986. *Birth Certificate of the School of Three Worlds.* Havana.

Blau, Andrew. 1992. "The Promise of Public Access." *The Independent* 15, no. 3. A survey of access in the early 1990s in the United States.

Blumberg, Skip. 1977. " 'The TVTV Show': Behind the Scenes and between the Lines." *Televisions* 3, no. 4.

Boyle, Deirdre. 1996. *Subject to Change: Guerilla Television Revisited.* New York: Oxford University Press. Starting with the invention of portable video, this chronicles the utopian movement of U.S. artists and activists.

———. 1997. "Oh, Lucky Man: George Stoney's Lasting Legacy." *The Independent* 20, no. 8. George Stoney has been called the "grandfather" of public access, having started with Channels for Change in Canada and initiated the Alternate Media Center at NYU, from which dozens of interns spread across the United States as activists/artists-in-residence at cable stations.

Bradford, George. 1984. "Media: Capital's Global Village." *The Fifth Estate* 19, no. 3.

Brecht, Bertolt. 1964. "The Radio as an Apparatus of Communication." In John Willett, ed. and trans., *Brecht on Theatre*. New York: Hill and Wang.

Brennan, Chris. 2000. "Another News Source: Independent Media Center Hopes to Be a Voice for Activists' Messages." *Philadelphia Daily News*, July 25.

Brown, Les. 1971. *Television: The Business behind the Box*. New York: Harcourt Brace Jovanovich.

Bruce, Steve. 1990. *Pray TV: Televangelism in America*. London: Routledge. How the conservative Christians learned to love and use television.

Bullert, B. J. 1998. *Public Television: Politics and the Battle over Documentary Film*. New Brunswick, N.J.: Rutgers University Press.

Calder-Marshall, Arthur. 1963. *The Innocent Eye*. London: Allen.

Carnegie Commission. 1979. *A Public Trust: The Report of the Carnegie Commission on the Future of Public Broadcasting*. New York: Bantam, 1979.

Carr, C. 2000. "Get Me Download: Reporting the Real Philadelphia Story." *Village Voice*, July 24.

Carroll, Paul B. 1994. "Foreign Competition Spurs Mexico to Move into High-Tech World." *Wall Street Journal*, July 5.

Cleaver, Harry, ed. 1994. *Zapatista! The Writings of the EZLN*. New York: Autonomedia.

Cohen, Roger. 1991. "For Coke, World Is Its Oyster." *New York Times*, November 21.

Couldry, Nick. 2000. *The Place of Media Power: Pilgrims and Witnesses of the Media Age*. New York: Routledge.

Dagron, Alfonso Gumucio. 2001. *Making Waves: Stories of Participatory Communication for Social Change*. New York: Rockefeller Foundation.

Davis, Susan. 1997. *Spectacular Nature: Corporate Culture and the SeaWorld Experience*. Berkeley: University of California Press. How "Nature" is sold to children.

Debord, Guy. 1995. *Society of the Spectacle*. New York: Zone Books.

Del Solar, Daniel. 1976. "Toward 'Unfringed' and Open Programming: Some Workable Suggestions." *Public Telecommunication Review* (July/August). This article is about the Open Studio, an experiment initiated by KQED in making studio facilities available to community groups and local artists and activists.

Demac, Donna. 1988. *Liberty Denied: The Current Use of Censorship in America.* New York: American PEN Center.

Derry Women's Workshop. *Mother Ireland,* available from Women Make Movies, 462 Broadway, 5th floor, New York, N.Y. 10013.

Devine, R. H. 1992. "Access in the 21st Century: The Future of a Public." *Community Television Review* 15, no. 6. Robert Devine has been an important figure in the grassroots public access movement and one of the most visionary strategists.

Douglass, Susan. 1987. *Inventing American Broadcasting, 1899–1922.* Baltimore: John Hopkins University Press.

Downing, John. 2000. *Radical Media: Rebellious Communication and Social Movements.* Thousand Oaks, Calif.: Sage.

Downing, John, Ali Mohammadi, and Annabelle Sreberny-Mohammadi, eds. 1995. *Questioning the Media: A Critical Introduction.* Thousand Oaks, Calif.: Sage.

Dunnifer, Steve, and Ron Sakolsky. 1998. *Seizing the Airwaves: A Free Radio Handbook.* San Francisco: AK Press.

Engelman, Ralph. 1992. "The Origins of Public Access Cable TV, 1966–1972." *Journalism Monographs,* no. 123. Available at http://ccsnet.com/c3tv.monograph.htm.

———. 1996. *Public Radio and Television in America: A Political History.* Thousand Oaks, Calif.: Sage. This book presents public access in the context of the turbulent history of noncommercial broadcasting in the United States.

Enzensberger, Hans Magnus. 1986. "Constituents of a Theory of Media." In John Hanhardt, Gibbs M. Smith, and Peregrine Smith, eds., *Video Culture: A Critical Investigation.* Layton, Utah: Peregrine Smith Books. In association with the Visual Studies Workshop, Rochester, N.Y.

———. 1974. "Constituents of a New Media Theory" (1971).

In *The Consciousness Industry: On Literature Politics and the Media*. New York: Seabury Press.

Espinosa, Julio Garcia. 1998. "Towards an Imperfect Cinema." In Michael Martin, ed., *New Latin American Cinema: Theory, Practices and Transcontinental Articulations*. Detroit: Wayne State University Press.

*Extra*, the bulletin of Fairness and Accuracy in Reporting. New York. FAIR's newsletter contains important studies of mass culture and many useful statistics.

Faris, James. 1992. "Anthropological Transparency: Film Interpretation and Politics." In Peter Crawford and David Turton, eds., *Filmography*. Manchester: Manchester University Press.

Fekete, John. 1977. *The Critical Twilight*. New York: Routledge and Kegan Paul. One of the best discussions of McLuhan.

Franck, Peter. 1988. "First Amendment: Friend or Foe?" *Propaganda Review* (San Francisco), no. 3.

———. 1989. "The Law, Peace, and the Mass Media: Special Issues and a Working Symposium." *National Lawyers Guild Practitioner* 46, no. 1.

Franco, Jean. 1989. *Plotting Women, Gender and Representation in Mexico*. New York: Columbia University Press.

Freire, Paulo. 1970. *Pedagogy of the Oppressed*. New York: Continuum.

Fulton, Jean. 1996. "DeeDee Halleck and Bob Hercules." In *Art Out There: Toward a Publicly Engaged Art Practice*. Chicago: School of the Art Institute of Chicago.

Gaffney, Maureen, ed. 1977. "Young Viewers." *Sightlines* 11, no. 2. A report on the 1976 Conference on Child-Made Films.

Garrison, Jim. 1989. *On the Trail of the Assassins*. New York: Sheridan Square Press.

Gaventa, John. 1980. *Power and Powerlessness: Quiescence and Rebellion in an Appalachian Valley*. Urbana: University of Illinois Press.

Gever, Martha. 1983. "Meet the Press: On Paper Tiger Television." *Afterimage* 11, nos. 1–2.

Ginsburg, Faye. 1991. "Indigenous Media: Faustian Contract or Global Village?" *Cultural Anthropology* 6, no. 1.

Ginzberg, Eli. 1979. "Professionalization of the U.S. Labor Force." *Scientific American* 240, no. 3.

Goldberg, Kim. 1990. *The Barefoot Channel.* Vancouver: North Star Books. This book explores the possibilities of community cable in Canada.

"The Gold Rush of 1980: Prospecting for Cable Franchises." 1980. *Broadcasting* (New York), March 31.

Goldstein, Neil, and Nick DeMartino. 1974. "FCC Weighing Crucial Access, Origination Regs." *Community Video Report* 2, no. 1.

Gouldner, Joseph. 1988. *Fit to Print.* New York: Lyle Stuart Publishers.

Hall, Doug, and Sally Jo Fifer, eds. 1990. *Illuminating Video.* New York: Aperture Press.

Hall, Stuart, and Bram Gieben, eds. 1992. *The Foundations of Modernity.* New York: Polity Press.

Halleck, DeeDee. 1993. "Community TV from Geostationary Orbit." *Leonardo International Journal on Art and Technology* 26, no. 5. A discussion of Deep Dish Television and the Gulf Crisis TV Project.

Halleck, DeeDee, and Nathalie Magnan. 1993. "Access for Others: Alter(native) Media Practice." *Visual Anthropology Review* 9, no. 1.

Halleck, DeeDee, and Monica Melamid. *Stone's Throw: TV from Cuba.* Catalog from Artists Space Gallery, New York, N.Y. A gallery catalog with several essays.

Hallin, Dan. 1992. "Sound Bite News: Television Coverage of Elections, 1968–1988." *Journal of Communication* 42, no. 2. A devastating look at how our public dialogue has been literally truncated.

Hamelink, Cees. 1977. *Corporate Village: The Role of Transnational Corporations in International Communication.* Rome: IDOC.

———. 1994. *Trends in World Communication and Development: On Disempowerment and Self Empowerment.* Penang: Southbound.

Harding, Thomas. 1997. *The Video Activist Handbook.* London: Pluto Press. This excellent British handbook includes a section on Paper Tiger and an introduction to the series *undercurrents,* which has provided alternative programming in the United Kingdom.

Hazen, Don, and Larry Smith, eds. 1996. *Media and Democracy: A Book of Readings and Resources.* San Francisco: Institute for Alternative Journalism. This useful manual for activism was put together for the Media and Democracy Congress.

Heath, Stephen. 1990. "Representing Television." In Pat Mellencamp, ed., *The Logics of Television: Essays in Cultural Criticism.* Bloomington: Indiana University Press/British Film Institute.

Hénaut, Dorothy. 1970. "A Report from Canada: Television as Town Meeting." *Radical Software* 1, no. 1. A report on one of the first community experiments with video.

Herman, Edward. 1995. *Triumph of the Market: Essays on Economics, Politics and the Media.* Boston: South End Press. This is a brilliant overview of corporate media.

Higgins, John. 1999. "Community Television and the Vision of Media Literacy, Social Action and Empowerment." *Journal of Broadcasting and Electronic Media* 43, no. 4.

Horowitz, Andrew, and Bert Cowlan. 1976. "Should People Fight for Satellites?" *Televisions* 4, no. 1.

Hoynes, William. 1994. *Public Television for Sale: Media, the Market, and the Public Sphere.* Boulder: Westview Press.

Hulser, Kathleen. 1986. "Many Tasty Morsels Fill This Deep Dish." *The Guardian,* June 11, New York.

Hurtado, Maria Elena, and Judith Perera. 1988. "The Science of Suppression." *South Magazine* (November).

Institute of Lifelong Learning. 1986. *Community Television: A Handbook for Production.* New York: American Association of Retired Persons.

Jackson, Janine, and Naureckas, Jim, eds. 1996. *The FAIR Reader: Review of Press and Politics in the '90's.* Boulder: Westview Press.

Jancowski, Nicholas W. 1995. "Reflections on the Origins and Meaning of Media Access." *Javnost: The Public* 2, no. 4.

Johnson, Nicholas. 1972. *How to Talk Back to Your TV Set.* New York: Bantam.

Keen, Ben. 1987. " 'Play It Again, Sony': The Double Life of Home Video Technology." *Science as Culture* 4, no. 1.

Kellner, Doug. 1990. *Television and the Crisis of Democracy.* Boulder: Westview Press.

Kellogg, Rhoda. 1970. *Analyzing Children's Art.* Palo Alto, Calif.: National Press Books.

Keydel, Julia, and Brian Winston. 1986. *Working with Video.* New York: Watson-Guptill. This book is a video primer which emphasizes community television work.

Koch, Kenneth. 1971. *Wishes, Lies, and Dreams.* New York: Vintage.

Korot, Beryl, and Ira Schneider. 1976. *Video Art: An Anthology.* New York, Harcourt Brace Jovanovich.

Kovel, Joel. 1988. *In Nicaragua.* London: Free Association Books. A personal journal of life in Sandinista Nicaragua.

———. 1994. *Red Hunting in the Promised Land.* New York: Basic Books. Anyone serious about understanding U.S. history needs to read this book.

Kunzle, David. 1995. *The Murals of Revolutionary Nicaragua 1979–1992.* Berkeley: University of California Press.

Kupferberg, Tuli. 2000. *Teach Yourself Fucking: Political, Social, Cultural, Artistic and Idiosyncratic Cartoons and Collages.* New York: Autonomedia.

Larsen, Roger, with Ellen Meade. 1969. *Young Filmmakers.* New York: Dutton.

Lazar, Mathew. 2000. *Pacifica Radio: The Rise of an Alternative Network.* Philadelphia: Temple University Press.

Lazere, Donald, ed. 1987. *American Media and Mass Culture: Left Perspectives.* Berkeley: University of California Press. This is a good compilation of some classic articles; see especially David Kunzle on Donald Duck and Tom Englehardt on Kamakazi Pass.

Ledbetter, James. 1997. *Made Possible By . . . : The Death of Public Broadcasting in the United States.* New York: Verso.

Lee, Philip. 1986. *Communication for All: New World Information and Communication Order.* Maryknoll, N.Y.: Orbis Books.

Lewis, Richard. 1969. *Journeys*. New York: Simon and Schuster.

MacBride, Sean. 1980. *Many Voices One World*. New York: UNESCO Unipub. This report from the MacBride Commission addressed issues of information equity in a manner that was threatening to the U.S. State Department. This is why the United States has been so remiss on paying their UN dues.

Mander, Jerry. 1978. *Four Arguments for the Elimination of Television*. New York: Morrow.

Marcos, Subcomandante. 2000. "On Independent Media: Address to the Meeting of Free the Media." In J. Ponce de Leon, ed., *Our Word Is Our Weapon: Selected Writings of Subcomandante Marcos*. New York: Seven Stories Press.

Masmoudi, Mustapha. 1978. "The New World Information Order." Document 31. Paris: UNESCO. The key issues of the rights of states to information parity.

Mattelart, Armand. 1986. *Communicating in Popular Nicaragua*. New York: International General.

Mattelart, Armand, and Ariel Dorfman. 1975. *How to Read Donald Duck*. Available from International General, Box 350, New York, N.Y. 10013. This classic deconstruction of Disney was developed during Chile's Popular Unity government as part of a popular study of mass culture.

Mattelart, Michele. 1982. *Women and the Cultural Industries*. Paris: UNESCO.

M'Bow, Amadou-Mahtar. 1984. "Address at the Opening of the Conference of Journalists of Non-Alligned Countries on Media." New Delhi. UNESCO Document DG/83/49. The director general of UNESCO states his position in the debates around the "new world information order."

McChesney, Robert. 1995. *Telecommunications, Mass Media and Democracy: The Battle for the Control of U.S. Broadcasting, 1928–1935*. New York : Oxford University Press. McChesney provides an important historical background of the struggle for democratic media.

McLuhan, Marshall. 1964. *Understanding Media: The Extensions of Man*. New York: McGraw-Hill.

Mearns, Hughs. 1935. *Creative Power: The Education of Youth in the Creative Arts*. Garden City, N.Y.: Doubleday.

Meiselas, Susan. 1981. *Nicaragua*. New York: Pantheon.

Milam, Lorenzo. 1972. *Sex and Broadcasting*. San Diego: Mho and Mho Works. Milam was the founder of many community radio stations throughout the United States.

*The Miners' Tapes*. 1984. *The Lie Machine*. Available from Paper Tiger Television, 339 Lafayette St., New York, N.Y., 10012.

Moore, Rachel. 1976. "Woman Cooking, Woman Spending, but Not 'Woman Alive': Corporate Underwriters Buy an Image on PBS." *Televisions* 4, no. 1.

Moore, Rebecca. 1992. "Marketing Alterity." *Visual Anthropology Review* 8, no. 2.

Morgenthaler, Eric. 1993. " 'Dittoheads' All Over Make Rush Limbaugh Superstar of the Right." *Wall Street Journal*, June 28.

Mumford, Lewis. 1934. *Technics and Civilization*. New York: Harcourt Brace.

Mwalimu. 1995. "Radical Television: DeeDee Halleck's on a New Vanguard." *Mountain Herald* (Catskill, N.Y.), August 17.

National Institute against Prejudice. 1988. "Bigotry and Cable TV: Legal Issues and Community Responses." Institute Report no. 3. A very useful look at issues of censorship and bigotry on cable.

Negt, Oskar, and Alexander Kluge. 1989. *The Public Sphere and Experience*. Minneapolis: University of Minnesota Press.

Nettime. 1999. *Read Me!* New York: Autonomedia. Available through www.nettime.org.

Nicholson, Margie. 1990. *Cable Access: A Community Communications Resource for Nonprofits*. Benton Foundation Bulletin no. 3, April. Washington, D.C.: Benton Foundation.

Nordenstreng, Kaarle, and Tapio Varis. 1974. "TV Traffic—A One Way Street: A Survey and Analysis of the International Flow of Television Programme Materials." UNESCO Document no. 70. Paris: UNESCO.

Not Channel Zero. 1992. "Not Channel Zero Untaped." *Felix: A Journal of Media Arts and Communication* 1, no. 2.

Paper Tiger Collective. 1986. *Dou Dou Dienne and Claude Robinson on the New World Information Order.* New York: Paper Tiger.

————. 1991. *Roar: The Paper Tiger Television Guide to Media Activism.* Columbus, Ohio: Wexner Center for the Arts.

————. 1992. *Paper Tiger Guide to TV Repair.* Catalog of the San Francisco Art Institute.

————. 1998. *Putting the Demo Back in Democracy: March against the Moguls.* New York: Paper Tiger.

Penley, Constance, and Andrew Ross, ed. 1991. *Technoculture.* Minneapolis: University of Minnesota Press.

Percq, Pascal. 1998. *Les Caméras des favelas.* Paris: Les Editions de l'Atelier/Editions Ouvrières.

Plagens, Peter. 1993. "Fade from White: The Whitney Biennial Gives Center Stage to Women, Gays and Artists of Color." *Newsweek,* March 10.

Preston, William, Edward Herman, and Herbert Schiller. 1989. *Hope and Folly: The United States and UNESCO.* Minneapolis: University of Minnesota Press.

Radical Science Collective. 1985. *Making Waves: The Politics of Communication.* London: Free Association Books.

Reyes Matta, Fernando. 1981. *La Communicacion alternative come respuesta democractic.* Mexico City: ILET.

Rice, Michael. 1978. "Independents and PTV." *Public Telecommunications Review* 6, no. 5.

Roberts, Jason. 1994. "Public Access: Fortifying the Electronic Soapbox." *Federal Communications Law Journal* 47, no. 1. Available on-line at http://www.law.indiana/fclj/fclj.html.

Rodriguez, Clemencia. 2000. *Fissures in the Mediascape: An International Study of Citizens' Media.* New York: Hampton Press.

Rodriquez, Maritza. 1992. Interview with Kelly Anderson, Havana, July.

Roncaglio, Rafael. 1991. "Notes on the 'Alternative.'" In Nancy Thede and Alain Ambrosi, eds., *Video: The Changing World.* Montreal: Black Rose Books.

Rosler, Martha. 1990. "Video Shedding the Utopian Moment." In Doug Hall and Sally Jo Fifer, eds., *Illuminating Video*. New York: Aperture.

———. 1998. *Positions in the Life World*. Cambridge, Mass.: MIT Press.

Ross, Andrew. 1989. *No Respect: Intellectuals and Popular Culture*. New York: Routledge.

Rowland, Randy. 2000. "Breaking the Bank." *Z Magazine* (July/August).

Ruby, Jay. 1991. "Speaking for, Speaking about, Speaking with, or Speaking alongside—An Anthropological and Documentary Dilemma." *Visual Anthropology Review* 7, no. 2.

Schechter, Danny. 1997. *The More You Watch, the Less You Know*. New York: Seven Stories.

Schiller, Dan. 1999. *Digital Capitalism: Networking the Global Market System*. Cambridge, Mass.: MIT Press. This comprehensive book traces the political economy of Silicon Alley/Valley.

Schiller, Herbert I. 1969. *Mass Communication and American Empire*. Boston: Beacon. Herb Schiller's seminal work in the critical political economy of communications was the impetus for the founding of Paper Tiger Television and has served as a standard for passionate and committed research in the field.

———. 1973. *The Mind Managers*. Boston: Beacon.

———. 1976. *Communication and Cultural Domination*. White Plains, N.Y.: M. E. Sharpe.

———. 1981. *Who Knows: Information in the Age of the Fortune 500*. Norwood, N.J.: Ablex.

———. 1984. *Information and the Crisis Economy*. Norwood, N.Y.: Ablex.

———. 1989. *Culture Incorporated: The Corporate Takeover of Public Expression*. New York: Oxford University Press.

———. 1996. *Information Inequality: The Deepening Social Crisis in America*. New York: Routledge.

Schiller, Herbert I., George Gerbner, and Hamid Mowhana. 1992. *Triumph of the Image: The Media War in the Persian Gulf, a Global Perspective*. Boulder: Westview Press.

Schrage, Michael. "Karaoke Battles a Case of Laryngitis." *Los Angeles Times*, March 25, 1993.

Shamberg, Michael, and Raindance Corporation. 1971. *Guerrilla Television*. New York: Holt, Rinehart and Winston.

Shulman, David. 1992. *Everyone's Channel*. Still the very best tape about the history and potential of public access. Distributed by the Cinema Guild, New York City.

Singh, Kusum, and Bertram Gross. 1981. "MacBride: The Report and the Response." *Journal of Communications* 31, no. 4.

Solomon, Deborah. 1993. "A Showcase for Political Correctness: The Whitney Biennial Easily Qualifies as the Most Disturbing Museum Show in Living Memory." *Wall Street Journal*, March 5.

Sontag, Susan. 1975. "Fascinating Fascism." *New York Review of Books*, February 6. Reprinted in Karyn Kay and Gerald Peary, eds., *Women and the Cinema: A Critical Anthology*. New York: Dutton, 1977.

Spivak, Gayatri Chakravorty. 1987. *In Other Worlds*. New York: Methuen.

Starr, Jerry. 2000. *AIRWARS: The Fight to Reclaim Public Broadcasting*. Boston: Beacon Press.

Stearns, Jennifer. 1981. *A Short Course in Cable*. New York: United Church of Christ. A concise description of cable franchising and the potential for public use.

Stone, Allucquere Rosanne. 1994. "Cyberdämmerung at Wellspring Systems." In Mary-Anne Moser, ed., *Immersed in Technology*. Cambridge, Mass.: MIT Press.

*Stone's Throw: TV from Cuba*. 1990. Catalog from Artists Space Gallery, New York, N.Y.

Stoney, George. 1971–72. "The Mirror Machine." *Sight and Sound* 41, no. 1. Stoney has been the primary leader of the public access movement.

———. 1992. "On Censorship." *Community Television Review* (fall).

Sturken, Marita. 1987. "Private Money and Personal Influence: Howard Klein and the Rockefeller Foundation's Funding of the Media Arts." *Afterimage* 14, no. 6.

Sullivan, Lawrence. 1992. "The 700 Club: Electronic Imperialism and the Satellite's Healing Shadow." *The Squealer* (Buffalo, N.Y.), March.

Tankha, Brij, ed. 1995. *Communications and Democracy: Ensuring Plurality.* New Delhi: CENDIT. The proceedings of the 1994 Conference on New Technologies and the Democratization of Audiovisual Communication held in New Delhi in 1994.

Teasdale, Parry. 1999. *Videofreex: America's First Pirate TV Station and the Catskill Collective That Turned It on.* Catskill, N.Y.: Black Dome Books.

Thomas, Wes. 1994. "Four Arguments for the Redemption of Television: Video Pioneer Stephen Beck." *Mondo 2000,* no. 9.

Turner, Terence. 1992a. "Defiant Images, the Kayapo Appropriation of Video." *Anthropology Today* 9, no. 6.

———. 1992b. "Visual Media, Cultural Politics and Anthropological Practice: Recent Uses of Film and Video among the Kayapo of Brazil." *The Independent* (New York) 14, no. 1.

Vidéazimut. 1996. "Vidéazimut: An International Coalition for Democratic Communication." *Media Development: Journal of the World Association for Christian Communication* 43, no. 3.

"Video Vigilantes." 1991. *Newsweek,* July 22.

Videofreex. 1973. *Spaghetti City Video Manual.* New York: Praeger.

Vogel, Amos. 1974. *Film as a Subversive Art.* New York: Random House. Vogel's inspirational compilation is enhanced by exquisite photo illustrations, which were edited by Babette Mangolte.

Wasko, Janet. 1994. *Hollywood in the Information Age.* Austin: University of Texas Press.

Whisnant, David E. 1995. *Rascally Signs in Sacred Places: The Politics of Culture in Nicaragua.* Chapel Hill: University of North Carolina Press.

Williams, Raymond. 1974. *Television, Technology and Cultural Form.* New York: Schocken Books. Williams was one of the first to really grapple with the essence of TV viewing.

Williamson, Judith. 1986. *The New Statesman,* December 5.

Youngblood, Gene. 1970. *Expanded Cinema*. New York: Dutton.

Zimmerman, Patricia. 1981. "Independent Documentary Producers and the American Television Networks." *American Screen* 22, no. 4.

———. 1982. "Public Television, Independent Documentary Producers and Public Policy." *Journal of the University Film and Video Association* 34, no. 3. This article is the best summary of the struggle between independents and public broadcasting.

———. 2000. *States of Emergency*. Minneapolis: University of Minnesota Press.

# FILMOGRAPHY

16 MM FILMS

*Children Make Movies*, 1961, produced for Lillian Wald Settlement (producer/director)

*Mural on Our Street*, 1965, produced for Henry Street Settlement (producer/director)

*Minimoviemakers*, 1967, documentary on a film workshop (producer/director)

*Mr. Story*, 1972, 28 minute documentary on an old man (co-producer/director)

*Jaraslava*, 1973, documentary on a Ukrainian woman, 1983

*Self Portrait: Jean Dupuy*, 1974, documentary on the artist (producer/director)

*Meadows Green*, 1976, 28 minute documentary on Bread and Puppet (co-producer/director)

*Railroad Turnbridge*, 1976 (camera and editing)

*Bronx Baptism*, 1980, documentary on a Pentecostal church in the Bronx (producer/director)

*Haiti: Bitter Cane*, 1983, 71 minute feature film, made with Haiti Films

*Haiti: Reasons to Flee*, 1983, PBS special on Haitian refugees (co-producer/director)


VIDEO

*Sari Dienes Masked*, 1978

*Waiting for the Invasion: U.S. Citizens in Nicaragua*, 1983

*Barco de la Paz*, 1984, made with the Fellowship of Reconciliation (producer/director)

*Stones' Throw: TV from Cuba: Island in Goliath's Sea*, 1992, four hour-long compilations of Cuban TV (co-producer/ curator with Monica Melamid)

*The Gringo in Mañanaland,* 1995, 61 minutes, compilation archival film (producer/director)

*Ah! The Hopeful Pageantry of Bread and Puppet,* 2001, 80 minutes (producer/co-director with Tamar Schumann)

PROGRAMS THAT HALLECK INITIATED AND WAS A PRINCIPAL CO-PRODUCER:

*Paper Tiger Television, 1981 to Present, Founder and Co-Producer*

*Herb Schiller Reads "The New York Times"* (series of six), 1981
*Brian Winston Reads "TV Guide,"* 1982
*Ynestra King on "Seventeen,"* 1982
*Martha Rosler Reads "Vogue,"* 1982
*Sheila Smith Hobson Reads "Newsweek,"* 1982
*Sol Yurick Reads "The New Criterion,"* 1982
*Joel Kovel Reads "Psychology Today,"* 1982
*Murray Bookchin Reads "Time,"* 1982
*Karen Paulsell Reads "Computer World,"* 1982
*Conrad Lynn Reads "Commentary,"* 1982
*Sheila Smith Hobson Reads "Newsweek,"* 1982
*Joel Kovel Reads "Covert Action,"* 1982
*Teresa Costa Reads "Biker Lifestyle,"* 1982
*Tuli Kupferberg Reads "Rolling Stone,"* 1982
*Natalie Didn't Drown: Joan Braderman Reads "The National Enquirer,"* 1982
*Stuart Ewen Reads "The New York Post,"* 1982
*Stanley Diamond Reads "Scholastic Magazine,"* 1982
*Brian Winston Reads "U.S. News and World Report,"* 1983
*Serafina Bathrick on "Working Woman,"* 1983
*Harry Magdoff Reads "Business Week,"* 1983
*Alex Cockburn Reads "The Washington Post,"* 1983
*Archie Singham Reads "Foreign Policy,"* 1983
*Myrna Bain Reads "Ebony,"* 1983
*June 12 Disarmament Special,* 1983

*Tom Weinberg Reads "The Wall Street Journal,"* 1983
*Joel Kovel Reads "Life" Magazine,* 1983
*Tim Haight Reads "Channels" Magazine,* 1983
*Chris Choy Reads "American Film,"* 1983
*Richie Perez Reads "Fort Apache, The Bronx,"* 1983
*Michele Gibbs Reads "The Free West Indian,"* 1983
*Elayne Rapping Swoons to Romance Novels,* 1983
*Peter Rossett and Others Read the Nicaraguan Press,* 1983
*Tuli Kupferberg Reads "Sports Illustrated,"* 1983
*Bill Boddy Reminds the FCC of the 1934 Communications Act,*
   1983
*Bill Tabb Reads "U.S. News and World Report,"* 1983
*Jim Rix Reads "Organic Gardening,"* 1983
*Herb Schiller on the Selling of the New Technologies,* 1983
*Bob Edelman on Sovietsky Sports,* 1983
*Gabor Rittersporn Reads "Pravda,"* 1983
*Nolan Bowie on High Tech Snooping,* 1984
*Patty Zimmerman Reads "Variety,"* 1984
*Pearl Bowser Looks at Early Black Cinema,* 1984
*Renee Tajima Reads Asian Images,* 1984
*Eva Cockcroft Reads "Art Forum,"* 1984
*Video Art Special with Max Schumann,* 1985
*Flo Kennedy Reads the US Press on South Africa,* 1985
*Herb Schiller on the Crisis Economy,* 1985
*DouDou Dienne Reads the MacBride Report,* 1985
*The Trial of Tilted Arc,* 1985
*Peter Wollen Reads US Press,* 1985
*Ellen Stein Reads "Vanity Fair,"* 1985
*Elayne Rapping on Soaps,* 1985
*Molly Kovel Reads Kiddy Books,* 1985
*Rereading "The Year of the Dragon,"* 1985
*Brian Winston Looks at Black Sit Coms,* 1985
*Joan Does "Dynasty,"* 1985
*Nidia Bustos on Mecate, Nicaraguan Theater,* 1986
*Archie Singham on the US Press and the UN,* 1986
*Paper Tiger Celebrates 100 Shows,* 1986
*Joel Kovel Reads "El Tayacan,"* 1986
*Ed Herman and the Famous Pope Plot,* 1986
*Bill Schaap and Ellen Ray on Vernon Walters,* 1986

*Paper Tiger Scans the (Inter)national Audio Visual Fe$tival,* 1986

*Jasefina de Zayas and Isabel Languia Read the Cuban Press,* 1987

*Joel Kovel on the Shrinking of "Amerika,"* 1987

*Not "Top Gun,"* 1987

*Dan Hallin Watches CBS News,* 1987

*David Avalos Reads "The San Diego Union,"* 1987

*Donna Haraway Reads the "The National Geographic,"* 1987

*Sheila Rowbothan Reads "The Star,"* 1987

*Red Ink: Rebecca Zurrier Reads "The Masses,"* 1987

*The Pedagogy of Telecommunications,* 1987

*Judith Williamson Consumes Passionately in Southern California,* 1988

*Fred Landia Digests "Selecciones,"* 1988

*Page DuBois Reads Plato,* 1989

*Terry Odendahl's Glamour Workout,* 1989

*Fred Landis Reads "The Washington Times,"* 1989

*From Woodstock to Tiananmen Square,* 1989

*Herb Schiller Vs the Bat Lords of the Global Village,* 1990

*Unpacking the Revolution in a Box,* 1990

*The Devil and Mr. Moyers,* 1991

*Tetsuo Kogawa Cooks Up a Transmitter,* 1992

*Somalia: Kill to Feed,* 1993

*Herb KO's the Sponsorship of Sports,* 1993

*Twist Barbie: Lyn Spigel on Barbie,* 1994

*The Power Elite in the Bohemian Grove,* 1994

*A Cry for Freedom and Democracy,* 1994

*Shredded Hopes,* 1994

*Super Barrio,* 1995

*Dan Hallin Unmasks Jacobo Zabludosky,* 1995


· *The Gulf Crisis TV Project*

*War, Oil and Power,* 1990

*Operation Dissidence,* 1990

*Getting Out of the Sand Trap,* 1990

*Bring the Troops Home,* 1990

DEEP DISH PROGRAMS

*Kids Playback,* 1986

*The Border: Where Do You Draw the Line,* 1988

*The Underground Voices of the Panamanian People,* 1988 (co-produced with CheChé Martinez)

*Stone's Throw and TV Marti: Anatomy of an Electronic Invasion,* 1988 (co-produced with Monica Melamid)

*Ends and Means: The History and Consequences of Anticommunism,* 1988 (co-produced with Catherine Gund)

*Let Nicaragua Speak!* 1989 (live presentation by Daniel Ortega)

*Ideas and Power: Super Barrio,* 1991 (co-produced with CheChé Martinez)

*Ideas and Power: Tiempo de Hibridos,* 1991 (co-produced with CheChé Martinez)

*Beyond the Browning of America: Latinos and Labor,* 1992

*Hands Off Cuba TV Teach In,* 1993

*Unconventional Coverage: Breaking Conventions: The Republican Convention in San Diego,* 1996 (development and satellite coordination)

*Unconventional Coverage: Off the Record: The Democratic Convention in Chicago,* 1996 (development and satellite coordination)

*The Killing State,* 1996 (co-producer/director)

*Lock Down USA,* 1996 (co-producer/director)

*The Last Graduation,* 1997 (co-producer/development)

*Bars and Stripes,* 1997, 12 hour series (co-producer)

*Critical Resistance,* 1998, compilation from a Berkeley conference (co-producer)

*Too Soon for Sorry,* 2000 (associate producer)

*Democracy Now Television,* 2001, 20 hours of live coverage of the 2001 political conventions (coordinator)

COMMUNICATIONS UPDATE

*The Ant and the Elephant: Bertram Gross and Kusum Singh,* 1979

*Eddie Becker's Washington,* 1979
*Mom and Pop TV Stations: Michael Couzens,* 1979
*International Communication Conference,* 1980


DISTRIBUTION INFORMATION

Paper Tiger
339 Lafayette St.
New York, NY 10012

Deep Dish
339 Lafayette St.
New York, NY 10012

All others available from
Viewing Habits
Box 89
Willow, NY 12495

# INDEX